The Private Thoughts of a Traveling Preacher's Wife

Other Books by Jack Crowder

Victory or Death: Military Decisions that Changed the Course of the American Revolution

The Story of Yorktown: Told by the Men Who Were There

So You Think You Know George Washington? Stories They Didn't Tell You In School

Women Patriots in the American Revolution: Stories of Bravery, Daring, and Compassion

The First 24 Hours of the American Revolution: An Hour by Hour Account of the Battles of Lexington, Concord, and the British Retreat on Battle Road

Strange, Amazing, and Funny Events that Happen during the Revolutionary War

Underage Warriors: Over 600 Stories about Courage and Hardship of Children, Ages Seven to Fourteen, Who Fought in the American Revolution

How Disease Affected the Military during the American Revolution

Massacres: The Dark Side of the American Revolution

African Americans and American Indians in the Revolutionary War

Chaplains of the Revolutionary War: Black Robed American Warriors

Abby's Secret (Historical Fiction)

We Were Once Warriors (Historical Fiction)

The Private Thoughts of a Traveling Preacher's Wife

---

*The Journals of Malvinia Louisa Foster
Central Texas, 1847–1870*

Transcribed and annotated
by Jack Darrell Crowder

Fort Worth, Texas

Library of Congress Control Number: 2024044550

TCU Box 298300
Fort Worth, Texas 76129
www.tcupress.com

Design by Bill Bramer

To Ralph Walker
my cousin and longtime member
of the Mansfield Historical Society

CONTENTS

Preface

———

The Foster journals were donated to the Mansfield Historical Society in 1985 by Mrs. Jean Marie Foster Crowder. Jean was the great-granddaughter of the Rev. Finis Foster and his wife, Malvinia Louisa Phillips. Louisa kept a diary consisting of eleven books from 1847 to 1870, which she wrote in ink, though some pages are written in pencil. Her wish was for her children to read them upon her death.

The Mansfield Historical Society was chosen to receive these diaries because of the Fosters' connection to the founding of the Texas city. John Collier Foster, Louisa's youngest son, married Mary Etta Feild, whose father, Julian, was a cofounder of Mansfield.

In the spring of 2021, Marilyn Gerloff, of the historical society, contacted me about the journals and asked if I had any suggestions about what to do with them. I agreed to look them over and did so in June of that year. Initially, I thought there was not much that could be done with them. However, once I started looking through them, I realized they did have historical significance.

I suggested to Marilyn that I take them home and begin transcribing each journal. She agreed, and for most of the year I prepared them for publication. I quickly became absorbed with Louisa's entries and looked forward to working on them each day.

In one entry, Louisa expressed a wish to have her writings read by others, especially mothers and their children. Louisa also wrote of her desire to be a useful person and to leave something behind after she died. The more of her entries I read, the more I felt that I had been chosen to make her wishes and desires come true.

Louisa Foster's eleven journals and John's three journals provide an interesting insight into life in Texas during the latter half of the 1800s. They document their experiences of many historical events, including the Civil War, the assassination of President Garfield, cholera epidemics, the advent of the telephone and electric light, and the important people they met, such as Sam Houston, Thomas J. Rusk, and Judge Robert Baylor, cofounder of Baylor University.

Louisa wrote with little punctuation, and her writing has been transcribed as she wrote it, with no changes to content or spelling. I have also underlined words that she chose to underline. If I could not determine a word, I indicated it by "___?___." Any comments inside square brackets are made by me to explain what was written or to make a historical observation.

It was necessary to edit her journals because of the large amount of content in each book. No historical information was edited out, only passages that did not contribute to the overall substance of the journal. Removing these passages made the journal easier to follow and more interesting to the reader.

I think that the reader will find, as I did, that Louisa was an interesting and remarkable woman. As you read her written thoughts, you may find some of them offensive. Before passing judgement on her, consider the standards of the time and place in which she lived rather than the standards of today.

Introduction

When Mexico gained independence from Spain, it received control of much of what is Texas today. Mexico felt threatened by the Indigenous people who dominated the region and by the United States' proximity to and interest in the area. In order to gain better control of the territory, the Mexican government encouraged settlers to move into Texas.

The Mexican government worked with land agents, called *empresarios*, to bring outside people into Texas. The empresarios and settlers received titles to large areas of land. Stephen F. Austin, one of the most famous empresarios, brought in three hundred families to settle the land, known as the "Old Three Hundred." Each family received 4,605 acres of land.

Many of these settlers came from cotton farms in the South and brought enslaved people with them. Even though some settlers renounced their US citizenship and became Mexican citizens, they still supported the United States. As a result, distrust and hatred toward the Mexican government soon developed, and many of the settlers later fought for Texas independence.

Louisa Foster's parents were Nancy and Isham B. Phillips. Isham was probably a cotton farmer in Alabama. He served under General Andrew Jackson during the Creek War in 1813–14. The family came to Texas as part of Austin's "Old Three Hundred" colonists. On May 9, 1827, Isham received a sitio of land in Wharton County and another league of land in Matagorda County on March 9, 1829. A sitio (from Spanish) of land equaled about 4,338 acres and in this area of Texas was often used for grazing livestock, including horses, mules, and cattle. A league of land was about 4,428 acres. Isham owned another league of land in Gonzales County on Snell's Creek. The family home was located on the north side of Peach Creek in Matagorda County.

Isham also served as a judge in 1836 and as a postmaster. In 1841 he died at home several days after the death of his wife, and his estate was divided equally between Louisa and Marion, her younger brother, who was a minor at the time. In addition to the land, the estate consisted of ten enslaved people, horses, cattle, pigs, a home, and furnishings.[1]

Malvinia Louisa Phillips was born on December 3, 1821, in Washington County, Alabama. The county is in lower southwest Alabama, and borders Mississippi. Her brother, Leonidas Marion Phillips, was born on December 9, 1823, in Alabama.

Louisa married Benjamin M. Clopton on May 15, 1839. She never mentioned where they lived, but I suspect it may have been in Matagorda County. Louisa suffered many losses over the next two years. Benjamin died on June 1, 1840, from unstated causes. Shortly after her husband's death, Louisa gave birth to their son, Isham Benjamin Clopton, on July 21, 1840. In March of 1841, Louisa's parents died within two days of each other. Louisa said her father suffered from a disease for ten years that eventually led to his death. Louisa then lost her one-year-old son, who died in her arms on August 8, 1841.

Louisa's second husband, the Rev. Finis Ewing Foster, was born in Wilson County, Tennessee, on February 26, 1816, and died on August 14, 1879, eight years after Louisa's death, near Mexia, Texas. Several sources mentioned who his parents were, but they offered no proof. The 1850 US census showed his birthplace to be Tennessee.

Finis came to the Republic of Texas sometime in 1840 or 1841. Texas had recently won its independence from Mexico, and many people were moving into the region. It would have been fertile religious grounds for a young preacher.

Louisa said she first saw Finis at a religious camp meeting in November 1841. I speculate that Louisa attended the meeting because she was still mourning the deaths of her parents and young son earlier that year and her husband's death the previous year. She wrote that her earlier life had been one of gaiety but that she had wanted to die after the deaths of her parents, husband, and child. Now she was probably seeking the comfort that religion might

[1]Matagorda County Book Committee, *Historic Matagorda County* (University of North Texas Libraries, The Portal to Texas History, Palacios Area Historical Association, 1986), 1:83–84, texashistory.unt.edu/ark:/67531/metapth992181.

provide. I suspect that this wealthy young widow probably had many suitors.

Louisa wrote that she and Finis fell in love immediately. They began discussing marriage in December of 1841, which alarmed her friends. Finis was new to Texas, and many young men had been coming into the area fleeing debts or a wicked past. I am sure some believed that this poor, unknown preacher might take advantage of an attractive and rich woman in mourning.

To his credit, Finis tried to warn her of the life she would be getting into if she married a poor traveling preacher. Louisa wrote in her diary, "He drew a dark picture indeed of the trials of a minister's wife." His honesty made her love him even more, and they were engaged on April 27, 1842, and married in Matagorda County on September 1, 1842.

Their first child was born on March 10, 1845, and they named him Finis Robert. Tragically, after a long illness, he died in February 1847, soon after the family returned from a trip to Ohio and Missouri. Louisa wrote that the illness that led to his death was an inflammation of the brain caused by teething. While living in East Texas, the couple had another son, Thomas (Tommie) Wilson, who was born on November 11, 1847.

In January of 1848, the family moved to Houston, Texas. Finis was still preaching, and had gone to work for a company that published religious books. They then moved to Austin in February 1849, and Finis served as a full-time preacher in Austin and the surrounding area.

On August 7, 1850, the couple was blessed with a girl, whom they named Louisa Clemantine. Sadly, the girl died on June 3, 1851, in the same room in which she was born. Another boy, Finis Andrew, was born to the couple on December 14, 1852. Louisa wrote that the new baby had blue eyes and resembled the departed Louisa Clemantine.

In March 1853, the family moved about sixty miles north of Austin to Belton, Texas, and lived on a twenty-acre farm there. The small town had first been settled in 1850 and a year later became the county seat of the newly formed Bell County. In twenty years the population would still be fewer than three hundred people. Finis was a Cumberland Presbyterian preacher (sometimes referred to as a missionary), and shared a church building with a Methodist congregation. He was also one of the founding members of the Masons in the area in 1855.[2]

[2]George W. Tyler, *The History of Bell County*, ed. Charles W. Ramsdell (San Antonio: Naylor, 1936), 143, 161, 381.

In October 1855, the family left Belton to spend the winter in the Gonzales area. Finis preached in the area and attended various church meetings. On November 7, 1855, Louisa Cathrine (nicknamed Lou Katie) was born. During much of the time, Finis was out of town attending meetings with church elders. In order to pay the bills, Finis traveled to Wharton County to sell some of the land Louisa had inherited. When he returned, he discovered that little Lou Katie had been sick off and on for several weeks. On February 2, 1856, the little girl died a few days short of three months old and was buried in Gonzales.

Louisa kept these eleven journals for two reasons, as she explained in 1856: "One object of my life I had in view was my own satisfaction in being permitted by it more closely to retrospect my past life, and by it more carefully to guard the present & with Christian resignation & prayers to wait patiently the events of the unknown future. Last, but not least I fondly hoped it would have a solitary effect upon the morals & hearts of my only child, my sweet Tommie W. Foster."

Note: As you read Louisa's journals, you will notice that she called many people "cousin." It was not uncommon, especially in small towns, to refer to very close friends, usually around the same age as oneself, as a cousin. Louisa also referred to numerous people as "aunt" and "uncle." They were usually close friends who were older than Louisa. Some people were called "brother" or "sister," and they were members from her church or members of a like-minded church, such as the Methodists. Members of other churches, such as Baptists, or nonchurch friends, might be referred to as "Mr." or "Mrs." or just by their given name.

Many times, Louisa gave the names of the men who preached the church sermon. Because so many men were mentioned doing this, I suspect that many were her neighbors and not real preachers.

Where the Fosters lived (map by webmaster@d-maps.com)

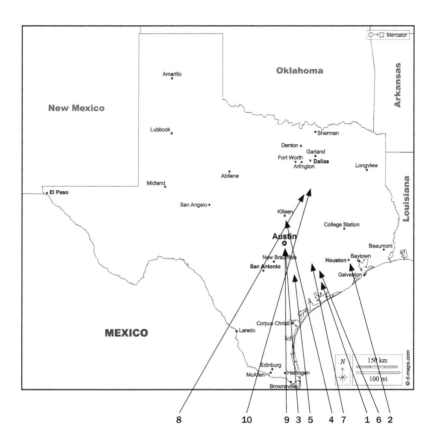

1. Matagorda County, where Louisa lived, met Finis, and married in 1842.
2. The Fosters lived in Houston in 1848.
3. The Fosters lived in Austin 1849.
4. Belton, where the Fosters lived from 1853 to 1858.
5. Gonzales, where the family spent the winter of 1856. Daughter Lou Katie is buried there.
6. Wharton County, where Louisa had land. Finis went there in 1856 to sell property to pay bills.
7. La Grange, where the Fosters bought property and moved in 1858.
8. Bosqueville, where the Fosters moved in the summer of 1862.
9. The Fosters moved back to Austin 1866.
10. Tehuacana Cemetery, where the Reverend Foster is buried.

Journal #1

November 11, 1847–February 9, 1850

Thursday morn 11th [1847] O yes! Be it ever so humble I do <u>feel that home is a sweet place</u>, our visit to our dear relatives in Missouri and attendance at the Camp Meeting, and Genl. Assembly Lebanon Ohio was delightful to us and I was happy then and am so still. We this morning were blessed with a large sweet boy we call him Thomas Wilson for our beloved brothers. We dedicate him to the Lord and pray that he may be spared to us and us to him, to be permitted to raise <u>him</u> the second <u>sweet pledge</u> of our conjugal affection for the Lord, here our sweet Finis Robert was taken from us, and here our previous little Thomas Wilson was given to, and we know that "the Lord giveth and the Lord taketh away," and blessed be the name of our God.

Tuesday 16th We are doing well, my dear husband started this morning to Crockett [about 120 miles southeast of Dallas] for the purpose of attending our Synod, may the Lord bless and prosper him on his journey, and may the way be opened up for our being more useful, as servants of the true and living God.

20th No accident or misfortune has befallen is, to day we are well also, nothing to mar our peace & happiness, save the absence of my dear Finis, and when I think of him, it is a pleasure to know he is now living in the discharge of his duty as a minister.

December 3rd 1847 This day I am 26 years old. O how faithless I have been. Many precious moments of that time I have spent in folly. My husband is gone again to the vicinity of San Augustine [about thirty miles east of Nacogdoches, in far East Texas]. There to close his preaching there forever, I presume.

December 7th To day my feelings are of a mixed nature for it is the last day my husband and Bro will spend with in 5 or 6 weeks, perhaps longer.

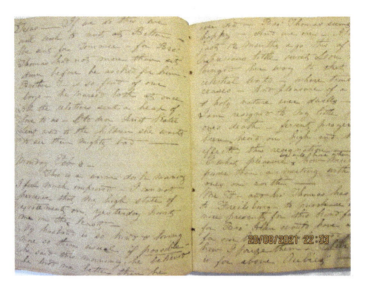

Sample page of Louisa's journal

And owing to the unexpected tour of my husband and my late confinement, I am in a great press to make necessary preparations for the trip. This evening Miss Julia Newton came to spend some time with me during my husbands absence. Mr Foster this day sold our home residence, we are to give possession in March next.

8th I feel almost sick with a headache, and quite lonely, nevertheless I know it was my Dear husbands duty to go hence and select for us a home, and for him a newfound preaching place.

14th This day is passing away, and it is a lively bright one too, and all we need to cheer us of the merry laugh of my absent beloved F, our sweet little Tom is improving in looks, and goodness. He has heretofore been pretty cross but is now some little better.

15th Another day is gone and Mr F has been gone a week this morning. I am glad that one week has passed away, that he is to be absent, to look ahead in imagination 4 weeks longer seems distant. But the time I hope will soon roll round that will bring his welcome return.

Sunday 18th Another Sabbath has passed away and we are all enjoying good health. J Parilee Newton and Salina Smith are here again. I had to give Jeff [an enslaved child] a lecture for misbehavior on this the Lords day.

Wed 21st This is a lovely day, but still I feel lonely, not so much so as I did yesterday. I felt cheerful & happy after my husband & bro Wilson started, knowing or at least believing it was my Finie's duty to go hence and seek another home. I prayed to the Lord to give me a cheerful heart, and he granted my petition. Jeffs misbehavior on the Sabbath has caused me many serious moments of reflection. I fear the lectures & warnings will all prove abortive and of our praying for him will only sink him lower in to hell.

Thur 22nd My husband has been absent just 2 weeks today. In 2 more I will begin to look for him. I do trust he will be favored with good weather and soon will return safe to his own home & Town. O I do feel so anxious to look upon that smiling face again.

Fri 23rd To day is rather dark & cloudy I fear that we will have rain. I trust not our sweet boy is well. I think he had the colic last night. I gave him 5 drops paregoric which eased & caused him to slumber sweetly immediately.

25th We have a very beautiful Christmas day, but a general dull time. I have company all the time but still I feel that I am all alone.

Jan 4th O I feel so lonely. I wish more than ever if possible for the return of my husband.

Wed 12th Houston is the point of our destination now, then perhaps my husband will labor as a stationed minister, or a colporteur, as God may seem to direct him. O for more grace. [A *colporteur* is someone employed by a religious society to distribute religious books and literature.]

Thurs 13th We are well & have fine health, are busily packing up & selling our things that we cannot carry with us.

Thurs 27th Beautiful morning. We traveled only 12 miles to Mr Bighams an acquaintance of my. There we spent the night agreeably passed thro' Douglass & got our boorish horses shod, our team traveled west of Douglass 5 miles to Maj Durnsts corn & fodder. [Douglass was about 10 miles west of Nacogdoches.]

Fri 28th We traveled 22 miles to good water struck camp, made a big fire, & now I am writing by its light, ferriage over, the Naches corn & fodder cost us $2.50.

Sat 29th We traveled 25 miles to Bro Gossetts, arrived there bout dark.

Sunday 30th We are at still at father Gossetts, this is a lovely morning. We did intend to have gone into Crockett, for the purpose of attending Church at 11 o clock, but owning to the rain on yesterday we are compelled to remain in town & spend the night with Bro & Sister Nevils, the team will remain here until Monday. We spent an agreeable night at Bro Nevils. My husband was solicited to preach tonight, but he could not consistently comply with the request on account of a rising on his jaw.

Mond 31st We traveled 16 miles & camped near a prairie a cool but pretty day $1.50 [cost of fodder].

Feb Tue 1st We traveled 17 miles through a prairie, a cool ride it was truly. Corn & fodder $3.75.

Monday 20th [It is March and the Fosters are now living in Houston.] A very pretty day. My dear Finis returned & met me with his wanted smile, that ever cheers & animates my heart.

Thurs 23rd We made several pleasant calls to day and my husband was appointed agent for the Houston Bible Society which is auxiliary to the American Bible Society. He is now making all the preparations that are needful for a tour west with a quantity of Bibles & books.

Friday 24th This is another pretty day, about ½ after 3. My husband and Bro McGowns started to Presbytery. I could not for my life refrain from weeping. O that I could compose my feeling more at the time of his leaving home. I cannot as yet but perhaps in future I may do better; I trust that I will. I sat in the door and watched my husband as he drove out of the City. It was consoling thought to me that he was conveying in his boroush [a type of carriage].

Wednesday 29th I am still gardening and got thro' planting seeds. Soon after dinner this employment to me is a delightful one, Jeff. When I finished reading I felt that if I would bow down, with & pray, perhaps it might an impression that would do some good. I did so, Lord bless my efforts this day and help to be faithful and may I see these little precious immortal souls connected. That they may make proper impressions on the young & expanding mind of our sweet babe. And that in Heaven we may meet to extol the lamb forever. has just finished throwing up a beautiful walk, on either side I intend to sow first the Missouri running rose a native plant or vine rather of that state. Then the flower arbour bean, then Butter & lima Beans, that will answer for good vegetables, and shade also.

Thursday 30th I arose this morning which was a damp rainy one. Feeling rather sick, dressed myself & washed my face & hands hoping this would cause me to feel better, but I got worse. Could not sit with any comfort, therefore was compelled to go to bed and had to remain there almost all day. This evening I fell very weak indeed, but think & trust I will be almost well by morning. I desire very much the tender hand of my dear husband to distribute comfort to my little wants and that kind voice I wished to hear in its wanted kindness.

Sat 1st April We are all in fine health. Our sweet boy is growing finely & is very forward & playful. He has learned to hallow & make a noise that pleases him very much to listen at his noise. That will delight his Pa when he returns.

Sunday 2nd Am returning home after morning service. I met with an old acquaintance, during my former association with him he was irreligious but since that time he has obtained a blessed hope and has attached himself to the C.P. church [C.P. stands for Cumberland Presybeterian].

Thurs 6th This is a cold day, but tolerable feeling. No special change save Jeff's learning to cook better, Mary [a young enslaved girl] is very dull, the babe is well cheerful & knows his uncles voice, Sarah loves to talk with him & he notices Ma near a very great deal.

Thursday 13th About 12 Mr Foster & bro McGown returned, my husband as usual met me with pleasure beaming in that eyes, which to look upon ever affords me pleasure. He affectionately kissed his little Lou & Tom as he is ever want to do on his return. He sold all his books & could have disposed of more, he is pleased with his agency.

Sunday 16th Mr Foster Preached our rented room at 11 O clock. Brother Nevils at 3, a respectable audience. The Baptist showed us much courtesy in attendance inasmuch as their Pastor was absent on a short mission to the Brazos. Our minister proposed organizing a church here soon & forming a missionary society.

Wed 19th To day I visited a Baptist Lady, was kindly received. We had a good religious & social conversation. I said to her, Sister Smith, we expect to organize a church here & endeavor to cooperate with all the evangelical churches, in spreading the gospel colors to the __?__ she seemed gratified and said in this City there is sufficient number of inhabitants for each church to have a goodly share. [The population of Houston in the 1850 census was 2,396.] O for more Christians inbred with that spirit. Bro Matthews, a minister of our church arrived at our city to day. The Houston Bible Society met tonight, had an interesting time. They practically assigned Mr F his field as agent commencing here, placing in his hands every citizen of this City & County first, the Bible and then. Houston, and here may we witness the conversion of scores to the worship of the true Living God.

Sat 22nd By the request of my husband, I tried sell some Bibles. I sold 2 books & bargained 5 bibles for next week, this was my first effort to assist my husband in his agency and I felt happy.

Monday 15th May 1848 This day 9 years ago I was first married [to her first husband, Benjamin Clopton]. I was blessed with a tender & affectionate husband, but he was spared to me only little over a year. I then thought the cup of happiness on earth from my life had passed forever. On the 21st of July following I was blessed with a sweet little solace. Soon all my earthly affections were rendered on the dear pledge of our conjugal love. Alas! I loved him too well, on the 8th July next he too was torn from his youthful & widowed Mother. To lay beside the father that never was permitted to look up his son and between the demise of my beloved husband and babe I was called upon to bury at the burial ground my dear and revered Parents, all my props for earthly happiness was gone. I had fondly expected that My babe, my own son would be spared to rock the cradle of my declining years, but mistaken idea, the thought of my lonely condition almost crazed me, my friends in after life told me. They feared for my reason, "but I then turned to thy gospel Lord," & found consolation in believing and on the 1st Sept, 1842 I bestowed my widowed heart upon Finis Foster, Minister of the Cumberland Presbyterian Church.

We each loved at first sight, and until this hour that deep ardent love has been deepening and widening. I do not love him just as I loved my former companion for himself alone, but because God gave him to me. To sooth my sorrows, and dry up the fountain of grief that was perfectly undermining my Constitution, and more than this my mind. He has been a solace to me, a help in divine things, things that pertain to heaven. O may our efforts be more firmly united to do good, to work and to give for the advancement of our dear Redeemers cause.

Thursday 18th Our gardens are much refreshed from the rain that fell on yesterday. As yet Mr Foster has no carriage to prosecute his agency with much success.

Sat 20th This is a bright lovely morning. My dear husband this morning after kissing his Louisa & babe as is his invaluable custom, left home for the purpose of visiting a member of our church & taking a short tour & try to sell some of the societies books.

Tuesday 23rd A bright morning, we are all well and old gentleman a Baptist minister called to day to sell us some butter and Mr Foster invited him in to look at the books he has on hands. And now I am the wife of a minister of the same church, and a book agent. May the good Lord assist me to be his helpmate and attend each Vol. distributed each with a prayer & address delivered to good souls. And the means of saving thousands.

Thursday 1st June 1848 A very warm day, I am very much pleased studying natural Philosophy & revising Geography & several of my old studies. It is a delightful task.

Friday 2nd Mr Foster west on a tour, and to attend some camp meetings and see Sister Clementine.

Friday 16th I think Judge Noble paid me over 7$ to day. Our sweet boy is getting still more interesting every day. He can say Pa, Papa & Daddy perfectly plain. He a few minutes ago called Jeff bad boy, that little incident called to mind our beloved departed little one that now rests in the bosom of the Savior.

Sunday 18th I had just dressed early for church, the rain began to fall & prevented. I regretted it very much indeed, but the good Lord will act right. I had in the forenoon a feast of reading the Bible for my own special instructions. Then I read & explained as well as I could to Jeff & Mary the dedication of Samuel to God. They were interested and I felt deeply.

At dinner Bro A hurt my feelings exceedingly by saying that I kept Mr Foster from going off on his agency. I must say this assertion was not true, and told him so. When he saw that my feelings were wounded he observed he would call it back, that he was jesting, he left immediately for his office.

I spent some time in weeping. My heart was pained to think Bro McGown would think such a thing. I have stood up for him thro' thick and thin, many have been the objections to him, that have been told me, but I have invariably argued for him, A tender cord could not be easily touched in my heart, than to say I try to curtail my husbands influence in doing good. I scarcely ever express my humble opinion, but leave all things for him to act upon. It may be just because I weep when my husband is forced to say farewell, but it is not because I do not wish him to go, but I feel a tender sorrow that that causes my hearts to bleed and suffuses my eyes with tears, but this transcends __?__ of sorrow cannot disturb that settled peace which is deeply settled in my bosom.

Wednesday 21st A bright pretty morning. I visited a house where lay the corpse of a little infant 2 weeks old. We feel satisfied its love wrap spirit is now in heaven, death is its everlasting gain.

Friday 30th As usual on Friday night Bro McGown was out late preparing his papers for the mail. I read to my little servants [enslaved persons], Jeff & Mary and asked them some questions on the part of scripture I read and tried to expound to them last Sabbath week, some they answered promptly. This was comforting to my soul.

Sat July 1st We look for Mr Foster this evening, I do desire much to see him, our boy has improved so much since he left. About 4 O clock this evening my dear Finis returned. The first thing that met my eye was a bright cheering smiles which ever repays me for days of absence, when duty separates us. Mr Foster ever expressed much pleasure on returning home, but this time he seemed more delighted than ever. O he said I did want to see you & our sweet boy so bad. Said he never wanted to see us as bad before, he believed. He wrote me from Huntsville but I did not get the letter until after he got home.

Tuesday 4th We went to the Presbyterian Church. There we had music by the choir, then a prayer by Mr Belvin, then music. The Declaration of Independence was read by Mr Williams, Music, an Oration was read by Music, Benediction pronounced by Mr Miller, we returned home pleased & gratified, that we attended the celebration of that great eventful day.

Tuesday 11th This day our sweet babe is 8 months old. He is very healthy & sprightly for which I do thank the Lord that bestowed such a treasure up on us. Lord may, O may we raise him for <u>Thee</u>.

Sat 15th A busy day as usual preparing for Sabbath, so our servants will have time for rest and attend church. Lord bless my little servants. I have reared them from infancy. I desire more than language can express their conversion.

Friday 21st It rained all night, bad roads, but duty calls <u>him</u> to depart. And I have desired much for him to be with me. But when duty commands I submit. I feel more than a usual willingness for him to go. Lord strengthen that willingness.

Thursday 27th My babe of late has taken up a notion that he will cry & hallow all the time he is being dressed and on account of his being so strong it is with hard struggles & much difficulty that he can be dressed. A five minutes ago I was compelled to change his dress, he was in a perfect good humor until I commenced to undress him. He kicked & cried a great deal, I have always been a strong advocate for firmness in decision in raising children, but have been of the opinion of all the writer on the subject, before Father

Rev. Jacob Lindley, a Cumberland Presbyterian preacher, wrote a book published in 1846 titled *Infant Philosophy*. He startled the mothers in his congregation by urging that they ought to commence governing their children, at least, by the time they were six months old. He implied the use of corporal punishment. However, he did not come out and say it. Source: *Brief Biographical Sketches of Some of the Early Minister of the Cumberland Presbyterian Church*, by Richard Beard. 1874.

Linly that 1 year old was plenty early to commence corporal punishment, but according to Father L's [Jacob Lindley] code of reasoning, the child's habits in a great measure are fixed for life. So, I think this about it, we had better begin too soon than too late, and I have always had a great anxiety for my child to be more than common in goodness, & intelligence and prompt to obey its parents. I have been and am now reading prayerfully that aged Fathers Infants Philosophy, which added to my own views on the subject.

I determined more resolutely the Lord being my helper, to try and do my duty towards the pledge of conjugal love, the good Lord has bestowed upon me for some <u>wise</u> purpose, it is painful for me to whip, but this morning I smacked my little one until his tender skin turned red, and that made my heart ache, but still I felt I had discharged my duty, my child <u>must be</u> obedient and do not feel that I did wrong. I then set him in his crib, he commenced crying again. I thought what shall I do, I knew. One or the other must conquer, my Tom or myself. I then calmly laid him down in his crib &

smacked him pretty severely & rocked him telling him firmly but kindly he must mind Mother, he hushed immediately, and would sweetly murmur Pa.

O my precious little one, how my heart yearned over him, but I dared not take him up I left him in a few minutes he cried out. I dreaded the result but kept writing, he soon got quiet of himself, and is now playing so sweetly in the crib. Lord give me firmness & fixedness of purpose to raise by beloved little one, for Thee.

Our sweet precious was a good boy played a long time. After a while he took another little spell. I smacked him a little and bade him hush & immediately he obeyed, this was a source of gratification to me.

Thursday 3rd [August 1848] A very pretty morning rather warm. As yet I have not received a line from Mr Foster, neither one word since he left. I am anxious to hear from him, and his success in his good work. I have just been looking upon his picture. I felt that I wished to press it to my lips and did so. And those eyes seemed to look a kind reproof, perhaps it was imaginary. Yes! Doubtless it was caused by the simple fact that my husband (when first he gave it to me, I pressed it to my lips) he said O Louisa that looks like idolatry. I am afraid its wrong to do so. I prized my loved image much, and desire much to see the (original). Tomorrow he will have been absent 2 weeks and at the least it seems to be a month.

Friday 4th I received one of the kindest letters I ever read from my beloved husband. Lord bless him and may he be useful to the great & good cause in which he is so engaged. O ever O Lord in his meanderings may they smile, attend to cheer him, and urge him on to duty.

Sat 5 I have just been reading my Dear husbands letter over. It breaths the spirit of love, love to the good cause in which he is engaged. And love to his precious Louisa & sweet Tom Wils, as he fondly terms us. So far I have done well since he left. I have daily prayed for him and constantly think of him. But it is not with regrets, but I know he is trying to unfurl wide the gospel banner I am happy.

I finished my lesson in Philosophy and began my letter to my dear husband before dinner. Afterwards I finished it. In it I poured for the effusions of my soul to him that I love, that is engaged in trying to do good for the human family. This morning my babe is rather fretful, so much so that I had to slap him, painful as it is to my feelings.

Wednesday 16th I had hoped to get a letter from Huntsville from my dear husband but failed. I think quite strange of it fear he is sick, he surely would have written to be at this favored time. When he knows I am so anxious to hear from him, and more particularly when he is indebted to me an answer to an affectionate letter sent by Bro McGown, which unless something happen. He has doubtless received, but I trust he will write next mail. I judge the course is he was unaware that the mail starting from Huntsville was changed to an earlier day that had been customary. Lord I ask thy protection to be extended over us both during our absence & health & safety may we meet.

This morning I got up & went in the kitchen, our babe was asleep, when I returned in about 2 minutes he had gotten up & was sitting up, looking in perfect astonishment for his absent ma, & when I came to the bed, he gave me one of those sweet looks, that none but a parent can appreciate.

After breakfast I went to dress him. O what a fuss he did make. I smacked him severely he would not quit. When I finished dressing him calmly laid him the bed slapped him biding him firmly to hush, until he looked scornfully at me & obeyed. How my poor heart did ache but I felt, I love my child, but I must make him obey me, & that is the best way to express affection for a child rear them right. An old adage often occurs to me, spare the rod and spoil the child, as tenderly as I love my sweet Thomas Wilson, and as loth as I would be to give him up, I would rather follow him to the narrow cell prepared for all the dead than to raise a disobedient & wicked child.

Thursday 17th To day is quite pretty O with what intense anxiety I waited Bro Carroll's return from the P office fondly expecting a tender letter from my absent loved <u>one</u>. And I cannot describe my disappointment when he returned and no letter for me. I was glad to learn by a letter from Bro McGown to Bro Carroll that Mr Foster was well. I must still believe that he wrote me and the letter miscarried some way. I wrote to him a long letter again tonight.

Friday 18th Last night was the stormiest night I have witnessed in many months & I believe I might say years. It rained & blowed all night long. O how I did wish for my dear husband. I was fearful the house would blow over.

Tuesday 22nd This morning I dressed our sweet little babe in his solid pink gingham, and put on his cap, and Jeff asked in as much as he had to go to __?__ some flour, if he might not take sweet little Wils with him. I consented he started off in triumph as if proud to bear the little treasure along. He said one of the gentlemen took him behind the counter and gave him some loaf-sugar to eat. I thought when the little one when he returned looked sweater & prettier than I ever witnessed.

Tomorrow I expect a letter from Mr Foster and to day week I expect his return, and I do fervently ask, God that I may be disappointed, if I just could get a tender letter from him. Speaking to me thro that silent but eloquent medium in his wanted language of tenderness & affection & happiness would be much enhanced and my poor heart would be greatly encouraged to bear & endure with perfect submission, "thus to live apart."

Wednesday 23rd To day is quite pleasant. Roll along ye wheels of time and bring the anxiously expected day when I shall again be pressed to that bosom in whose happiness I live. To day I received some of the tenderest letters from my dear & beloved husband that I ever read. Even that kind letter breathing such ardent conjugal love for me & tender paternal affection for our sweet boy, has already repaid me for my hours of loneliness since he bade me adieu, beside this I live in anticipation of more happiness in sweet converse together than language & pen could give.

Wednesday 30th I expect perhaps Mr F's desired return in his last letter which I received a week previous to this date, he observed that it appeared like it has been almost a year since he has left us, and now I feel the same. Our sweet boy is well and improving finely. I must here relate for his satisfaction when he grows up, to be a large boy & perhaps then his anxious & fond mother that watches with delights each little endearing action, may repose runeath [sic] the cold __?__ of the earth, but to my story. Our precious Tom Wilsy, first pulled up by a chair & stood there awhile. And I was standing near him & turned round and looked and behold my precious babe had gotten up and was standing in the chair, holding a post in each hand to support his little body. Lord do bless & save our little one to us, & us to him and may, O may we rear him for the Lord. He was 9 months old the 11th of this month.

I called at A. J. Burks, according to promise to bid Miss Dunn an intimate acquaintance farewell. Mr Foster got home and met me on my return home. He as ever expressed great pleasure on meeting with his little wife & boy and my happiness cannot give utterance to the happiest hours of my life, as when my dear husband returns from his mission of love with his soul having been blessed during his arduous work in the discharge of the holy duties of his ministerial office.

Thursday 31st My husband & I to day had pleasant interchange of thoughts and talked over the gracious revivals he witnessed during his tour of labor of love.

Friday September 1st Well to day we have been married six years. Many changes, both adverse and prosperous have occurred since that auspicious hour, in which I gave my heart & hand in the holy bands of matrimony, but we still find pure conjugal love, the best antidote against the trials and difficulties of this life.

We took a ride in our boroush [carriage] with our precious child. On our return Mr F presented me with a beautiful pink silk bound advice to a married couple. [There was a book, first published in 1793, called *The Christian Minister's Affectionate Advice to a Married Couple* by James Bean.]

Tuesday 5th We are well as usual only Bro C. has a cold. It is pretty certain that the Yellow fever is in our City. O may we do some good for the great & good cause. That we have expounded this. [One of the Houston doctors noticed a case of yellow fever on August 30th. He stated that he saw more during the first week of September 1848, and in a few days the epidemic was fully developed throughout the city. Several hundred people eventually died from during this outbreak.]

Thursday Sept 7th 1848 It is now 20 minutes after 5 O clock, and we will soon be off for the City of the Hills (Austin) for the purpose of attending the Presbytery and at the same time Mr F will attending to the arduous duties of his agencies. We have traveled steady all day, arrived here about sundown. We had a pleasant but warm drive. Mr F sold no books to day but granted some few tracts, Lord we ask humbly thy holy aid, we desire this trip to be one of joint usefulness. We were kindly received here. We traveled 25 miles to Mr C's, good road, am entirely level poor country. I think the citizens of this immediate portion could not sustain themselves were it not for keeping entertainment. Bill $2.20

Friday 8th Quite a change in the weather very much like autumn as it is. We traveled 25 miles to Bro Durhams, very kindly received indeed, spent a very pleasant night, no bill. Mr F sold a good many books.

Sat 9th We traveled some 6 or 8 miles stopped to sell some books & found an old acquaintance of my youthful days. He would have us spend some time with him & had we dined with them, & enjoyed ourselves well. Capt Hoth is a Roman Catholic. He bought a book. I purchased 45 cents worth of muslin for a harvesting bonnet. We traveled on to a small commencement of the town. The citizens purchased some books, they observed they hoped the citizens of the surrounding county would now give them a better name in as much as they had bought the scriptures and so many religious works. At night we were informed that their town bore the name of Devils Bend. [There was a community by that name northeast of Austin, but it would have been out of the way for Louisa to travel there. I found nothing by that name on the way to Austin. It was probably named for a creek in the area.]

Sunday 10th We arrived here last night, our host & hostess & daughter are worthy members of our Church, Bro Green's a delightful place to spend the Sabbath.

Monday 11th We arose tolerably early and bowed together in our bedroom and engaged in humble prayer as is our custom, and then we came down the stairs & met the kind family around the altar of prayers. Now we desire to spend this day for God. I have some books of our order to sell for Bro McGown. I sold 3 vol. this morning to Father Green. It is now 7 minutes after 6 and we are now at Mr Prestleys after traveling some 10 or 12 miles. About 10 O clock in the morning we arrived at Jacksonville.

Mr Foster sold some books & I dined with Mr Day an old acquaintance. [This could have been one of Austin's Old 300 that, which arrived in Texas with Louisa's family.] We had a hard rain about 12 which detained us some, and was partly the cause of our short days travel.

Tuesday 12th We passed through Brenham [This puts the couple about halfway to Austin]. Called to see Sister Pipkin, she was very low hardly expected to live. We traveled some 23 miles to Bro Tom Bells, here we spent an agreeable evening. But an almost sleepless night on account of heat, our sweet babe is well.

Wednesday 13th We drove half mile to Father Duffs. Here we met a kind reception, by our old friends. A pleasant morning we will remain here a day or 2. At 5 in the afternoon Mr F preached by request, he selected this passage "If you know these things" & to a small but attentive congregation. How delightful to spend the day with friends we love.

Thursday 14th We have spent another pleasant evening here. Lord bless every word spoken to day & forgive any error. They all seem fond of our sweet child.

Friday 15th We are now most ready to be off again. We left Father Duffs about 8 in the morning. Dined at Mr Muckloroys spent several hours at Bro Clem Allens, we have a pleasant time to day.

We at last stopped to spend the night at Mr Abner Kuykendalls. [This may be the Abner Kuykendall that came from Tennessee in 1831.

There was a man by that name in the area who had earlier fought the Indigenous people.]

We are now in connection in going to Presbytery & and our agencies, visiting old acquaintances. I have not had the pleasure of seeing for some 4 years. Lord bless our meeting and bring together to our mutual good.

Sat 16th Then we traveled about 10½ miles & stopped at an old acquaintance, a dear friend. We were kindly met indeed.

Sunday 17th We spent Sabbath at Clear Creek. Mr F preached morning & evening. Our sweet boy is quite unwell. This is the first sickness he has ever had. May he soon be well again, he has a cold.

Monday 18th We drove 10 miles to LaGrange, stopped at one corner of the square. We remained in our carriage & witnessed the Masonic & military parade around the square & then saw the possession form & march in order towards the point over the river when then intended to bury the bones of some of our chivalrous fellow citizens who had fallen in combatting the Mexicans. It was a solemn sight to look up on the hearse & horses. [On September 18, 1848, the bones of fifty-two Texan men were buried on Monument Hill in a commemorative ceremony attended by many dignitaries and citizens of La Grange. The men were from the Dawson and Mier expedition, which fought against raiding parties by the Mexican army in 1842.]

We went in our boroush, the distance being too great for me to walk. A sermon was delivered by Bro Kinney, a Methodist E. south. We returned to Bro Farrell's & spent the night. [Methodist E. south stood for Methodist Episcopal Church South. In 1845 the Methodists, after a long struggle, split over the issue of slavery. The churches of the North were opposed to slavery and those of the South supported it.]

Tuesday 19th We drove into LaGrange dined with Bro & sister McFarland, in the evening we called on Bro & Sister Waller, also Sister Oats. We then drove 5 miles to Cousin Moore's was affectionately received in the rain.

Wednesday 20th We are now spending agreeable time with Cousin Betty Moore as Cousin Edwin is absent, their Servant girl & our boy done up of clothes neatly.

Friday 22nd It is now 25 minutes after 8 in the morning. We will soon leave. I sold 1 Burrow, Mr F family pocket Bible. We traveled 12 miles to Mr Young's, his Lady is a dear friend of mine, here we were most warmly received. To day we called to see the consecrated spot where sleeps the mortal remains of our beloved & lamented Bro John Foster, he was doubly dear to

A barouche carriage that the Foster's took was probably similar to this carriage. It had to be large enough to accommodate the Fosters, their servant Jeff, personal luggage, and the books they sold. It may have had two horses for such a long trip. Jeff probably did most of the driving. Public domain.

us, for he was a Dear brother of my husband & then a faithful minister of Christ.

Sat 23rd We traveled 20 miles to a pretty town situate in a valley, here we were met kindly by the widow of Bro Morgan, one of our talented & beloved ministers. My husband's acquaintances.

Monday 25 Some appearance of rain, we hope it will shower a little the dust is very troublesome. I called to see Uncle this morning he was absent. When he returned Aunt Indiana sent for me. In the afternoon I called & met Uncle. He said he accompanied me over to Sister Morgans & had Mr F with us to spend the night. They seemed they could not treat us kind enough. I do feel happy this night for there was a coolness existing caused by my marriage to Mr F. But the breach is closed and by our going along and attending to our own business & letting others alone.

O my Dear child when I am gone to eternity read this and practice it out in your whole life. It is for you my little one I endeavor to write this journal. May God bless it to your souls eternal interest, & my <u>highest aim</u> will be attained.

Tuesday 26th We started about 9 in the morning. Traveled 18 miles to Webbers Prarie. [Webber's Prairie, also known as Hell's Half Acre, became Webberville in 1853. Anglo-American John F. Webber, along with his African American wife and children, settled in this sparsely populated area of Texas in 1839 in order to escape the racism they had experienced in towns and cities. It was fifteen miles east of Austin.]

Sold a great many books of American Bible and Tract Societies. [The American Tract Society was an evangelical organization founded in 1825. Its purpose was publishing and disseminating tracts of Christian literature.]

May Gods spirit attend the books sold & may they prove to be effectual preachers long after we lie down in the silent tomb. Our sweet babe is unwell to day. I think nothing however but teething.

Wednesday 27th Mr F sold some more books, started about ten and we are now seated in our Boroush in Webbers prarie. Jeff has gone back to get my veil that the gentle southern gale blew off my sun bonnet, as I pass along on my journey. We got to Bro smiths about 4 in the evening, spent an agreeable time here. Mr F sold to him 7 or $8 worth.

Webbers prarie is one of the prettiest Praries I have ever seen, it is level & good land. I see it produces fine corn. Our Babe is entirely well to day for which invaluable blessing we do thank the good <u>Lord</u>.

Thursday 28th We traveled six miles to Austin. [Without all the stops, the trip to Austin would have taken about five or six days. The Fosters took twenty-one days to make the trip.] Passed over some pretty country. Arrived at the City of the Hills truly just before 11 O clock. Presbytery met at the appointed hour & the opening Sermon was delivered by Rev. H. Renick in an able forcible manner he brought to bear the duties of the ministry, Eldership and Laity. They then constituted by prayer.

We have a pretty full Presbytery. We do pray the good Lord to hover us and bless our efforts to do good. Presbytery met again in the evening, at candle light. Mr F held forth from John C 13th V 17 followed by Bro H Renick in a short feeling exhortation.

Monday 2nd The Citizens of Austin would not consent for Mr F to leave and he could not get away unless he would just tear off. So he consented to remain and preach at 11 again. He did so from Hebrews.

There remaineth therefore a rest & then they expressed a desire to me for us to make our home with them. We started late & traveled to Bro A.

Smiths, there we spent an agreeable night, he spoke to us of the desires of the people of Austin to get Mr F as their minister, which I think now would be agreeable to me. I am pleased with the people and look upon Austin and its vicinity as the prettiest Country I ever saw & it bears the name of being healthy.

Tuesday We traveled 12 miles to Webbers prarie and dined & thence to Bastrop 35 miles.

Friday 6th We drove 12 miles to the Clear Creek Camp Ground. I was much fatigued late I retired to the grove to supplicate a throne of grace. I returned they had already surrounded the stand. I seated myself near the altar. I could not be satisfied until I would go and we were Jeff was with our Babe. I was fearful he would go to sleep & let Tom fall. So I arose & walked to the tent. I was taken with a dull hurting in my breast, which seem to go through to my shoulders. I felt strange indeed. I sat down & nursed my babe. Jeff wished me to let him go attend preaching. I felt so bad. I thought I had best retire to rest & take a good sleep. Which would I expected refresh me and by that means be better prepared for usefulness, so I undressed myself & babe. We got up on the bed pointed to me, & told Jeff to go and attend the preaching & try & pray & be benefitted.

But alas! Sleep fled from my pillow I had a fever then a child then my fever returned & I spent one miserable night. Today I met Sister Clemantina Foster for the first time in six years. She is much changed in appearance.

Monday 9th I am so sick I can attend public worship but seldom.

Tuesday 10th I can hardly sit up at all. We drove to Bro Kellough's, thence to Cousin McClelland's where we spent the night, quite restless.

Wednesday 11th Drove back to Bro Kellough's retired immediately to bed. Unable to be up at all. Mr F sent for Dr Gregory, he came, & pronounced my case pneumonia, gave me, a mixture of Lobelia Quinine & Paregoric, 1 dose of purgative pills, no Calomel.

Thursday 12th I am too sick to write, we are weaning Tom.

Sat 14th I am still confined, but I perceive the medicine is taking the desired effects.

Monday 16th I still better I think. Mr F went to the Camp Ground again, sold $24 worth of books & preached at 3 in the afternoon, returned home at dark. To day I dressed myself & set up part of the time. I feel much strengthened. Our sweet Boy is pretty well weaned, but he would nurse if I would let him. He is a pretty good little one.

Wednesday 18th We are now at Dr Lafertys. I am doing well our sweet Babe is completely weaned, but he has not forgotten the breast. We traveled some 5 miles to Bro Atkinson. They expressed joy to see us, we had some singing. I felt my poor heart warmed & knew it to be pleasant to serve God.

Thursday 19th Mr F said try Tom & see if he would suck, he grabbed his tity with eagerness and seemed so glad. O that I could let him nurse again. But the Dr says it is best for both of us on account of my bad cough, that I never let him nurse again. He eats any thing we give him. We traveled 20 miles to Bro Carrs, his Lady is an old acquaintance of mine. Our little Wils was rather cross to night. I do to day finish reading my Bible regularly through for the first time. Our friends here treated us kindly indeed.

Friday 20th We traveled some 33 miles to Washington & passed through Independence. At night I was much fatigued. I was fearful I would relapse. I commence to day to read my Bible through again. [Washington is now a ghost town and is about ten miles east of Independence, which is around seventy miles east of Austin. Independence was founded in 1845, and the next year Baylor University opened its doors there. About twelve miles to the south is Brenham.]

Sat 21st We traveled 10 miles to Bro Elisha Floyd's here we were kindly received. They expressed a desire for me to remain until Mr F return from Synod. I would do but desire to go as far as I can with him, for we are compelled to be separate so much, for the yellow fever is now raging in Houston. So I cannot safely return & we think I had better travel together. Our sweet Tommy appears so sorrowful and I think he wanted to suck. Oh! It hurts some sorely to see the little one sorrowing over what he knew not the cause of his being deprived of.

Sunday 22nd We are here and intend to spend the Sabbath. Quite a rain. I tried __?__ he laughed and bit the tity, but would not suck, that relieved me much.

Tuesday 24th Traveled 15 miles to Huntsville. I felt very serious indeed, but knew no cause for it. It is now night & Mr F has gone to Church to endeavor to preach, he feared for me to turn out in the night air. Therefore, I remained here to write letters to Houston.

Wednesday 25th Mr F was busily engaged packing books for his agency, he could not attend church on that account. I was present at 11 when Bro Peal preached from 1st Psalm we dined at Bro Yokums. Left for Marshall. Traveled 12 miles to Cincinnati, no bill, only for horse feed. [Cincinnati, Texas, was twelve miles north of Huntsville. Cincinnati was hit hard by yellow fever in 1853, and after it was bypassed by the railroad in 1872, the town died out. Marshall was about 160 miles away.]

Thursday 26th We traveled 35 miles to Crockett. In the night again. Bro Nevils was absent, on his route to Synod. We were kindly received by Sister N. [Crockett was named for Davy Crockett and was founded in 1836. It was a training center for Confederate conscripts during the Civil War. It was about 118 miles to Marshall.]

Sat 28th We traveled 30 miles to a Methodist Camp Ground near Rusk in Cherokee County. [They were now about seventy miles from Marshall, in the heart of East Texas. Thirty miles in one day was good time considering Mr. Foster was traveling with a sick woman and a small child.]

Monday 30th The meeting at the expiration of days service, closed this morning, a great number of converts, may they all prove an ornaments to society & living Pillars in the Church of God. Mr F sold some books. We drove 2 miles to Rusk. Dined at Dr Moores. Mr F sold $28 worth of books in a few hours. I spent the time agreeably with Cousin Martha & Mrs Hayden & Erwin who called on me at the Dr. we drove six miles to Sister Halls, kind attention.

Tuesday 31st 1848 We traveled 25 miles over a wooded County to Mr Windells bill $2.00.

Thursday 2nd To day our Synod convenes at Marshall, Harrison County, Texas. 17 miles from here so fearful we will not arrive early enough. [This could take about five to eight hours, depending on the terrain and the speed of the horse. A horse travels at a speed of 2–4 mph when walking and 8–10 mph at a trot.]

I hate so much to see minister's marked as absent. I love promptness in all things, but particularly in attending the Judicatories of the Church. I do feel thankful, by hard driving we arrived here just in time for Mr F to record his name. I am commenced the use of Wistars Balsam of Wild Cherry.

Friday 3rd We are comfortably situated At Mr Freeman's half mile from Marshall. On account of being so far out I fear I shall hear but little preaching. To night Mr Foster with 11 other ministers were iniated as sons of Temperance. [The fraternal society was founded in 1842.]

My cough & the rain prevented my attending Church. I have commenced wearing flannel next to my skin for the benefit of my lungs. [A medical book

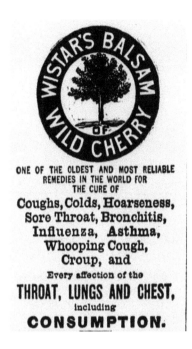

ONE OF THE OLDEST AND MOST RELIABLE
REMEDIES IN THE WORLD FOR
THE CURE OF

**Coughs, Colds, Hoarseness,
Sore Throat, Bronchitis,
Influenza, Asthma,
Whooping Cough,
Croup, and**

Every affection of the

THROAT, LUNGS AND CHEST,

including

CONSUMPTION.

Wistar's Balsam of Wild Cherry was created by Dr. Henry Wistar around 1840.
It was made of cherry extract, alcohol, and opiates. It was supposed to be a cure
for any throat, chest, and lung disease, including consumption. Public domain.

written in 1847 wrote, "In every obstinate cough we must not neglect to wear
flannel on the chest. Which is often sufficient of itself to cure."[3]]

Sat 4th Snowy morning I fear I shall not be permitted to attend Church.
My cough is evidently better, may it continue to improve. Our sweet babe is
doing fine, forgetting his tity, getting cheerful again.

Thursday 9th Quite a flattering prospect, a large number of mourners.
[According to the *Century Dictionary and Cyclopedia*, a mourner can also be
a penitent, especially one who makes public announcement of a desire for
salvation; the term was used in Methodist churches.]

Tuesday 14th We had meeting. Bro Handy Preached. Mr Foster followed by give a brief detail of the Doctrines of our Church. We then spent

[3]Christoph Wilhelm Hufeland, Caspar Bruchhausen, Robert Nelson, Bristol Royal
Infirmary Library, and University of Bristol Library History of Medicine Collections,
*Enchiridion Medicum, Or the Manual of the Practice of Medicine: The Result of Fifty Years'
Experience* (New York: William Radde, 1842), 183.

the night at Mr Freemans, he & Lady professed religion during the meeting & blessed be the Lord our feeble prayers for them were answered.

Friday 17th We will stay here, I am busy making my boy some linsey dresses. [During this period, boys and girls wore similar dresses and this was sometimes up to the age of five or six. It was usually the mother who decided when the boy should stop wearing a dress.]

Sat 18th We all attended Church. A very cold day. I never suffered so much with cold at Church in my life.

Tuesday 28th Started for home, arrived at Genl. Rusk's about 4. [Thomas J. Rusk was a political and military leader in Texas. In 1848 he was elected a US senator.]

Wednesday 29th We started late on account of being detained on business. We drove 3 or 4 miles to Mr Whitikars. To night our babe was very sick I was truly alarmed. He is teething. I feared he would go into fits.

Thursday 30th We started for Douglas, broke a Boroush spring, rained on us all day.

Friday Dec 1st 1848 We stayed all day at Bro Binghams. Sewed hard and gave our sweet babe a combination of Lobelia, Quinine & Patrgoric. He had fevers for 8 days in succession, after I gave this combination he had no more fever, but improved rapidly.

Wednesday 6th We are safely housed at Bro Hevits. We to day witness something uncommon for Texas, a snow storm, the ground is almost covered.

Monday 11th A cold pretty morning. I do trust it will continue so. We have some agency business to attend to here in town. I fear it be so late e'er we leave, that we will make but, a short days drive. I am anxious to get home & make preparation to move to Austin in as much as the CP Church [Cumberland Presbyterian] & People of that City have made known to us their desires for us to make our home with them. O for Mr F to take the Pastoral charge of the Church there.

Tuesday 12th We traveled 12 miles to Bro Folk's, we could not cross San Jacinto, reports of high water.

Tuesday 13th We traveled some 15 miles to Mr Rogers a good start pretty bad road, pretty morning but bad evening some rain at night.

Friday 15th We have a lovely morning, we are now on the road in a black level Sandy Prarie, we arrived in Houston early in the afternoon, on the general road pretty good. [They have been gone nearly two months.]

Sat 16th We are now at home. Bro Andrew Foster has a prospect of selling horses. Our sweet babe is well but spoiled from traveling. When he wants anything he says Gibben, gibben, gibben, supper, supper.

Monday 18th We took a morning ride in our boroush to try a fine Missouri horse. He performed lively, we are all together undermined whether to stay here or go to Austin. We are so pleased with Houston we hate to leave, but these fatal epedemics.

Tuesday 19th A warm <u>unpleasant</u> morning. O our sweet little boy is so badly spoiled by being necessarily nursed so much. He crys awhile then stops & looks at me to see if I will take him up. For moral courage to enable to us for judgement to overcome sympathy and bring up our child properly, it pains my heart to correct him, but must be done.

Wednesday 20th A warm day, Bro A sold another horse, our Babe is some better of his crossness. I was necessarily compelled to slap my boy, his little words when he gets mad is nappen bappen.

Thursday 21st A warm morning. Mr F & his brother would have started to day but for Mr F's indisposition. I fear he is going to be sick. At night some rain & a north blow.

Friday 22nd A cold rainy morning. Mr Foster was loth to leave home. But his brother would not consent to remain here any longer. He has been absent so long from his family. Therefore about 10 O clock they started in the rain. Mr F an his agency & Bro Andrew to look at the Colorado Valley. It has been a dismal day for traveling, but I passed off this day better than I expected. I heard this that the Cholera is in town but I hardly believe it. [With little or no knowledge of sanitation or hygiene, it is not surprising that the early citizens of Houston were the victims of frequent and fatal epidemics. Around 1846 Houston had its first cholera epidemic. African Americans appeared to have been the main victims, although many white people suffered from it, also. Between epidemics they would have scares.]

Sat 23rd Another cold day, very unpleasant. I felt very contented, until I heard this evening that it is quite likely that the Cholera is in town commencing its ravages among our citizens. I do trust what I have heard is a mistake.

Sunday 24th A dark day, sun shone out twice to cheer us, but gloom has again settled around us. This bad day & wet streets forbade my attending church.

I have a severe headache, I read my Bible, and laid down and endeavored to rest & see if my head would get ease. I could sleep. I fear I will have a spell. I feel so strange. May the Lord sustain me from what I have heard this evening I am convinced that the Cholera is now in our city and O what a lonely time my husband is far from me and it is certain the cholera is making its ravages in our lovely Houston.

Monday 25 Another Christmas is here and I am alone as usual. I am packing up, preparing to leave Houston, in the Thursday stage. I cannot bear the idea of staying here all alone, no fire side in case of sickness to sit by. If my husband was here with me it would be different. But his affairs call him hence, our babe is so lively & fascinating, but when I look upon his bright smiling face, a melancholy steals o'er my poor heart at the thought perhaps in a few days that <u>one</u> may fall a victim to that fell destroyer, but in God I put my dependence. I received a letter from my dear husband informing me he had heard of the scourge here & would return tomorrow or next day at farthest. O my heart did thank God for his goodness. About dusk I heard a rap at my door on opening I beheld my dear Finis returned to his own Louisa with him his brother A. My husband had heard an exaggerated account, & when he arrived at home he was almost sick with head ache caused by excitement, for he said he knew not but when he entered his own dwelling, he would behold his own dear wife or child a lifeless corpse. We cannot imagine or describe his feelings, but thank the good Lord the destroyer had not come to our dwelling. We kept packing up until 11 at night getting ready to leave Houston.

Tuesday 26th We are thank the good Lord almost ready to start. We finished packing Mr F took our goods & chattels [property other than real estate] to the wearehouse & returned. We all started about 4 in the afternoon and traveled 18 miles by 9 O clock at night muddy bad road.

Wednesday 27th We drove to Mr McMahans & dined kind attention indeed. Old Alabama friends of Mr F's. thence we drove to Mr John Borden a tutor of mine in my young days.

Thursday 28th We started in the rain to get over the Bernards [San Bernard River] before rain made then swimming. It rained so we feared another thunder storm was coming and stopped at Mr Fosters 5 miles from Richmond [about twenty-five miles southwest of Houston], when it let up a little we started & had a pretty evening crossed the east Bernard liked a few inches of being swimming. We stopped at Ezekiel Georges, our bill was $5.00

Friday 29th Mr F had to give him six dollars to haul the boats to the west Bernard end. We had to unbound and boat over. We got over safely and thanked the good Lord. We then drove 13 miles to Uncle Jim Osburns, and was again pressed tenderly to the bosom of my Dear Aunt Polly, whom I had feared I would never see again. She could scarcely speak. Years had elapsed since we had met. She was an old acquaintance of my Father & Mother in Alabama.

Monday 1st Jan 1849 My husband & his bro left for Austin this morning, a pretty day. [Austin was 123 miles to the northwest. Also, Fort Worth was founded on June 6 of this year.]

Sunday 7th 1849 A dreary misty day. I am still at Uncle Jim's, pleasantly situated. We spent the day in reading the Bible & religious works & conversation.

Our sweet babe is so cheerful, for which I do thank the Lord. Today our blessed little one walked along, 2 or 3 steps for the first time. O may he still improve. Mr F preaches in Austin today.

Wednesday 10th I felt quite unwell this morning. Such an aching in my bones I never before felt, & I was compelled to retire to bed. I kept my bed until about 10 O clock. An old acquaintance of mine visited me and I ventured to get up and converse with her. This has indeed been a distressing day to me. So sick & my husband away from me, but I look to god for divine assistance.

Thursday 11th I think I now never remembered spending a more restless night than I did last night. I am very sick, late this evening we called in Dr Stannchfield and old friend of ours he prescribed.

Friday 12th I am very sick indeed, Dr S called again, says my disease is one of the family of small Pox, only one shade lighter, it is called very silly. [I wonder what she meant by this.]

Sat 13th I am very sick. Dr called again says the medicine is having the desired effect driving the disease to the surface.

Sunday 14th Well to day I have suffered great. I vomited almost all day. Great God sustain I beseech <u>thee</u>. I felt that great is my affliction but I know the Lord is able to deliver me out of them all, and may I trust in Him in a proper manner and be submissive. Dr called again says I am doing pretty well. O, I was so glad to see him it is alboysa pleasure for me to see my Physician.

Monday 15th To day thank the good Lord I am some better. Late this evening my husband stepped in the door before I knew he was on the place, the room was so dark he could not see me, he said, Oh! Where is Louisa, he was pointed to the bed, he came to see me and knelt by the cot side &

kissed me. He could scarcely talk for a several minutes. Deep were the tender feelings of heart strings touched at that meeting. He had not heard I was sick until the day he got to me. He rode 50 miles & led a horse that day.

Tuesday 16th I am improving a little but little. My suffering is not near so great as it has been. Lord for grace.

Sat 20th I am decidedly better but very weak yet. I now have hopes I will soon be up again.

Sunday 21st I got up & dressed to day. I found if possible that I was weaker than I anticipated. I set up a small portion of the time, this is a very unpleasantly warm day. Mr F is with me & has been ever since his return.

Tuesday 23rd Jan 1849 We started about 9 for Austin, our future home at least for this year. The church & people of Austin have called & subscribed $400 for Mr F's supports their as minister of our church. It is my humble & constant prayer that we may be useful. We dined with Bro John Osburn & Lady, traveled on & spent the night with an associate of my girlhood days.

Feb 2nd 1849 We are here [Austin] kindly entertained, no prospects of a house to rent. I do not know what we will do.

Sat 3rd We became acquainted with Mother Mills. I have a horrible bad cough. I am trying a new simple remedy, warm sugar water. I trust it will relieve me.

Sunday 4th Mr F has gone to fill his second appointment for the year in Austin. Mr Smith accompanied him. It was so cold we could not go. They returned, so few turned out on account of the coldness of the day, there was no sermon.

Monday 5th We are here no house rented yet. I trust all will work for our good & that we will prize more highly home privileges when we get to enjoy them again.

Monday 19th A pleasant day. Mr F returned from town this evening with glad news. He had rented a shantee [a crudely built cabin or house], we will move in a few days. Lord may we do what is best for the interest of our beloved Zion.

Sat 24th We moved this morning. We are at house. I feel more if possible than ever, home is a <u>sweet</u> spot, consecrated by its association, grateful were our feelings when we surrounded our little board and dined for the first time under this humble roof, but still more deep were our feelings when we came to kneel around & here raise our family altar.

Monday 5th [March] We to day are well, but have a boil beginning to gather, I fear I shall suffer with it.

Wednesday 14th A tolerably pleasant day. Our babe disobeyed his Pa and he was compelled to correct him. How severe it was to us, but we knew it was our bounden duty to make the little treasure mind now whilst he is young, or he never will.

His Pa completely conquered him, but the stripes were many, our little one has such a high temper. My sincere & frequent prayer is for Divine assistance that we may bring <u>our precious child</u> up in the fear of admonition of the Lord.

Friday 16th We are still improving, we are now able to sit up and sew & read all day. When we reprimand our sweet babe he cries and tries not to make a noise & says baby, baby so pitifully.

Sat 17th An unpleasant morning, dark & cloudy, appearances of rain. Two gentle Ladies called on me this morning. The ladies of Austin are treating me with marked kindness, all this I feel grateful to them for, through God, two ladies called on me this evening.

Sunday 18th A pretty day. I was by my boil and weakness prevented attending church, which I regretted much. But my morning was, I trust profitably spent. I read 20 chapters of scripture and a good many pages in a religious work entitled Anecdotes for the family. My husband to day preached on the Sabbath. Jeff attended preaching at the Capital at 11 O'clock. When Mr F held for the black people of Austin requested my husband to preach to them at half after 3 this evening in the Methodist Church. He did so our little black servants Jeff & Mary attended they took our sweet Tom with them. He behaved well.

Thursday 22nd A pleasant day but rather cold for the season. The sons of Temperance organized here this evening. Had meeting of the sons tonight, 23 members & good start. Lord bless & prosper them & may they soon cause every __?__ to disappear from our lovely Austin. [The Sons of Temperance was founded in 1842 and began spreading rapidly in the United States.]

Friday 23rd We are all well save myself. My boil is such that I believe it rather impairs my general health. But I feel thankful that the boil seems some little better.

Thursday 29th Tolerable pretty day. No news, but the Golden Country, all excitement for California. Mary returned home sick. [Gold was discovered in California on January 24, 1848. The peak year for the "forty-niners," people going there to seek gold, was in 1849.]

Friday 30th Nothing of interest, my determination on __?__ more & still more, to live for the cause of my blessed master. Sons of Temperance met tonight. I believe 7 was initiated, 30 petitions laid before the Division.

Thursday 5th [April] Dr just paid Mary a visit. He says she is fast improving. I do feel thankful, we were all vaxinated this morning [possibly against smallpox]. Our sweet babe is walking good, and calls his Pa so sweetly.

Wednesday 11th Gloomy weather, the grasshoppers are about leaving and ruining almost every garden. Our sweet babe is 17 months old to day. [Every few years there was an invasion of grasshoppers in Texas. The years 1846, 1849, and 1857 were especially hard years.]

Tuesday 17th We are all tolerable well, the grasshoppers have not left us yet and we fear they will not soon.

Tuesday 24th We are only tolerable. Mr F is much complaing, all the rest save Mary are well. At 11 O clock this morning we attended a little wedding Party. My husband said the ceremony for Dr J A Horne & Miss Harriet Gouch, all of this city. [In the Travis County Marriage Records, 1846 to 1882, it is noted that James A. Horne was married to Harriett Gooch on April 24, 1849, by Finis Foster.]

Wednesday 25th Rather a cloudy morning. Mr F is quite sick, it is now 20 minutes after 11 and he has not arose from his bed. He has taken violent cold. Our sweet babe had quite a fever last night. I arose often. I had retired to rest & gave him a tepid bath which cooled his fever & gave ease & he went to sleep immediately & slept well all night. He is quite lively this morning.

Friday 27th A pretty morning. Mr F was much better about and he left for Bastrop for the purpose for attending a two day sacramental meeting. It seemed doubtful about my getting company whilst he would be absent, and I could not refrain from weeping, which I was very sorry for it was the first time I had given way to weeping on his departure since we left Houston.

Wednesday 9th [May] Nothing special, but the Cholera is still doing it work of death in San Antonio. [The cholera epidemic of 1849 lasted six weeks in San Antonio and had killed at least five hundred people by May.] We expect it here e'er long, but pray God to stop the destroyer. O of consistent may it not visit our city.

Thursday 10th A pretty day. Bro Whitson called on his way to California. I fear it will be a death trip for him.

Friday 11th A lovely bright day. Mr F started on his Agency & to fill an appointment at Bastrop. He expects to return Tuesday. I wept not on this departure thank God. I felt calm & collected to a great degree. To day our sweet child is 18 months old he is running all about & speaks sweetly. He is a precious child, he sings at prayers & says mama so sweetly.

This is **Sunday 9th day of Feb 1850**. I have just finished my bible regularly thro' twice. Lord impress truth upon my heart. I regret I forget so much that is good & remember so many foolish things. Father direct in all things. Mr F preached today in Bastrop.

[The last entry was almost a year after the previous one, and there won't be another entry until March 19, 1856.]

Journal #2

March 19, 1856–April 21, 1856

Malvinia Louisa Foster has not written in a journal since February 9, 1850. She is now thirty-four and has been married to Rev. Finis Foster for thirteen years.

* * * * *

March 19th 1856 About 9 or ten years ago I commenced the pleasing, and I think profitable task of writing a journal fully intending then to continue it until the close of my life. One object of my life I had in view was my own satisfaction in being permitted by it more closely to retrospect my past life, and by it more carefully to guard the present & with Christian resignation & prayers to wait patiently the events of the unknown future. Last, but not least I fondly hoped it would have a solitary effect upon the morals & hearts of my only child, my sweet Tomie W. Foster [Sometimes Louisa spells "Tomie" with one *m*, rather than "Tommie," with two *m*'s]. I have had been blessed with two dear little sons. My oldest Isham Benjamin Clopton by my first dear husband, we were married May 15 1839, little Isham was born which was July 21 1840 over a month after his beloved Fathers death which occurred 1st June 1840 & lived to be a few days over a year at this interesting age, the dread monster tore him from my fond embrace & left me desolate. Yes! The evening of the 8th of Aug. 1840 was to me a dark & gloomy one, one that can never be erased from memory. That evening when I last had my lifeless babe in my arms. I thought my misery was complete. The March previous I had consigned to the narrow limits of the tombs. My dear & reverenced parents in two days and a half of each other. In attempts to express my feelings & heart rendering sorrow at that crisis in my history was to be vain & fruitless.

This is the marriage certificate of Louisa's parents, Isham B. Phillips and Nancy Lewis, March 9, 1820. From the Alabama county marriages 1809–1950 database.

The fond affectionate hearts of [a] <u>tender woman</u>, that has been schooled in afflictions furnace can only imagine my sad state. Deep in my heart my sorrow lay & there I nursed it. I did not desire ever to be happy again, I prayed for consumption to settle upon my vitals.

Although my life had well nigh been a life of vanity. For I was one that delighted in the gay giddy dance: I merely laugh. My Father was called wealthy, he had but two children. A sweet little brother two years younger than myself his name was Leonidas Marion Phillips. I remember he was a dear little black eyed boy. He was truly his mothers darling. He was born in Sonisanna [I could not find this place.] Dec 9th 1823.

I was born Dec. 3, 1821 Washington County Alabama. [Washington County was located in the southwestern part of Alabama. In the nineteenth century, the county was largely developed for cotton plantations, with labor supplied by thousands of enslaved people.]

I am proud of my native state. A mere mention of that loved name touches a sensitive cord in my fond and patriotic bosom. I was to use the treasured words of My father "his Jewel". My beloved aged father was closer to me than life itself, when disease laid him on his bed, which was almost constant 10 years before his demise, I never wearied in waiting on my Dear Papa. My station was near his bed. Many sweet talks we had. They are now fresh on memorys tablets, they made lasting impressions for good on my young and tender mind.

Mother, loved Mother, you two still retaining a place in my fond heart, the seat of all true affection, would that I could say as I can truly in regard to My Father. I never remembered to have given you one unkind word. But O I cannot, this though, ever gives me pain. I never hear a child speak unkindly to a Mother. But my mind with the rapidly lightning recalls the past, and it gives me and I think I know not what cause for anguish they are treasuring us, yet to be revealed to their hearts alone. But Mother (sweet name to me) when I think of you, all is not painful, often did you speak sweet words of comfort and counsel to your daughter, which has ever benefited me in every station of life. I thank you my Dear Mama for all your acts of kindness, they shall last whilst life remaining. If I am anything I owe much, much to the strict care with which you ever watched over me—in my youthful days.

Mother would the awful fiat had not passed so soon, until I could have felt every pulsation of the Mothers heart, that I since experienced. And could have asked your pardon for every unkind word or loss.

But Alas! It was not so. I knew nothing but the love for a healthy lovely & good babe. I was a stranger to the anxieties & cares of a Mother for children of riper years. But it is past forever,

At this juncture I met with my present beloved husband. We first saw each other at a camp meeting. He was in the sacred desk, I in the congregation, our eyes met, we loved, and a purer flamed since no! never burned upon the alter of the two faithful loving hearts in that day or since.

This occurred in Nov 1841. He began addressing me in December I thought him the most candid man I had ever seen, he drew a dark picture indeed of the trials of a ministers wife, and it is well he did for my life had been spent in gayety. I was a total stranger to such things.

It gave me some little preparation for what awaited me, in after life, and made me love him still dearer. My relatives & friends that I loved with a tender affection and some that had shown me great kindship—in sorrows trying hour were bitterly opposed to our marriage. He had just come to Texas a stranger in a land of strangers, where the population was a mixed mass, from almost every quarter of the globe, and at a time when many fled to Texas to prevent paying their debts, & often the man whose name was linked with crime.

Yes! & whose hands had been but recently imbibed in the innocent blood of his fellow man, found asylum in this new fair and happy land of ours, to which I presume (to some extent at least) has been the fate of all new countries. I made this subject of prayer. I prayed almost as hard to know If I ought to marry Mr Foster as I did to get religion. <u>My children</u> you must do likewise, imitate your Mothers <u>virtues</u> & pass by her faults.

I received thoughts (I believe firmly now) on the 27th of April 1842 we were engaged. Sept 1st 1842 was the auspicious day that I gave myself away, to my betrothed & beloved Finis E. Foster. In him I have <u>ever</u> found a trusting confidential heart, one that proved able to extract the thorn from my aching and disconsolate bosom—& implant his dear image there. To dwell upon the many happy hours we have spent together which seemed to have more of heaven than earth connected with them would fill vols. But our little bark [a small sailing ship] has been well nigh shipwrecked with the enemy—on the 10th March 1845 we were blessed, with the birth of a sweet darling little boy, well do I remember our joy when we first gazed together upon the beautiful features of our, now sainted little <u>one</u> "who is not lost but gone before" [quote was from a hymn that first appeared in the *Evangelical Magazine* in 1829]. There was one idol I became resigned to the death of my Isham B [son from her first marriage]. Feb. 1847 on that blessed day of rest we were called up onto give up that inestimable treasure, after protracted illness of near twelve months he was teething, inflammation terminate to the brain, never shall I forget that look, those bright dying eyes, and the sudden paleness that spread over those angel features. It was a fearful beauty. O: I cannot describe it. I thought that paleness so mournfully beautiful. I came near after going into spasms. My grief was immoderate, was it sinful? I know not, My dear Husband wept like a child, talked to heaven & our angel babe. Had it not been for his words of consolation I cannot take what would have been my fate I prayed for resignation to Gods will. [Throughout history, teething has been held responsible for a wide variety of childhood illnesses. In the 1800s, it was often listed as a cause of death.]

After our returning from Ohio & Missouri it was on a dark and drizzly night Nov 11th 1847. In the same room where as again (we thought) quaffed the bitter __?__ to the dregs near where we walked with breaking hearts our dear one take its everlasting flight to the realms of endless, our little Finis Robert, there we received with emotions of joy and gratitude; our other little boom from heaven—our great big babie boy __?__too. Thomas Wilson Foster, O we were so proud of him. My husbands brothers came to our house. Bro Wilson he too rejoiced with us & named our son, he was very cross until he was 4 months old, this annoying as it was to a fable another gave me pleasure. But it made me hope I would raise him. I suppose merely because our other little boy had been so good & docile, well bless the lord he is now alive healthy, now at school & delighted with it 8 years old. O Tomie is a treasure to Mothers sweet resignations was mine.

[18]48 My husband was called to the Austin Church as Pastor. I was delighted when he accepted the role. My health bad.

Aug 5 I thought I was going into consumption which made me think of my wish with honor for now. I had dear objects to love. I had a skillful Physician an elder in our own beloved Zion Dr. Horne who with assistance of Townsend sarsaparilla [a popular cure-all medicine that could cure everything from consumption to face pimples] which I took by his advice in connection with other medicines. My health became much improved. I enjoyed better health than I ever expected again on earth.

Aug 7th 11 o clock at night 1850. Heaven bestowed upon us another treasure O yes it <u>too</u> was of incalculable value. What joy it brought to my husbands fond & affectionate heart. It was our first daughter. She was a perfect beauty, you never looked upon anything more lovely.

A great many said that she was the prettiest babe they had ever saw, when she was a day old she looked like she was a month old, she was all our hearts could desire on earth. Her Pa often called her a model of human perfection. She had a fine body & mind, also mood. I had little thought of her death. I remember thinking (perhaps it was wished) god had afflicted me enough. I really felt I would never lose another child. Why I felt this I cannot tell, unless just because I wished it to be so—our sweet infant was beloved by all at home & abroad. Tomie after 4 months old became very good & pretty, some said he was the smartest & most obedient child they ever saw. But I regret to say of you my dear child they could not say so now. But I am aware you are not as disobedient as some. But do try to be obedient so I can write it in this diary.

On June 3rd 1851 about 4 O clock in the same room where our daughter was born & where we had so much enjoyed her sweet winning ways, where nights & morn <u>she, little as she was</u> (seemed) to have some ideas of devotion, kneeled at the altar of prayer. If she was far from her Pa & Ma she would sit still during the reading of the scriptures, when her Pa shut the book of books, she would kneel & continue still until he would say Amen. Then she would rise sit in her little rocking chair, rock herself & look so happy at Pa & Ma for a smile of approbation, which thank heaven she never failed to receive, from eyes that looked at her with beams of love. I such a child I never have seen on this broad green earth. But 3rd of June closed & you might have seen her lovely form covered with the emblems of Purity, such a corpse. It looked heavenly, I thought I had never behold so sweet a sight now sorrow & gloom took possession of our hearts & home Louisa Clemantine was her Papa's idol. It was a Father loved a sweet daughter it was my husband he was absent on church business once six months, he wrote me often, he wrote one sweet little letter to Tomie & one to Lou Clemie, & said she must love him just like her Ma did her Pa. This wish was gratified to the letter. She would always run to meet her Pa & say my Pappas' come back, my Pappas' come back. O those sweet and happy days to us. She has escaped the turmoil of this sin polluted earth "In that far off home of bliss" she dwells without ever committing an actual transgression my Precious loved little one has gained that "Port called Heaven"—sweet consoling thought. ["In that far off home of bliss" was from a poem found in the *Christian Ladies Magazine* 1847, and "Port called Heaven" was from the hymn, *Prayer of the Dying Californian* 1857.]

I have often been heard to explain from my innermost soul was ever anyone's lot as hard as mine. I have often thought my troubles were greater than ever fell to the lot of mortals here below, but when I reflect I know it is not so. I have ever been blessed with kind friends. And above all earthly considerations, my own beloved Pious husband, by his kindness has soothed & comforted my disconsolate heart, how many in sorrows distressing hour has one found virtuous bosom on which to recline in perfect safety. Sometimes I think I ought to be happy & content. In some respect I have been so highly favored of heaven. My little Tomie is again my babe. I so much different. Twice before I gave up my only child & truly realized I was a childless Mother. O heaven grant this may ever be my fate again. O God spare my Tomie & may he be a great, good man. My health tolerable good—

Dec 14 1852 9 O clock in the evening. God bestowed upon us another sweet boy, he is very large weighed ten pounds & a half, he was called very beautiful, some said he was the prettiest new born babe they ever saw. When he was about ten days old I took child bed fever [a common cause of death much feared by pregnant women until the end of the nineteenth century], inflammation commenced in my bowels & stomach. When he was a month old I began to __?__ alone. I have always thought Finis Andrew ought to be so kind and good to Mama, because she came so near dying after his birth. I felt resigned almost like I had Lou [Louisa] back again Finie resembled her so much in features, blue eyes, & good to. But I often look out & think if she was sitting between the two dear boys I would be so much happier. But alas! This will never, no never be the case. My husband often says if little daughter was here the chain would seem complete, is this wrong? I hope not. In March 1853 we moved to Belton. There I formed many organizations that I dearly love, & I have every demonstration of their love to me & mine. Oct 1855 we left here expecting to remain here with a friend all winter, Mr F, attended Synod met with some dear old friends with whom he became acquainted too soon after his arrival in Texas. They persuaded him to come after me at Austin, promised to board us & and wait on me and children, to pay him besides to preach to them. He felt he ought to go I was willing to do so, I felt I was willing to anything that I thought was right to be taken care of. For Mr Foster had moved & preached and depended upon the church until we had nothing to support upon and if we remained at home we remained at home we would still be adding to our indebtedness, we have plenty of property left to me by my fathers estate to make us comfortable if we could sell it. As yet we cannot. All the good it does is to pay taxes on it yearly. We arrived at Gonzales last night remained until Monday. My husband preached twice Sunday. I could not attend, several ladies called on me, among them was sister Peck, also her husband. Monday we drive out to sister Barnetts the widow of Dr. Barnett an elder of our church, such a touching welcome reception. Dear Sister Barnett gave me a nice little snug room upstairs with good fire place.

Nov 7th 1855 we received another new gift from heaven—about 11 O clock at night, Wednesday our eyes were blessed with beholding another sweet pretty little <u>daughter</u>. I had constantly desired her to be a girl. When they told me it was as I desired how my heart did rejoice. But it was with fear & trembling I fondly hoped not to suffer as I did after I beheld my little Finie, and most earnestly desired to raise my precious little daughter it seemed that name was sweeter to me than ever before (daughter sweet name) when she was a few days old her Pa names her Louisa Cathrine, we called her Lou Katie. O it did seem & still does that this is the prettiest name I ever heard, (my Lou Katie) there is music in the name, her Pa thought so too. Am I foolish or am I not tell my sons remember Mother wrote for you pleasure & profit. My children you must love. I feel so much for you. If ever a little treasure was idolized and caressed it seem to me it was our Lou Katie. Our little boys could stay out a play—they were so fond of their sweet sister. Oh it seemed to me that my joy was complete. I thought I never knew what pleasure was before. I still feared and trembled when I look upon Tomie and Finie gazing on that sweet face and their Pa as to gaze as they. I tremble and I fear I saw idolatry in their eyes. I never saw such look, little did I imagine the danger that was all with me. O God forgive me poor unworthy me. When Mr Foster left me to attend Presbytery [a body of church elders] our Babe was three weeks, we thought she was doing well. During his absence she was very sick. I sent for the Doctor she got well immediately.

Mr F returned we enjoyed beyond description. He had returned from discharging his ministerial after an absence of 4 weeks, was well found wife and Babies well. The Presbytery would not consent for him to leave them & they promised to do something for him as to a support but I put no faith in that.

We were detained at Sister Barnetts about a week with bad cold weather. We then traveled to town, Gonzales, spent two or 3 days with Sister Peck. Our sweet Babe sweeter and better than ever. O I was so glad and feared to take her out so much. We traveled ten miles to Mr. Braches. There Mr F left me and went to Whorton County to try and Sell some land My Pa left me. While he was gone, our dear little infant got sick. I sent for Dr. Coleman, she recovered immediately, and seemed more playful than ever in her short life. I was so proud of her, she was chief joy. I hourly thought of returning home with her, and the pleasure I want to have in showing my little beauty to my friends was hurrying get my work thro' for my little song so I were to make her some nice clothes. But alas Mr F returned Monday night evening daughter seemed well as usual but, fretful. O I was well satisfied about her then. Tuesday evening she took the fever again. I was not so much alarmed, it had previously yielded so readily to medical treatment. Mr F went in town next day and got medicine from Dr Coleman. Dr said he would come to see her next day, but it poured down rain all day. He did not come. I dressed her sweet & clean that morning in a white chassed muslin slip, to see the Dr. O I thought she did look so pretty, so lovely to me. Mr F spoke that day and said what a beauty she was. O had we know death was so near, so miserable we would have been. Mr F, had traded some of my land for stock. Soon as the weather got better we intended to start with our little lamb home. My friends I flattered myself would have rejoiced, but God ordered it otherwise.

We had one of kindest most sympathetic Christian Physicians to attend her, his words of consolation was balm on my poor wounded broken heart.

Feb 2 1856, My Babe breathed its last in my arms, it seemed my sun of happiness had set, to rise no more. I love my children dearly. And I hoped to raise them. I had already buried 3 of 6 and I had built so much upon <u>my daughter</u>. I thought this summer I would be so happy to have my sweet Lou Katie with me when Mr Foster would be off preaching, Tomie at school. But alas, it seems that fate is against me. I felt could I but to know why I was again bereaved of my only Daughter & she so lovely. I would be resigned.

How I loved her so well, Gods ways are not our ways but they are just & upright. I often thought of God you visit our happy loving home circle again, with his bereavement. I would not grieve as I had done, but be cheerful and submissive under <u>His</u> dispensation let them be ever so painful, knowing he afflicted us for our good.

But the happy heart know not what it do in sorrows disconsolate hour. For I had a beloved husband, two little precious boys that I love so dearly, left to me. Still my grief was so immoderate, and I so little resigned as (I thought I would be) that my husband told me, if I did not submit God would send other bereavements on me, or I would die, and then said what would he do alone in this wicked world with his two little boys. Sweet word. I strove to be more resigned at times. Then again I thought cold, sinful & indifferent thought & be happy when I had.

[This ends Louisa Foster's entries about the events leading up to this journal. Her first entry in this journal is dated March 20, 1856. Since her marriage on September 1, 1842, she has lost two daughters and two sons. Her oldest son, Tommie Wilson, is now eight years old and the other son, Finis Andrew, is four.]

March 20th I now begin what I trust I will continue this life. I pray God to direct my pen by his <u>unerring</u> rule of right. May this <u>journal</u>, bad as it may be written, and foolish as it may seem to the sophisticated mind, prove a blessing to those way like spirits that I so tenderly love, and that God has given me to train for him, and my highest aim will be attained.

March 21st Today is another lovely spring day which animates my desponding heart a little. I hope to become resigned to the death of my little Lou Katie. I did hope to hear that little tongue talk to me and say ma and papa. But O that never never will be. I thought if she could only have been spared so my friends & dear relatives could have looked once upon those lovely features and caught but one glance from those deep "wells of passion," those bright eyes, and could have heard her say Papa, Ma and brothers. I could have given her up with so much more fortitude. But I now know this is not so. For it's not in my nature, if I have sinned in my grief. O my God forgive one, and may I do so no more.

March 22nd Mr F has gone down in town to purchase Tomie a pair of shoes. This evening we to drive out 5 miles to Bro Jophings. My first visit to the family. Bro Jophings & son had been at our house several times. My heart was so pained when Sister Jophings asked me where our babe was, she had not heard of her death. It filled my mind with gloom. I do hope I will never be asked that question again it hurts me so bad. My own Lou Katie would I could have you with me. What exquisite pleasure it have been to your Dear Mother.

Sunday March 23rd Another Sabbath has dawned upon us and a bright & lovely one it is. Mr F & B J [Brother Jophings] rode 6 miles above to attend church where my beloved husband expects to preach. One main reason why I did not accompany them was I dreaded to meet my friends, & fared they would look in my arms for my darling babe & then ask me where it is, which is like a dagger to my already wounded heart, which has been caused to bleed at a thousand pores. Now as I write the table is spread for dinner with such a neat white table cloth, it would do your heart good to look at it. And last night I slept on sweet clean sheets, these two particularly are essentials which all good neat housekeepers ought to observe with tenacity when a friend or stranger calls to stay all night.

My two precious little boys are very well and sweet to Mother. My husband & Bro J returned & dined here after 3 O clock, we all then white and black attended church, with a respectable attentive congregation. My husband, Sister Jophings & Mr Miller spent the__?__ singing hymns, some sweet soul cheering ones, but there was such impenetrable gloom resting on my mind I could not shake it off. I knew the cause I could not tell whether I had thought of Lou Katie more than usual or not. My mind mediates continually on her lovely looks and her present happy state. I was to force myself to laugh & talk. But soon as I was to stop that gloom was there. I fear those feeling forbade some ill to my family.

March 24th This Monday morn is a dark cloudy one, we expect to return home, I don't feel very well or cheerful.

O my Lou Katie, sleep sweet innocent in grace & serenity. Peace be to thy ashes. Dear as tho are to my retentive memory. Let me not disturb your sweet repose with my vain & perhaps sinful regrets. Sweet animating hope in the blessed morn of the resurrection. <u>All</u> will be joyous.

March 25th We are all well, Tomie at school is now in the spelling class, but fool I am sorry for that, he never went to school until this session. I taught him at home. Malvinia Smith called on me with her infant sister who is one year old. Finie kissed the little thing until he made her cry, they have just left. Finie went too. This evening good news. Tomie turned down two little boys in the spelling class, one had been in school 2 or 3 years. Strive to get head my son so that I can write in my journal, where you can read of it awhile. I have just finished reading Goldsmith's History of Rome [published in 1834]. I am now reading the Escaped Nun written by herself. [This book was written during an anti-convent wave in the United States in the 1850s.] A regular rule which I have observed for years is to read one chapter or more every weekday, spend part of Sunday reading my blessed bible.

March 26th 1856 Belton Bell County Texas, a lovely day. My husband has acted a conspicuous in the days drama. This morning with his wanton, playful smiling face, he said to me (May I go to mill) I said yes with an answering smile. He started at 9 o clock, to returned with a load of planks to make a gate for our littler farm.

In the meantime we had received a very polite invitation to witness the solemnizations of the rites of the marriage between Miss Mary Rugendale and Mr Davidson a pleasant good looking young man.

There were about 200 to 300 persons. The Bride dressed upstairs. Mr F was invited up to converse with them. The groom was a stranger to us, he handed Mr F a license, he opened them to read (herein he found a $20 note). Then all parties came down stairs. Mr Foster & Bro Smith came in at one door, opposite through another door, The Bridal group entered consisting of the lovely Bride arranged tastefully in her white bridal vestments. Two lovely girls, her brides maid dressed to suit the occasion and the position they occupied, all well dressed. The groom and his attendants, gentlemanly in appearance.

Friday March 28th A bright morning Aggie arrived, I was as glad as if some great personage had come. We had most every thing out in the sun scald and scour. It clouded up, I was so uneasy fo'r fear it would rain. I helped her scald. We got through scalding and scorning 7 minutes after eleven, that was the home she had to return home to cook dinner for Cousin Hen. So I finished rinceing the floor, and while she is gone I thought I would improve time by taking care of the moments and write in my diary. And when she returns be ready to assist in gathering through scalding by boxes & fitting up my house with as much taste as I can having all in one room. On account of boarding, as we love to rent the other rooms. Aggie returned after dinner, we went to hard work, about 5 Aggie got thro, she is a good & nice hand to work.

I was fixing until 9 O clock. Finie fretted until about midnight. I was fearful he was sick. I calmly gave him a slight slap or two, and all was quiet, and sweet slumbering came to my weary eyelids. Tomie returned all joy and glee and said Mother I turned down four in the spelling class. I was so glad I encouraged my little son, hope he will soon stand head.

Sat 29th March I rose late, dressed eat a small breakfast. My dear girls, Ellen Amanda & Eliza Smith are helping me. Which they say is a pleasure to them. And it is to me. I have tried to be a friend in <u>need</u> and will ever be while they are so kind to me. My husband returned from hunting, Finie Andrew chewed and swallowed tobacco which made him sick, I ought to have more fortitude.

Sunday 30th March Mr F had intended to attend Bro Clarks appointments. But heard it was 12 miles distance, he had previously been informed that it was only 6 miles, therefore it was too late to go. On the eve we drove a short distance to Mrs Chandelys. They insisted on our spending the night with them. I hate to keep Tomie from school. I now of late hate to be in company because I am compelled thro' due courtesy to smile & join in the conversation, which generally is irksome to me, unless it is with someone who has been bereaved as I have been.

That is one reason why I enjoy Cousin Hen's society so much. 2nd Feb last my own sweet infant Lou Katie was taken to that fairer world on high. On the morning of the 10th of the same month and year, Cousin Hen's little Beloved infant daughter Mary Ermaine was summoned to join in that celestial throng of which my Lou Katie had only participated one week. My beloved cousin Hen & I had been intimate friends for years we loved each other dearly. Our Babes were near the same age. Mine died 10 [miles] below Gonzales and hers in Belton. Almost every symptom of disease was the same. Both the little innocent Lambs had severe spasms. My Lou Katie & Mollie seemed at death's door several days previous to their deaths. But we bathed them and gave medicines to prolong life. Yes! Alas hoping to yet remove the disease which purged upon the brains of those lovely fragile flowers, doubtless we prolonged those little lives that was so <u>dear</u> to us a few days, but made the struggle at last more severe.

Monday 31st March 1856 Bro Phillips says Tomie beat himself spelling, I am so proud, study hard my boy. Tonight Tomie still retains his place in the large spelling class. Whilst Mr F was finishing reading the Escaped Nun aloud, Tomie had the slate & the arithmetic and set down a sum and done it so well. Made such good figures that his teacher brought it in to our room, to show it to Mr F & myself. I do hope my boy will be studious & be a intelligent & useful man. And remember my dear boy the only way to effect this is to study your book. Mr F and I alternately read <u>the escaped Nun</u> through. O such trials the poor nuns have, Protestant parents beware. The author, Margaret Moult, wanted to be a nun as a child. She thought the nuns' singing must be angels, and she could think of no better way than to devote herself to Christ than by becoming a nun. What she found instead was a closed community of petty jealousies, cruel punishments, and extreme misery.

April 1st Tuesday One boy turned down Tomie in the spelling class, for which I am very sorry. Today Mr F put a letter in the P.O. containing 3 dollars subscription money for the Pearl and took a certificate. Tomie stands above 4 pupils in spelling class.

April Wednesday 2nd In my heart there is sadness, 2 months ago my own sweet Lou Katie closed those little angel eyes which had cheered my lonely heart many an hour, in death. Yes! Over that form in which we gazed with such intense delight, was that day covered with the emblem of purity. I do not feel that keen anguish that I did that fateful day. But my heart is still desponding. I join in conversation the merry jocular laugh often when my heart is sorrowful. Often to please my own cherish husband, he says it pains him so to see me gloomy.

Past evening after tea we walked down to see old Mr Martin, he seemed so glad when Mrs Martin had told him Mrs Foster had come to see him, this caused my heart a mournful pleasure. She said to him you know you always liked to see her. I drew near the sick bed & conversed with the old man as it truly seems almost on the threshold of an eternal & unknown world & without any preparation for that awful feat. What a deplorable condition. May children listen to the words of that old dying man. He said to me, Mrs Foster I know we must all die, <u>health</u> is the time to prepare for death. I am so weak, so sick I can't pray. I have sinned so long & so deep. I told him Christs blood was sufficient, he said O yes, but I am so low, if could be spared to set up again. His sorrowful wife asked him if he wished if Mr Foster to pray for him, he said I don't care, then he said I am fearful it would harass my mind. She said you must not let it harass you. He told her to tell Mr Foster & Mrs Foster too. He said I know they are praying people, he stopped could say no more. She added you wish them to pray [for] you. He said yes. He said the Dr told him he would have him up in a few days. How candid Physicians ought to be, under such circumstances, when a poor immortal soul has but a few days to prepare for eternity to which there is no change.

Friday April 4th There is a little Norther whistling around our north door. This bids fair to a lovely day. Mr F requested me to go with him & let us decide where to hang the Loot gate. I must do so and then go and spend the day with the friends of the old sick gentleman.

I went and spent most of the day with Mr Martin and his friends. Tomie is above 5 schoolboys in his spelling class, I am so proud, study hard my own sweet child and get head and you shall have a saddle to ride. We returned after tea to Mr Martins sick room and stayed until after 11 at night. The poor old gentleman seems sinking, seemed in more pain. I had a conversation with Mrs Roseborrough. She said if he was only prepared, how unwise to put off the obtaining the seal of great price to a dying hour.

Sunday Apri 6th This is the sabbath of the Lord. Mr F is to preach at 11, near here in a school house. The dearest aim of my life is to be a faithful devoted Christian to live an act so that after I have long rested from my earthly toils & cares and that I may again speak & wield an influence that is in favor of that cause that is dearer to me than life itself. My children read this imperfectly written book, & think it was dictated by a fond loving mothers heart for your good in life and this a bondless & never ending eternity. Your Mother fondly deserves that you may live so as to be an ornament to society and living examples & pillars in the church. As I write Finie standing near my side prattling. I've drove to church, Bro Jopling drove his family in their hack.

Monday April 7th This evening 2 months ago our precious beautiful Lou Katie breathed her last and bid adieu to her parent that loved her too well. O joy, heavenly joy to her little soul [that] will be remembered by me until life's pilgrimage close and eternity shall open upon us. Perhaps sad as it is to me, as I write tho' the boundless & endless roll of ceaseless years it may be a sense of rejoicing. [I don't know why she says it is the anniversary of her daughter's death. The two-month anniversary occurred on April 2, which she wrote about in this diary.]

About half after 9 O clock Tomie started to school, I must read my chapter and finish my answer to Bro __?__ letter, and attend to my domestic concerns. Children & teacher returned home at noon. [Some one room schools practiced what was called *boarding round*. The teacher would move around to each student's home to stay with them for a day or two. Teachers received little or no pay, so this enabled them to survive.] Tomie had fine lessons, hardly missed a word, I am so glad, study hard my own child, never stop my own big child until you get head & stand there. O may your teacher come home & tell me you are a good studious boy again this eve. He did bad yesterday but he is good today now I am happy in my boy's goodness. McCorde is a son of one of my old playmates, a smart little boy, he has been going to school about 2 years, he turned Tomie down, & then Tomie turned him down, there are 4 below Tomie this evening, O I am sorry you are getting down, my child, I hope, I hope you will study hard & get head.

Tuesday April 8th A pretty morning, a rather cool north wind. Tomie at school, Mr F at work, we have just laid our beds out to sun. Tomie's teacher let him sit with the large boys awhile today, which made my little boy very proud.

Friday April 11th This morning is cool I rose at six, dressed made up my bed, dusted the things, wrote two pages and this much in my journal, breakfast is now ready I must go. Tomie looked angry at me this morning, which gave me sorrow of heart. His Pa asked him to run out [and] bring him a knife to cut some meat to sell. Tomie looked angry and disobedient. O my son when will you learn to listen to Mother's <u>loving</u> voice and be obedient. Do as to make Pa & Ma happy. Tomie has not returned yet. I hope he is getting up in the class. I know my child has a mind if he will only apply himself to his studies which I trust he will soon. Tomie has come from school, hallowed [*sic*] at the gate and said 5 scholars below me. I am so proud my little man.

He with Jimmy & Bobbie Smith also his precious little Bro Finie are playing on some planks in such a gleeful childlike manner that it cheers my heart & caresses me to smile. While Tomie was at school, Bobbie, Jimmie, and Finie packed up a fine quantity of wood & chips for me to make fires these cools evenings & mornings. I am not well, eat no supper, but not __?__ I was so sorry for that.

Sat 12th April We attended church, listen to a discourse delivered by Bro Phillips. Bless be the pure in heart for they shall see God, he dwells upon the heavenly pleasure the pure in heart will have when the[y] recognized their loved sainted <u>ones</u> in that blessed clime. He said parents you will meet your children there. I wish he had said Sainted Babes, for I know I will meet my treasure Isham Benjamin, Finie, Bobbie, Loy, Calammie, & Lou Katie. But will, O will I clasp my sweet Tomie & Finie to my own fond bosom in that haven of eternal repose. Heaven grant it may be so, Tommie, behave pretty at church. Finie got choked, I left him with Carrie. I saw from the church window something was wrong. For all Bro Smith's children were gathered around him whilst Carrie held him in her arms. I sent Tomie to see, he had returned. Said Finie had been choked, but was alive. O I am so foolish about my children, but I can't help it.

Sabbath eve April 13th This day almost throughout has been rather cool and cloudy. My own cherished husband requested me to go prayer meeting at 10, with Carrie I did so, he remained at home to mediation & private prayer. This afternoon Carrie, Mary Jane, Ellen Smith & myself with my two little boys attended preaching, for the colored people at 3. I have ever felt a deep and abiding interest for the colored population.

Tuesday 15th April We are about ready to start on our trip. We started about 9 in the fore morn, traveled to sister Elliotts, a widow lady and an old friend from Nacogdoches County. She seemed so glad to see us, had a pleasant time. Miss Penelope Carns was there is a pleasant sweet girl, a Methodist, we had a fine good dinner. Some delicious biscuits & butter. I told Sister E. to bake a biscuit and send to Bro S. & he would be sure to come and preach, feed our good horses and gave them salt.

After dinner traveled over some pretty county & some ugly. Stopped at the night at Sister McDonalds a C. P. widow, a sweet home she has, in a lovely grove mostly hack berry a fine spring & a large stock.

Wednesday 16th April We started about 8 O clock, traveled over some pretty country. Some rich land, some not so good, passed some lovely building sites. Beautiful groves and saw about 1,500 to 2,000 head of cattle. Some of fine durham stock [Shorthorn cattle]. One cow in particular was as large as a work ox, we arrived here after dinner, which I presumed was about one, sister Ragsdale, another widow C. P., she was absent, at her married daughters. Old Aunt Minnie, the colored woman met us warmly, sent from her mistress & then asked me if we had been to dinner. I told her no, she said must get you dinner, but we have nothing but meat & bread, away she went to cooking.

Here comes Sister Becca Ragsdale in a pace, says howdy bro Foster, I am glad to see you. "Where's the children" I called them & she kissed them, asked where's your babe. This made me feel mournful. I have been acquainted with Sister Becca 14 years, about 6 years she has been a widow. She too has drank deep of the bitter cup of affliction, yes truly she has been tried in [the] afflictions furnace. She has a fine family of children, but all the large children are at Clarksville eastern Texas at a fine institution of learning [Clarksville was about 130 miles northeast of Dallas].

Today we have passed some beautiful farms, we eat a good dinner, nice fried ham, egg corn puffs, wheat Butter cakes, some of the nicest butter, sweet & butter milk. Neat white table cloth, Sister Becca has a good house, 6 rooms, wide entry[.]

Thursday 17th We bade Sister Becca an affectionate adieu drove off, the river San Gabriel was quite low where we crossed it, on its banks were a great quantity of drift wood & tree saplings cut down. I said I wish Bro Smith had it piled up at home for here it will waste and do no one any good. We journeyed on to Brushy [Brush Creek was about thirty-five miles north of Austin]. There we saw an old man with a jug to his mouth. O dreadful sight, it caused me sad feelings, but I thought maybe it is water. We drove near him as he sit in his neat borough. He asked Mr F if he was from Socklins [?] his tone & manner proved to me he was a tosser [drinker], how awful to see intemperance at any period in life. But how doleful to see the aged old man with frame bowed down with time, his head white, blaspheme and almost re-alized for the grave, deeply intoxicated. But my own dear loved boys beware, if you touch it at all in youths joyous & sunny hours, if you feel its buoyants & exhilarating effects, at first on your young & tender minds remember it will at last sting like an __?__ & bite like a serpent. Yes your fate will like the wretched dirty looking man we behold on banks of bushy this morning. I repeat with emphasis. My own loved treasures "Beware, Touch not, Taste not, Handle not." [from Colossians 2:21] The unclean & unholy beverage. O drink slake your thirst at the cooling, running brook, the Simple stream, the gushing stream or the "Old darken bucket that hangs at the wall." Yes, drink of this pure beverage that nature has so beautifully in most regions prepare[d] for weary toil & care worn man, draughts from the crystal fount will soon bring remorse my Babes. The children & I got out walked down Bushy Bank got in drove across, got out walked up. The Banks were awful, but thank fortune the rain did not reach there last night. We drove over some tolerable land, not so good or pretty a country as yesterday, no good improvements or large farms. We drove about 14 miles, stopped at a little creek in Burleson county [about seventy miles northeast of Austin] where we found good grass for our horses, staked Tecumpsak, turned Prince loose to graze, we all eat a luncheon that Sister Becca put out for us, had milk and now as I am writing I am sitting under a tree with rich green foliage which affords good shade, when the kind hands of my own cherished husband placed a carriage cushion & blanket for me to rest on. He sweetly reposes with his head on the other cushion, every now & then my ears are saluted with the silvery tones of two little pratting of boys at play in the road. Tommie says 3 and 4 lessons every day in the carriage as we journey on & I knit as Mr F drives. I finished healing & almost footing him a pair of socks, am now footing Tommie a pair, economy requires I should do this. I think it is our duty to be saving, but not stingy, nor extravagant. I try to avoid each extreme. I am happy in my husbands love & confidence, he said to me today what inexpressible happiness little Lou Katie would have been to us if she had been spared.

We have passed only 4 houses since we crossed San Gabriel Creek, and they were little cabins, any other improvements. This country is poorly watered, which I miss so much coming from such a fine watered county as Bell. We traveled on over some lovely country, still in the lower cross timbers, the timber is larger & fine, the country much more handsome & land richer. We passed 10 or 15 houses & farms, some small & some as large as 60 to 100 acres, at almost every place however new settled. I saw young peach trees growing finely. The building sites were most beautiful. Just before dark we drove through Lexington [about sixty miles east of Austin and founded in the 1840s] a small, but neatly arranged town. I was agreeably surprised. The town & county surpassed my closest conceptions of its beauty richness. The very appearance of this town, its neat white houses, its well attended and arranged farming that lie adjoining its __?__ taste & intelligence. We drove up to Mrs Doaks, all strange to us, called for lodging. Mr D absent, Mrs D sent us word to the gate to come in, she met us __?__ at the door. This is a neat white house of 6 or 7 rooms, two fire places, they are sealing it up with brick inside, something new to me. Just eat supper, fine for, among various things I must mention the nice butter, buttermilk battercakes, & some of the very best peach preserves, which made me think of my dear old Mother. Mrs Doke has best prospect for a garden I have seen this year. What a pity this country is badly watered. Mrs D seems to be a very pleasant lady & neat housekeeper. She has lost 3 infants in succession teething in Mississippi. Her sister is here she has lost a little girl & has 4 little boys, one is very low now. I feel for her distress & its Pa is a Dr. Mrs D's sister is here, she is a resident from Fayette County, Peach Creek. [Now it's a ghost town, and it was southeast of College Station.] She has had 10 children all living near her here, but one. How happy she must be. She is well acquainted with my loved friend and Sister in Christ Julia Martin, that resided near me at Austin. Tommie & Finie behaved well at supper.

Tommie said 5 lessons today & I knit, today we had a nice little room to ourselves. Clean beds for us & our little boys. I made my sleeves a little larger to my spencer. Mrs D Johnson had a baby Washington, on her removal to

Friday 18th April We rose early after a sweetly reposing. It is a few minutes after 6, breakfast seems ready. Mr F is putting our goods & chattels in the carriage. The sun is shining bright & cheerfully through the window. I am again seated on the cushion & blanket placed by the same kind hand under a large tree but the shade is not so dense, because the foliage is thinner. We have just taken a lunch & a cup of coffee & milk put up for us by our friendly hostess, our bill this morning was three dollars. We were among strangers. The country so far is not near as beautiful or rich as yesterday afternoon, very few improvements. We passed one old settled place. The old gentleman was making some substantial chairs, the house poor, the people plain, a nice farm, a man plowing, a fine Peach Orchard, a young chance of small peach trees. Such sight does me good. My husband has brought the horses from grazing & is harnessing them I must stop. I resumed our pleasant journey. This morning we passed thro' San Antonio Prairie, we crossed in it, the old San Antonio road which was made about 100 years ago in this prairie. [The road is not a single road but groups of several trails. When Texas belonged to Mexico, the road was the main route between Mexico City and East Texas.] There were several tolerable good houses, some pretty with flowers. This evening we traveled over a fine portion of Texas, more water but not clear & pretty. We passed some very fine large wells. Saw glowing wild flowers, lilac & scarlet & purple which were very attractive to the eye of the weary traveler. Almost every settler has a good Peach orchard & among where the luxuriant rosebushes spread out to view almost a complete bed of roses of the richest here. I have today seen many most beautiful building situations. Where were my husband one of that happy number of retired farmers. I could joyfully spend the remnants of my days on earth. But fate seems to have allotted to me a more lonely life. I often try to look into the future & discern my future destiny. But how vain such attempts.

We drove 35 miles today to Bro J Killoughs an old friend of 10 years acquaintance also he & lady are members of our Church. They live about a half mile to Round Top, a small town in Fayette County. Sister K had a nice plain supper. I eat a little. She had just received the March no of the "Ladies Pearl." [*The Ladies' Pearl* was a monthly magazine devoted to the literary and moral culture of women. The first one was published in June of 1840.] We are all well. Sat Ellen Killough came home from spending the night with Sister Flack, owning to her husband being absent. Just after I was seated in the carriage she kissed me & we all parted. Louisa my namesake was absent, on a visit to her sister Hall's this I regret. We drove over some good country & my some good houses where there were some Peach Orchards. To our old & much esteemed friends Mr Mike Muckleroy's, he was absent. We were met in the most joyful manner by Mrs Muckleroy who smilingly impressed an affectionate kiss upon my lips. [Mike Muckleroy was born in Tennessee and came to Texas in 1840. His wife's name was Elisabeth. The family had a two-story log house with a watch tower to guard against raids by Native Americans.]

She kissed my children. I kissed her little Jamie & Willie, who are lovely children, we took a fine dinner, by the way she has a splendid Peach Orchard, the result was we were treated with some of the ve[r]y choicest preserves, which could not be surpassed. We enjoyed ourselves in a teat-a-teat. Mrs Muckleroy made me a present of one yard & a quarter of thread edging, cost 50 cents for a yard.

Sabbath April 20th '56 What a pleasant time in conversation with Sister Minnie, the Dr's wife, but in despite of me when I would gaze upon sweet little Josephine the lovely & beloved infant daughter of my old & much esteemed Bro Carroll & Sister Minnie, a mournfully sad feeling would creep over my heart. For here I had fondly & proudly hoped to show our own sweet daughter, Lou Katie & thought Bro Carroll, Sister Minnie, Mr F & myself would enjoy so much together comparing our little babies. But alas, my little innocent sleeps alone in the masonic grave yard in Gonzales. Long have we loved Bro Carroll, make our friendship warmer still strengthened into purer esteem, & may our affection increase for his lovely dear wife & sweet Babe, he has not returned. I am so anxious to see him. We are going to church directly.

Monday 21st April Breakfast not ready yet, Mr F fixing to start. I presume we will be off in our hour. We breakfasted, I eat but little. I never remember as had a little appetite during my life as I have had for the past months. Do not look well or feel robust. We start, drove a mile or so. Mr F left his saddle, we drove back, got it, drove on.

Journal #3

April 21, 1856–July 14, 1856

———

April 21st 1856 Left Dr Wm. Carroll McGowens after we with him who is one highly esteemed friend, & his lovely wife. Had breakfast. Drove thus for about 2 O clock we stopped ungloved our good animals, staked to graze. Mr F made a fire, I washed our tin cups, put some coffee on to boil. Mr F brought it near me, after it boiled. Now we must eat our dinner.

We have just completed our cold reposes, saved the good warm coffee with milk in it. Our little boys had a cup of sweet milk, which we did love to see them drink, with their wheat cake & puffs & grape preserves. We were seated as usual on the cushion & blanket, placed by those hands I love so well. We drove on to Mr Hubbard's and with him his amiable lady we have been acquainted, some 13 or 14 years, he met us at the carriage with warmth, she did the same at her door, their affable manners made of feel at home, her eldest daughter is at school. I had a glass of very nice Clabber [the curds formed when whole milk is left out for twenty-four or more hours] for supper, which I enjoyed, the result was I partook more largely of supper. We conversed & kindly she has lost 3 children, has 5.

Tuesday April 22 We arose dressed, all well, a dark morn. I heard a number of mosquitoes whizzing around my pillow last night, which sounded strange to me of late years. I am near my <u>childhood home</u> where I spent in gayety halcyon [calm] girlhood days. Some where I listen to kind instructions and admonitions from my own & beloved revered parents. Yes! <u>Home</u> where I first tasted of the sweets of communal bliss, home where I first attempted with fear & trembling to take upon me the yoke, and perform the arduous duties of a ministers wife.

Mr & Mrs Hubbard's have a garden paled with seed cane [sugarcane] they have a large magnificent farm of between two and three hundred acres, work about twenty hands [enslaved persons], the servants seem happy & cheerful, at the negro quarter they have a dozen or so fruit trees, good cabins, we passed by several very large plantations. Drove to Uncle Jim Osburn's, who was an acquaintance of my parents in Alabama my native state. He lost his dear & beloved wife about 15 months since.

Wednesday April 23rd Mr Foster, Uncle Jim, & Tommie are off on a fishing excursion about 2 miles distance. This evening Eliza showed me her Ma's & Pa's daguerreotype. They are very striking, especially Aunt Pollie's looked like I have so often look on me with a fond affectionate gaze.

I must cut out a white jacket spencer for myself. And a pair of pantalets [undergarment covering the legs worn by women and girls] to needle work for an amiable for a little girl as a kind of present, as a memento. I gave Uncle Jim's old black woman, who washed my clothes at Eliza's biding to day a pair of yarn stockings also a few quilt scraps.

Thursday April 24th A dark morning it was, but now the sun is shining brightly, it is a warm morning. Finie awoke with a croupy cough, I gave him some squills. [Squills, also called sea onion, is a bulb of the lily family. People cut it into thin slices and used it in medicine, mainly as an expectorant.] He is now seemingly as well as ever playing sweetly with bow and arrow.

Tommie is now studying his last lesson before dinner. He is improving. Mr Foster started to ascertain when our stock is to be delivered, he expects to return, try to sell more of the land, my father left me at his death, for cattle and horses. He says he will brand them **L F**, my old brand he made for me soon after our marriage. I had not thought of that idea, but it pleased me very much, as I think it such a pretty one.

Friday April 25th I am at Mrs Young, we call her Aunt Manda, she is remarkably kind, pleasant, and affable, takes notice of my children, this always pleases a fond Mother. She has one grown colored woman, & a young girl & several little servants. She is a good housekeeper, & manages & makes good crops, from & to ten bales of cotton a year. Her daughter Virginia is her only child with her. She is an interesting, industrious, good look, lively young lady, helping her mother. O how pretty to see a young fragile creature, thus engaged in soothing the sorrows & disease of a fond aged widow mother.

Monday April 28th Looks like rain, we are getting ready to start. For Mr Hudgins, where Mr F is to receive our stock. I do hope we will make the other trade we have in comptemplations at the offer Mr F made but we cannot fale in any price of the western land, 50 cents is cheap, but we will save ourselves in the exchange of land with <u>my brother</u>. Last winter was a year we swapped our improved labor consisting of 177 acres of land a dwelling house. Kitchen, smoke house, hen house, and a 20 acre field, that my own dear Father deeded to me soon after my marriage with Mr Clopton my first husband, to my brother Leonidas Marion Philips for this land of over 3,000 acres on San Francisco Perez [Medina County] about 30 miles west of San Antonio. It was the head night of Mr Nicholas George, a good little.

This land over 3,000 acres we have swapped to Mr Joel Hudgin for horses & mares, to the amount of 1,600 dollars. [According to the book *Hudgins, Virginia to Texas* by Edgar H. Hudgins (1983, page 82): "In May of 1856 Joel Hudgins purchased a tract of land from Finis E. Foster and his Wife, Malvina Louisa Foster, of Bell County. This land contained 3,206 and was located in Medina County, Texas, on Perry Creek."]

In the trade with Brother we got one hundred fifty dollars cash which made our labor bring us 10 dollars per acre and one bottom land off the league 9. We took dinner at Capt Heards an old friend of Mr F who lost his wife last June, he went on to Miss [Mississippi] last fall, now has just returned with a new wife. She is the very lady that waited on his first wife when they were married.

We drove to Mrs Hudgins where we are to receive the stock. I must sign the deed. Mrs Rachel Hudgins was my schoolmate, a member of our church, a previous friend I always loved. She met me with a smile & a kiss. O friendship how dear thou art, she looks & talks so natural. I do love to look at her & hear her, her converse. [Rachel Ann Hudgins was born February 18, 1821, and died April 25, 1903. She is buried in the family cemetery in Wharton County.] She says I look & talk natural. It does my soul go to hear her say <u>Louisa</u>. With the rapidity of thoughts it carried me back to my halcyon girlhood days, days of unsuspecting pleasure, days long to be remembered, days the recollection of which is indelibly impressed on memorys fair leaflets. Never <u>no</u> never to be obliterated, but will ever stand out with prominence as long as time endures, & I trust will not be entirely forgotten in that "far off home of bliss." [The quote is from the poem "Two Brothers," found in *The Christian Lady's Magazine* 27 (1847): 151. Louisa liked to read this magazine.]

Tuesday April 29th Mr F rode over to see Doc Myres to see if he would sell him 500 acres of our bottom land but could not. He had the stock wished to sell for cash & negros.

Wednesday April 30th Mr F & Mr Hudgins rode out expecting to meet Mr Quiman, to survey the land. Mr Miller the gentleman Mr F let our cattle has come, with three hands to drive, home. They said we had a fine rain at Belton. At night Mr F & H had much difficulty in trying to survey, it seems the former surveys are wrong some way. Some prospects of selling more of the land my Father left me at his demise, to Mrs Lucinda Tilley, formally Mrs Virgil A. Stewart, wife of the man that detected Murrell, for horses & cattle. [Virgil A. Stewart wrote a book about Murrell's capture and exposed the "Great Western Land Pirate." Murrell was a criminal and bandit operating along the Mississippi River in the early 1800s. Stewart also wrote an account of Murrell's involvement in a plan to incite an uprising of enslaved people in every slaveholding state in 1835. Murrell died of tuberculosis in 1844.[4]]

Thursday May 1st 1856 An ugly morning, all well, Mr F is gone to see Mrs Tilley's horses & to complete surveying. I must needle work today. I commenced needle working a collar, for a loved friend, as a pennant. At twilight hour Mr H & Mr F returned, saw Mrs Tilley's horses, pleased, traded for all of them I presume, near two thousand dollars worth, to be paid in land off the J B Philip's league.

Friday May 2nd Mr F & Mr Hudgins have swapped carriages, swapped mares. Mr F got more with a colt & six head of cattle. Mr F let Mr H have 18 acres of more land at 9 dollars per acre. The way seems to be opening so that our property could be in a tangible form & do us some good O if our own sweetest Lou Katie was here, where we would both look upon that fine baby face & catch the love looked glance from those treasured little eyes. I feel I would be happy. But her lot is infinitely more happy in those blissful climes. May O may we all meet her there. Yes this day three months ago our little angel one took her everlasting flight from this woe stricken, sin polluted world, world where sorrow comes near holding a ceaseless reign. This three months have dragged heavily with me, seems like six long tedious ones since we gazed upon that marble brow waxen face and with bleeding broken crushed heart stood & had to see that lovely & love little thing of clay con-

---

[4]H. R. Howard and John A. Murrell, *The History of Virgil A. Stewart, and His Adventure in Capturing and Exposing the Great "Western Land Pirate" and His Gang in Connexion with the Evidence: Also of the Trials, Confessions, and Execution of a Number of Murrell's Associates in the State of Mississippi during the Summer of 1835, and the Execution of Five Professional Gamblers by the Citizens of Vicksburg, on the 6th July, 1835* (New York: Harper & Brothers), 1836.

signed to the narrow limits of the tomb, there to sleep until the last trump shall sound to awake the pale nations of the dead.

Saturday May 3rd Mr F has gone to see Mr Milburn my cousin Lucy's husband & try to sell him some timber land. I hope he will succeed. So soon as we sign the deeds today before a Notary Public, we propose driving to Uncle Jim's, there I expect to remain until Mr F starts with his cattle, unless he makes another trade & I am compelled to return to sign another deed. As all the land we are trading was left me by My Father, J B Philips & the law of our land makes it necessary to secure a valid title to the purchase, that I must sign every deed. The notary has come, Mr F returned, the deeds signed, the notary has taken them to Wharton to affix to them the seal.

Mr F is now gearing horses to drive to Uncle Jim's. I must soon say farewell to my old schoolmate. May we meet again & enjoy happy days in each others society.

We rode up in the carriage Mr F swapped out for & gave a hundred dollars to boot in the land trade. We are pleased with the exchange. The one we swapped for cost $175, was said to be worth $200, the work we have put in it made it cost at least $200, soon after we got it, before we have used it all, I have taken a bad cold from taking off winter clothes, My head aches.

Sabbath May 4th I felt so badly that I could hardly get up this morning. I hope it is nothing serious my head hurts much worse than it did last night. I have not read my Bible any today, I have had such a headache all day and there has been a crowd of strangers & old friends here today.

Monday May 5th My headache was released, but I have a heavy drowsy feeling. My husband has gone to see a gentleman or two to try to get them to assist him driving his stock several days at least. I fear Mr F will have much trouble & lose some of our stock as he has 200 head of cattle, two cavyards [Spanish, a drove of horses or mules] both cavyards amounting to 126 horses. Mrs Dr. Stanchfield, Aunt Manra & Miss Jinnie Young called on me. Miss Jinnie insisted so hard on my going home with them, I am now ready to start according to their urgent request.

Tuesday 6th May Bedtime, Mr F, returned late this afternoon with the cattle & horses. He sent to Aunt Amanda's for me to come to Uncle Jim's, which is a few hundred yards. I did so with pleasure immediately. He went back & drove the stock right by the yard. Eliza Jinnie, my children and self were standing on the old fashion style blocks & truly did we enjoy the sight, it reminded me of my girlhood days. When my dear old papa was a planter & stock holder. Yes, I have some of my identical old stock my papa gave me some brand **MP**, some **LF** the brand Mr F, made for me soon after we were married, he had the same brand made for me, as his choice without my thinking or asking of it or wishing for it. He said to me a minute ago it is the prettiest brand he ever saw.

May Wednesday 7th This morning found us sleeping soundly, a slight pressure of my husbands hand on my arm awoke me. O I hated to get up so bad, but I know it was my duty, I jumped up dressed, we had family devotion, breakfasted early. Mr F & Mr Miller & hands drove the horses out to graze & Mr Miller, Bobbie Bigham a little boy from Belton & an Irish man remained to heard them. Mr F (Uncle Jim, John M, his son) (Mr Lores, a Mexican) Mr Sledge & Mr Graves returned to brand the Cattle. Eliza, me and the children went out to see them brand after Tommie said his lessons good. It did not seem to hurt them as I imagined it did. I think with Mr Foster I think it is the prettiest brand I ever saw. I was so pleased I remained so long in the hot sun, my headache returned. Eliza & I returned to the house. I laid on a cot & got a little nap but it was too short to do me much good.

About 2 O clock a very hard rain came up, it is not needed by farmers. And it stopped the branding they had over 80 branded. They started with them to drive them out to eat grass, for they must be very hungry. We sat on the front Porch and watched them. My dear husband rode in front & the cattle followed gently along. I looked upon the manly form of my husband with a mingled feeling of pride & pleasure to see him joyfully engaged in the very vocation that for years he has so ardently desired. Lord bless him in the laudable undertaking to make a livelihood for himself wife & his Babies. They penned their cattle at Mr Juchin's pen drove the horses and penned them as before, all was wet as drowned rats. I fear the results to all.

Thursday May 8th Mr F has on his hickory shirt he purchased purposely for this drive. I never have seen him wear one before this (he laughed & said I look like a cow driver) Uncle J thinks he does. I believe in persons dressing to suit the business in which they are engaged. It is now 11 O clock Mr F drove his horses to Mr Juchin's pen where had his cattle penned, last night, turned them out, grazed both droves, until a hard rain compelled them to pen at Dr Stannchfield's pen above here.

By eight O clock my precious little Tommie said three good lessons, & my sorrow is gone about my little Tommie & his lessons. Finie came & stood by me & pestered me so I could hardly write. I bade him get away, he disobeyed me & I took him by the arm & set him on the floor. He looked angry at me & with all a Baby's resolution said I won't love you now, I told him I was going to write it in my journal he said he wanted me to do so. I told him he would be sorry after a while when he would read this himself, he said write it in your journal.

Friday May 9th 1856 About 9 O clock it slacked raining, they move the horses out to graze after partaking a cold luncheon & some warm coffee. Remained until late this afternoon Mr F Mr Lores & John M came in a few, moments & then rode out to Mr Mc's pen, they remained until most dark returned after branding 15 head of cattle, just as they arrived in sight with the drove of horses, the rain poured down & wet them all. John M was wettest of all, he roped to brand. When will it cease raining. It is ten minutes of the night. I hear the time piece tell the moments as they pass. Now & then I hear the distant muttering thunder. I hope the horses will not get frighten to night, as they did last night, none heard it but Uncle Jim, but no damage done.

Sat May 10th Tommie has just said some splendid lessons & is now through his spelling book for the first time. We are so all so pleased my sweet dear boy wage your way up the hill of knowledge, until you gain the very <u>highest</u> pinnacle, then joy will be your fond parents portions.

Sunday 11th May They have driven the horses out to graze. I felt bad to see Mr F at such work on Sunday, it seems so strange. But it is a work of necessity, the stock must eat. It would be sinful to starve them all day. Mr Lee Borden a nephew of one of my teachers came down from Aunt Amanda's where he & his young wife had paid a visit the previous evening. Eliza my children & self, accompanied him back. [H. Lee Borden was born in Wharton County, Texas, on January 18, 1832. Louisa described him as having a young wife. He married Jane Osburn in June of 1855. When Louisa met the couple, Lee would have been twenty-four and his wife just eighteen. Lee's father was Gail Borden, who became famous for concentrated food, especially condensed milk.]

Monday May 12th We have commenced to retrace our steps homeward. Tommie broke the string of our Spanish gourd today, & told me a story about it, which gave his Pa & me great sorrow. I am pained to record it, but I hope by thos means to do my dear earing boy good. Finie's so sweet today. The cattle are penned near here, the horses have to be hearded all night. Mr F hired two more choice drivers.

Tuesday 13th May A dismal morning for cow drivers, & traveling families, Mr. F's grooming the horses. Our two newfoundland puppies that Mrs Wear gave us, are whining at my feet as I write seated on my carriage cushion under the shade of a pretty tree. They are so pretty, black with white necks, white stripe down their foreheads with white tips on their tails. They are almost perfectly alike. We are proud of our puppies. Tommie & Finie nurse them like they are babies. Late we drove into Freilsburg [founded around 1837, Freilsburg was fifteen miles north of Columbus], there we stopped to try to purchase some white, red green, orange goods to make a quilt called a rose of sharron. In the quilt line it is the prettiest thing I have ever seen yet. It was on the bed I slept last night. It looked more like a fine painting, the border was formed of roses & large green leaves. I desired it to present to my husband. I procured yards of white domestic at 18 cents, 2 yards of very handsome red, there was no orange, & no pretty green. This belated us we got to Mrs Mike Muckelroy's after dark, they were eating supper, Mr M met us cordially at the fence, took Finie who was asleep into the house, seated me on the front porch until the family room was lighted up, then invited us in. Where Mrs M soon met us warmly saluted me with a kiss, here we waited supper a short time, was conducted into the dining apartment where we partook of a fine repast. Nice biscuits, butter cakes, preserves, & some of the very nicest pound cake. I care so little for coffee I like to have forgotten to mention it, & clobber & sweet milk. I have a very severe headache I presumed it was caused by having the carriage curtain up & the hot sun shining on me, which happen because I hated to shut up so closely. Were invited kindly to a bed chamber where we have prospect to repose sweetly.

Thursday 15th May Table set, chairs up all waiting on the cook for breakfast, Puppies seem very well, old Aunt Jane took care of them in her house last night. It was quite a relief for me they seem to grieve so for their mother that I could hardly sleep. Finie is sleeping near me on a nice little mattress. Tommie is out playing with his puppies. Finie has just awoke, I must dress him. The bell has rang I imagined it was the signal for all to repair to the breakfast room as is the custom with the family. I did so. But the servants informed me it was some to arise. So I returned smiling at my mistake to my bed chamber, where I have not time to dress Finie. Well I hear the Bell again.

My precious Tommie is a great help to me when he does pretty. But I am sorry to say when I told him to dress his little brother, as I entered the dining room he looked angry, and whilst dressing him he made him cry. I hate to write this but I must attempt to give a true history of every days occurrence. So My dear boy if you want me to present a good one for your future perusal you must be a good boy & be a blessing to you parents & afford yourself pleasure of a pure nature in after life <u>my son.</u>

Friday 16th May We all arose late, I have completed my toilette, and as I attempted to write in my journal Mary the servant cook is bring in breakfast, Josephine is fretting, Finie & Tommie are playing with her. Finie awoke before dog & wanted water but there was none in the room & I could not get him any. About sunrise Mary came in and she gave him a drink, then he asked for piece of bread and brought him a piece from the kitchen. Finie calls Josephine, Finie Joe, a new transposition of the name. When I awoke I felt sorry to think my husband either had to herd cattle until midnight, or sleep on the ground beneath some tree. I hope he will yet receive a reward for his toil. I hope he will succeed well with his drove.

Sat 17th May Finie awoke after light and asked for a drink, after a short space of time he asked for another. I don't know what the child, he seems well & not feverish at all, plays all day, breaths hard at night & cries out often. Bro Carroll says nothing is the matter with him of a serious nature. But that he is the stoutest, strongest muscle child he is acquainted with I know he is a great boy in regards to both body & mind. I look forward to the future with my sainted loved little ones that have gone before, we have sweet confidence of meeting my kind affectionate beloved & loving husband and my two precious and fondly cherished boys on the sunny banks of that sweet smiling Eden[.]

Little Josephine is very sick indeed, it grieves me to listen to her little plaintive moans & when I gaze upon her dear little sick face it recalls vividly to my mind the intense suffering of my own sweet darling, Lou Katie, & then whenever I think of her the power of association immediately brings to my mind sweet little Mollie Embree.

Bro Carroll brought a Physician home with him this morning just from Georgia, he seems to be quite pleasant & intelligent. Sister Minnie looked quite animated whilst she was presiding in her easy graceful manner at the head of her table. Bro Carroll was very conversant. After supper he invited Dr. Green into the family room. Bro C told him we were both old Texians. This new Dr that has come him looking a location, extolled Texas highly. I should feel much complimented. After Bro Carroll lighten Dr Green upstairs to his bed chamber he returned & took a seat right close to Sister Minnie & myself, & here we enjoyed a sweet social laugh & talk.

Sun May 18th 1856 I & dear little boys are very well & cheerful. We breakfasted, our children waited without a mummer which pleased me so much, they did not even attempt to enter the breakfast room, were not noisy at their little gambols on the front porch on the pretty grassy lawn at the front of the dwelling. We all conversed on various topics during the meal.

I regret to say after breakfast Sister Minnie took a fever. As I write she is lying on a palate with her feet to the fire. I do hope she will be well again soon, Bro C has gone to see a patient, there are 4 persons on the front porch for his return. Great deal of sickness, keeps him stirring. It looks hard when he is in duty, compelled to leave his own sick wife & babe. But he must be true to his trust. When as it were the life & happiness of a large circle, one with confidence placed in his hands. Surly a faithful practicing Physicians life is an arduous one fraught with anxiety, toil & care. I have just assisted Sister Minnie in giving sweet little Josephine a dose of quinine left by her father. It distusses me she cries so much, won't nurse or be quieted in any way. If she were my child I would be so uneasy. But Bro Carroll say he has not the least doubt he will raise her, says he has just that much confidence. But a few years ago he lost a lovely amiable sweet wife & young infant, he says he believes it wrong for a parent to live in dread of losing their offspring that god has given them.

This is for my own experience, is not true, I lost two lovely babies, my first son & my first daughter, and had no dread of it, but firmly believe that I would be permitted to raise them. My two I yet have with I had a perfect daily dread that they too would be taken from me. My second little son, second daughters that sojourn with me. I was the subject most of the time miserable almost unbearable forebodings of an early death. But at times I believed that God had surely afflicted one enough & in mercy would spare these loved dear & treasured ones to my fond embrace to train & nurture for Him. But alas, the fell destroy came in all his painful tenor. Out of six of as sweet "Cherub Babies" as ever was bestowed upon a fond & doting parent, we have but two on earth.

Bro Carroll has returned. I fear my husband had to sleep on the ground last night. I hope & trust that he is pleasantly situated today where he can preach.

I have just partaken of a good dinner of vegetables, & a nice cup of coffee, & egg bread & butter which is nicer to my taste that the best biscuit. Sister Minnie could not preside me at her table on account of her hot fever. Therefore Bro Carroll, my children & myself eat alone. I miss her smiling face very much. Bro Carroll praised Tommie said he was a better boy than Finie because he hit his little Josephine today when she was sick and a sleep. I said when I take him home I must stake & bell him. Finie as usual looked as independent "as some lordly little Elf" and began to carelessly talk about Budda losing his string, as he calls his brother.

Bro Carroll looked at me & smiled at the child's tact to get him to think of some other subject & then said it was not a pleasant subject is it Finie. Treasured Finie said no sir. Bro Carroll say Tommie always was a better child now than he was when we were here 15 months ago. This he has remarked a number of times since I came here. At dinner he said that Tommie is getting so steady and that in 2 years more we can trust him with anything. This pleased Tommie a great deal. I think it will stimulate him to be still better.

"But sorrow trod" as in often the case, "quick upon the heels of joy." I called Tommie & kindly told him to wash his mouth & hands as is my regular habit after eating, he would not. I still spoke kindly & bade him to do as I commanded him with all a mother's tenderness. He just walked clear round the corner of the house and me calling him every minute distinctly, firmly but tenderly. He went on as though he felt he intended to have his own way. I went through the room & met him where he had come in a back door & was coming through two rooms to get to the wash pan & water bucket. I made him go back & go the way I first told him. This is my rule if I tell my children to do the most trivial thing & they refuse. I compel them to do it, by this means of uniform government I hope my own beloved treasured sons, of whom I am so proud & happy will at last "all a fond mother wishes meet."

Tommie is very naughty again, looks angry at me and says he will 3 years hence be neither good nor bad. O my son mind what rash sayings you make use of. When you can read these lines with those little blue Foster eyes of which I am so proud, you will be sorry. When if Perchance your fond Mothers loved form, should be moldering in the dust, and her spirits flo', where you could never give her over a look of gratitude for all the great anxiety which you will perceive is breathed in every page of this journal for you.

As I write sweet Finie has just come before the door, to look upon that flaxen head ever affords me pleasure. About the twilight hour Bro Carroll was called to another patient 3 miles distant, it seemed not later than 8 in the evening when he returned. To his sick wife and babe.

Monday May 19th Tomie watered Prince one of our carriage horse and staked him out to eat grass as he has done every day since his father started with the drove. And went to school after he had helped me so sweet. My heart glowed with gratitude when I looked upon the receding form of my manly looking little son as he walked off to school. I am daily interested & daily yes hourly, pray for my child.

Finie my sweet little Flaxen headed one, is playing so sweetly with some string by my side, as I pen these lines. And that voice is sweeter to my ear than any melodious music. O how kind & wise it was in the God of our fore fathers, to implant <u>such love.</u> And deep concern in the parents bosom for their young pledges of conjugal <u>affection</u> that makes our duties to be performed for them delightfully pleasant. And their little winning wags ever new, treasured and happyfying in their tendency to bouy up the often woe stricken soul of the parents.

Finie eat breakfast as usual played a few minutes & then came to me & with a sorrowful countenance said (my little bosom hurts) I laid down my journal took the loved little one in my arms and rocked him a little. He would get down to play with Josephine, he loves the sweet little, little thing dearly. But I am sorry he is so rude with her, she loves to look & laugh at his sweet little maneuvers, but when he comes close she begins to shut her eyes, look uneasy & fret, she is so afraid he will hurt her. My little dear loved boy, you must be more gentle. Tommie is very fond of __?__. She loves him dearly. I called Finie to me asked him if his little bosom had got well. He said yes. I told him let me read what I wrote about him and little Josephine; and told him he must be a better boy.

He said I'm going out doors now. I observed, let me read it then you may go. He said O I must go & rope my horse then I will come. Placed his string in his hand the way the Mexicans do to rope anything, showed to me & off he went. He is an independent boy, never still one moment scarcely through the day. When I rose the first thing I thought of was my husband. Did he sleep on the ground last night? I hope not.

Finie and I just taken a walk, when we got out to a flat block of wood, where we sat down and talked last evening. He said lets have a little talk. I said well we sat on the block, I said now talk. He began saying "A little boy snubbing and crying, a little boy snubbing & crying, then he got up laughing.

We kneeled to pray, he said I'm going to sleep. I prayed with feeling, he gazed so sweetly in my face as I prayed.

Finie played some & then got rude, I took him [to] task made him sit near me, and switched a little with a very small peach twig, spoke in strong & tender tones to him. I did not get the least angry. I kept him sitting by me two or 3 hours. After dinner I allowed by sweet little prisoner liberty to run and play.

I sewed on Tommie a black moimo sack, until my little boy came to me where I was sitting on the porch in a chair. And said to me sit on the bench & take my head in your lap (my little bosom hurts) I did so after sending my work into the bedroom I occupy, and he said I am sick. I thought strange of this, for he very seldom will allow me to nurse him when I wish to. But I wish he had just got into a loving fit. I went into Sister Minnies room dressed him for bed as he desired it, and it was a pleasure to me I rocked him to sleep and nursed him an hour, I presume. Whilst Bro Carroll set near me conversing socially near the sick bed of his wife, also rocking his babe, all at once it seemed to me Finie had a fever. I asked Bro Carroll & he said O no this quieted my mind. Finie cried out as if frighten, more than usual I took him up. He looked like he would go into spasms, so nervous that he trembled all over. Bro Carroll said lay him down & let him be quiet, that children are often thrown into spasms by speaking to them. I layed him gently down, he slept until after prayers. When we aroused him for Bro Carroll to give him a dose of calomel[.] [During this time, this powder was viewed as a miracle drug that could cure anything from syphilis to ingrown toenails.]

He looked more frighten than ever, I was exate but kept quiet, by summing up all my fortitude, he took the medicine well. I laid him on the bed after he fell asleep. Bro Carroll said he thought he was going into a spasm in my lap, his little body was the object of such nervous excitement. Which produced the same trembling from head to foot. I made a palate for Tommie near. All retired to rest. I put on a dress & laid beside my sick treasure, he would talk in his sleep, throw open his eyes seemed to look wild as well as I could decern by the light of the moon whose gentle rays entered my window by the bed side: as I was fearful of throwing him into a spasm to have a light. The time piece ticked the passing time. All slumbered sweetly but myself & my sick child. As it was the first nightly repose Sister Bro C, and little Josephine had been blessed with for near a week.

About midnight Finie would toss his little body from side to side, throw his tender little arms around my neck, hug me tightly affectionately. He kept yawning almost incessantly. O I hated to awake Bro Carroll so bad, but I could not rest. I arose stepped to the door of his room and told him how Finie did, he said be quiet, keep him still. After a while his medicine acted freely, vomited him several times, after which he seem to sleep more calmly, just before day I dropped off in a sweet little sleep & slept until Finie awoke me by saying Ma, his medicine acted again, he said where is daddy. I feared to tell him his Pa had gone home. I said he will be back after a while, he said where's budda. I pointed where he lay on his snug little palate. He said I want to lay on a palate too. I persuaded him & he willingly returned to bed, he noticed I had my dress on, he said put on your gown & lay by me. I laid down by him, he talked sweetly, about some cats upstairs right over his head. I was so glad they did not frighten him as I feared they would, he was by this time more composed. I kindly & smilingly said lets go to sleep, Mothers so sleepy, he shut his dear eyes in a few minutes was reposing.

Tuesday 20th May Finie awoke laughed, hugged, & kissed me. I had a tub of warm water & bathe him all over, dressed him, he said that Uncle Carroll gave him some medicine & cured him, asked often if those of the family that had been sick were well. Said sweetly, I am well now. Bro Carroll said he must take oil, we coaxed & tried to hire but were compelled to hold his nose and pour one spoonful down him, the other he took & eat it, he cried & said I'll tell my daddy, I'll tell my daddy. Bro Carroll killed a dove & gave to him & all was well again.

He was so anxious to play, little negro Tom made him cry. I took & put him on the bed he laughed & played, then got up, & took in the door & then asked me if he might lay on the floor. I told him yes he did so, dropped into a sweet slumber, did not snore or breath that hard breathing. Lord bless & spare my lived little darling boy. Finie is better he hates to take Quinine so bad, at times I have to force him to take it. Bro Carroll has gone to kill birds for the patients. Amelia went & halled [sic] Josephine in her little gig. Finie is on the style blocks calling Uncle Carroll, he has just shot.

All the children gone by from school, Tommie was not along, I went most to the school house about half hour after they passed by here. At length I saw Tommie & a boy coming this way from a creek. Tommie said whilst he was drinking the boy who was named Sam knocked & pushed him. Now

Tommie you see disobedience often brings a just retribution.

You know that when you started to that creek you were breaking my command, for at dinner when you bade me goodbye, as is your usual custom, I said my son as soon as school is out come home. My child you will find out that to obey your dear parents that loves you so dearly is the best, safest, & happiest for dear little fellows.

Finie seemed pretty cool, he has become a good boy today, so loving & kind in playing with, and dividing his play things with little Josephine. I got him to take his last dose of Quinine just after dark by telling him Uncle Carroll would say he loved him when he would come in & I would tell him little Finie took his medicine good. He was then sitting on the large cushioned rocking chair, rocking himself so sweetly. When Bro Carrol came in I told him how good Finie took his medicine, he said that's a pretty boy, I love you now. I asked Finie to get in my lap & let me rock, he said no I want to go to Uncle Carroll, he went to him when he was sitting on the sofa. Bro Carroll took him in his lap, nursed him to sleep. Held him a long time. I hope I will get a good nights rest to night as I slept very little today. Finie seems so well, cool, & quiet, My spirits are brought up, but I am very sleepy.

Wednesday 21st May After we retired last night to bed between 9 & 10 I was restless, felt badly. Finie began to yawn, I made Tommie lay across my feet he disturbed Finie so much, he is surly one of the most restless little bedfellows I ever saw.

Just as at length I dozed off, dear little Finie vomited on my shoulders, neck, & one side of my face & head. I called the little Dutch girl Amelia who was sleeping in my room, & asked her to go into Sister Winnie's room asked Sister Minnie and light the lamp for me. She said O shucks. I went to the door & asked Sister Minnie if the lamp was near. I got it by reaching my arm in the door. My gown & cap was so wet I began to feel cold & very unpleasant. I struck match after match they would blaze, but could not get the wick to burn. Sister Minnie said hand it to her, I did so (well thanks I to myself) if you can light that lamp you are pretty smart. She failed the wick was most burned out, well thought I, what am I to do. Then she requested to me to awake Amelia. I tried but failed, she called her again, and again at last got her up. Sent her to the kitchen for the cooks dutch lamp made of iron. Maria brought it, no oil in it, here I stood all this time my gown so wet it made me chilly. I had to wash my face & neck in cold water. Dear little sick Finie was sitting on a chair, but fortunately, he behaved like a man. Sister Minnie got up came to table, filled the dutch lamp with fried meat gravy out of a dish of bacon from supper, which happily was left on the table. I had brought but one night dress on account of the bulk, so I had to get out a jacket sack wrapper, that had just been done up neatly at Uncle Jims, rather than ask for a night dress. And I was glad I had that.

I scrambled & fixed around, rather awkerly I reckon heretofore, being accustomed to having at least the kind hand of my husband to assist me on such occasion. Tommie has come from school with a fever he has been eating green mustang grapes. [These grapes have leathery, astringent skins that can irritate the inside of your mouth. They are edible, but it is recommended that you not eat them off the vine.] Well I will do the best I can for my two sick boys. I am thankful that I am in the house of a good Physician, I trust the Lord will bless his efforts to restore my dear little ones to health again, before their dear papa's return. Finie is so good & sweet & sleeps a great deal & when he is awake is not ill or fretful, ask only now & then for water.

After 5 in the afternoon Bro C is now on a visit to a patient, he told me give Finie oil this afternoon, I did. It has had the desired effect. Finie seems a little better but has kept his bed all day, as not played any at times like he did yesterday. Whenever I go to give him medicine he says he is well now, he woke up a little while ago & said O I want to see my daddy. Tommie is better, he has intermittent, & Finie remittent fever. Tomie is now playing with Josephine, her tongue looks badly still, falls into profuse perspiration when asleep. Tomie says his legs pain her [him] very much this evening.

Thursday May 22nd Finie's fever is getting a little cooler. I do hope he will soon be entirely cool. Bro Carroll says he will not let his fever rise again. Tommie is entirely cool, they are both under the influence of medicine. Tommie rested well all night. I had the dutch lamp burning by my bed side. Finie awoke in another fright, throwed his eyes up toward the wall, hollowed fretfully, hit at me and looked wild, I watched him trembling kept myself quiet, said not a word to him, nor touched him, remembering Bro C said he had known children to be thrown into a spasm, by speaking one word to, or touching them, he says we must guard his head well, he at length looked right. I talked to him, he got up, his medicine acted, he talked sweetly I began to needle work a very fine linen shirt for a present to little Josephine.

Friday May 23rd I am sorry to record again Tommie has fever that attended with chilly sensations, and severe headache which attended his fever all night. I kept a wet cloth in cold water to his head most all night. In pure pleasure in regard to Finie he is cool, and very playful. Slept well last night, breathed so still & peaceful. All the difficulty with now it seems, he cannot obtain enough to eat. Bro C let him eat one butter cake a little molasses on it, no milk, I tried to get him to drink a little coffee, he would not taste it, he sit in the large rocking chair, where he could see himself in a mantle looking glass.

I have just persuaded Finie to lay in the bed. I rested better last night, than any night this week excepting Sabbath. Finie just said that I am mad at you cause daddy don't come. O I want to go home. I have 4 new powders to give Tommie today. I do hope he will be well tomorrow. Very late Friday night has come. Tommie has been the sickest today I have ever seen him.

I hoped & felt assured by morning that Tommie would still be better. Owing to these facts I felt that I could have slumbered pretty well. But Finie when ever I would in a doze, would cry out and be so mad I could do nothing with him, until he would go to sleep. I hated to whip him so soon after being so sick. Bro Carroll said there is something wrong, he says he acts mighty like a child with worms, he is still free from that hard breathing.

Sat 24th May Tommie awoke much better, called me & told me it seemed strange that he was so weak, said he had just been up & would have fallen, but it not been for a table near, he is not aware how sick he was. Finie awoke whilst I was at breakfast, and when I came in looked as bright as a dollar, laughed when I told him I would bring him breakfast. I brought him some cold batter cakes & molasses, he cried because he could not eat them on account of a sourness in his mouth caused by fever. I then brought him some soft egg head & molasses & a little coffee, he eat the first time since he was sick. I could get him to drink coffee, he begs for milk so hard. Afterwards I gave Tommie 2 tea spoonfuls of castor oil & Finie one. Tommie took his like a man. Finie acted as ugly, as ugly could be. He would clinch his teeth so I could not get the spoon in his mouth at all. I was forced to give him a lick or two with a little peach switch. Then he would open his mouth and I would put it into his mouth.

Tommie has powders to take 2 times through the day. My mind has been so engaged with my sick boys, I almost lost sight of the probability of my husband's nightly reposing on the ground beneath the broad spread canopy of heaven, although I have hourly thought of his loved person, & desired return. But I know duty took him away. As soon as possible I know he will be here. I am anxious to leave this sickly country, and get up into that lovely healthy, hilly region.

May this make Tommie attentive to dear Mother when she is sick. Sometimes he is very kind to wait on dear Mamma, sometimes gets angry & looks so ugly at Mother. Finie looks so sweet today. Tommie is in a perspiration. I hope tomorrow to see him well & lively like Finie.

The sickness here seems like it used to in the low country in midsummer. There are hundreds of acres of land broken up south of this, it is thought probable this is one cause of sickness. A young gentleman has just returned from Houston City, reports the roads in a miserable condition. Bro Carroll sold his first place here for $3000 paid down, he says he is glad he has sold. I must write to home, Bro Smith. Who would live here & bring up children, amongst such disease, and such a degraded population where they would be debared [sic] from almost every social pleasure.

Monday May 26th I was so sick all day yesterday with a touch of cholera morbus [This was an acute gastrointestinal illness that usually occurred in summer or fall. It is characterized by cramps, diarrhea, and at times vomiting.] That I did not write a line in my journal although I thought frequently through the day I would. I was very weak & nervous, am better today, but still weak, have not dressed yet. Eat a batter cake and drink a little coffee, the first refreshment I have taken since Sat supper.

My two little dear boys are getting along finely, Finie playful as a kitten, Tommie so ill and cross I do not know what to do with him. Every moment they need a Mother's watchful eye, to prevent their eating too much, and playing in the sun. I make me as it were, a palate across the foot of the beadstead this afternoon. I rested well with Tommie by my side trying to sew some scraps together for past time, he laughs & talks to me so quietly, so sweet that precious to me will the reminiscence of this evening of pleasant quietude.

I am very nervous. I cannot write with ease. I am going to relate a singular reminiscence, last night after I laid myself down to repose, I thought suppose a tarantula was to get on my foot. I took hold of something on a side table near me it was my sponge my hand touched. A few minutes afterwards there was an outcry in the yard and the end of the room next my feet, and the servants killed a tarantula as large as the palm of ones hand. This sounds like an old man's story, but is true, and I can't remember when we had talked to those hideous poisonous spiders.

Tuesday 27th 1856 I am so weak & trembling I can scarce walk steadily across my room. Dr thinks it is loss of sleep weaken my digestive organs, and some article of food disagreed with me. Last night & night before, I fixed my bed and it was as much as I could do. I was completely wearied out. My heart beat quick & fast. I was in a compel tremor. Husband I miss thee, thou kind faithful loving one, I must quit writing. My back begins to hurt. I slept well last night. I arose about 10 this morning dressed, had to lay down immediately. I have eat nothing today, although I have had several kind solicitations to do so.

I have been drinking London Porter. [Glasgow's Anderston Brewery was famous for its porter beer. They exported it to London in the 1790s, calling it London Porter. In the 1850s breweries in the United States began brewing their own porters. I am surprised that Louisa would drink any beer. Perhaps her doctor prescribed her to drink it. I wonder if she knew what she was drinking.] I feel hungry for the first time since I was sick. I hope I am going to get well now.

Bro Carroll says we contracted our sickness in the low country, says it was a good thing it was impossible for us to go with Mr F we would have been certain to be sick, and perhaps could have got no physician. And my dear boys would have died if they had been deprived of successful aid in time. Bro Carroll said I must eat, and sent me two nice irish potatoes, a piece of superb egg bread, some butter, a fine cup of coffee. I did relish it all well. He sent me a small piece lean boiled bacon said I <u>must</u> eat that. I had starved long enough. I wanted butter milk or clabber but he said wait until evening. I was mighty sorry, but I knew it was right, did not entertain a murmuring thought. I sent back for more coffee, Sister Minnie sent me most another cup full. I drank it <u>all.</u> A rare thing for me to drink one cup of coffee once.

It is now about 3, I feel so much better. My dear children had clabber, I could hardly keep from drinking a little. I feel so much better.

Wednesday May 28th One of the sweetest mornings, I feel still better & so much stronger. Tommie swept the room nice, after I had adjusted it the best I could. My sweet boys are playing pretty outside beneath the window, as I pen these lines. Tommie to sadden my peaceful heart got mad and stamped the ground. Finie had made a hole in the ground, and Finie with that sweetest little voice asked me to look at it.

Finie came to me crying, told me Tommie hurt him. I whipped T for it, although Tommie denied it, for I am sorry my child has told me so many stories of late. I cannot believes a word he tells me. I have brought forward every inducement, to get him to quit it. O What shall I do. What must I do. Ana J that hates a liar so bad, to raise one in my own bosom, one in my own son, God forbid it. My rule always has been with servant or child, if they confess a fault or misconduct no whipping. But I warmly & tenderly embrace & kiss my child. Tommie my dear child. I am driven to record this, to see if it will break you from telling storys. God knows when you tell the truth. My son act so that this maybe the last time, I will have to write, "Tommie told a story." Will you my dear beloved boy, In the name of heaven do. For Mother's Father's and your own honor's sake, break this low & mean habit right off, now delay not one time. When you do wrong, look me in the eye & say Mother I did. You shall receive a Mother's fondest embrace right off, & you will give Mother so much pleasure.

[Circled at the top of this page was a sentence added later. It read, "8 Flowers my little Finie brought me, told me to put in my book May 27th." There are indications that several flowers were placed in the book. Their moisture left impressions on the pages. There are also several small dried leaves that remain.]

Journal with flowers and leaves

Tommie is standing by me & says he will try to quit telling stories. Lord grant to help him. I whipped Tomie wrong this time from what Amelia told me. But this is the fate of a story teller, when he tells the truth, he cannot be believed. Tommie think of this.

Tonight I listen with interest to Mrs & Bro Carroll's conversation in regard to farming. They say farms are generally more grassy than they ever saw them. They say if you work black land at the proper stage, after rain, it works sweeter than any other, and it will last longer, but as long as sandy land is not worn out, it produces the most kindly generally. These thoughts to me are new. And I wish to profit by them in as much as we expect to purchase a new home soon. And I wish Mr F to make the very best selection, with a good cold gushing spring with white pebbly bottom, close to a high elevated & nother sandy building site, with a Majestic grove on it of various large handsome forest trees, so that the yard lots & will be <u>almost</u> a dense shade. Not enough so, however to create dampness sufficient to cause sickness. I wish the view in either direction to be, romantic, picturesque & commanding.

In the valley beneath, at the base of this lovely eminence, I wish a place a little lower for <u>Our</u> garden, Orchard's etc. And still a little lower I wish a large smooth level tract of at least 250 acres of the richest tillable land, for <u>our</u> farm. I wish this 250 acres planted in neatly, or hedged in the best style. I wish hands, trusty faithful servants of <u>our</u> own to till this amount well.

I wish to have 2,000 to 3,000 dollars worth of horses, cattle, and sheep & fowls of every description in one Poultry yard. On this eminence I wish Mr F to have a neat substantial abode erected with of sawed white rock or brick, wood near, near us a large splendid Church, and Seminary of learning: Precious neighbors around, born faithful, sympathetic loving hearts. [I suspect that the farm she described may had been what she remembered of her family's farm when she was growing up.]

Thursday 29th May Bro Carroll sold his place to a Bohemian family they have a servant, man & wife, & child, they live in the yard. But I cannot understand one sentence they utter, the women go half dressed. My mind since I have been at this place has been made to imagine how can <u>woman</u> the pure & softer sex be so lost to modesty. At my favorite twilight hour, I occupied my evening seat, upon the porch, & watched two of the Bohemian girls, enjoy their wild frolicksome gambols [to skip about in play]. One seemed to be about ten years old, the other 8, they would get on their knees and one would put a string, for a bridle in her mouth, the other would do as if it was a horse. Such wild peals of laughter comes often from the childrens lips. These Bohemians are roman catholics. Now I am here with my little family these 6 families in this yard. The Bohemians make their stables joining their dwellings.

I feel strange & lonely. I do not think I can stand of another night, there are several pleasant acquaintances that have invited me to visit them during my sojourn here. I hear the cords of a violin being played by Perry, Marys husband. It recalls my mind to my gay, wild, girlhood days that I regret I have passed so gayly. The candle bugs are so bad I must quit & retire to repose between by two noble boys. [Candle bugs were also called lantern flies. They don't actually emit light, and they have fake eyes on their wings to scare predators.]

Sat. May 31st We had a nice breakfast, chicken biscuit, fresh butter, butter milk jelly & so forth & so on. My husband had his horse shod, we waited on him half hour. We then drove to Mrs Adriances there we partook of a fine dinner, cake pies & custard tame Plumb & Peach preserves & chicken pie.

June 1st Sunday 1856 We supped at Mr Muckelroys. I am now ready to retire. As I was preparing my children for bed, Tommie brought a pan of hot water, before he had time to cool it, or speak to Finie he stuck his hand down into it, he screamed out. I got a pan of water put his hand in it, while his hand was in the cool water he would have ease. I laid him on his mattress put his hand in the cool water, he took a short nap awoke crying. Mrs M mixed castor & spirit turpentine and anointed his hand well, tied it up he laid down, he said it will drip on the bed. Mrs M told him it would made no difference, he fell asleep immediately. Bro Carroll gave Finie a pretty spotted puppy, called pointer & setter, bird hunting stock of dogs.

Monday June 2nd We have breakfast. I am sorry to write our good old Prince is sick with botts. [Botts was a disease caused by the maggots of the botfly when they infect the stomach of a horse.] Mr F rode Tecumpsah down, left him, borrowed a horse from Bro Jopling. We are in a great hurry. Presbytery meets on Thursday at Bro B. O fear we can't get there.

After Mr M & Mr F doctoring Prince he got seemingly over it. We started between 9 or 10 O clock, traveled 11 miles. We have eat our good cold luncheon put up by our kind friend Mrs M. also a cup of coffee, made by the hand of my husband, whilst I took a nap. I felt very drowsy & wearied, caused by my late sickness I presume. In a few minutes we will start. Mr F showed where he slept under a tree the first night after he left me & started home with our stock.

Our two newfoundland puppies, are so fat & playful, can begin to eat meat. I never have seen any thing grow & fatten as they did while Aunt Jane kept them for me. I gave her a skirt, & a shirt pattern for her husband, gave

Harriett a shirt for her babe. Tommie calls his puppy Fido, Finie calls his Fidel, they are perfect beauties. I believe we will call the little pointer, after our good Hector. Late we arrived at Mr John Bells.

June Tue 3rd A pleasant morning. Mr Bell kindly helped Mr F fix his carriage, all well, most ready to start. Drove 17 miles, stopped under a large black hickory tree. I am still seated in my carriage writing, as Mr F unharnesses his horses. So that [they] can rest & eat the nice green grass that surrounds them. Our puppies are crying for dinner Tommie has taken them out, the little pointer is begging for dinner still. Fido & Fidel are playing prettily with Finie. I feel much improved, I am not fatigued like I was yesterday. So soon as Mr F makes <u>our</u> nice little campfire I will with pleasure make <u>us</u> a cup of coffee & take our luncheon as usual. I finished the pair of socks finished Finie's gingham apron commenced & almost completed a calico for him.

Mr F mended his harness, left after 2 O clock, we traveled until about 10 at night, got to Mr Guthries, they were all up, which pleased us, for we hate to disturb any one after they have gone to rest. It The lady put a clean sheet on our bed, treated us kindly, charged us only 50 cents for the corn our horses eat.

Wednesday June 4th We got an early start, travelled well. I took a nap in the carriage the first I ever did traveling in a carriage I believe. Stopped paged a blacksmith, by the name of Gay Lend 25 cents to repair a little damage done by our last nights travel.

Thursday June 5th We traveled 15 miles to sister McDonalds took dinner spent several pleasant hours, traveled on to home. Sweet, sweet home, got there about dark. Soon after we got in we perceived Tommie had fever, Mr F went immediately after Dr Embree, he came said Tommie was very sick, gave him medicine.

Sat June 7th My dear sick boy needs Ma's attention. I have just given the last powder, he appears a great deal better. Dr said he had no fever this morning, but the irritation was caused by vomiting, and it originated from the quinine. I do trust my children will be well again. I always dread a relapse worse than the attack.

Sat 10 minutes after 7 in the evening, Tommie still has some fever, feels well save sick stomach he vomits green, blue, & yellow. Dr called to see Tommie, left me directions returned home attended church, and after preaching came here. I told him I followed his directions closely, he was delighted with the effects. I am so glad, so glad.

Sunday June 8th 20 minutes of 10 This is one of the bright lovely mornings of which poets sweetly sing. As I write, my two dear loved boys lay on palates at my feet. Tommie seems better fever still, Finie had a chill about 10 now his cheeks glow with fever, burning fever.

Dr E has been up twice today, says Finie will not be sick long. I am glad to see Tommie look so cheerful, his blister drawed [sic] well, is doing fine, he is so good today, not ill toward Mother. Yes, as I try to open a few thoughts in my journal the delightfully pleasant south breezes fan my heart. Which is soothing to me since my last nights broken rest, I kept, watchful vigils by the sick couch, attending the Dr's directions until 3 in the morning all alone. My dear husband being sick, and being under the influence of blue mass could not assist me as is, his invariable custom (nor would I desire it). [Blue mass was a widely used medicine for treatment of various ailments; unfortunately, it contained deadly mercury. It was also given to President Lincoln for his depression.]

I have dreaded an attack of fever with him ever since his extreme exposure, while attending to our stock, he is better, he is at church, said he hated to go to church & leave me to attend to our sick children all alone. I persuaded him to go. I told him I not mind staying here alone. & he had better go to church.

This evening I got frighten about Tommie, his discharges were so dark, and a red spot appeared on his cheek. I sent for the Dr, for my son cried for me to send for him, he said the medicine is doing as fine as he ever saw in his life, we all believe Dr Embree is a great Dr.

When Mr F returned from listening to Bro Collier preach about ten or eleven at night, he said to me he feared Tommie was worse than we thought for, said he wondered if he [Tommie] was accountable. I replied I didn't know. He said have you ever talked to him on the subject. I said surly I have ever since he could talk or understand me. Tommie's mind is well informed on the subject of religion, he often talks to me about it with great sense & feeling.

Monday June 9th A lovely but very warm, supper over, the wind is from the north, we do hope it will rain, crops need it so much. Our corn looks well, we had irish potatoes for dinner raised at home. Dr Embree eat some potatoes with us. 10 O clock at night Dr Embree has paid my children a visit. Did not leave anything but slippery elm mucilage for my <u>Dearest</u> Tommie. [When slippery elm preparations were taken internally, they caused reflex stimulation of nerve endings in the gastrointestinal tract, leading to mucus secretion. The treatment was effective for protection against stomach ulcers, colitis, diverticulitis, gut inflammation, and acidity.]

Finie has another hot fever. Dr left two powders, a little calomel in them for him. Half after 11 O clock, I have given Finie his last powders, he has slept well. I do hope he will soon be well. Tommie slept sweetly until a few minutes ago with his blister, says he feels very well. The clock has just struck 12 Tommie rests sweetly again. Finie said I want to get into your lap. I took him up & nursed him, then he said I want to get into the big bed. I laid him in his dear Father's arms, who is not well tonight but threaten with fever. Lord grant that he may be well tomorrow.

Tuesday June 10th A bright cool day, 15 minutes to 1 in the afternoon. My Dear children seem better, as far as I am capable to discern. Finie made a rhyme today, he said to me laughing,

I'll whip you, you'd cry, cry all day

And I'd go galloping away

O my sweet Finie is a treasure to me. Dr Embree was call off last night has not returned yet, consequently has not visited my boys. Finie's fever has risen very high this evening 7 O clock, but he is playful. They are the strangest fevers I have ever seen in my life. Tommie seems improving, very cheerful & playful wants to be up & walk about, but I compelled him to be still, this evening it seems to me those little red spots appear on his cheek & chin. I hope it is only imagination with me. Dr was called off some 14 miles last night, has not returned yet. I do regret this bitterly. I fear my dear little <u>ones</u> need his attention at this moment. Ellen is with me. At sun down Dr Embree came, said it was impossible for him to come any sooner. Says the children are getting along slower than he would wish, but it is a slow fever.

Says Tommie's fever is no higher, but some more excitement, but he cannot tell the cause, he cut sticks all day, & in the evening became so anxious about the Dr's return, is the only cause I know, for I stay beside them night & day, & keep them both as still as possible.

Wednesday June 11th Dr Embree came said Tommies tongue better than it has been yet. Finie tolerable cool, says he left a note on his table requesting Dr Bradford, his partner to call up & see our children at 12 as he was compelled to pay a professional to the country. He says Dr Bradford is as good a Physician as any. I am not acquainted with his practice, trust I will find him such. But when I try a Physician & he proves to be a good one. Mr F returned from the Baker shop & failed to get any light bread. Mrs Payne said she had some of her own make, and when she returned home she would send the children a piece.

She did so, it was very nice, the children eat eagerly, the servant girl brought P's little Mollie along, she is a sweet child sitting alone. When I looked at her it made me think of <u>our</u> sweet little innocent that sleeps in Gonzales, but not with vain regret, that I used to do. No if God spares & raised my little sick though still playful boys, I will endeavor to be more resigned to my (I deem) premature loss. Sisters Austin & Smith, Miss Sallie Keese, Miss Minnie Graves & "Puss" came to see me the girls paid a short call but however it was prized by me & mine. Sister S & A stayed a good while.

Sister A is much dissatisfied with Texas, says she don't see one thing in Texas to interest anyone. She cannot bear the ideal of raising her children here. To my <u>full</u> surprise Sister Smith joined in with her, & said more than she did, that it did not speak much for anyone's intelligence that would say that the Texians were the most intelligent people they had ever seen, but it proved that they never had seen much before they came to Texas. But these remarks from Sister Smith would have had little effect on my mind being convinced I have often, <u>very, very often</u> seen persons raised & educated in Texas, without even in infancy breathing the atmosphere of another clime [climate], equally so intelligent as she is, and even I think after hasty reflection. I don't really remember of seeing a Texian possessed with any <u>talents</u> than sister S.

But what surprised me I had so often on previous occasions heard her praise Texas & Texians when conversing with any one that praised Texas, or when conversing with me. And really I think if she would only look at the improvements of <u>herself</u> and family since she came to <u>Texas</u> even after living in 5 states, she ought never indulge in the strain she did yesterday, if perchance she is conversing with a merchants wife. If I admire country or person, and am called upon to speak of it before those that hate or oppose. I extoll its beauties & worth more highly. Yes I love candor. Cousin Hen says if I have any faults in the world (is I am too candid) Dr, wife & Mattie came up after supper, Mattie kissed & embraced me, but would tell Tommie & Finie howdy. They wanted her to be loving to them so bad, her Mother & Father rebuked her for <u>not</u> speaking to my children. Dr says our boys are clear of fever, both must have quinine in the morning. I am rejoiced my heart is glad, I hope my boys will soon be well.

Thursday June 12th After dark Dr & lady came, Dr gave Mr F medicine. Tommie & Finie better, each one gave Mattie some flauce for her Ma to work her a pair of pantalets. Sister Smith has been up several times today.

My skin feels hot & dry, I feel a little uneasy, fearing I will get sick, then what will we do? Mr F spoke of trying to hire a servant, but I told him not, unless his sickness was protracted. I would try to do the best I could. Aggie has washed about twenty-five pieces tolerable well. Carrie made some nice chicken tea for my sick ones.

Sat June 14th I hired Ellen to iron for me today. I am helping her I have ironed 8 pieces. I slept better last night than usual, notwithstanding this. I have a headache, feel very tired & badly. Lord grant I may not be sick. My husband has been very sick, vomited all evening. I gave the pills according to written prescription Dr Embree sent up and he & Dr Bradford came to see Mr F after dinner.

It did make my heart glad when he said I did right to send for him & told me to send for him at any time & he would cheerfully visit us. Mr F says he surly never suffered as much in his life as he did about 4 this evening until dark. Mr Robert Miller came up to see Mr Foster & rented the house across the street from us for $8 per month, place for garden & cow lot.

Sunday June 15th I rose at daylight, gave my husband med as directed. Although my rest was much broked through the night, Tom Smith got sick, Mr F rested pretty well considering. Eliza, Bobbie & my little boys have just returned from a short walk, at sundown.

O I am so glad to say my dear husband is better. Dr says he is most well, no febrile excitement, pulse rather low, I gave him some wine, he says it helped him so much. I feel tolerable well, save the aching in my feet, caused I presumed by me being on them so much. Tommie's puppy went to church today. I feared I would ever see it again. I got old Aunt Sarah, a colored woman, to go & get it for Tommie. Finie sat on my lap & said I am not your child, I'm your baby. I'm a negro woman's child.

Monday June 16th My dear children at play. Sister Smith was kind enough to go to the store and purchase at Mr F's request a bottle of Port wine, 30 cents worth crushed sugar, 50 cents of very nice rice, indeed all the articles are superb, the most refined crushed sugar I think I have ever seen. The wine has a bracing tendency, I am boiling some rice now for those I love.

Mr F did not sleep well last night & awoke me often to wait on him. I did comply with his request with pleasure, but it made me feel badly, almost like vomiting when he took his pills the last time.

I sent for Dr Embree, he came, bo' Woods with him, Bro Woods said he had not heard Mr F was sick until this evening or he would have been up to see him. Dr Embree gave Mr F three blue pills. Cousin Hen canvassed some ham, said the next one she cuts she will send me a boiled bit. I hope some one will make haste & go to see her so she will have to cut one. Dr says wine will do Mr F & children good.

Tuesday June 17th Another sweet, bright morning, my all are still improving. My head aches yet, Sister Smith came up & took Mr F's pants that commenced to finish for him, which is a kind favor to me, that I do appreciate, He stills relishes the rice & milk. I gave Tommie & Finie all a little butter milk mixed with water, this morning, Mr F sweet milk & water, rice in it. Dink, Dr Embree little negro boy brought my camphor bottle home filled by the Dr but it is stopped so tight I can't open it. Mr F is worse, vomiting again, I sent for Dr Embree, he came gave him medicine, opened my camphor bottle, it was very excellent.

Wednesday June 18th Mr F is much better, I feel rejoiced. I cut out the linen gingham dress I purchased in Freilsburg, and basted the waist, made my apron Mrs Muckelroy gave me sewed buttons on Mr F's pants Sister Smith made & altered them, darned Tommie's night drawers. Mr F feels worse, heaviness in his head again, vomited yellow bile & seems quite weak.

Friday June 20th With an aching heart I am compelled to write my precious Tommie has another fever. His hands & feet were cold, I do hope it is only chill & fever & that he soon be well again. Mr F & sweet Finie are still improving. Finie runs out so much I had to tie him in my rocking chair, he said O Ma if you will untie me I will stay in the house. I did so & he is lying on a palate on the floor.

Our children have great notions of being Drs, have their pill bags made of cloth, & vials in it. Tommie's fever seems gone, he is up & playful. I just about __?__ Tommie's fever rose again. I sent for Dr Embree. He came and examined Tommie and said he was not going to be bad sick. This lighten the burthen that had began to gather upon my heart.

Sat June 21st Dr sent bitters for the children & a note begging to be excused for not attending himself on account of being unwell. I have a miserable headache. Mr F wants to send for Dr Embree. He gave me three pills, says I have taken cold.

Monday June 23rd Looks like rain. I feel much better, confined to my bed all day yesterday. I don't believe I ever suffered so much in my life with head & jaw ache. I did not write a word.

Wednesday June 25th 1856 Bro Philip rode his young horse, he did well, he loped, trotted, galloped & walked him. After partaking of a nice well cooked dinner, of eggs, bread & chicken, I finished my spencer that I cut out at Dr McGowrs & cut out a dress body & sleeves for Sister Jopling, & showed Finie a little about needle work & Mrs Graves about leaf tape trimming.

The woman and the boy in brown are wearing spencers.
Public domain.

Thursday June 26th The clock is just striking 5 in the morning, our sweet Tommie & myself are up dressed & I have given him his bitters. Finie is still sleepy sweetly, he did not rest well last night, got very much frighten in his sleep, wanted to get a light & get in the beadstead, because I preferred & requested a straw bed on the floor. Tommie & I were reposing on it. Finie on a palate touching the straw bed. I then after he cried put him in between Tommie & myself, he would jerk every minute. I feared he had a little fever, but now breakfast over. Sister J, Fannie & Stanford, her son are out milking. Finie up dressed eat his beef, batter cakes & butter, seems well lively & playful. Tommie has improved so much since we came here. Whenever my eyes meet Tommie's pretty solid blue eye, & Finies bright mischievous blue eye, My heart of Hearts leap forward with all a <u>Mothers</u> pride, joy & love.

2 O clock in the afternoon, Bro's Smith, Collier & Philips have gone on to town. Mrs Miller & Thomas have gone to hunt Bro J's cow that they supposed were near the hunting ground. And now how many deer do you suppose these 5 big most hearty, talented gentlemen killed (listen) <u>ONE</u>, two dogs engaged in the hunt, Mr Thomas killed it. I think the hunters are rather plagued & I know these two are hungry. Sister J is getting dinner for them. Mr F says Bro Philips horse does well. Licked salt out of his hand, then kicked at him. Quarter of seven, we all have partaken of a delicious supper, cooked in good style, out of the venison, is choice, had some of the nicest __?__ __?__ I ever saw, one of our cows is lying near here dead. I made Sister J the waist of a dress & most made the sleeve.

Sat June 28th At sweet home again, it only sprinkled on us a little as we came in. I left Fannie as Sister Jopling desired me if I went away with Sister Smith. Dressed in my new linin gingham. Tommie, Finie & myself walked down to Dr Embree, Cousin Hen met me warmly with a kiss. Miss Sallie soon came out to see me. Mrs Holbert, a lady Baptist was at the Dr's. She dressed slowly, at last came out to see me. I was introduced to her, in a few moments Mr F drove up in our carriage to take us to Mrs Kuykendalls to see them & their sister, my much loved old friend Sister Mary Young, Aunt Marie & Uncle Abner met us friendly, sister Young affectionately with a warm kiss. I formed her acquaintance soon after Mr F's & my marriage. Since I last met with her, she has quaffed the bitter bitter cup of affliction to almost to the dregs. Near 3 years ago her kind loved respected husband was assassinated riding along the highways, attending to his lawful business. She wept & talked over our past & yet fondly cherished moments of social intercourse,

& of her sore trial & said Sister Lou your precious babes were dear to you, it was hard to part with them, but God took them in a natural death, but just think my poor dear husband left me in perfect health.

Sunday June 29th We gave Bro Collier a seat in our carriage, returned home to attend church to listen to a sermon to be delivered by Judge Baylor a Baptist Minister. [Judge Robert Emmett Bledsoe Baylor (1793–1874) moved from Alabama to La Grange, Texas, in 1839. That same year he became an ordained Baptist minister, and after Texas became a state, he was appointed judge over the Third Judicial District. While judging cases around Texas, he preached perhaps the first sermon in Waco. He later became a cofounder of Baylor University.]

Monday June 30th I cut out 9 garments, finished Finie's mansheen pants. Mr F went to purchase himself & Bro C some materials to make each one a coat & pant. If I would go & solicit to have a preachers sewing, I did so. I obtained the promise of $4, Mr F, succeeded & purchased me a pair of shoe, 4 pairs of ladies hose, 2 dozen swiss, himself 2 pair short hose, our little boys a black hat each for taking bitters good. All is as I wish save the shoes, they are very pretty, nice & good but to low in the ankle & thick soled for summer. But I have not told my husband, for I always desire to be pleased with every article he purchases for me. As I have a burning in my feet they will be very warm for this hot season.

Wednesday July 2nd To my sorrow I must write my Finie has taken chill. I have finished my husbands coat worked until my back aches.

Thursday July 3rd 1856 Finie seems well, I gave medicine according to Dr Embee directions, have more for him & Tommie. Mr F is fixing my trunk. If Bro Collier is well enough this evening, we expect to start to Bosque giving him a seat in our carriage, to look us & him a home there & a stock Ranch. Mr F & Bro C are on a trade, he is about to purchase about half of our mares & colts & go in partnership with us.

This morning Mr F & Bro C Drive up to Mr Kuykendall's to made the last preparatory arrangement to starting to Bosque. 9 O clock in the evening my husband just returned left Bro C, very sick again, chill & fever, vomited blood, perfectly prostrated, sent for Dr Embree. Dr & Cousin Hen & Miss Sallie, came to see Finie he says Finie has not much fever now, says it was caused by eating roasting ears, his fever rose today about 1. I have sewed hard all day, made a pillow slip, & new swiss sleeves trimmed with swiss inserting & edging close at hand & put into my white swiss dress.

Friday July 4th Sweet dear Finie had hot fever, attended with symptoms of spasms all night, very restless, we slept very little, up & down all night. He would frighten in his short dozes like he did at Bro Carrolls. Quarter after nine, he has fever yet, seems to be cooling. Mr F arose at daylight and went after Dr E, he had not returned from his visit to Bro C at Mrs Kuykendalls.

Dr promised to come & see Finie this evening. 7 O clock in the evening Finie has a burning fever all day, he vomited a great deal, phlegm & bile, he seems to be sleeping better than he has today. Tommie had fever a little while, seems pretty well this evening <u>we</u> are so uneasy about Finie, he is not willing to take any medicine from anyone but his Pa, he will take anything if Pappa gives it to him with his own hand.

Sat July 5th Dr came to see Finie after tea, he has little fever tonight medicine acting well, he laughed & played some today. Early Mr F arose & gave the children their medicine. I slept late, finished, finished me a pretty black silk apron it is one yard wide scolleped in small scollops, then notched them round, cut four little inlets in each scollep, fined strings same way, all say its pretty to wear over white, this is all the fashion. I cut Tommie out a suit of clothes, showed Vianna how to make her a bonnet, & begin to hem a pillow slip. I have patched & darned. Must now retire to rest between my dear sick boy & my loved husband.

Sunday July 6th My Finie yet has fever, Mr F has rode up to see Bro C & he will be compelled to stay until the cool of the afternoon. I will be glad when he returns. I have read as I have kept the flies off my sick little dear one 8 chapters in the bible & the "Ladies Pearl", though, O I am thankful when this sweet breeze fans my sick child's fevered brow.

Wednesday July 9th In the morning we leave for Bosque in company with Bro McKee. Mrs Walker our female teacher called on me we have spent a pleasant evening in social intercourse.

Thursday July 10th We are almost ready to start to Bosque. But am disappointed again Bro Mc could not travel as slow as we with our children, so he is gone. Mr F bought me a pair of traveling gloves, 3 little blank books and an alpaca apron. We started about 10 this morning. This afternoon we drove to Bro Joplings, had a good supper, such nice butter, My children seem to be improving. I do hope & pray they continue to do so. I have most made Tommie a pair of pants since I left home today. Made my apron before I left home. It is so dusty, if it continues so our trip will be anything but a pleasant one.

Friday July 11th A pleasant morning after a night's repose. We had rain last night about midnight. I am so glad, not enough for a season yet, but it will lay the dust. I finished Tommie's pants. Made them with suspenders, the first I have made him without a body. I don't intend he shall know it until he goes to put them on. I know his blue eyes will sparkle he has begged for suspenders for so long. I made him a shirt out & out today after putting a watch fob in Mr F's pants also hemming them. I made a shirt with a standing collar, he was very proud it & asked if I would starch it like Fathers. I told him yes he was still prouder.

Sat July 12th When I awoke my Tommie was up & dressed. My smart boy. Finie is sleeping yet. Breakfast not ready, 10 minutes of 1 we had a nice well cooked breakfast, fried chicken, some of the lightest best biscuits I have eat this summer, made of Texas flour, honeycomb molasses, good coffee & clabber. We have traveled about 18 miles thro' a long lonesome prairie, but few inhabitants some houses & 10 miles from timber. We came to a delightful spring near one of these residences & little farms which was indeed a treat to us, this intensely warm morning. We filled our traveling keg, & feasted on a tin cup full ourselves, we surly have passed by 2,000 head of cattle today which looked fat & fine, notwithstanding last cold winter. We are now stopped to eat our snack on Harris creek [west of Waco] I washed out all our tin cups, put coffee in the quart cup & filled it with water. Mr F put it on the fire, it is made, Mr F boiling our bacon on a stick over the coals. Tommie gone to the creek for a cup of water, our good horses are feeding on pretty good grass. My fine husband cuts with our little ax all the bushes down then rolled our carriage under the branches of a large spotted oak tree, where I now sit in a cool shady place to write in my journal, where every now & then a slight cool zephyr fans my brow. We saw two large loafer wolves today. [This wolf is also known as a Great Plains or Buffalo wolf.]

We drove half mile off our road to see haunted hill, we stopped at __?__ base, hitched our horses. Mr F took Finie in his arms, I took hold his arm Tommie ran on beside us, we ascended its summit I presume it is 30 feet high, 60 feet long on the top about 4 feet wide, where one could ride on horseback. Our keg of water is so warm it is not fit to drink, no spring, O how I want a cool drink, what shall I do this hot afternoon, it is several miles before we meet with a well. Mr F is going to fix to start, I am glad, so I may get a cool cup of water, ee'r long. We got to Mrs MacClellans, got directions to the spring. Mr F hunted a long time, met a negro man he conducted him to it. It seems to us we never tasted better water. We were fully prepared to appreciate a drink from natures pure fountain. We drove on got to Bro Sparks just before dark. We were met warmly, I received many kisses.

Sunday July 13th Mr F & Bro Sparks & his two daughters Onortha & Ellen drove 7 miles to White Rock to church. I was anxious to go but feared Finie might take fever, they returned about sundown, with invitations with me to visit them. I have been gloomy all day, this evening my favorite hour I could not enjoy at all, for a sadness almost unbearable weighted heavily on my heart. I know no cause unless it is seeing little Laura Sparks, who is near the age of my own precious departed <u>Lou Katie</u>. And the thought of making a location here, away out in the country, where I will be left alone many a night & day, and spend hours, miserable hours, unpitied and almost unknown.

Monday July 14th 1856 We had a sweet nights repose, awoke & rose refreshed. Mr F & Bro Sparks rode out to look at a place that is for sale not far distant, said to be good for a Ranch for stock, where there is everlasting water. I am so fraid I want to be satisfied, so far I don't like as well as our lovely home at B. I fear we will never get to live on as pretty place again.

Why is it my lot to be ever roving here & there, when I love <u>home</u> so intensely? But stop let me be contented, my husband I see is pleased here, his heart is set on this country. I hope when I see more of it tomorrow, I shall be delighted for his sake. It is so pleasant always for me to love the place that he does. May heaven direct us.

Journal #4

December 16, 1856–May 11, 1857

––––––––––

Dec 16th 1856, Started up our trip to close up my poor bro's estate, traveled nine miles to Sister Elliotts. She seemed so glad to see us, had fine supper & splendid biscuits & butter for supper & breakfast next morning.

Dec 17th I rode to Mr Bon__?__ , met warmly, had nice sausages for dinner which pleased me very much. Our good old horse has the bellowses traveled sluggishly. We arrived at Uncle Tom Thaxton's a quarter before six O clock. The good girls soon had us some nice biscuits & butter & good coffee. We all ate heartily.

Sat morning 20th Dec So cold we gave out going to meeting, Mr F purchased a pair of heavy green blankets for our trip. Tommie a nice overcoat & a nice suit of brown jeans, for me to make Finie a pair of brown pants, each one of our dear boys a nice brown __?__ cap, he has now gone to get me sewing silk & needles, all from which I am very grateful. A very cold afternoon. This indeed a pleasant family. They speak of visiting Belton next summer, <u>we</u> do hope they will. My husband returned with some splendid needles, but forgot the silk. I do not need it right now. I patched Tommie's pants, cut myself out 3 prs. of drawers, made two pair, & a good deal more work. A good days work.

Sunday Dec 21st A very cold morning. My kind husband warmed a brick, put it between our new green blanket & pulled the end up over, sweet Finie & my Papa. Drove to Father McDavids took dinner. I ate hearty for I had a big dish of winter collards.

Dec 24th Wednesday Drove to Bro Andrew Renick, took dinner nice preserves & sausages. Late in the afternoon drove to Bro Willis. Mr F is near sick with cold, I am suffering intensely.

Dec 25 Thurs Mr F felt too bad to travel on, Bro Hill family & us drove to Bro At & us went home with Kinston, had a splendid dinner, his birthday, so we had some nice pound cake, Bro A's family & we all drove back & appointed Mr F to preach at Bro Hills. But the appointment was out for prayer meeting at Bro Spencers a Baptist. They thought Mr F wanted to attend there, and would not consent for the meeting to be moved. But Mr F was too sick to go. And I was suffering more intensely than ever.

Mon Dec 29th Got up & tried to dress, but was so weak, but I laid down again. A very warm evening perspiration started up on my face.

Tuesday Dec 30th A very cold morning, I arose, dressed, & laid down. Started we drove to Bro Hills. I fear the results of my drive. Lay down to rest twice today, feel better tonight.

Wednesday Dec 31st Last day of December, I am much improved, and my husband, Tommie, Finie have returned from having caught 11 birds. We drove to Bro Jacks, nice supper, enjoyed ourselves well.

Thursday Jan 1st 1857 Rose pretty early, had prayers breakfast about 7 O clock, very nice. Started on our journey, feel much better, Stopped at Dr McGowns, took dinner, spent several hours in conversation, then he rode with us some distance. We drove to Sister Uptons a Cumberland Presbyterian. My husband gave me 20 drops medicine Dr McGown prescribe for me. I feel so sick at my stomach so giddy headed, __?__ hands perspiration stood in great drops over my face. Very nervous, Mr F sent for Bro Carroll. He rode over to see me, said it was only the effect of the spirits in the laudanum. [Laudanum is a tincture containing approximately 10 percent powdered opium.] Said my circulation is good, left morphine for me to take in place of laudanum. I felt much better & active tonight.

Tuesday Jan 20th 1857 Yes we did start on our way Jan 3rd 1857 after taking a dose of morphine. Am trying to eat breakfast, but I felt so sick at my stomach that I could eat nothing save a little boiled chicken. I felt so sick while the carriage was being prepared, I laid down on a couch. I felt O that I could lay here all day. But our business was so urgent, I would not tell my husband how sick I felt. Dr White said it would not hurt me to travel. Dr McGown said he did think it would by taking laudanum and morphine. But by the time I traveled 2 miles or more, I became so deathly sick. Mr F noticed it & said had we better turn back. I said I don't know. But I am so sick, he immediately turned and drove back to Mrs Uptoms. I soon took my bed. De McGown attended me __?__ my bed for three days, the coldest weather in an open house with a dust chimney ever and a more the cry was heard chimney's on fire. Then the water dashing would take place, the fire put out, all still. But one fire place all had to stay by the same fire place. I never had been sick before where I did not have a private room. Mrs Uptom took sick and was lying in a room more open & no fire place. I was miserable. I became convinced it became impossible for me to accompany Mr F to the low country. I asked him to ride to Bro Allen an old esteem friend and Bro Camberland who has a good wife a Methodist & a good lady, and ask for board, they said cordially come on & if I could put up with their bad fare & bad children. Dr said it would not injure me but would put some back a little. Wednesday it rained all day & Mr F feared to take me out. He went knetting and caught 5 partridges, came in late, I was worse he went to see the Dr he sent me medicine to take & preface be to be moved. O how I dreaded to get up out of a warm feather bed and go out in the cold. Next morning came still drizzling. I felt I must move Mr F dreaded to move me. But he fined horses & carriages, come & dressed me. O I was so weak I tried to walk into Mrs Upton's room to bid her farewell, I found I could not walk alone. Mr F led me I said good morning & left. Mr F had closed up the carriage so no wind would get to the children & me. Every once in a while my kind husband would say my dear how do you feel. I ask him & my dear boys to pray for me. I was so afraid the move this cold drizzly day would kill me. I had no fear of death but I hated to leave my beloved companion & children. O I thought what would become of my beloved sons without a Mother's hand to guide them thro' this wicked world.

We arrived at Bro Allens about one O clock. Mr F took me in his arms & carried me in the house. Sister Allen & Mary her step daughter met me & kissed me. Mary said I was so fraid you would not come. I soon took my bed again. Mary said excuse our clothes Mother & I have been cooking all day. Directly Mary said don't you want something to eat, some cake, we have plenty pies & custards if you wish any. I still thought how strange, liked to ask what's to pay? Sister Allen said did any body call to see Bro Foster this morning I observed no. I began to smell a mouse.

She says Mary is going to marry tonight My Bro Samuel Hancock and he said he was going to see Bro Foster this morning. Mr Hancock in the course of the afternoon called at the fence & asked my husband to marry him. Mary dressed in fine neatly trimmed white swiss dress, low neck short sleeves. Satin bows & long streamers over her hair & waist, she had on a neat breast pin, on her sleeves she had a pair of gold cuff pins. I put my breast pin on her satin bows. And have since regretted that I forgot to put my chain and pencil on her neck. She is a large fine looking woman. She married in the same dress she married her present husband's cousin in a year ago.

Thereafter receiving from me power of attorney to settle my deceased brothers affairs he embraced and affectionately kissed our children & me. Started for __?__ & Wharton. I have not heard a word from him. After he left I got a little worse and sent for Bro Carroll, he talked so kindly to me, and assured me I would be well after a time, if I would exercise patience. This was Thursday week after I got to this house, he told me to get up & dress next day. But sit up very little I did so, said I must not sew, read & write very little. I fear I am now transcending my limits which is my apology for writing so hastily.

I have improved every day since yesterday, I walked across the room twice, last night we heard a vehicle, Tommie & I thought it was my dear husband. I left my supper & went to the door. O I became so excited I feared it would injure me. I composed myself. When I found the mistake as the vehicle passed and the sound died away in the distance. Today I am 17, I have walked about the room several times, feel much stronger, [Some readers may think it strange that Louisa says that today was her seventeenth birthday. What she was implying was that she had been very sick and now felt much better. She was saying that she felt like seventeen again.]

The lovely bride I spoke of above has been sick for several days, with pleurisy, caused by dressing in low corsage of such thin materials in a cold room without fire such a freezing cold evening. I whipped Tommie a little today I feel badly since, and I have written too long.

Wednesday 21st I rose, don't feel as strong as I did yester morn. I still grieve about whipping Tommie yesterday. Although he needed it badly. I accidently left a little mark of a switch on him. This has cause gloom of mind ever since, although he laughs and says Mother what you grieving for it don't hurt. I believe it is well now. Lord forgive me. And my dear little boy too. And as Finie prayed last night "Make us good."

Thurs Jan 22nd A cool morning. I don't feel so well. My back hurts so bad I sometimes eat my breakfast before I dress. It still pains me very much.

Today is the day Mr F was asked to unite another couple in the holy bonds of matrimony. I hope he will do so. Mr Jamie Muckelroy to Miss Hale below Wharton.

Friday Jan 23rd Mrs Judy Walker came to see us today. There does not seem to be that friendship among neighbors as is the case in that hilly region where my sweet little cottage home is. My dear boys are well & out at play. In drawing up my sketch on account of weakness & debility I was compelled to be brief & forgot to mentions Sister Allen's twin daughter babes. Allice Ann and Ada Byron. They are very sweet, are 4 months old, Allice weighs 8 ¼ lbs., Asa 8 lbs. They are very smart, laugh, take hold of things. It seems so strange & they less than most of my babes at birth. Allice can almost sit alone, Tommie calls her his, Finie claims Ada and says we will take her home and give her some of his cows milk. Bro Carroll came to see me says I need nothing now, but still take my Iodite of iron twice a day [an iron supplement]. The norther blew up in the afternoon.

Sat 24th Jan A pleasant norther, I slept well last night. I spent this morning reading Reeve's Bible History to Tommie. We were both deeply interested. My Tommie cut me a nice pile of wood, and has gone to take his play. I darned the stockings & socks. Now must rest I am still very weak. This afternoon Judge Walker on his return from Columbus was kind enough to stop and send me in a letter from my ever dear husband, it brought glad tidings to my heart. I had to hold, for I felt I was in danger of being too much excited. It informed me he was in good health and business all right. Which has moved a mountain off my desponding heart, he informed me he had worked one of our horses we have down there in the carriage & he worked finely, he is worth about 150$. I am so glad, so our dear old prince will rest from his arduous labors. Mr F said he was going to marry the couple mentioned above.

Tommie has stayed in all evening until now about sundown, having me to continue reading Bible history to him & explain & I have never seen such a child. After 9 O clock he will come & sit on the floor at the low trammel bedside where we sleep & beg me to talk to him every night of Christ, the Prophets, the Martyrs and religion in general.

Monday Jan 26th I feel stronger. But this kind of weather always has a bad effect on me. Tommie has just waited on me well & just swept the floor of my room, & placed the chairs so prettily in a circle around the fire. I told him I must write it in my journal, he said I must not & turned in and swept the room nice again. And then I let him go with Willie Meales & Clemmie Allen to hunt Rabbits in the pasture in the late afternoon, they returned in triumph with a rabbit. I wrote home to Bro Joe, filled a sheet, I felt very much wearied, layed down & rested until after dinner. I eat a very hearty dinner, felt much better. Began Finie a pair of pants sitting propped up on my bedside. At the close of evening I felt badly. My back & limbs ached. My head felt heavy. I was truly alarmed.

Tuesday Jan 27th Soon after I heard my children praying I retired to rest. Tommie seated himself on the floor near my side and begged me to talk to him. I tried, for I hated to refuse a good & praiseworthy a request as to talk from my child of Christ. But I presumed he noticed my weariness and retired to bed. Soon we were all locked in sweet refreshing sleep. And this morning I awoke feeling stronger, much better and happier, than I have since my protracted sickness, before dinner I finished Finies pants, they fit very pretty.

Wednesday 28th I received a note from my dear husband & informed me that he had sold the negroes acquired by me at the death of my poor brother at $3,300, a small lot of the cattle at 137.50, rented the little farm at $75 cash in advance. Today I finished Tommies pants they fit nicely. I am so weak I sew awhile & lay down awhile. Martha servant girl presses for me. I went to the table today at dinner.

Friday 30th Last night it began to rain, and after we retired to rest the lighting played in vivid flashes and the thunder rolled so awful. It shook the house so I felt a little alarmed, so I could not get to sleep early. This morning is still dark.

Sunday Feb 1st Mr F brought over three thousand dollars in cash, after paying all my poor dear brother owed. He sold all the balance of cattle on time to be payed next spring. O God [keep] us from getting proud & from forgetting the hand of the bestower of this may be dedicate a portion to thy cause. How thankful I feel that so soon as we get home we can pay every debt we owe. Then what peace will dwell in our hearts. We have been in debt for three years. O may we never do so again.

Bro Allen, myself, & some others were on the porch, Mr F was in our room. I was standing by Finie to get him to wash I saw a gentleman riding up the road. I observe to Bro Allen, there's a traveler. I judge from wrappers & saddlebags, he said he looks so, by this time he had got to the gate, said you don't know me. I screamed out (before I had time to think of my weak state & all the Dr's directions to be calm), Yonder Bro Thomas, Mr F laughing said don't hollow so maybe it ain't him & said yes it is. I thought of my condition & tried to compose myself, husband & I met him at the gate. O it was a sight to see the two talk. Manly forms that was our dear affectionate brothers locked in each others embrace. Bro Tom then imprinted upon my face a brotherly kiss. We came in my hands were as cold as ice, my back ached, my husband would often say to me how do you feel, he was so afraid it would hurt me. When Brother Tom arrived at the next house he called for directions. [Finis had five brothers. Thomas was born ca. 1812 and died in Texas ca. 1862.] He observed the gentleman came out and as he had a familiar pleasant looking face, he thought he might know his brother. So he asked him, he said yes & informed Brother, that the children & I were here and looking daily for Mr. F.

So he returned & hence the happy joyful meeting had, he had been out our house all right at home, but Bro Philip's had left our house & all to the mercy of the public, because Mr F had failed to sent him money. My protracted sickness was the cause of that failure. Perhaps it is all for the best, as we are now anticipating selling more land below for horses, and drive to Missouri, hope to get through in time to attend Genl. Assembly of our church at Lexington, Mo. And spend the summer with our dear relations & perchance to get some of them to move to Texas. [The Foster family had lived in Missouri. Finis's mother and father had died there several years earlier.] If we do this we will wish to rent at Belton. We sent for Tommie, for Bro Thomas had not more than sit down before he asked for him. Bro T is so fond of our boys, he nursed both at once. All the relatives sent a heap of love to us.

Monday Feb 2nd I cannot perceive that my high state of excitement yesterday hurt me in the least. My husband is so kind & loving more so than usual if <u>possible</u>, he said this morning he believed he loved me better than he ever did. Bro Thomas seems so happy. And we are. Although just 12 months ago this afternoon our precious little sweet Lou Katie winged her way to that bright celestial world, where tremble ceases & pleasure of a high & holy nature ever dwells.

Mr F & bro Thomas has gone to Freilsburg to purchase some nice presents for this kind family, for bro Allen would not have a cent for our board. After they leave Freilsburg they will call by to see Bro Carroll to see if it will be safe for me to travel. And for Bro Thomas to become acquainted with our old friend, and make Josephine a present, for Bro Carroll never charges us for his medical services.

Bro Thomas & Lady came over I was glad to see them. Mr F returned with the presents. A muslin dress for Sister Allen & an apron of the same for Puss, a jacket dress for each one of the twins, 8 yards of prints to be divided between 3 negroes, 25 cents to old Uncle Calvin for making fires. Bro Carroll accompanied Mr F & Bro Thomas. We partook of a nice dinner another nice roasted turkey & delicious turnips. Bro C said he did not think it would hurt me to travel slow. So off we started Bro Thomas leading Bill [one of their horses]. Tommie ride a pretty gray pony his Pa traded for & gave him today, called Rattler. Tommie got very tired & wanted to get into the carriage, to night he was galled, but I used salve with seemed soothing in its effects.

Came to Bro Jack's all gone, dusk was compelled to drive 3 miles in the dark to Bro Hills, Bro Jack's family was here. He & Bro Hill rode up from La Grange, we were soon surrounded by smiling faces & received many kisses. I lay on the bed & Sister Hill & Sister Jack set near us as they could. We had a sweet time. Sister H after family worship had our bed made in the parlor. We retired to rest at 10 O clock.

Feb 4th Wednesday Drove to Cousins Eanes. This is the public fast day set apart by our synod. Mr F left one here with my Cousin's that if possible seem more kind than ever. Rode back to preaching at clear creek, I had cabbage for dinner, green grape pies for desert.

We can keep fruit of any kind all winter when properly put up. Late in the afternoon Mr F returned, had early supper, we remained grape tarts again. On account of the open house I told Cousin Betise I could not remain all night, she offered me her room & bed. I would not accept it. She being so weakly I know it would make her sick. She regretted it so did I. She drove back to Bro Eanes.

Feb 6th Friday I felt badly this morning. After I started I felt I could not travel all day for my back was so weak. I was convinced that dressing again this morning from the fire gave me cold. But thank the heavenly father as my day advanced the better I felt. Arrived at Bro Ben Dechard's at dusk. O I felt so well, but supper & worship I retired to rest earlier than the family.

Sat Feb 7th Well the norther is here. Arrived about 3 O clock before day. We started late, drove with a blanket in the front of the carriage 16 miles to Bro Newell Strayhorn's Webberville [less than twenty miles east of Austin]. Here we received a kind reception. Jef our negro boy that we had hired near here for more than twelve months was here met us at the carriage, his face weathered in smiles. [Louisa sometimes spelled Jeff's name with one *f*.] Seemed glad. O I felt rejoiced for this was an answer to my prayers that what I had heard about him was false, and that we ought to take him home.

Sunday Feb 8th After prayers, we partook of a nice breakfast prepared by our own Jef's hands of sausage, spare ribs, & sauce. It seemed like old times in my old sweet home to see Jef cooking around. He is so anxious for us to take him home. Bro & Sister Strayhorn say he is perfectly satisfied now.

Monday 9th Mr F begged me to walk with him to the store. I told him I did not wish to go, he insisted. About 12 we arrived at the store in company with Bell Strayhorn & my husband. Tommie to school to (Mrs Barre's the wife of a Methodist minister) this afternoon. I purchased myself 2 pretty dark calico dresses one a bit a yard, One 18 ¾ cents a yd. 42 yrds to send as presents to Bro Smith's daughter a dress a piece.

Myself a velvet Basque, black with crimson stripes. 4 bits a yd, black velvet trimming, a bolt at one dollar, a fine ivory comb, Tommie a comb 20 cents, & knife for Tommie, Finie, & Davie Bro Strayhorn's little boy. Jef is delighted, seems so cheerful & happy, said when he was first hired to Mr Hill he did not want to see us, But soon he found out the difference he wanted to see us, that he had often heard of our being down and hoped he would get to see us some time.

He never knew until last Christmas but that he was sold to Mr Hill. When Bro Strayhorn went after him & told him we would take him home, O he said he was so glad. I do think Jef will be a good negro now, I trust he will.

Mr F & Bro Strayhorn have just returned with a load of wood, they worked Bill one of our new horses. I hemed Mr F a silk pocket hdk. I bought a nice collar from Mrs Strayhorn she needled worked herself, price one dollar.

Wednesday Feb 11th Tommie purchased for me 50 cents worth more of French cotton. Mr F started home with a wagon load of corn, no corn nears, awful times, he is to be absent 2 weeks, in the mean time he expects to attend Presbytery & thank the lord pay every debt we owe. As to our trip to Missouri, some doubts about it at this time. I sent by Sister Strayhorn for 25 cents of yarn to make me two collars. Some ladies here called and I am invited in the room to see them. I was introduced to Mrs Nichols the hostess of the hotel and Mrs Wawivick wife of one of the teachers of this pretty little village Webberville. Seemed to be pleasant ladies.

After they left I returned to my room which is very comfortable. Darned up my children's socks, put them up, cut out a little garment, made it after supper. Sister Strayhorn & Bell when to prayer meeting. I feared to walk so far, for my back has hurt me worse all day. I have commenced taking nuriate of iron.

Friday 13th Feb A very warm ugly morning. Tommie lost his book again . . . which is very troublesome to me. If he does not do better I must correct him. I eat very little for breakfast, I must read my chapter & go to sewing. I finished my sack wrapper, it fits neatly. [The wrapper was fashionable in the 1850s. It was usually worn in the privacy of the home or in a rural setting. It was a loose one-piece dress pleated from neck to hem and belted for shape, sometimes with an apron.]

Sat Feb 14th I sent Tommie to Mr Smith's store for 50 cents worth of cheap domestic, he went & told him I wanted 8 yds or 2 or 4 he did not know which. I am sorry my little boy did like he had no little sense. I sent him back with the money, he got me 4 yds that suit very well.

I then sent him to Mr Brown's store for a sample of llk [sic] silk & the price he told me the kind he bought me cost 2.25 cents. I sent him for a piece to make an apron with one dollar to pay for it as it would take less than a yd. Mr B sent it with him with word to send 50 cents more I sent the money. And the price that Tommie told me, he wrote me a note telling me he told Tommie the price of the silk was $2.00, but I might have it at $1.75 per yd, as Tommie had asked for the finest piece he had. So my apron cost 1.50. It seems to be a superb piece of silk. I hope it will be cheaper at last, than the courser silk would have been. Although I told Tommie to get a scrap of the cheapest, I made it, trimmed with one row of velvet band bows of the small scallops. I am well pleased with it. But sorry my boy acted so awkwardly today. He generally does well when I send him shopping, for he does most of my shopping for me, as I hate to go to the store so much. I cut out my other dress which is a beautiful very dark purple, fitted it partly made the waist, ran up the shirt, made & put in the pockets, gathered it, basted the hem, fixed my morino ready for another.

Monday Feb 16th Tommie attended church. Bro Talliforo, a missionary Baptist preached immersion to the letter I am told [immersion of the body in water during baptism].

In the afternoon Jef & Tommie went Bro T baptized a negro man. Jef informed me my son Tommie laughed & throwed sticks in the water. I am so sorry, so mortified, I cannot find language to express my grief, at your behavior during the worship of the Most High. Little did I think when I consented to let you go that <u>my own</u> dear child would act so disgraceful. I would much prefer you misbehave at our own church, that at a sister demonization [sic], especially during the performance of an ordinance that is well known that your father does not administer by immersion. I am fearful that those by standers will attribute your horrible behavior on a sacred spot to your parents training. But you know better my child, & for your dear parents sake that loves <u>all</u> Christians, & ever endeavors to pay due difference to opposite sentiments of other Christians, and for heavens sake, <u>Never no never</u> do so again. I read a book through yesterday evening & this morning. I fear it was a novel. I was told it came out of the Sunday school library here, & such I read it. I am most sorry I read it, although it was good, I hate novel reading so much. I have sent Tommie to get me 10 cents worth of calico like my purple dress & then I will have a sufficiency to make my dress, also a ruffles spencer, with only two cents addition, to the cost of my dress pattern. I gain this by the width of the goods. This was a dark damp ugly morn. Tommie acted so foolishly again at the store. I felt it to be my duty again to whip him, I do so.

Tuesday Feb 17th 1857 An ugly morning still very warm. I look for a cold time yet in this month, for generally this is the coldest month of the year. I got my purple dress most finished. But as the day is warm, thought I had better cut my velvet basque & get sister L to fit it as she is such a good hand.

About midnight Bro's Golden & Strayhorn returned. Bro G stayed home, where tonight glad hearts will welcome him. Bro S has started to plant corn. I addressed my husband a letter. Bell took it to the office for me. I sent a dollar by her to get me an alpaca apron. Mrs Brown sent me the prettiest & finest piece of black alpaca I ever saw & five skeins of nice black silk for the dollar. Well I have had a time, so dark I cannot see how to sew. I hate to use Sister L's candles, these hard times, and my basque not ready to sew together yet. I have fitted 8 basted all day long & must confess got somewhat fretted. I hope the Lord will forgive me for being so foolish. I heard Sis Riggle had received a pearl. [*The Ladies' Pearl* was a popular magazine during this period] I was so anxious to examine its contents I sent for it, looked over it read a little. I was fearful she wished to read it & sent it back. I see they have reduced the price in case a club is made up.

Thursday Feb 19th Rather cold, a rainy, it rained a little last night. I hope I will finish my basque today. I feel very well, for which distinguished blessing I feel gratitude to God. I have gained strength enough to kneel at my bed, as is my usual custom, the last thing at night & commit my all & self into the hands of <u>our</u> great Creator.

I finished my basque. It is a neat a fit as I have ever seen. Tommie came from school in the worst of the rain. I made him change garments from foot to head & bathed his head & feet in cold water. After dinner he went with Jef to the crib to shell corn, returned very cold, he thought he had a chill. I made him a palate before the fire, & slept a sound long nap, woke up & said Mother I am well. This was sweet music to my heart. I dreaded his being sick now & Mother too weak to attend her offices of kindness.

Friday Feb 20th A pretty clear, tolerably cold morning. I look & feel better. My dear Tommie is well & he and sweet Finie are enjoying their childish sports as I write. Jef made me a cozy little fire.

Sat Feb 21st I slept well last night. In the same room with Sister Riggle & daughter. Tommie beg me to let him sleep in a bedroom with Reuben, Sister Riggle's daughter. I consented, Sister Riggle had the blues, she spoke sorrowfully of her dear departed husband. I tried to comfort her. Last night & evening I made Finie a nice apron. Today I cut him out of his dark half moon calico a gathered body with a yoke, made it, fits very well. Left Sister R much more cheerful than I found her, they are a pleasant family. Mrs Burres has given Tommie a word to spell & if he misses one she will keep him in but he has spelled them all to me. Tommie has bathed in luke warm water, ready for the approaching Sabbath, put on clean clothes, standing near me as I write. Will O Will my dearly beloved boy, be good or will he be a bad man after his fond Mother's many prayers & good talk to him. O God save my children. I have just written Jef a pass at his request & go around town & black boots. [Jef was enslaved and needed a written pass to wander around town to shine boots.] O send watch over our servant & may he not do wrong.

Monday Feb 23rd Tommie returned to dinner joyfully, he spelled every word that his beloved teacher gave him to learn. And I am glad too, my dear boy.

Tuesday Feb 24th We had a delightful rain last night. Fine for crops, I do hope it reached to Belton. O may we all be blessed with a good crop this year. I sent Jef all over town to get suitable trimming for Finie's velvet sack but cannot get it.

I cut out Jef's pant sister Strayhorn gave him for working for her one day in the Christmas holidays. I worked the button holes, done the stitching, basted the pockets, for Jef to finish.

Wednesday Feb 25th I felt so much better than I did last night, not tired, I attributed it to my walk. I must endeavor to walk every evening.

Thursday Feb 26th After all my good feeling last evening, I could not sleep until after midnight. I was so surprised that my husband has not written to me, when he promised me to do so. I can't not avoid being very restless

& uneasy about my husband & home. I looked for him last evening & he did not come. If I had have received a letter from him informing me <u>all</u> was <u>well</u> I should not have spent such a restless night. And woke up this morning with the headache. But he will have some excuse. My husband has never done so before in my life. And this makes me fearful <u>something</u> has happen. Today I hope to hear from as the mail comes down. I sent to the office the stage driver had forgotten the mail & left it at Bro Hornsby. I never heard of the like. I wrote 3 letters this morning one to my husband, one to my cousin at Le Grange, Texas, one to Mrs Miller, my nearest neighbor at B [Belton].

Friday Feb 27th Late yesterday I walked up to see Sister Hill's hoping to see the Dr at home, so I could get a mouth wash from him. Soon he came in with two strings of fish. They insisted on sister L & me to stay until after supper, but we could not. Dr said he would bring me a mouth wash. I ate no supper, retired early, rested well. My mouth is still very sore. But does not throb & pain me as it did. Dr Hill brought me the wash, I have used it once. Says I must wash with it 3 times a day, each time using cold water before.

My husband's not come yet. My fears are much dispelled. I am composed, and shall endeavor to wait patiently. Tomorrow I expect the arrival of the mail that was left above. Then I do trust to receive a letter from him. Then if all are well & right, I will be perfectly satisfied for I am daily praying [for] our board. In the services of our negro man Jef and have corn that we payed our own money for in the crib for our horses. I have a comfortable room to ourselves except Bell sleeps in here & I wish her to do so for company while my husband is absent.

Sat Feb 28th My mouth is most well, I feel as well as usual, for which I do trust that I feel gratitude to God. I hope to get a letter today. This afternoon has been a bright lovely one. I received a letter from my Dear husband, One from Bro Bob Wear to my husband & I answered both.

All was well at home. My husband had commenced sewing wheat, had planted one bushel of irish potatoes, some garden seed, my husbands letter breathed his usual kind tone. And said he was so glad my health was improving.

Said he had taken Milla our house woman home, and that she was so glad to get home. She sent me word that she was well & wanted to come soon as I could. He said she was doing finely. And wished me if I thought if I could do without Jef to send him home, as we needed his assistance, but he kindly let it to me. As Sister Lucy had her work to do when Jef would leave & I could not have her cook for me. I came over to Sister Riggles, spoke for boarding obtained us until my husband comes after me, at $20 per month. Monday early I expected to start Jef. Jef brought all my things over so I now write in my new home, which hope I'll like as well as the comfortable kind one I left.

Sunday March 1st 1857 We are all well. I did not sleep last night until after midnight. But my reflections were happy ones, save when I would think of writing Jef a pass & forgetting to sign my name to it. I fear the Patrols would whip him. Save enough he informed me that they saw him examined his pass, & told him that was no pass at all & if they had not known him so well, by law they were compelled to whip him. I think this will be a lesson for me <u>forever.</u> [There was a fear among people in the Southern states of enslaved people rising up or freeing themselves through escape. To protect themselves and to control the people they kept in bondage, enslavers had local courts appoint patrols to look for any fugitives from slavery and those without proper passes to leave the place prescribed to them. Male citizens were required to serve on these patrols for various times during the year. Usually they earned fees for captured freedom seekers. Enslaved people found without proper passes could be punished severely before they were returned to their owners.]

Monday March 2nd I washed & ironed all mine & childrens dirty clothes. Then I swapped Bill to Mr Boyed for a large sorrel horse with blaze face. [A sorrel horse had a wide stripe down the middle of the face.] Several persons that I know are reliable told me that Bill is a splendid carriage or buggy horse. I waited for the last week on the thought of swaping horses still hoped my husband would come for I feared to make a swap as I never had done the like. But Wednesday Mr Boyed speaks of leaving, and I knew we must have a horse suited to our and my husband wrote me to sell Bill as we had no use for him, and said better take seventy dollars than keep so I thought I had better pay 50 dollars in cash and get a horse of such good qualities than to work dear old Prince any more hard trips. And we were compelled to have a gentle horse to work with Carrie. It would not be safe to rush a wild young horse with so young a horse as C is 15 minutes after 12 Jef started home Riding Bill & leading Pony. My swap scared me as it was my first effort fearing I have made a bad one. I do believe Mr B was sorry he told Sis when I was out of the room he rather than 10 dollars I would say no. I would not give the boot required. I am not afraid my husband will uphold me no, I know he will be satisfied. If it proves a bad exchange he will be sorry & so will I. Late this afternoon it rained very hard. I fear Jef got wet, but he

Kathairon ad from the *American Farmers' Magazine*, vol. 1, issue 7, 1857, page 10.

had on his Kersey sack & a heavy overcoat, had his own two blankets so I hope he did not suffer & I trust it will not cause him to be sick.

Tuesday March 3rd Tommie begged me to give him ten cents to go & purchase a pencil a piece for Bro & Sister Bruues. Said he had never made his teachers a present & wished to do so. I gave him the dime, he has done as his benevolent heart desired. I know his sweet blue eyes glowed with happiness at the time. I wrote to my dear husband & sent it to be mailed.

Wednesday March 4th I went to the store & bought Tommie & Finie a pr of shoes. Tommie's one dollar, Finie's 75 cents, myself a plain white swiss dress & sun bonnet pattern for 50 cents per yd, 10 yrds, the lining hooks & eyes & thread thrown in. I purchase one yard & half of handsome lace at 20 cents for the whole. At Mr Browns I bought myself a pair of shoes $1.75, 25 cents for a bottle of Kathairon for the hair. [Lyon's Kathairon was first made in 1850. It was advertised to be a cure for baldness, gray hair, dandruff, and even headaches. It was also used for hair styling.]

Thursday March 5th Mr Boyd, Sister Riggle's cousin is about to leave here for his fathers in Sabine County eastern Texas. I feel much better than I expected. I am sorry so little exertion seems to over do my weak frame. I fear I shall never get over my late protracted spell of sickness. I cut out my swiss sun bonnet and run the cases for the splits, wrote a long letter. A sheet full to my husband. I told him I am homesick.

March Sat 7th I heard a wagon drive up. I rose to the door it was my beloved husband, all well & safe at home. My husband complains of his back so much says he is satisfied it is rheumatism, which distresses me very much indeed. Milla & Jef is at home at work, misty evening. All the wheat, corn, oats, Milla planted, good many garden seeds sewn. Milla has made about 3 gallons of nice soap. Mr F says Milla does finely.

After supper I finished Finie's velvet sack. I gave Sis one dollar & one dime for some pink silk gimp to trim it with, sent to Mr Rayons got 10 cents worth more. It is beautiful indeed, the only fine sack I every made Finie. It has twenty-four silk buttons on it. I must make Tommie a pretty sack, head prayers, Tommie bound two balls of factory cotton.

Monday March 9th A cold norther came up just before day, half after 4, so cold I fear we cannot travel. I feel like I shall take the blues if I cannot start home today. And the prospect is very unfavorable. Uncle Henry stayed here last night. We had a delightful talk with him about building up a high school under the direction of our beloved church of <u>our</u> own church. The prospect seemed fair & flattering. I now think it probable now that we will move there. And do all we can to assist in building up the school and educate my sweet boys, in a school under the patronage of our church. I wound 4 balls of factory cotton. Sister Riggle doubled the two that Tommie wound which was a great favor. I doubled all the balance, hemmed sis bonnet strings, to pay for Hannah the servant twisting 2 broaches for me. I put on a sack for my husband. Mr F purchased me a small oven lid for my oven, that brother Smith's children broke the lid of—price $50.

Tuesday March 10th We will soon start home. I feel like never leaving home again. Mr F got me 4 bottles of Kaithairon for my hair. I gave one to Sister Riggle. We bought another oven lid all $50. We drove to sister Mary Miniels, took dinner, drove to our dear old friends, Bro E.S. Johnson near Austin here, as ever, we were kindly met by all of this dear family.

Monday April 20th A pleasant day, we have no fire except a few coals on the hearth. South wind rather high. Soon after I arrived at home, I took sick with my old disease, and a severe cough, with sourness all through my chest & shoulders. I had great fear that my cold had settled on my lungs. And that my fate was to be a consumption. And sorry to leave my sweet humble home. Beloved & affectionate companion and my dearest boys in this world. O this thought to me was almost unbearable. Altho' I felt no serious dread of death, I fell conscious my dear husband would most meet me in heaven. But O my children left in this world without a tender Mother's kind hand to guide them amid shoals and quicksand of this sinful world.

I have been much exposed. My affliction has been great but I am reconciled if God will spare me to my husband & children. And here I covenant to try to live nearer to God and to endeavor to raise these sweet little olive plants [her boys] he has placed around my table so they will be the bright & useful ornaments in society, and living pillars in the Church of Christ.

I am walking about the room tolerable apetite headache yesterday & today, cold feet. My limbs ache a little. I feel pretty cheerful and have not ventured in the go for over 3 weeks. We had a snow storm on the 11th. A thing unprecedented in the history of our state.

April 25th I have commenced to use coffee out of my four gallon jar. Bro Philips returned from the low country with some of our horses. Our cattle were not delivered, we failed to get the expected money. Bro P returned yester eve.

Tuesday April 28th We received a kind precious letter from our brother Robert. We both answered it on a sheet and a half of letter paper. We tried to prevail on him to come & live with us. I feel well save a little hurting in my breast & shoulders, at intervals. I do pray to the good Lord that this symptom may soon be removed permanently.

Wednesday 29th We have cloudy weather ever since the rain (which has been favorable, so as to enable the parched earth to receive all the moisture) until this afternoon the sun has shone mildly, for I have written two letters, one to Bro Hilbelts, I enclosed 20 dollars to constitute my Dear Tommie a life member of the Missionary Society, 20 dollars for Mr F, to constitute Finie a life member of the same. [The Church Missionary Society was founded in 1799. In 1829 they began to send medical personnel as missionaries.] One to Bro Langoon enclosing ten dollars for the educational fund. To educate young ministers of our church. Lord send Blessings that little nite, and bless our souls abundantly.

Friday May 1st I made Tommie & Finie life members myself which was forty dollars. Mr F mailed them both. I feel so well, I sat up all day, company came in, Mr James Allen, he is Tommie's teacher, he is an old friend of ours. We sat up late. I got very tired, did not sleep until after 11 O clock.

Sat May 2nd I do not feel so well. My breast hurts me worst. I feel nervous. I hope it will soon pass off, ugly damp morning. The symptoms of my disease has stopped & I hope will remain so. I laid now most all day. This afternoon I feel much better. My chest is almost entirely easy, Mr F, Bro Philips, Mrs Allen and Jef they all went fishing & hunting. The river was up so the fish would not bite. But they brought in 2 nice squirrels, Milla has cleaned up, almost ready for Sabbath. Baked 2 nice loaves of raised bread.

Sunday May 3rd I feel almost entirely well, no hurting in my chest, shoulders and limbs. I do hope I will soon be entirely recovered. Tommie attended Sabbath school as usual, when he is at home. He brought home a question book I am so glad. This evening he has already learned all his question lesson. This Sunday evening I trust my 2 letters are on their way with my fifty dollars. O may it do good to some poor missionary.

Monday May 4th A cool morning, I arose an hour earlier. Could eat but very little breakfast. I felt sketchy sorter coolish, very weak and nervous. But very little if any uneasiness in my breast. Dr Williams came in. She is a daughter of Rev Haynes a C.P. [Cumberland Presbyterian] Minister. She stayed with me until dinner, while her husband had some repairing done on their hack in town.

I was pleased to have her company especially as my husband rode out to the Cedar break to see if we have rails enough to finish our fences. My face became very much flushed, about 10 or 11 O clock I felt so very warm. I fear I have had a fever. O what will become of my dear precious children if I must die & leave them in this most God forgetting world.

If it should be my last request, Remember your fond dear Mother's many words & lectures to you two sweet dear ones, and above all be virtuous & religious. O my sweet babes. Meet me in heaven, the bright place that is eternally fair. That bright & peaceful shore where Christian Mothers & children never part. But where they together may enjoy an eternity of bliss, O my children live so that you may be bright & shining in this dark world of ours. And O be an honor to your dear father & mother that loves you so <u>dearly</u>, never disgrace them Would that I could wield an inspired pen today, that I might trace words here than would be lasting as eternity on your plastic minds & wax-like spirits, that God has committed to my trust. "to be rendered back with interest."

Tuesday May 5th Dr Embree came to see me last evening, he said I had had fever during the day but it was cooled, medicine. And he knew just what I required and that he would cure me in a short time now. He said I must have a blowing horn, and blow it 2 or 3 times a day to exercise my lungs. He gave me 3 blue mass pills. I fear my liver is dormant again, left mitre I am taking it, it is to act on the kidneys and deplete. I felt very bad until my medicine acted, which was about 8 O clock this morning, it is now 10 & it has acted 4 times.

My heart is entirely relieved of that heavy dull aching which I had when I arose. But when I get up suddenly it is rather dizzy. Dr says now I am too full of blood. I still use Iodine on my breast, my breast & shoulders are all most if not entirely easy this morning. I do think the Lord. O may I now get restored again. My Shanghai hen laid 23 eggs in one litter. I have her up now to break her from setting. Mr F has just set one common hen on 7 Shanghai eggs and 11 common ones. I have a yellow turkey hen who has just hatched 10 pretty little turkeys one is dead 2 more eggs piped [pipped: to break through the shell of an egg]. I have another turkey sitting on 5 turkey eggs and 17 Shanghai ones. I hope I will have great success this year.

I feel better this evening, sun has gone down behind the western horizon. O may its dawn tomorrow find me much improved. O may the medicines I am taking with Gods blessing restore me to health, one sweet boon of earthly happiness. What O what is this worlds treasures without. I have had a warm sensation in my bosom, I fear it is inflammation in my lungs, but I trust not. I felt a little uneasy in my breast a few minutes only today. I am thankful. I hope this is a good symptom. Tommie & Finie behaved so ugly today when Bro Beasly and Mr Willis was here.

Wednesday May 6th I feel weak & nervous this morning. Before I arose my breast & shoulders felt uneasy. At the breakfast table I burst into tears. I have wept most all morning. Tommie kissed me & went to school. I just clasped Finie in my fond embrace and wept over him & asked him if he would meet in heaven, if I had to die & leave him, the sweet little looked lovingly in my face and said "Yes Ma" and in that good world. I again presented him to my bosom and said who will take care of my little boy if Mother dies. He promptly replied "God." O my God disappoint him, but not let him run into sin in youth. But O early in cline his heart to seek thee.

My children excuse the imperfectness of these pages, you are a stranger to the emotions that agitate your fond Mother's bosom, whilst tears are fast falling from her eyes. I feel a deep concern for your souls. O will you meet me in heaven, that home, true sweet everlasting home. If I have raised you, you know how I have prayed for you. Milla be good to my poor babes. Don't say ugly or vulgar words before them. O remember remember this, O my husband I hope my life will be prolonged and I may again be cheerful and make you happy as I have done. If not forgive all my errors treasure my virtues, if

I have any. O be kind to Tommie, I fear your harshness will prove his ruin. Don't listen to much to what others may tell you of his faults. They will not make allowances as they do for their own children, my boys have generous noble hearts. O cherish every opening bud. I know you will often, yes, daily speak them of your fond Mother. Try to smooth your own temper and "speak gently" to our little lambs. Keep them near your side as much as possible. Never let them sleep with girls. Teach them as I have done it is sinful. Early as practicable teach what virtue is and tell them without they cannot be pious and get to heaven to meet their fond Mother, little sweet brothers and sisters. I know you will meet me in heaven.

Thursday May 7th I feel better, when I arose my breast & shoulders hurt me a great deal. I took a walk, went where Mr F was clearing brush off the oats, they are growing so nice. Everything in the field look so green & pretty. We have a most excellent stand of corn. Uncle Henry said he had never seen a better.

I returned after I had fed my little turkeys and my husband started to work. Mrs M coughed a good deal. I coughed more than usual perhaps it was sympathy. Late in the afternoon I suddenly took the blues, I attempted to come, Mrs M, begged me to stay, I told her no I must go. I walked home Tommie met me at the gate coming from school. He begged me to remain, I told him I could not. I felt so gloomy. The children & I came on we went to pen our hen & little turkeys, fed them. I went and stirred my sack kettle. I saw Jef coming with the wagon, I thought, well I will stay till he comes. I know he will be glad to see me out in the yard. So I walked back & forth. I went to the pile of planks and crouched upon it, looked in the open squares to see if I could not find a hen nest. Jef drove up and said with a delighted face, "You are getting young, I saw you walking about when I was way round the field."

I came in the house & became cheerful. My husband came got him a drink out neat brass bound bucket and started after some more onions to set out as he did on yester eve that Uncle Jonnie Blair was so kind as to give us. I saw Mrs Miller & Luther her babe at the gate. I know she was coming to see if I had the blues. I was glad that I had become more cheerful. With a smile I said come in Mrs Miller. Then I laughingly said I know you came to see if I have the blues. She said yes I did. She observed I saw the gloom over spread your face so quick before you left my house, that I could not rest. But I am so glad to see you cheerful now. Said Mrs Foster I do think a cheerful heart and exercise is all you need. We went to see them set out onions. I dropped a few to be set out. Mrs Jack Smith sent me as a present 8 Shanghai eggs of the yellow stock I am so proud of them. Mr F put them under another hen he set with 15 common ones today under the stable loft. When it got so late I was afraid of the night air I came to the house and set the table as Milla was complaining. I eat a little corn bread & gravy with onions, it tasted so sweet, drank pretty near two glasses of milk. I trust to the good Lord that I will get well.

Friday 8th May My breast & shoulders still hurt me. But I feel much improved, much stronger. I swing as the Dr required, by my hands several times a day. Today is a busy day. Mr F is moving out the middle string of fence to take in the fifty acres. They have come to dinner, it is waiting, I must stop, a dieu, My dear husband it is for your good I write this book.

I called and spent the principle part of the afternoon with Mrs M. Finie had a fine time pulling her babe about in its little willow wagon. Mr F sent for me to walk up to where he was loading the wagon with rails. And then Finie, Tommie & I rode on a load of rails up to the back of the field. The first time I ever rode on rails.

Sat May 9th A lovely morning, as soon as I eat my breakfast I started out, I helped Mr F, hoe out our little garden. Then children & I got on the wagon & rode out to where he begin to load rails. And was sorry we had to dismount. Then we gathered a bunch of wild flowers with which we made 3 beautiful bouquets. I place one by the clock & 2 by the toilet, one on each side of the glass. [Toilet glass is a looking glass for a table or dressing room.] Tommie then brought me a small Bouquet of wild verbena. I placed it in Finie's china vase over his puppy. I placed my tissue paper flowers that I made myself in the children's vases that Jef gave them long ago. I have them on each side of the toilet glass also. I know my husband will be pleased & think our little home a wilderness of flowers. I have arranged my book table placed my large family Bible, my husband had locked up in my trunk, as a sweet surprise for me when I came home and the album on the spot. O I am thankful I feel so well. My breast hurts a little. This is the first time my room looks like it used to do, before my protracted sickness, which adds much to happy feelings.

Journal #5

January 20, 1858–May 19, 1858

Wednesday Jan 20th 1858 A most lovely day, it reminds of spring with its green verdure, blossoms, fruits and flowers. My precious young friends Mary Scott & Ellen Kuykendall spent the morning & dined with us. We then paid convalescents friend a call. She is fast improving & very playful, jocular, which afforded us much pleasure. It reminded me of the past pleasant I have passed with dear Sue. I must now pack my trunk, sachel & carpet sack ready for my anticipated trip. Mr F purchased 3 yds. calico for Finie's aprons, a remnant of 2 1/2 yrds. for his pants. I am trying to get he & Tommie a pair. Lord bless us on our trip, and aid us in making a proper decision.

Mr F rented all of our farm here today to Mr. Wade, that we do not wish to sew in wheat. Which is about 16 acres. Sat Jan 16th my bad symptoms left me. Jef sold 2 doz chickens, the whole amount $3.60 cents. My husband's spirits are much revived at the expedition we have made today in arranging matters for our contents, plated trip, We received a letter from Bro Dechard President of our Institution at La Grange, requesting us to come and attend his examination, and then judge of his institution, in regard to educating our dear sons. [There was a La Grange Collegiate Institute that later, in 1860, changed its name to Ewing College. When it opened in 1860, the president was R. P. Dechard. The school was charted under the Colorado Synod of the Cumberland Presbyterian Church and was described as suitable for ministerial students.]

Mr F will attend I presume, Bro D says many of our friends would be pleased for us to locate there. Lord, direct our goings.

Jan 21st Thursday Jef is packing the carriage, getting ready to depart. My head aches. Jef sold all my turkeys at 75 cents each, I had 6. I presume will start after early dinner. We had fine success, sold all the wheat, turkeys, &

chickens enough and shock corn, wheat chaff, which amounts to about 37 dollars. Started between 1 & 2 O clock, feeling happy and like we were doing right. Traveled 10 miles to Mr Reeds were kindly met.

Friday Jan 22nd Arose, dressed, attended prayers, breakfast about 7 O clock. It began to rain about midnight. Still drizzly, south wind, we are safely housed until a clear sky. I do hope it clears away by twelve. I have just read of Mr. Edwin Dean, agent for Mr. Singer's patent sewing machine, St Louis, Missouri. [Before Isaac Singer built his famous sewing machine in the early 1850s, he toured with the Edwin Dean theater company. This may have been the same Edwin Dean who was listed in the St. Louis City Directory years later as an agent of Singer Sewing Machines. He also ran ads for it in the agriculture publication called *The Valley Farmer*. This might be what Louisa read.]

Jan 23rd Sat A very dismal rainy day, arose attended prayers, breakfast, started traveled 20 miles to Florence, through mud & water, but I was so glad to see rain, that I felt quite patient. Passed by our lots and buildings we purchased lately, they are beautiful lots. [Florence was about forty miles north of Austin and was settled in the early 1850s.] Pretty grove and real snug little buildings, arrived at Bro Redding's just before dark, he is a baptist, his wife is a member of our church. They met us so open & frank that immediately I felt at home.

Tuesday Jan 26th I was so sick yesterday, I did not write in my journal. I did not rise this morning until about 10. Dr Adams paid me two visits and relieved almost immediately. I wrote down this recipe for Sister Redding who was so kind to me while we stayed. It is on dying yarn. One ounce Cochineal bugs, well beaten. [This bug was a scale insect from which the natural dye carmine was derived.] The same amount of crème of tartar, the same of muriate of tin, boil the bugs first , then add the balance, boil all well in a brass or tin vessel, then put the hanks in and boil, then take out the hanks & dip in water, they dry, then wash in a nice warm suds.

Wed Jan 27th We have the carriage ready packed & expect to get to our place of destination this evening. Well, we have arrived safely, at last, after tugging thro' the mud. Bro Gid McFarland was from home, sister Gid met us kindly. Had a nice supper of spare ribs, and as we had traveled all day without dinner, (a new thing for me) I ate a very hearty supper, which made me feel much better.

Friday Jan 29th Mr F kissed & pressed me to his fond heart, bade me not have the blues, imprinted a fatherly kiss on each one of our boys & bade our friends adieu. Started on our big mule kit, for La Grange to attend Bro Dechards examination at his request 4th of Feb I regret it is now raining.

Sat Jan 30th A very rainy day, high south east wind, I am sorry that Mr F will be compelled to ride facing it. But one consolation he will only have to ride 8 or 10 miles to where he expects to preach tomorrow. I cut out and made an apron for Finie.

Sunday Jan 31st I hope it will not rain but continued pleasant until my husband's return. Which I presume will be next Thursday week. And bless him in all his efforts to do good.

Marian McFarland, Gid's brother, had just told me Dr Owens will be out to see me today. I feel as well as usual. Tommie & Finie behave so ugly that it causes me great pain of heart. I must stop & read my bible.

Monday Feb 1st Dr Owen called on me again I commenced taking the medicine as prescribed he said he can help me a great deal but did not say he could cure me entirely.

I feel rather gloomy today, Tommie & Bro Gid has just returned from the woods with a load of firewood. Finie has taken a cold, I gave him a dose of castor oil by promising him a black frocked coat & a pair of boots. He readily took it.

Tuesday Feb 2nd 1858 Spent the day pleasantly, after I got over my weeping spell. I felt that I was in the way of everyone, but Uncle Sam, Aunt Jane & sister Pollie talked so good to me that I became quite cheery. In the afternoon we returned home with Sister Barton.

Thursday Feb 4th This day Bro Dechard's examination in LaGrange commences. May my husband be protected and attend the teaching of the Holy Spirit, <u>now</u> & ever. Attended family prayers, retired for the night.

Friday Feb 5th Sister Barton is very kind, she kindly offered to wash our clothes, so I told her I would pay Margaret (her daughter) to wash for me, she said she would have no pay. I told her I would pay her, she then said I might may, any thing I wished she would gladly work for me. So this difficulty is removed. Mary is knitting socks for sale and says she would just as I've wash for pay as to knit for it for she can make the money she needs so much sooner.

Saturday Feb 6th May my husband be cheered by this delightful morn & guide him. Finie must know his A,B,C. Tommie, Bobbie and Lizzie spell together, they learn very well. Sister Barton speaks of having a room built for our accommodation, which is very good & kind in her & her husband. I finished my chemise, made Tommie 2 or. Of suspenders, darned his socks, my stockings and Bobbie Barton's socks.

Sunday Feb 7th O I am getting so anxious to see by husband.

Tuesday Feb 9th A very misty morning, faired away a pleasant forenoon. As usual heard Tommie, Bobbie, Lizzie & Margaret spell, as I have classed them, they said a poor lesson. Dr Owens passed here late this evening, did not come in, said he would be out to see me in a few days.

Wednesday Feb 10th The thought gives me pain that my husband most likely riding facing this cold cold wind. My health seems much improved. O Lord grant Dr Owen may cure me entirely.

Thursday Feb 11th A cold morning, but much moderated since yester morn. No Snow yet. I now feel the need of a private room. I am sewing on Mr F's drawers. A very rainy day, Mr F did not come.

Friday Feb 12th I feel very well this morning. I hope my old symptoms will soon pass away. I feel better and more healthy than I have ever done since my long spell last spring.

But if I get sick I will surely give some praise (as an instrumentality) in bringing about my restoration, to Graffenburg's Cathlicon, surely it has benefitted me. [These were pills that were advertised at twenty-five cents a box and claimed to cure everything from constipation to loss of memory.]

I have read my Psalms, Bro Smith came changed his voice, fooled us & made us think it was Mr F, so we had a great laugh. He told me Milla & Jef are frolicking at home with a gang of Negroes at our nightly, which made me uneasy & unhappy. I could scarcely eat my supper & did not sleep until after one O clock.

Sat Feb 13th I am so glad my husband has returned, he bargained for a 5 acre lot with a neat flank house on it. Consisting of 3 rooms, kitchen, meat house, stable, a never failing well, several pretty cedar bushes in the yard, at 1800 putting in Milla & Kit at 1200, twelve months time. O I am so grateful to God. Mr F says Bro R.P. Dechard is the best teacher he ever saw.

The idea of educating our dear boys under such a man and in an institution under the patronage of our own beloved Zion. I sent to Hamilton by Bro Gid for 4 years of __?__ blue __?__ it was 25 cents a yard, and five cents to purchase flax thread, he got 10 cents worth.

Monday Feb 15th A most lovely day, we drove to Bro Hill's. Mr F thought I had better spend the time he is absent at this place. All seemed kind & pleasant. Caroline E. McAshan is the lady that the bill of sale of Milla is to be made to if we confirm our trade. Which I do hope we will be able to do so, in as much as it will give us a beautiful, pleasant retired home in La Grange where we can educate our dear boys in Texas. And in a school under the patronage of <u>our own beloved Zion</u>, and taught by a member of our own church, which I must confess is a most delightful idea to me and the thought makes my fond mother's heart leap for joy & gladness.

Make it happen to present a very needy field for my husband to labor in which is quiet an item also, which would not have been the case if we had located near the Bosque College according to our desire last autumn. [Bosque Academy was about five miles north of Waco and headed by John C. Collier, a Cumberland Presbyterian. There will be more about him later.] In which we were very much disappointed but now I look upon it as a providential occurrence. May it prove to be so indeed. A norther has blown up.

Wednesday Feb 17th Dr Owen called to see me. Mr F had a private conversation with him. He says he can cure me, and will soon have my cheeks to look rosy. O may the Lord grant it may be so and I covenant afresh to try (God being my helper) to live to be more faithful to raise my children in the fear & admonition of the God of our fathers, & to do all the good I can in every way. Mr F said he hated to leave his little wife so soon, but duty compelled, he pressed me to his fond bosom & imprinted an affectionate kiss upon my lips, and started for Belton to arrange home affairs & return in a week or two, to break unto this people the bread of eternal life, until we get ready to move to LaGrange. There I would be glad if it is the Lord's will & my husband can be useful to remain the balance of our days.

Monday Feb 22nd A very warm morning. Bro & Sister Hill wished to ride out somewhere & I thought as I felt so badly perhaps it would help me. So we started to Uncle Sam's. Tommie drove Bro Hill rode horseback, just as we started up came a norther but on we went. When we got to there, all were gone so we turned & drove to Bro Jack McFarland. Pretty cold by this time, but they have a very close room. Dr Owen & lady came. I was glad to see them. The Dr said the medicine was having the desired effect, he again remembered that the rose would soon return to my cheeks. This would of course afford me pleasure, but I fear he is talking to encourage me. Partook of a nice well cooked dinner, added to the balance was nice honey comb. Drove back in sweeping trot, Kit, Bro Hills buggy mare biting Cassy every step almost. Made a big fire, the coldest night I think we have had.

Sat Feb 27th A pretty morning, my head seemed relieved. Have not breakfasted yet, must read. I hope my husband will soon return. I finished Finies coat all but sewing the velvet trimming on the breast to make it resemble a vest & coat collar and would have done this, but my velvet was at Bro Bartons, it was a tedious job as I had to cut patterns & fit & cut & so on until I finished. But it is beauty & nice fit, when on my previous boy will repay me for all my trouble if <u>he</u> will only behave pretty at church. I swapped some of Finie's pantalets he wore when a babe to Sister Hill for 3 cuts of yarn then I doubled it ready to twist. O my back ached so when I got done. I feared Dr Owen could never restore my shattered system.

Sunday Feb 28th A sweet morning, I feel so much better. I am going to work Kittie Hill a pink calico shirt, sleeves bands & belt. Then ironed about a dozen pieces for Sister Sallie, in lieu of her twisting & washing out my yarn. I feared I could not twist it well as I had not done so in about 14 years as I have been so fortunate as to had a sufficiency of knitting yarn given to me until now. And Sister Sallie said she did not wish me to iron for her, but I would do it, as I do not like to get any one to do any thing for me & not repay them.

Then I traded her out of 4 cuts of nice yarn. I was most done doubling it when I was called to supper. Soon after I eat, Tommie told me father's coming. Children & I went some distance to meet him, he fondly kissed us. We returned to the house, I finished doubling my yarn, wound two nice balls of that which is twisted. It is very fine & nice, I am so proud of it. I will now knit my husband a nice pair of socks & foot several pairs for the boys.

Mr F told me Mr McAshan will take Milla & wished him to bring her down as soon as possible to close the trade. O we both feel so grateful to the good Lord that we will soon have so beautiful convenient & retired home in La Grange, where there is so fine a prospect to educate our dear boys properly, and where there are so few ministers, and where we have so many <u>precious</u> relatives & dear friends. We hail this as an indication that we ought to move there. It seems that everything has prospered in our hands in attempting to prepare for this move. And another comforting thought is that the people it seems here from what I hear have in my husband's services obtained their favorite preacher.

Monday Feb 29th [She put in the wrong date here—1858 was not a leap year.] In the afternoon I read aloud in the family an interesting an[d] thrilling account of a young lady who died of that awful & raving disease consumption. The title of the book is "The withered branch revised." [Possibly it was *The Withered Branch Revived, from Gathered Fragments,* by John A. Clark, published 1848.] O I earnestly prayed that I might not fall a victim to that fatal disease.

Friday 5th Had nice batter cakes & butter for supper last night. I am most done with patching. Lizzie patched one of Tommie's shirts.

Milla did not finish coloring but I sent her to wash & scoar for Aunt Jane. All are busily & cheerfully engaged. Put up the neat shed room for us to occupy this summer. I finished Aunt Jane's neat muslin cap & sent it to her. Milla has returned after the days labor with a nice mess of greens.

Sunday 7th A cold norther, I hope my husband will not however be prevented from preaching. Maro bit Finie, I put turpentine on it he rubbed it in his eye, which cause him much pain and alarmed me sorely. Milla rode over to Bro Hills.

Monday 8th A beautiful bright sunny morning although a little cold. Milla will have a fine day to wash.

I must write several letters this morning. I spun two broaches of wool, the first I ever did & doubled them. Sister P says they are nice. I finished Aunt Jane's cap.

Tuesday 9th 1858 A cool but pretty morning. I must read & get to work. I am needle working on my shirt. I am about to commence to teach Mary, to needle work her a handsome shirt. Tommie is breaking my wool. I began to learn Mary. I spun & doubled myself a small bale of yarn. Mr F returned but after riding 10 miles facing a norther last Sunday did not have __?__, which of course was discouraging. He looked on his return on Monday & Tuesday for our horses, but did not find them.

Wednesday March 10th I fear my system is getting out of order again. A beautiful spring morning. I feel that I am fast improving if I was house keeping only. I would be so happy. "No place is like home." If it is a board cabin. ["No place is like home" is the last line of the 1822 song "Home! Sweet Home!"] It seems to me next year if the good Lord spares us all and if we get home again & have my friends to visit me, especially our beloved ministers, we will be so happy & contented & fix up home so neatly. I have just written for the Moores Western Ladies Book published at Cincinnati, Ohio. [First published in August 1841, it was a thin pamphlet of around twenty-eight pages containing stories of heroic women.]

Thursday March 11th A beautiful spring day. We drove to Barnett & back again, the view of Colorado Mountains in the dim distance was magnificent.

I went in to sign the bill of sale of Milla before a notary a public to Mrs Caroline McAshan. [The following transaction for Milla was found on online at the Fayette County, Texas Slave Transactions: Caroline E. McAshan purchased on March 11, 1858 Milla female age 32, Deeds M 462-463, Know all men by these . . . sum of $1000 to us in hand paid by Caroline E. McAshan, . . . have this day sold & delivered to the said Caroline E. McAshan, a negro woman named Milla about 32 yrs of age yellow or copper color or complexion and we warrant her . . . Given under our hand . . . this the 11th day of March A.D. 1858 M. Louisa Foster (wife of Finis E. Foster).]

Mr F purchased one beautiful calico dress & he said I made the price of my dresses clear by going in instead of the notary riding out here. Mr F got 2 skeins of blue silk. Tommie & Finie nice drab colored hats, Finie a pair of shoes, Jef a pair of shoes. Milla a white checked muslin dress & ruffled spence. I hated that I got back to late to spin. We crossed the divide between the Colorado & Brassos today.

Friday March 12th An ugly dull damp morning. I moved my things into my room. I have written 2 letters. One to Sister Langdon, and one to Mr J Wardsworth & E. B. Stevens, No. 611, Western Row between Everest & Wade, Cincinnati, Ohio, to have Ladies Pearl & Templars Magazine changed to this point. [The *Templar's Magazine* and the *Ladies' Pearl* were monthly publications.] We went up to Uncle Sams to spend the night. I rode Fly, Bro B's mare, the first time I have rode horseback in 6 or 7 years.

Sat March 13th I walked over to Bro Gid's last evening and set up with her until one O clock. Milla & I returned it was so dark we could hardly see the road. We had a time getting over the branch. Mr F is fixing to start to LaGrange with Milla, he wished me to go 20 miles with him & spend the time he is absent with sister Brown Davis & Bomers. I am anxious to go. Mr F says he loves me too well to leave me behind. I cut out my dress.

Tuesday March 16th It blowed & rained furiously last night our new beautiful room leaked so we were compelled to seek quarters in Sister Pollie's room. Mr F carried me in his arms. I felt achy in my bones, drowsy & awful. I took salts the symptoms of my old disease had returned. Mostly finished my dress. Milla worked all day for Gib.

Thursday March 18th A dark lowering morn. I started & traveled 22 miles on to Bro Ray Bomer's. Kind reception & the nicest biscuits for supper

& plenty milk & butter. O what a treat. I feel pretty well but tired & sleepy.

Thursday March 25th A beautiful morn. We are still at Mrs. Kincheloe's, a very pleasant family. My gums feel like they were touched with blue mass. [Blue mass was recommended as a remedy for various problems from tuberculosis to toothaches. Abraham Lincoln was known to have taken it for treatment of chronic melancholia—a disorder characterized by depressed moods and bodily complaints. It is possible that Louisa was or had been treated with blue mass.] I felt very badly yesterday, but feel some better this morning.

Lourena Bomer's children & I walked down & spent the day with Sister Bettie Bomer, kind & friendly, returned to Mrs Kincheloes. Here we have a private room with a good fireside which is very pleasant to me.

Friday March 26th A beautiful morning Sister Ruth Kincheloe intends to have a quilting today. I will return at it & assist. We have a pleasant time at the quilting. I received a letter from my husband he informed on account of braking his carriage, he would not return as soon as anticipated.

Sunday March 28th We all rode in a two horse wagon to church 2 ½ miles to & heard Bro B. Returned & at 3 went to hear him fill Mr F's appointment. He then started for Georgetown, which would surely take him until bedtime. How often we are reminded of the hardships of an itinerant minister life. Full well I am prepared to sympathize them, when for the almost entire part of my "married" life I have been the wife of one that has almost exclusively devoted his life & all to the service of his God.

Wednesday March 31st A mild northern, but bright & sunny. Ray started to Austin. I am anxious to see my husband. Uncle Burkett came up & invited me to a quilting of his wifes. He desires one to write Whig Rose on two of the white squares. [The Whig rose quilt pattern was often linked to the American Whig Party formed during the winter of 1833/34. It contained a floral image circled by smaller motifs.] Which I hope I will be able to do & neatly, if I should have the pleasure of attending. Jinnie Davis came up & stayed all night. She is to me a lovely girl.

Thursday April 1st Jonmie came & invited Sister Hila Bomer to the quilting, also Sarah. The invitations are to be quite extensive and a fine dinner to be prepared.

If I have luck I will finish the first width of my skirt, which is worked a row down front. & cross the bottom of it. I enjoyed my reading in Isaiah very much this morning. Jinnie went home before breakfast & took Finie with her he was so proud to go with her & walked as big as a man. Jonmie brought him back on Teddy behind Sam a few minutes ago. Just about 12 my husband returned. We ran way up the road to meet him, he kissed us as usual. We are all glad & happy now. He closed his trade in La Grange & he is still much better pleased than before. O thank the Donor of all good that we have a comfortable home where we can educate our boys. Cousin Mc sent me word that I had the prettiest place in town & must make haste & come, but all seemed sorry that we were compelled to delay so long. I do hope & pray that God will help our removal to that place.

April 2nd Friday We attended the quilting, had a very nice dinner indeed. I preformed the parts for which I was invited, that was to write in large Italian hand, Whig Rose one side of the quilt & American Democrat on the other & quilted them. Mr F preached tonight at Bro Davis' from "If ye know these things."

Monday April 5th A pretty morning. I rested very badly last night which makes me feel dull. I have patched Finie's pants & he has them on. My husband returned just at twelve in the afternoon. Mr F went upstairs in the room that we occupy & took a nap & then read. After I knew he was awake I went up & we enjoyed a feast that is of rare occurrence with us in our new field of labor that is being alone together in sweet converse. About six I went with him to stake his animal.

Wednesday 7th April A very dark gloomy morning, but I was compelled to have some washing done, as usual I brought all our things home dirty. Jef is now washing at the branch. Mr F sent an appointment this morning to Hamilton. But this evening presents a forbidding prospect for it to be filled. Very dark, rainy & lightning vividly. Received a letter from Sister Criss, she writes affectionately, says is sorry that the money crisis has caused her to fail in paying us the money due us, and that she & Mr Criss will leave nothing undone in their power to raise the money. [There was a financial panic in the United States in the fall of 1857 that began to spread through the states. This may have been the money crisis written about.] I drawed all the flowers that I intend working on my skirt, made me a plain linen collar & most made a scalloped one, patched & darned after Jeff ironed.

Thursday April 8th We expect to start to Hamilton after dinner, in the meantime we intend writing several letters. I must now read my chapters. I wrote a letter to our only sister, Mrs Weeden & also one to Mrs Mills of Belton in compliance with my husband's request, as his tenderness sensibilities were recently aroused by Mrs Mills sad bereavement in the death of her only child her dear darling little Mary. In writing this letter I became very much enlisted for the poor bereaved Mother, for full well did my poor heart know the deep sad sorrow that now crushes Mrs. Mills to the earth. I endeavor to pour in the "oil & the wine" [from one of several Christian hymns]. O God bless it to the doing of good. We drove to H__ or Burnet as it is properly termed, as the name has been changed. [In 1858 the name of the town of Hamilton was changed to Burnet because there was already another town named Hamilton in Texas.]

Dr Owen says I have improved so much he gave me the amount of medicine he said will cure me. O Lord grant it. Mr F preach at night to a large audience. We spent the night at the Dr's pleasantly.

Friday April 9th We drove to Father Joy's, kindly received, some of the best egg bread I have eaten, the kind Mother Joy prepared for our dinner. I wish I possessed language adequate to the task of describing the delightful scenery that was presented to our view today on our way out here. As far as the angle of vision extended on either side & in front, the Colorado Mountains could easily be seen with the natural eye. The prospect was magnificent & caused a thrilling sensation, akin to the feeling that I experienced on beholding the Gulph [the Gulf of Mexico] in the days of my sunny youth.

Monday April 12th A pretty morning, we are preparing to go Marble Falls on the Colorado River to have a fishing frolic. We drove to the falls, Father Joy rode in our carriage, Mother Joy in Bro Chessers carriage with his family.

Wednesday April 14th We walked to church, thence to Bro Chessers [?] for dinner, then the gents rode down to the falls to fish again. A very warm pleasant afternoon, children & I walked back to father Joys before supper. I never have seen people seem so anxious for me to teach a writing class as here.

Thursday April 15th I drew up an article and left it for Mother Joy to circulate and see how many subscribers could be gotten by Mr F's next appointment, which will be second Sunday in May. We then started & drove the roughest road I ever did in my life. But the scenery was grand indeed. Took dinner at Uncle Sams.

Friday April 16th Finished packing up, walked to Bro Gid's, took dinner then drove to Bro Jacks, had a nice supper. Candied honey comb & venison which almost cried Mr F "bad cold." My old symptoms returned, so I decided to remain here & forego the pleasure of attending the two days meeting which began today.

Sat April 17th My husband gone on to preaching. Old Uncle Bennie Gooch, Mr F's old Missouri friend stayed here last night. This morning he took occasion to speak of teaching writing. I <u>ever</u> anxious to catch items on the subjects & prepare me better to teach this ornamental art and beautiful accomplishment. Got Mr F to shew him my book. Old Uncle Ben said it beat anything he had ever seen. Said he would not pretend to teach where I was.

But we insisted on his going into a school with me and he almost promised me he would do so. I hope he will for I feel that his age & experience will be of lasting benefit to me. I hope yet to make this useful art., useful to myself and to my fellow creatures.

I worked very steadily today after my reading & writing was finished, which was about 9 O clock. I completed a leaf on my skirt. O I am so sleepy & tired tonight. I laid down while Sister Sally Jack was milking which is so unusual for me. I fear I am not improving as I thought or I would not get so <u>wearied</u> & tired.

Sunday April 18th I slept so sweetly last night. I did not know when Sister Sallie retired for the night, this is uncommon for me of late. I read my 8 chapters in the Bible, since have been reading Watts on the mind, improved by Emerson. [*Watts's Improvement of the Mind*, revised by Rev. Joseph Emerson, was published in 1833.]

But amidst all this, my heart pants to see my own "sweet home" in La-Grange. I think I am so well contented as any woman could be without the enjoyments of home, which is precious to my soul, treasured as blessings from heaven. But all this cannot fill the vacuum caused by the loss of home, sweet home & its dear associations.

O how sweet to have our friends to come to our own dear home & there with gleeful faces around our own happy hearthstone enjoy the social laugh & then surround my humble board & partake of my fare, let it be ever so homely, last but not least of all, together with husband, children & servant bow the suppliant knee around our own dear, prized family alter. O roll on ye wheel of time & bring the wished for period when we will enjoy again our own little "cottage home." Then methinks I will be as happy as a mortal could possibly be on earth.

Monday April 19th Ben Gooch has come from Burnets, brought a new lot of fish hooks & line, got a top put to his buggy for a fish frolic. Mr F has not returned yet. Mr F returned & was disappointed in his anxiously expected fish frolic.

Sat April 24th Heard that the hooping cough was at Round Rock. Mr F all persuaded me to leave Finie with Sister Gal, so I did and drove to round rock & attended church, dined with our elder Mr Davis. Drove out to Uncle Tom Thaxtons & stayed all night. I had the blues about leaving my babe, my Finie & feel very badly.

Sunday April 25th I was so feeble that after breakfast I took my bed and kept it until just time to dress, and then we drove to church. Heard Bro Smith preach. Then took drive with Mr Askue & then drove to Bro Davis & then fondly clasp our boy in our arms. They all say he was such a good boy.

Tuesday April 27th We dined at Bro Anderson's. As we were driving along to Florence, my husband took my hand in his, & gently pressed it imprinting a kiss of affection on my lips. Said this day sixteen years ago, we became engaged. O how vividly the reminiscences of the past rushed up before my minds eye and <u>we</u> almost felt young, buoyant & gay again. O how endearing is the enduring love of a faithful fond heart, thro' years of suffering, sorrow, & pain.

Wednesday April 28th Mr F started for Belton. I have an appearance of cold. Aunt Kesial Gray, Aunt & step Mother of My Uncle's wife came over to see me, she looks natural. She is now in her sixty-first year.

Thursday April 29th An ugly morning, it has dropped a little rain. Aunt Kesial stayed all night with us last night & slept with me. We talked until late. I have cold. I dread my old cough, but I feel much better.

April 30th I rose to see Aunt Kesial according to promise & kept Finie with Sister Redding, as Aunt Kesial thought perhaps her grand child (Louisa Gray) my namesake was taking hooping cough. Miss Josephine Wales, the old Auntie's Grand daughter, a sweet lovely girl came over to see me. All persuade me to send for Finie & as I became convinced little "Louisa" did have hooping cough I did so. The little fellow was so glad he jumped up & down, every thing is so neat here, nicest dinner I have seen lately, cake & pie. Mr F returned just before dark. Our house at B has been broken open, but he said he would not miss anything.

Sunday May 2nd It was muddy & had so much the appearance of rain that I could not go to church. Mr F preached 3 times today.

Thursday May 13th My old symptoms returned. We drove to Burnett, stayed all night at Dr Owen's. He changed my medicine, he says I don't look as well as I did. Mr F preached to night very few in attendance.

Monday May 17th We are at Bro Jones, kind people. Drove to Bro Davis after dinner. Mr F cut off some chaparral sprigs which were full of berries. Sister Gall made some choice pies out of them for supper.

Tuesday May 18th With sorrow we heard to of the death of an acquaintance of ours, Mrs Hymus, she was formally Miss Berthe Haven of Austin. She died in the triumph of the Christian faith. She was a firm friend of the noble cause of Temperance. She was a daughter of Samaris in Austin. We attended her burial, she was interned with Templars honors, although she was not a Templar. The scene was solemn & imposing, especially when he met the brethren of the Templar in their regalia who had come 15 miles to pay his beloved wife the last sad tribute of respect. Her little one & infant of a day old was buried with her in the same narrow "prison house," but sweet reflection she left evidence behind that she was prepared for all the bless of heaven. Mr F has gone to Bro Bartons to move our things there.

Journal #6

October 6, 1858–July 14, 1859

———

Oct 6th 1858 Wednesday evening we arrived at Mr Peck's, Gonzales, Texas. His wife is a member of our church. She kindly met us near the gate. Surprised the children & myself, said laughingly to Mr F have a great notion to kiss you. She showed us into a neatly furnished parlor. A neat well completed & furnished upper bed room was soon prepared for us. I repaired to it, bathed, combed, powered. I went below into the parlor. Soon we were invited to the supper table. There we partook of a very plain but well cooked supper. Attended family worship in the parlor & retired to our beds.

    Thursday 7 Synod convened, the former moderator being absent in a different state, Uncle Henry Renick was selected & he preached the opening sermon, after which we returned to our room.

    Sat 9th Had a good rain last night, which I think will be of much benefit in allaying the great dust, as the streets here are very sandy. Preaching at 11 & night. Rainy & sunshine. Mr F at Synod, we were much perplexed about attending church. Sister Peck sent me word up to my room we would go. So I closed my letter of rejoicing to Bro Joe Philips on my hearing of his good determination to continue at college.

    Sunday 10th Dressed early, attended church, listen to Uncle Henry Renick preach at 11. Then we were blessed with a gracious sweet communion, a great may commanded. Mr F preached to the colored people at 3. [Rev. Mahlon Henry "Hailstone" Renick was called Uncle Henry by Louisa throughout her journals. He was born on February 17, 1802, in Kentucky and died May 24, 1874, in Manchaca, Texas. He was a Cumberland Presbyterian circuit rider and first moderator of the Colorado Synod in West Texas. He was called "Reverend Hailstone" for his way of coming down hard on frontier sins and sinners.]

Judge William Christian Menefee was born in Tennessee in May 1796 and came to Texas with his wife Agnes in 1830. He was a delegate to the state conventions of 1832, 1833, and 1835. He signed the Texas Declaration of Independence and was a member of the Texas House of Representatives when it was a republic and a state. In 1839, he was a member of the congressional committee that selected Austin as the Republic's capital. Judge Menefee died on October 29, 1875. Source: *The Men Who Made Texas Free* by Sam Houston Dixon, Texas Historical Publishing Company, 1924, pages 227-231.

Bro Smith preached at night. I was told by more than one that he made a poor effort. Butchered the English language awfully. I do wish our ministers would prepare themselves for the most important work that has ever fallen to the lot of man on earth, and not to depend wholly to zeal. How important I feel it is to have an educated ministry, <u>especially</u> that they use their own mother tongue with propriety. I did not attend tonight on account of the storm. The streets were flooded with water.

Tuesday 12th Traveled to Bro Herron's partook of a late dinner. Our little family then journeyed on 3 miles home with Bro & Sister Morris.

Crossed Guadalupe River in a flat boat, on the bank we were ushered into a neat bedroom, remained til supper, then we were invited into the dining apartment, then into the parlor which was very tastefully arranged. There we listen to Sister Maggie Morris play a few tunes of the Piano forte [an early piano]. Attended family devotion, thence we were lighted to a neat little bed room, joining the parlor. The drapery of which rivaled the snow in whiteness, neat mating on the floor, snug little wash stand bowl, pitcher & a stand bowl, pitcher & a nice Bureau & looking glass completed its furniture.

Friday 15th Attended morning prayers, then dressed again attended church. By invitation we accompanied Bro Campbell's family home, a spacious building 2 ½ stories cost $6000. We were conducted into Sister Campbells family room children & I, Mr F into the parlor. Both on the second story. Sister Lou Goode & her Sister Ann Morris were with us. We were afterwards led down into the basement story, there we partook of a sumptuous dinner. Attended worship at night, returned here. We were lighted up to the 3rd story, there we had a nice room, bed & turmel bed for our boys. All is nice. Here I felt assured of my condition and now from what Physicians tell me I hope my health will be much better.

Tuesday Oct 19th Arose, attended prayers, started in the rain, drove 32 miles without dinner, stopped at old friends. I was raised 10 miles from his house, Judge Menefee, nice supper, then prayers. Then a nice little room with snow white cozy pallet for my boys.

Wednesday Oct 20st Mother Menefee wanted us to stay all day, but we could not. We traveled to Bro Ferrells, took dinner, drove to ferry crossed Colorado. We had a fine passage which is new to us. Drive to Cousin McClelland, kindly met. Put out our baggage, then drove up to our own place we bought here. I find it most beautiful & retired. A sweet inviting place, in my present condition, with surrounding property. I don't see how I can leave it & rent or board & cast my destiny among strangers. But I won't say this to my husband, I don't wish to interfere with his woefulness. I am determined he shall decide. We drove to Bro McFarland, supped & attended the C P weekly prayer meeting. Some feelings, I felt deeply serious & prayed fervently. Lord teach us what to do in this strait. Returned to Cousins McC had nice clean sheets, nice room, retired to rest.

Thursday Oct 21st We rose early, attended Family worship. Then Jef borrowed a plow, we drove up to home, & Jef plowed ground & sowed turnip, collard, mustard, & lettuce seed. Mr F cleared the weeds out of our front walk. We then drove to Uncle Henry's dined & spent part of the evening, thence back to home & Jef plowed & sowed more seeds. Then we drove to Cousin McC's supped & spent the night.

Friday Oct 22nd A rainy morning. Mr F would have started to Wharton but the rain stopped him, & he will decline that trip. Bro McFarland called in, I asked him to give Uncle Henry to give him a gold fob chain, he took his off cheerfully & gave it to me. Uncle Henry came by going to see an appointment. I made him a present of a gold watch worth $40 and the chain from Bro McFarland worth I presume $15. Mr F & Cousin Mc attended the Methodist meeting, the Ministers failed to arrive. Mr Boomn, an old Presbyterian minister, Mr F said gave a good talk. The people prevailed on Mr F to put off starting to Belton until Monday & attend the meeting. My husband says there is deep serious feeling and say he hopes we will have a revival & told me after we retired for rest that he felt so easy & good in regard settling here in LaGrange. O this intelligence made me feel so happy, that I pressed that loved manly form to my boson & impressed a fond kiss on those lips that have so often caressed me.

Sat 23rd Alternate sunshine & clouds, attended prayers, breakfast. I am told that Mrs Dechard proposes to call on me this morning. Mr F children & Jef have gone up home to work. Prayer meeting at 11 O clock. Mrs Dechard came after us this morning to go & spend the day with her.

Sunday 24th 1858 We attended church at the usual hour. The celebrated Rev Wilson a Methodist minister preached, a very good sermon. He was formerly a member of the bar & a legislator for years in Texas. They first met today to worship at the Methodist Church, but it would not hold the people. The old Presbyterian church was kindly tendered to them, their Pastor being absent, so we repaired to that church, after which we drove to B McFarland & dined. Aunt Sallie Renick sent for us to go & sup with her as Dr Lone & lady had arrived, he is a C P minister.

We cheerfully did so, thence to church. Listen to a sermon again by Rev Mr Wilson. I think it was skimmy. I fear he aimed too much at show, but perhaps I am mistaken, it may be his natural manner or a manner acquired at the bar & not easily gotten rid of. Returned to Cousin Mc's we had a very heavy wind & rain last night.

Tuesday 26th Drove to Uncle Henry's spent a pleasant day. Attended church, listen to Bro Wilson preach his last sermon at this meeting. Some 6 mourners. [According to the *Century Dictionary and Cyclopedia*, a mourner can also be a penitent, especially one who makes public announcement of a desire for salvation; the term is used in Methodist churches.]

Thursday Oct 28th Sister McFarland & I drove to the store of Cousin Alfred's & bought us a nice besage Delane dress at 15 cent per yard, until they began selling out at cost, was worth 30 or 35 cents per yd. Jef is plowing up Cousin Alfred's garden to pay for it.

Sister McFarland & Miss Pope spent part of the afternoon with us, which made time pass pleasantly. We expect to attend church tonight. There was near 20 mourners last night, one embraced Christ.

Friday Oct 29th A pretty morning, I awoke before day. Sent Tommie to awaken Jef, he made a fire, fed his horses & began to wash before breakfast & breakfast was at 7. Cousin's Alfred & Kate are old Presbyterians, he is sick with neuraligia. [Neuraligia a stabbing, burning, and often severe pain cause by an irritated or damaged nerve. The nerve may be anywhere in the body.]

Sunday Oct 31st Sunday night we attended church again, Bro Hubert preached. Called mourners, had none. He fell on the pulpit and wept & groaned, the members went out and induced a number to come in.

Monday Nov 1st 1858 We had to call at several places to get things for cousin Betties wedding & purchased myself a piece of brown velvet for a sack & some lighter brown for Finie a cloak. We drove to Cousin Edwins, nice cabbage dinner. Here we will remain til after dinner.

Wednesday Nov 3rd A cold morning, the day has arrived for the wedding. I fear I shall not enjoy it. Tommie has gone to town to get him a pr of shoes. I must read & get to sewing. Tommie returned with a nice pr of shoes $1, very cheap. I dressed for the wedding in good time, company came early. Bro & Sister Atkisson & little Henry their son. He and Tommie fell in love with each other. After the marriage rite was performed by Bro Atkisson, the bride looked beautiful, arranged in her neat white suited to the occasion. She was firm as a rock, the groom, Mr Young Bowers was much frighten, the waiters look well. We partook of a very nicely trimed supper, the nicest Barbacued ghoat I ever eat, they had & nice baked turkey. Cousin Alfred wife & children Bro Adkisson wife & son, Jef & children & myself went home with Bro Lee & wife. Had a comfortable warm fire to sleep by.

Friday Nov 5th A cold morning, Bro Adkisson is here, his wife went to Cousin Betties, infair given by old Mr Bowers, nice breakfast dinner & supper, Bro Hill killed a nice shoot. I enjoyed the eating very much I hope that it is ominous of good in regard to my cold. Jef washed & ironed all my things. I bought a cow & young calf at $15 bargained for our years pork, of Bro Hill, he promised to like a shoot & send it to me week after next.

Monday Nov 8th A cold morning, after dinner Jef came after Prince, the ground was so hard one horse could not do good plowing.

Thursday Nov 11th A cold frosty morning, it seems that winter has set in with earnest. Bright & sunny. This is our dear boy Tommie's birthday. Today he is eleven years old. O may I be impressed to say something to my boy today that will make a lasting impression upon his mind for eternal good. O may we live to raise our little ones & see them grown up & useful & good men.

Friday Nov 12th Early after breakfast we started to Cousins Edwins, I wore my velvet sack found it warm & comfortable. I most made Finie's brown cloak, lined it with pretty red, green & white checked linsey & wadded it two ply. I will make my little boy very warm & comfortable & I will do for me a cape. He is very proud of it, it always does me good to make anything for my <u>sweet</u> boys that pleases them. Very warm & pleasant this afternoon.

Sat Nov 13th A cool morning. I prayed in my room with my children, breakfast heartily had such nice egg bread & butter & milk. I did as usual took my pile, picked my teeth & brushed them & read with deeper interest profit & pleasure my 3 chapters & must now to my sewing. Today I have written to Brothers Brown & Logan to direct my "Pearl" to direct to La-Grange in future & that I would soon send them Miss Campbell's name as a subscriber. [*The Ladies' Pearl* was a literary and religious journal for the ladies of the great West. The editors J. B. Logan and W. W. Brown published it monthly.]

About 8 O clock at night Jef came and said he had plowed about 5 acres for Cousin Alfred $1 ½ per day, got done Friday before breakfast, then worked for him all day, which came to about $7 ½ then Sat he worked for Dr Gregory, who paid him $1.00 this I gave him. He is a faithful servant. I begin to realize the sentiment the blessed bible inculcates bring up a servant tenderly, he shall become your son at last.

O may we make a livelihood to cut Mr F loose to go & preach all the time. And then in Heaven we will reap a rich reward, then an eternity of bliss will be ours.

Sunday Nov 14th Looks like rain, O I pray it might not rain until Mr F returns with our things. I must read my Bible. We gave Cousin Betsie a seat in our carriage. Jef drove us to the old ironside Baptist place of worship.

TABLE OF CONTENTS.

This is the table of contents of *The Pearl* from 1846.

O such ignorance, they preached their sing song against an educated minis-try. We listen to 2 sermons one exhortation in quick succession, which lasted from eleven to near 2 O clock. They had 2 mourners and some feeling not withstanding their ignorance they said some good & true sayings, but since I embraced religion, I have never heard a man preach without saying some-thing profitable, though ever so ignorant. We needed & had no fire in our room as it was almost as warm as summer.

Monday Nov 15th A cold norther blew up in the night & I was lightly covered as it was so warm when we retired to rest which was very early, as I felt badly. Whilst I was recovering children & self we all slept together, I got so cold I fairly shook, trembled & my teeth chattered as I generally do as I get cold in the night season I cannot divine the cause. Jef I hope has started back with our cow & calf as I sent for him after her. I am so distressed about him, as Cousin Edwin would not loan him a saddle, he had to ride bareback and I had made the appointment with Bro Hill for him to remain at home & start Jef with the cow & calf this morning, so he was compelled to go.

But it was Jef's fault he should have borrowed a saddle in town. Rather cold this morning. Tommie is about to read, Finie is playing on the floor and singing as gay as a May morning lark, which buoys up my spirits. But I am happy now, most all the time in anticipation of getting to house keeping soon & such a warm & comfortable house.

I finished my collar, just after dark. Jef came laughing & told me his ups & downs driving the cow to LaGrange, but Bro Hill kindly loaned him help to drive her about half the way & a black boy loaned him a thick coat. Thank the giver of all good we will have milk & perhaps butter. This afternoon Tommie rode Prince 2 ¼ to a place he had never been & purchased & paid for a 6 lb butter at 20 cents per lb.

I brought not quite half bushel of potatoes from a negro man at $1.00 per bushel, not quite half bushel dried peaches from his wife Clarissa at custom-ary price, not quite half peck the same from Fanny, to be paid as soon as I can do so. Cousin Betsy gave me 2 doz eggs.

Tuesday Nov 16th A cold morning, Jef rode 1 ½ miles to Bro Lee's before breakfast to get me a load of cotton seed to feed my cows, he gave him a wagon load. Cousin Betsy says she will give me 3 hens.

We drove to Mr Heradon & I bought 4 ½ more butter, it is extra nice. I gave Cousin Betsy enough for supper breakfast & dinner. Then we drove to Cousin Alfreds but came by home & left our things that I had obtained for housekeeping, gave Cousin Kate enough butter for dinner. Jef got a job of plowing & did it for Dr Gregory worth 25 cents.

Wednesday Nov 17th I awoke Jef before day, he is now gone to get the wagon he engaged last night at 75 cents per day to go & hall [*sic*] load of pecans & cotton seed. It is now a little after 7. I have arose dressed prayed with our children, read 5 chapters in the new testament about Pauls imprisonment, his conversations with the king & Bernice. Cut out my window curtain. Comb Finies head thoroughly, written in my journal, took my pile & made up my bed very nicely, and breakfast is not over yet. My Cousin here has no family worship. Tommie & Finie's time is now pleasantly engaged, looking at pictures. Jef was disappointed in the wagon he engaged, but got Dr Manly's a Methodist minister, by paying 6 pumpkins, & got back by time to drive out to Bro Lee's after cotton seed. He cannot return until tomorrow. I cut out & made me a velvet cape & finished my window curtain & began my bolster slip.

Friday Nov 19th I did not awake until light & I heard Jef up. I have made my bed, breakfast is not ready. Jef has gone up to scour the balance of our house. Tommie is to take his breakfast to him. Tommie took Jef's breakfast to him, he finished scouring the whole house & drove Sister McFarland & I to the store. I purchased sheeting to 3 pr's sheets & 2 window curtains, all cost $9.42, which I hope to be able to pay in a few days. Sister Mc bought some velvet.

It began to rain harder. We drove up to our new home, looks nice. Thence home, Jef loaded the carriage with corn for Cousin Alfred to pay him back. I told Jef to return early to get supper he did so.

Sat Nov 20th I am up & dressed & it is not daylight. I am such a hurry about making my sheets. I am done my bed, my reading & writing & ready to cut out my sheets as it is just ½ after 5 O clock. I gave Jef money to buy himself a pair of Kersey pants, he got the pattern for 73 cents. [Kersey was used for military clothing throughout Europe and North America. By the time of the American Civil War, it had become the standard fabric for army trousers and greatcoats.] I made 4 sheets, fixed Finie's sack, and knit near a finger length of my husband's socks by 10 O clock at night. I am so tired my back & shoulders ache. Cousin Kates girl has not returned since she ran away.

Sunday Nov 21st Arose after day, Jef is cooking for Cousins. I did not know there would be preaching until late. I did not go for several reasons. Jef is rather disobedient which fretted me today & I am very sorry for it.

Monday Nov 22nd I arose, dressed, made up my bed, read my three chapters & day is just a breaking. Jef has been washing an hour I reckon. We must be smart, we are in such a hurry to get ready for housekeeping. Tommie harnessed the horses, then we drove by & took Cousin Amanda in, drove home. I made her climb up in my windows & measure the length for a curtain, I gave her a spool of nice cotton then we drove to Mr Hayines to get me a fine set of colored window curtains. But there was none that suited me. I bought 5 yds 12 ½ cent domestic to make Jef a window curtain for his house, received a note from my husband, he is on his return, presumes he will not be here until the last of this week. But I shall look for him the middle.

We drove to Cousin Cates. I cut out my 3 domestic window curtains, Jef staid & swept & dusted the house, and before bedtime I made his window curtain & gave it to him. He was proud of it, he washed ironed cleaned out our well & Cousin Mac's also today. I cut out his Kersey pants & he bagan to make them. I bought him a pair of boots today. Price $2.50, also a pair of handsome Sunday pants. I knit a little tonight.

Thursday Nov 25th This is a warm cloudy morn. It is the day set apart for thanksgiving. [Thanksgiving had been celebrated nationally on and off since 1789.] There will be divine in the Union church at 10. Uncle Henry was to have preached but I am told that he is too much indisposed. Tommie harnessed our horses & drove us by & took Sister McFarland in, drove to church. Mr Boone, our old schoolman preached. A part of his discourse I liked very much, a part I thought was too showy for the sacred desk. I cannot bear anything like show in the pulpit. I like to <u>see</u> & know that the words come from the heart. We dined at Bro McFarlands also did Bros Bates & Andrew Renick, and Mr Rogan, the teacher in Mr Deckards school that Tommie will be under the charge of I presume. We had a sumptreous dinner, after dinner we drove to see Bro Henry. I fitted & began Tommies drawers Cousin Kate gave him, cut out & basted Jefs pants I gave him. Cut out & selected & drew a handsome pattern & began working me a bolster slip on the finest of bleached domestic. I knit half Mr F's sock heel to night.

Friday Nov 26th Arose as usual before day, made my bed, it is now about light. I sent Tommie up home to place the and irons in the fire place & put wood on ready to burn. After dinner I sent Tommie up to pack wood for burning purposes. Just as he got home his Pa drove up with a 2 horse wagon load of our things & sent for me. I helped Tommie harness the horses & he drove fast.

Sunday Nov 28th Family prayers, said our verses at the table, attended church at 11, heard Bro Herron preach a good sermon. I felt so tired. I thought it imprudent to attend church any more. Jef went at 3, when Mr F preached to the colored people & then at night.

Monday Nov 29th A rainy day. Bro H spent most of the day with us. I am so glad to be at home, I cout [sic] half work. I commenced Mr F a pair of drawers, Tommie starts school.

Tuesday Nov 30th Tommie is pleased with Mr Rogen, his teacher, says he is so kind to him. Tommie seems pleased & interested I am so glad, so delighted.

Wednesday Dec 1st A bright sunny morning. Tommie is at school. Mr F is pruning trees. Finie cutting & packing wood. Jef preparing to sew wheat for one calf. We sold Carrie to Cousin Alfred for $80, he is to get me a carpet & some furniture.

Thursday Dec 2nd In pay for Carrie, we received a nice carpet for our parlor price $40, also a bedstead washstand & mahogany centre table & pickle barrel. I am making my carpet.

Friday Dec 3rd My birthday [age 37] it is a gloomy day, feelings are more so. My birthday present from my husband is a bottle of cologn & a paper weight, from Bro Bates is a nice watch pocket. Mr F bought me 2 large oven dinner pots, & a set of small plates.

Sat Dec 4th Mr. F started out to help Bro Jack, out with a two days meeting at Clear Creek, and to try to get some of the pork that I engaged whilst he was absent. I finished my carpet, & Jef & Tommie put it down about 9 O clock at night, it looks pretty. Now I need a nice library for our books. Tommie, Jef & Finie finished shelling corn & Jef went to mill, get the meal Monday.

Sunday Dec 5th A bright sunny Sabbath morning. But my floors are so muddy it makes me feel badly. Jef, children & I stayed all alone last night for the first time in life. Jef slept in the parlor, which joins my room. I felt perfectly safe & rested well. Arose, had prayers felt refreshed. Jef attended church at 11. He & Tommie attended at 3 & heard a negro preacher. Mr & Mrs Dechard came to see me & spent some hours with me. I was so glad as Finie & I were so lonely. Bro Bates came also, Bro Dechard told him he must stay & take care of Sister Foster whilst Bro Foster was gone. He said he would & did so.

Tuesday Dec 7th Uncle Abner brought a convossed ham & presented me with, but this only added to my mortification to think a friend had to furnish his own meat at my table. I have made & cushioned with rich stamped crimson calico. Tommie & Finie a crochet for them to sit on at prayers in the parlor, cut out & began another table cloth. Cousin Amanda made Mr F a fine pair of brown jeans pants & sent them home yesterday. I made Cousin Mc a present of a pair like them, and loaned him our double barrel shotgun. Mr F returned with half hog, very thin & indifferent meat, one fat midling price 5 cents, a fine quantity of collards, near 12 lb butter 25 cents per pound, 13 dozen eggs at 12 ¾ cents a dozen. Uncle Abner & Mr Donorrson spent the night with us.

Wednesday Dec 8th It seems to me the coldest morning we have had this season. Jef has gone after the childrens trunnell bedstead Cousin Mc kindly made them a present of. Jef brought the bedstead, it is a nice present indeed, children & I are pleased. Jef hauled Mrs Wilcox a 2 loads wood $1 per load. I made another table cloth & commenced another, bound Mr F's vest, patched his old overcoat.

Thursday Dec 9th My husband kissed us & started to Belton on business. May the good Lord prosper him, this time. I must cut out my new double wove, homespun counterpane [bedcover].

Finie looked after his Dear Papa, this morning, when he got out of sight, he burst into tears, and said as he laid his little head on my lap, My father won't come back anymore. Althou it was the words of a child, it made my heart ache, for I feared it might prove prophetic, & those words I know in despite all my efforts to resist them, will haunt my mind until his [sic] the happy, joyful day of his return arrives. O I wish my little one had not said that. Jef worked for Cousin Alfred & he paid him $1 in candles, 16 candles.

I finished my table cloth & made 2 more, which makes 5 new homespun cloths, 3 cotton 2 linnen [sic] one, & cut out and my counterpane I have had cut out a number of years. I wrote 2 letters one to Mr F, one to Sister Brown Davis.

Sat Dec 11th A dark morning, Jef brought my oval table and is now bringing my bedstead from the cabinet shop. They look neat to be old furniture repaired. I wrote to Mr F. I awoke with headache, felt rather badly all day, took a dose of quinine. [The main use of quinine at this time was to treat malaria. In small doses it was not harmful.] Jef & children put up my old bedstead in my room & put the new one in the little bedroom. The old one is much the handsomest bedstead, it looks quite well. I made up my bed. I am thankful to have all my beds off the floor once more. Tommie cut some Sunday wood then he & Finie packed up all the Sunday wood and stacked it nicely. After supper Tommie & I arranged things more neatly in the parlor, it looks quite neat & fashionable. Thank the Lord for all his benefits. I felt so poorly I let my sewing alone all day, knot a little at night. Old Mrs Ashon called on me.

Sunday Dec 12th I feel a little better, I took a dose of quinine. Tommie has gone to attend Sabbath School. Finie is sitting before me. I must now begin my reading. I read my six chapters, some in Hills Select thoughts. [This may be *Select Thoughts on Religious Subjects* by Rev. Rowland Hill, first published in 1836. It was a small book of Rev. Hill's thoughts, which were pointed and sometimes witty. For example, "As we grow old, it is fit we should grow modest."]

Some in Tommies Jeny Gazette & Sunday school book. I took too large a dose of quinine its made my ears tingle all day. [That was a side effect of too much quinine.] I have felt badly all day, had to lay down an hour or so. I am sad & gloomy, know not the cause. Jef attended the Baptist meeting today.

Monday Dec 13th A gloomy morning arose & breakfasted early, feel better. Jef got thro' his work & started off to work a few minutes after seven, Tommie has shucked & brought in 6 doz years [*sic*] of corn to shell, to send to mill & have ground coarse for cow & calf. And is now studying his Arithmetic lesson. Finie is at play.

I am sorry to write I was compelled to whip both my dear boys severely this morning. O may they do better now. Finie has now gone to pack up cut wood from the pile & stack it at my door ready for use. Jef baked Finie 2 little cakes ready for his birthday. Finie said tomorrow he will be up to my neck, for it is his birthday. Jef says he ploughed over an acre today, which is worth $2 per acre.

Tuesday Dec 14th Jef washed off my room floor, porch & steps, put on dinner & started to work a few minutes after 8 O clock. Tommie shucked & brought in 2 doz years of corn to shell, shelled 6 or 8 ears then made a fire in my room, studied his speech, went bounding to school. Finie is shelling corn, well my littlest boy is six years old today. This is the birthday of my boy, my sweet Finie, this day six years ago, I was proud for to look upon that sweet infant face for the first time, with how much interest & tender solicitude have I watched over that little one. Only God grants this child as well as my beloved & dearest Tommie may be added another <u>star</u>, bright dazzling star in my crown of rejoicing in younders bright angelic & ever peaceful world. Finie handed around his birthday cake, I sent a quantity to school to the boys.

Wednesday Dec 15th A most beautiful delightful morning, the sun is shining so brightly, all nature wears a different aspect which enlivens my heart & happy home, sweetness & cheerfulness beams on all around. Jef was up and getting breakfast when I awoke which was at 7, a rare thing. Cousin Amanda is here and I am so cheerful & happy. I spent such a lovely day, Cousin A & I made a trade. She is to quilt me 2 comforts, which I have paid her, and 2 for which I am to pay her. I gave her 1 candle and my little dipper. Jef made $1.75 cents today.

Thursday Dec 16th I have been most sick all day was compelled to keep my bed most of this afternoon. Jef contrary to my daily orders, stayed away until almost dark, which fretted me & I had to lecture him, which I always hate to do. But I cannot have my rules infringed upon time after time & let it pass unnoticed. I finished binding my rising sun quilts & began to bind Finie's blazing star. Jef made 75 cents.

Friday Dec 17th A brighter prospect for a pretty Day. I feel very poorly, must lay down. I finished Finie's quilt. Jef made 50 cents today & came home in time to take down my parlor carpet. Sister McFarland came & helped us. Sister Morris McAshan called to see me, she has a sweet babe. I am all almost sick. Jef set out a doz roses, I wrote to Mr F today. Sister Mc brought me a mess or 2 of sweet potatoes, after I sent her some of our flour.

Sat Dec 18th Jef is most done washing. I have patched, attended & mended up many garments today. Jef has washed some for Cousin Amanda for which I make no charge, she sent me some nice fresh pork bones. I took 2 pills.

Sunday Dec 19th A misty day. I am sick, my head I don't think ever was in such a fix. I can hardly breath, almost incessantly sneezing. I am thankful my lungs seem right Cousins Mc & Amanda & children came up spent the afternoon with me, took supper. Billie Mc stayed all night.

Monday Dec 20th I am so sick today. I sent for Dr Gregory & Sister McFarland. She stayed with me until dinner, Dr sent me some cough drops, & some pulverised opium to burn on coals & inhale the smoke to open my head. [Throughout the nineteenth century, the inhalation of medicated vapor from aqueous solutions continued to be a primary mode of treatment of respiratory ailments.] Which I am thankful to say was of much benefit to me. Jef washed today, collected $5 dollars of money due us & bought me a pr of embroidered & swiss window curtains for my parlor. Cousin Mc spent part of this afternoon with me. A rainy day, Tommie & Finie began shelling mill corn.

Tuesday Dec 21st I have made my window curtains. Tommie bought for me, one dimes worth blk pepper, the same nutmeg, the same cloves, all for my Christmas mince pies, also 6 bunches tape [first developed in 1845]. I sent Cousin Amanda one bunch, & some blk pepper as a little gift. Jef is out at work, he is engaged to clear up ready for planting a 10 acre field at one dollar per day. I feel much better.

Friday Dec 24st Cousin Amanda stayed until the afternoon, whilst we were all busy making our Christmas mince pies. Uncle Henry & Bro Dechard came to see us, very pleasant & kind. I sent for Sister McFarland, she came & helped us and gave me grapes to put in my pies. Such a rainy bad day. O I wish my husband would come, we are all so lonely, now they are all gone. The ingredients in my mince pies are fat & lean pork, lean beef, biscuits, cinnamon, citron, cloves, nutmeg & spice. Jef baked 7 pies, baked some molasses cake. Sister Mc brought me near 20 lbs of mince pork.

Sat Dec 25th Christmas day, blessed event that gave rise to this day. Santa Claus visited our boys stockings and gave them a towel to keep their faces clean, as he writes to them he likes to see sweet clean faced children in the little pretty letter he put into their hanging stockings. Also a little cake for each one & today he put into their hose, some candy, almonds, tree cake sugar, & each a little toy safety bank.

I hope my little boys will be good and kind, as he writes to them, if so, next Christmas he will do much more for them. A very ugly gloomy rainy Christmas day. I feel very badly. My cough kept me awake a good deal last night. O how I wish to see my dearest best beloved one drive up.

I finished my last counterpane today and knit considerable on Tommie's socks by bedtime. We could see the light of the boy's Christmas fire up here at night. We made 2 cupcakes & 2 Wisconsin fruit cakes from 4 until 8 O clock. They look nice indeed.

Jef planed most of the planks for his table that sister McFarland gave him whilst he was cooking the cakes I made. Cousin Mc sent me a nice piece of pork, Cousin Amanda sent me some bones, some baked turkey & some sweet peach pickles which were mild.

Monday Dec 27th /58 I coughed most all night. I feel poorly. Rain & gloom, will my loved one come today? Jef intends making his table. Jef went up town & bought 40 cents worth of lumber to finish his table Sister Mc gave him & bought with him a letter from my love to me, he states he will be here Wednesday or Thursday next, and has apples for Finie, a chair for Tommie to sit on at school & says he is so proud of his advancement at school, which sentence filled my heart with joyful emotions, all my eyes, all most with tears of pleasure, he also stated he had some few things for me. I have finished my new toilets & put it out to bleach. Patched a change two of Finie's sacks & Tommie's riped [sic] the hem in one of my dresses & I faced it. Tommie rode to Sister Mac's & bought for me 5 lb of nice butter, Sister Walker had sent into to sell. Sister Mc gave Tommie some trap sticks, he brought them home & made his trap & set it and is now trying to make his sweet brother a little toy bedstead. Jef has just brought me in his table finished, nicely indeed for his first efforts. He is proud of it & so am I. I must give him some table cloths. I just made him a present of 2 course dinner towels.

Thursday Dec 28th Such fitful weather, alternate gloom & sunshine. I have made my blk silk apron. Jef is washing for me as Christmas is not over I hired him to do so. I did hope we would be blessed with a bright day.

My breast & shoulders hurt me very much. My cough seems better last night, & of course I slept more sweetly, & felt much better this morning. I am making me a nice swiss night cap trimmed with bobonet inserting & lace. Jef finished working, scoured 2 buckets, 2 wash pans, pr shovels & tongs & pr candle sticks. This afternoon is bright, sunny & beautiful. Sunset clear as a diamond. My chest & shoulders hurt so I felt compelled to lay down awhile, which made me feel much better.

Jan 18th 1859 This is the first I have set up dressed in 9 days. Suffered intensely with this prevailing cough & cold had 2 physicians Drs Gregory & Farley. I don't think I ever suffered such pain in my chest & bones, also fever. I am hungry now all the time. Jef ploughed this afternoon for Dr Gregory. We have all been sick, all mending. Mr F bought 2 plows, $15.00, 1 hoe at $1, 1 barrel irish potatoes for planting $7. Dr Gregory kindly offered to loan him money to pay for them, & did so. Mr F made & put in the hoe handle.

Wednesday Jan 19th 1859 I eat my breakfast in my bed, then Mr F dressed me. I feel better & stronger. Mr F & Jef went to the farm we rented to begin farming, I took a sweet little nap about 8, Mr F returned with me 2 vapors and has made 6 pins, & himself a handsome plough line 28 cents and has made 6 gluts for splitting timber. [Gluts were large wooden wedges. They were not driven into the solid timber like an iron wedge but into the cracks that had been formed by the iron wedges.]

It is near 10 & I am so hungry. Our little wheat looks fine, the horses & calf seem to enjoy grazing on it very much. Mr F & Finie are making hen nests. 25 minutes after 2, Jef had us such a nice dinner of chime & irish potatoes, we all relished them so much, but none more than I. I feared I had eaten too much, but I believed they helped me. Jef has gone to work long ago.

Tommie is preparing for his first examination, he is to say his speech this afternoon. I am writing as my strength will admit to Bro Joe.

Thursday Jan 20th Bob Davis arrived this afternoon, to live with us & go to school, to prepare for the ministry. O may he be a blessing to us & we to him. We planted a bushel of irish potatoes today in my garden.

Friday Jan 21st Mr F set out some shrubbery & fruit trees, peach, fig & apple.

Sat Jan 22nd Mr F & Bob went out to Mr G Killoughs and got a load of fodder & about 60 nice peach trees to set out.

Sunday Jan 23rd A beautiful day, our folks went to church. No one unlocked the court house door or rung the bell for Uncle Henry, so we had no preaching, O such sheer neglect is shameful, and killing to a ministers feelings.

May 16th 1859 When I pened the last page little did I expect it would be so long before I would write in my imperfect journal again. But it is even so. The events of life are uncertain, again (as often before) I have been reminded of the uncertainty of all human calculations.

My health continue so delicate up to the 16th of March, I neglected to write. Bro Thomas left us that morning after giving Finie & I a kiss. That night about 10 ¼ O clock God bestowed upon us another little daughter. She seemed delicate, suffered about one month with snuffles (what is called hives) and a very violent cold & cough. O how great was my anxiety about my little baby girl. My little bright eyed treasure, yes she seemed more precious because she resembled our precious little sainted Lou Katie, it seemed that she had returned to bless her fond mothers heart again, and that it was not a new babe. At times when alone I would look upon our sweet little suffer and when she would cough it seemed like a dagger piercing my heart. The tears would involuntarily roll down my sorrow stricken cheeks. O I prayed she might not die.

My little Tommie has just returned from the burial of Bro Bean, an old friend of my husbands youthful days in other lands & other years. An old member of our own beloved church. He died yesterday morning, he has left his second wife, many children & friends to morn his loss.

But amid all this sadness & gloom thank the good Lord our little broken family are well. My health has been <u>very delicate indeed</u> until within a few days my strength has increased rapidly for which I feel so much gratitude to God. O may it continue so. And our babe is so well, so bright & sprightly. She is two months old today. Has been cooing, talking, and laughing so sweetly a long time since, truly has Tupper written "A babe in a house is a well spring of pleasure." [This was a quote by Martin Farquhar Tupper, 1810–99, an English writer and poet.] How could it be otherwise when it is part of ourselves and then when we think of the Donor, thinks it comes from God.

We think our babe the sprightliest child we have ever seen of her age. She is so strong, she can almost stand & sit up without being held. She weighed 9 ½ lbs soon as dressed, but she had the most delicate little face of any of our babys. We think she is just pretty enough, large black eyes, can't tell yet rather they will be blue or black. We are both so anxious for them to have Mamma's eyes. But still we will be satisfied either way. We are all so fond & proud of our little sweet daughter. O may it please the good Lord to spare her to us & us to her, for she indeed is our "pet-flower" & Mr F says she is the center of attention in our little family white & black.

We have received money in the low country for the land that we sold that came by my Father's estate. My father labor & toil, O bless the Lord I had a good father. With the money we bought some 2 ten acre woods lots, near LaGrange, and a negro man named Isham and Mandy his wife. He is one of black complexion, she is a bright mulatto, we gave twenty-five hundred dollars for them, part down part Christmas.

We would not have bought them but (they perfect stranger) hunted us out & begged us so hard to buy them so they could live together and have a good home. They enlisted our warmest sympathies & we bought them.

I hope we can pay the balance before it is due, we can if we can sell land. Isham says he prayed the Lord to send him out to Texas where his wife had been sent 15 months before him and to give him a good home, and he believed the good Lord sent him to us to get him a good home in answer to his prayer. O may it be so.

O may they prove to be faithful servants and we be good to them. Would that I could be cheerful and happy as in days past. O may we as a family white & black live for God, & all meet an unbroken family in heaven. As I write now little sweet daughter is in her little willow wagon "Pappa" bought her, & Finie is pulling & singing to her. I am just beginning to believe that both our boys will be singers. I hope so. Mandy is washing & singing so cheerfully that it rebukes me for feeling so sad.

Jeff by hauling made $2.25 cents before dinner. He is now gone to hall us wood, to home consumption. Isham is cutting in the post oaks. I have spent all the intervals of the forenoon in writing, but now answer a letter I received from my little cousin Mary Figures Lewis, and I feel I can scarcely take time from my sewing.

Tommie has written 2 letters, I dictated the first one for him, it was to Bro Joe Philips, today he wrote to Sister Cummings at Austin & dictated & spelled for himself it surprised me, it was good for a child who had been writing for a short time. O I pray that my wild boys will make <u>devoted, pious Christians & had useful lives indeed.</u>

Thursday May 19th 1859 Mr F left for Wharton to try & sell some land.

Sat May 21st Mandy has done my work, she finished by dinner. I gave her this afternoon, she is now putting up some shelves in the kitchen, as I write sweet daughter is coming in the little willow wagon beside me. Tommie & Finie have gone to the store, Isham & Jef are ploughing & hoeing the corn. We have fenced in 2 ½ acres balance of the back parts of our lots here & have planted 33 rows of corn where we intend to plant potato slips. Mr F has 9 rows, he gave Isham 12 rows each.

Wednesday June 29th/59 A cloudy day, last Sunday we had a little rain, thunder & lightning the latter struck a house in town. The people at the church were very much frighten by it. Jef & our children set out a fine chance of sweet potato slips & vines yesterday late. [Sweet potatoes are grown from slips rather than from seeds. A slip is a rooted sprout from a mature sweet potato.] He, Isham & Tommie will set out again all this afternoon. Mr F started to a meeting at Gay Hill last Sat. has not yet returned. [This was a small town about thirty-seven miles northeast of La Grange. It is a ghost town today.] I feel sure they have been blessed with a gracious revival. O may it be so.

Professor Dechard's examination commenced on 21st June & continued until 24th, closed by an address on education by lawyer Shropshire. I do believe <u>all</u> were pleased. Tommie stood a good examination made his first efforts at public speaking, his subject was "Close of Term." He did remarkably well, O I was so excited that I was cold & did not get warm so long as I awake at night. There was one Original speech delivered by Robert Hodge one of the young candidates for the ministry under the care of our Presbytery. It was very good & well delivered. Jef took Ann Isabella out the night Tommie spoke, she was perfectly delighted & behaved so pretty & excited about as much admiration as the juvenile speakers.

Sunday July 3rd 1859 As Mr F is out at Clear Creek assisting Bro Jack in holding a two day meeting, I should have been with him but our carriage horses ran away & could not be found.

Sweet <u>daughter</u> is improving so fast, what a charm her little enchanting smile spreads on all around our dear "home circle." Last Sat, Sabbath, Monday & Tuesday Mr F assisted Bro Jack in holding a protracted meeting in Washington County. [A protracted meeting was a religious meeting held for several successive days.]

July Friday morn 14th We drove to clear creek camp ground yesterday morn, found 4 or 5 campers on the spot, quite encouraging. Stretched our fairly new tent, very nice, but I feel sad in the extreme. I never came on a camp ground as I now do. Had a missionary monthly concerts collected $6, Mr F gave Sissy a dime to give. We all joined that concert, Jef gave 25 cents. This morning is bright lovely & sunny. We are tented on the most pleasant spot on the ground. Would that I could feel as I have heretofore on this to me doubly blessed spot, for here Tommie embraced our holy religion, a short space from this ground where our church stands. I felt my change come, a change that has cheered me all along life's dark & gloomy or sun shining pathway, it has been my solace in afflictions hour & serve to gladden my brightest & happiest moments

Journal #7

July 30, 1859–February 24, 1860

July 30th 1859 This is a bright day, but the hottest we have had this summer. We left home yester morn drove to Bro Hill's, dined. I felt sick but could eat little dinner. But that little relived [*sic*] my sick stomach, but my aching knees continued into the night, then it ceased. I presume it all originates from extensive labor making up my preserves & putting up my fruits.

I feel well today. We arrived here just before preaching was over. I find Sister Atkinson to be pleasant, also her daughter, Mr Love & Miss Amanda who they call "Manke." We stayed last night at Bro Killoughs, enjoyed myself as in days past & gone which afforded us a pure pleasure. We were today traveling over ground that we traveled over 16 years ago passed Mr Matsons old farm residence where Mr F spent some time 20 years ago e'er we ever met. Mrs M started to Texas in last stage of consumption. Her removal to our sunny south clime acted as a charm, it restored her and she still lives, and is now an old lady, of course she blesses the day she arrived in <u>Texas soil</u>.

Near that dwelling we beheld the prairie dotted with most beautiful groves, where when we traveled here years ago there was nothing but grass & shrubs and all along the side of the road the old log huts have given place to <u>very neat</u> and some fine two story home <u>family residents</u>.

Left Jef & Isham at home. Bro Hill let us have Billie a little black boy he has hired to nurse Sissy, he seems kind & fond of her. She likes him but I have to send him back in a few days. Mr F wishes me to go to him to a meeting in Burlison [not Burleson because the town dates to 1881], then to my Uncles and then to Bastrop meeting. I reckon I shall go, but I don't know what I shall do for a nurse. I have never attended a meeting without a nurse, when I had a small babe. But I will trust the Lord. I hope that I will be useful

& do <u>some</u> good this trip, this is my dearest aim. Next is to take care of <u>our</u> sweet babe.

The arbor where we worship is in sight of this place, but a short distance. We today passed by a place where they were attempting to make a fence of prickly pears. The first I ever saw or heard of. This is a beautiful romantic country, but not so well watered because when limestone water abounds which I fear is not so healthy.

This is also the sentiment of my husband as expressed to me to day. Unless some blasting or mildewing influence comes yet, this country will be blessed with an abundant corn & cotton crop. We passed the air line road where they propose to build a rail road to Austin City.

July 31st Sab. We attended church, a large attentive congregation. Mr F preached at 11 "the other foundation can no man & C" ["For other foundation can no man lay than that is laid, which is Jesus Christ" 1 Corinthians 3:11]. I took daughter. She was so warm & fretful, that I could not pay that attention to the preaching that is <u>ever</u> my hearts desire. She was not used to her nurse & he is inexperienced, but the dear babies must be attended to.

Monday August 1st No preaching until night on account of election for Governor. Great & intense excitement I learned this afternoon that Genl Sam Houston in over 100 votes ahead in this County. This rejoices our hearts. Surely the <u>hero</u> of San Jacinto <u>justly</u> deserves that high honor. [Incumbent Democratic governor Hardin Runnels was defeated by Sam Houston, who received 57 percent of the vote.]

It was a joy to my heart that my husband was privileged with so much pleasure to vote for him once more, my father who has long since slept the sleep of death, my husband, Many friends & kindred are his warm friends how could it be otherwise.

Thursday August 4th Last night the glad news was brought me by my husband that 2 precious souls embraced religion, young men. O how much anxiety & deep solicitude I ever feel for young men, when I think of their proneness to be wicked & the many vain false glowing allurements of earth. I stayed at 11, & took care & nursed 2 babes beside mine.

Oct. 28th/59 Robert Millenburg, A Texas raised german of refined taste and feeling has been boarding with us all this session. He is a candidate for the ministry under the watch care of our Presbytery. [La Grange was in the center of the Texas German belt.] He bids fair for usefulness, he is very devoted & zealous. He is great company to the children & myself since Mr F left us to go up the Country & to attend to some business of a secular nature.

Mr F has been absent weeks. I have had not a word from him since the day he left home. Surely he has written. I feel a little uneasy about the Indians. May the Lord protect him & return him soon to the embrace of his family in love & peace & pure pleasure that is <u>nowhere</u> to be <u>found</u> beneath the circle of the sun save in a happy <u>well ordered home.</u>

Daughter is 7 months old & over. I said to her this morning something about crying, she really seem to say __?__. Just like she intended to imitate me. She often says Pa & Ma, as distinctly as I can, once or twice has seemed to say "titty." Young as she is I do believe she is beginning to talk.

Since I wrote the above I took her in my arms & she <u>really</u> appeared to say "titty" O what a sweet treasure. I nursed her to sleep & laid her smugly in her neat cherry crib & covered her with her funny little red blanket, I made just before her birth. Tommie attends school regularly, he has commenced grammar. I see him learning better than expected. I pray that my <u>fond</u> hopes may yet be realized in regard to <u>our</u> boys. Finie is learning at home. He has just read & spelled a lesson, but I had to switch him severely, he can learn faster when he can get his mind fastened on his book. He is a great boy. O may I give this plastic little mind its proper starts.

I pray oftener in secret, some times 3 or 4 times a day, and I feel, much more happy & humble. O that I could fully govern my temper, it is my <u>woe</u> beseting [*sic*] sin. Lord help me. Finie is sweeping the front yard. My children must work too. I am giving Julia Atkinson writing lessons, have written her 2 copies. I think she will learn fast. She has such a desire & taste for writing.

Jef is so disobedient and causes me so much trouble I do not know what to do with him. O how ungrateful he is after I have attended to his wants in infancy, raised him around my knees, <u>prayed for him</u> attended so closely to his morals, taught him religion & <u>tried</u> to <u>teach him principles</u>. But alas how little gratitude he feels toward my endeavors to make him a useful & happy servant and I taught & had him taught so that he can now read a testament I gave him so that he understands what he reads, that he is able to tell me about it. And still he will not obey my orders or kind requests <u>only</u> as it suits him. [Alabama, Georgia, Louisiana, Mississippi, North Carolina, South Carolina, and Virginia all passed antiliteracy laws for slaves. Texas did not have such a law.]

This afternoon I told him & sent him word again to come home time to have early supper, that I wished to attend prayer meeting, but he came much later than usual had supper way after dark. O how surprising and this is his all most daily course. It frets & perplexes me most to death. Would that I could get not to care, and let him slide on. But when I think of the pains and anxieties I have had with this negro, think of the immense trouble he has already cause me. Yes! Heart burnings I can scarcely bear it. But I got to put up with it. Isham bought on credit for me from Cousin Alfred $2 sugar 2 gals molasses $.30 cents worth, one jug $1.

Sat Oct 29th/59 I am most sick with a bad cold, how I dread my winter cough. I would be where there is no cold weather. All well, but poor me. Our sweet babe is all life & sweetness. A pencil of light in this darkly, lonely home.

I feel so bad my head aches. My heart aches. My heart aches. I fear I will be sick, if I get sick who will take care of me. I gave Jeff a long good natured lecture. I hope, I pray he will do better. I received a letter from Mr F.

Sunday Oct 30th I am under the influence of a violent cold & also medicine I have taken to remove that cold. Tommie as usual attended Sabbath School, Finie also attended for the first time. I put him under Robert Willenburg's care, he kindly promised to take care of him. Mr Boone the old Presbyterian minister enrolled his name, next Sabbath he is to be classed.

Jeff was more kind than usual done what he has never done since daughters birth, came & voluntary took her off her rug & kept her in the kitchen until 11 o clock or after and she never cried one bit, but was all life & glee when he brought her to me to nurse. She nursed & went to sleep & by this means I got to read & enjoyed my reading so much.

Monday Oct 31st Jeff halled [*sic*] Mr P Y McAshan a load of wood. Isham has gone to work for our beef Market Man. The wheat we have sewed is growing finely. A small portion of our turnips & Mustard are doing well. Robert & Tommie are at school. Finie is hunting eggs. Anna __?__ is sitting quietly on her sheep skin rug. Would that I could add where Mr F is this cold morning. O may he preach good & succeed in selling property so we may get out of debt.

I wish Mr F could get a salary sufficient to keep from every year selling property to pay our expense bill, for it seems to me we surely we will run thro' all the property we have. But I hope to be able to trust for the better.

But as it is he has no regular appointments & can of course expect no salary. And what preaching he does is here & there and anywhere.

Sometimes as it is now half his salary are in another Presbytery. And portions of his own destitute and would add to his pecuniary interest some little at least. If he would have regular appointments I told him I would be so much happier if he would have some work assigned him, he said he would be more happy, but he returned without any. I hope he will not continue so. His excuse has been he must try and arrange business. Well business is not a whit better arranged than it was last year. And I fear so that it will continue. We have no income save our rents. Jeff's & Isham's labor. And that could go on & Mr F preach all the time, and surely we would all be more contented & happy & woeful. What do we wish to live for if it is not to be useful in this our probationary State.

May our hardships teach our children a lesson of humility. We are in debt and when Mr F left home I presumed we had 50 cents worth of sugar in the house. Our house has been crowded all most ever since he left. And when Robert is paying board I cannot will not, give him tea without sugar. So I was under the painful necessity of getting Robert to ask credit for one dollars worth sugar for us (which is a cash article.)

After that was gone, I was compelled to ask credit again, if I had no boarder, I feel I would rather done without than ask such a thing. But I thought who could I go to with more satisfaction than my Cousin Abel Moore. Whose wife (a lovely woman I think) had lately begged me to trade with her. Husband saying he would willingly credit us to any amount.

But what was my mortification at the close of the bill I read a complete emphatic __?__. Well my children this is only a small part of the trials of a ministers wife. Yes, at times the very time my husband & your father was spending time & excellent talents preaching to others that at any other calling would secure at least $1,000 per year. We his wife and children are at home, as I feel all most begging the necessaries of life. For indeed it is very humbling to my proud womans heart to be compelled to write and ask for credit, for cash articles. Especially when it resulted thus.

But be it far from me to say that no other wife has troubles. I would rather suffer Martyrdom if necessary as a Ministers wife, than to suffer as a gamblers, drunkards, Libertines [a person devoid of most moral principles] or many other men's wife's whose callings are much less honorable than a Gospel Minister notwithstanding all this at times I hold that a ministers wife has joys __?__ holier & purer than any other woman on this green earth.

I have enjoyed my secret devotions today so much. Finie followed his dear Mama once or twice & knelt by her side and prayed with all the fervency of his little heart which filled me with inexpressible feelings. Robert Willensburg is to head the union laymen prayer meeting tonight. Children & I each went alone & prayed for him to perform this awful responsible duty, as he should.

The old Presbyterian, notwithstanding the union meeting went & had preaching at our Synod. We gave place to the union and the members of the Synod attended it. Jeff halled the last load of corn at last. I patched Finie's pants, began Tommie's a brown jeans pr, his Paps brought him last winter. [The union Louisa wrote about was the group of people that had ties to the North. This is the first mention of union people in a Southern state. Talk of secession had been going on for several years.]

Tuesday Nov 1st 1859 Jeff is going to hall punkings, Isham has gone to help Bro Beaumont fence a place to sow wheat, then his black man will help make nails to fence our ground to sow another small pasture. Sissy is lovely this morning. I had to whip Tommie for telling me a falsehood this morning.

O how distressing to my poor heart. Jeff measured one load of corn according to it, he says & parts of the corn is about 250 bushels. He had halled one load of punkins, one after another, some very nice ones. We had a mess of green ones for dinner, which Robert & children were very fond of. Our sweet & ever good babies had been better than usual today. I finished Tommie's pants soon after dinner & began Finie a pair like them. Tommie churned after dinner, got half lb butter, he was half hour churning. Jeff halled one more load of nice punkins.

Wed Nov 2nd Daughter is sitting on my bed playing so nicely & looking so sweet in her nice white neatly done up checked muslin slip & pink gingham baby apron. Jeff has gone after another load of pumpkins. Laura, Dr Manley's black woman is now washing for me. She is a nice hand at the business. My cold seems worse, My neck is so sore & sorta stiff, but I must get to my work.

Jeff is very kind this morning. O may he do his duty. Jeff returned before 11 O clock with another load of pumpkins. Finie swept the front yard nice and is now before me fixing his yard broom but he cannot do it. I will for him.

After dinner Jeff finished halling pumpkins there was only part of a load. I gave Cousin Amanda one doz and a half, gave Mrs P Y McAshan 3 pumpkins. Laura got done washing after dark, what Jeff would have washed in half or a little more half a day, & done the cooking. She had nothing to do but wash. I finished Finie's pants. This is Robert Willenburg's 21st birthday, we made him a nice light cake, had preserves with it.

Thursday Nov 3rd A bright coolish morn, most pleasant one since the norther. Isham is still at work at Bro Beaumonts, Jeff is going to hall wood. We had breakfast about sunrise. Jeff was from breakfast until after 10 halling one load up town for the lady for which he got $1.00, slow work indeed. Laura came some earlier to iron for me, she seems to be a nice ironer.

Friday Nov 4th I am just ready to start to spend the day with Cousin Amanda & try & sum up the fortitude to have two teeth pulled. It is now 25 minutes after 8 O clock at night. And we have just returned home.

Sat Nov 5th Jeff halled one load of ralls to make me a pig sty, also a little wood. He has gone to carry Cousin Amanda one bag of corn as a present, & hall Cousin Mc some planks. Tommie is now selecting & writing down some passages of scripture to prove the Divinity of the Savior to present to his Sabbath School Superintendent tomorrow morning the last Sabbaths request.

Monday Nov 7th A beautiful clear bright sunny morning. It is now after 8 O clock, Robert & Tommie are at school. Isham has gone to make rails to fence in the front part of our lot to sew another small pasture for our cows horses & calves this winter.

The back pasture & also my chicken wheat [wheat fed to chickens] in the yard is growing finely. Jeff has gone after one load of wood to hall up to Mrs Hopson. I read at my childrens consent request last night at prayers. After prayers Tommie beg me to read & I read 2 preceding chapters, just as we were to retire to rest. Finie was asleep. Tommie & I kneeled alone to pray. I ask him to pray, he prayed very well, thanked the Lord for a praying mother & bless the Lord we had been raised in a Christian land & were not like the poor heathen.

Yesterday Jeff & Isham gave me such a large nice mess of sweet potatoes out of their patch. O it did one so much good, such a spirit sharing so much love & kindness in the relationship of owner & servant, it always touches a tender cord in my bosom. I gave Isham a tin cup of sugar. I intend Jeff a present too. Isham gave Sissie a little water melon, she loved so to play with it, but Finie brok it this morning. Jeff halled Cousin Amanda one load of wood. A present from me, he halled one load up town received $1.00

Tuesday Nov 8th Emma washed for me today. I paid her 50 cents (price). I am making daughter a nice ruffled crib pillow slip. It seems to me she is becoming daily more lovely & interesting. Her eyes seem to talk, tity dady & Ma she seems to say dek for Jeff. I received short letter from Mr F.

Wednesday Nov 9th A damp misty morning, Salina, Dr Lewis' woman has come to iron for me. She is a nice smart looking woman. I answered Mr Fosters letter last night. I received another letter from my husband, he says there is a prospect of selling our Peppers creek farm for part pay in horses. [Pepper Creek was about two miles northeast of Belton.] Captain Erath had sold our labor on Bosque which was my Father, I.B. Philips headright labor. Capt E. head paid Mr F $210 in gold for it. [The Republic of Texas made many headrights, which were grants given to settlers that met certain conditions. The amount of land ranged from hundreds to thousands of acres, based on who applied and when they came to Texas.]

Friday Nov 11th A memorable day. Today my Tommie is 12 years old. I helped Jeff make him some nice cakes. We ate of them for supper, have sufficient for two more meals. And our valued and loved old horse <u>Prince</u> dropped dead in the wagon as he was halling a load of rails home. A hired boy drove the horses today & I fear he drove him too hard. O how it hurt us all, we all cried. He has been faithful indeed to us, eleven years in our service, he was 15 years old. O how sorry I am that we worked him today. I am so afraid the boy drove him <u>too hard</u>. Isham & Jeff say he did not, that he only halled four loads of rails.

Well Well, I am so sorry my heart aches at the idea of the probability that our poor good dear old horse was abused the last day of his life. Could that this last day had been one of rest. Isham & Jeff say he has been failing fast for several weeks, but they did not tell me until he was dead. O I might have prolonged the poor old diseased creatures life. But I <u>can't help it</u> now. I am sorry, I am sorry.

But thank God it was not one of our children or any of the family. Finie says he would rather to do without sugar that for Prince to have died. Yes he says he would rather every horse in the country had died rather both our other horses had died. He says he would rather do without dinner, for poor old good Prince to have died.

Sat Nov 12th Tommie is reading his lesson he has to read Monday. Isham is sick in the kitchen. Robert is studying in his room. Finie is with Isham, Jeff has gone to borrow a horse & wagon to haul our good old horses remaining off to burry [sic]. Mr F always said when the good old creature died he intends to have him buried.

My tooth trouble me a great deal. I must be careful with sweet, sweet Ann & myself this norther I fear our colds will be increased, but the lovely little plant [Ann] is doing well all life, sprightliness & glee. O what a "well spring of pleasure" in this house is our own sweet Ibbie. She is now taking her morning nap.

Jeff has just returned & got one horse & wagon for which I shane [*sic*] is to work for one day next week. Robert has kindly gone to see to Jeffs burrying my poor old horse. Robert & Jeff buried our poor dead Prince. While they were gone Cousin Mc accompanied Dr Huff up here, and he pulled three teeth for me. Cousin braged on my great courage.

Sunday Nov 13th A blue, cold day. Water was frozen in all our buckets this morning. Robert & children attended Sabbath School. Finie wore his new brown jean suit I had just made him. Tommie wore his new pants & his semi black coat. They looked very nice & comfortable. Robert & Tommie attended the methodist church. Jeff & Isham have gone to "black folks" preaching. Robert & Tommie have good to hear Mr King preach on relative duties of parents & children. Finie, sis & I are all alone & I feel so much more lonely than common. Robert attended church this evening.

Monday Nov. 14th Jeff has come with 48 lbs of pork at 8 cents per lb $3.84 cents. I have sent Isham, out to Bro Jacks to see about getting some beef Mr F bargain for before he left home. Conference will begin in a few days and I am ill proposed for it. I have waited for Mr F's return to make preparations, until I can wait no more. So all I could do was to send a servant trusting in the Lord for help. I feel so much relieved since my teeth have been extracted.

Tuesday 15th 1859 A cold morning yet, last night my ink stand was sitting on the hearth stone & the wooden part burnt half up, also the jam was burn some. I am glad it was no worse. I feel I have taken fresh cold. Cousin Mc called on us this afternoon. Julia is here come to stay all night with us.

Wednesday Nov 16th Surely Mr F will be home in a few days. Isham returned last night. Bro Spencer sent me in the quarter of beef, Bro Hill gave us. I have just traded for a turkey hen from Mr P Y McAshan. I had the promise of 4 from the country, but did not get them. I am much disappointed. Anna is 8 months old today, precious treasure most standing alone & talking. I received a letter from Cousin Mary Figures Lewis near Bastrop. I was so sure it was from Mr F that half my joy was over when I looked at the scrimption & found from the handwriting it was not his. Jeff has gone up town to sell his potatoes. I believe he has $5. worth in the wagon sold, fifty cents worth last night, has I presumed 7 or 8 bushels worth to dig yet. They are very nice, he gave us a fine large mess for breakfast this morning, which was so kind.

Thursday Nov 17th My chest & cough trouble me so much. I sent for Dr Gregory this morning again after a night of suffering. He says I must wean our babe, that nothing injuries my lungs so much as nursing. O what a trial. Well I can't begin until Mr F returns he must see her suck her tity once more, which is such a pleasure to him. Now I am so glad I learned her to eat. Dr says I must wear flannel next my chest and then a soft buckskin jacket over that to fit close up around the neck, buttoned up behind so as to protect my chest. He says the late affliction I had of my throat was Bronchitis which disease I feared I had years ago. But it did not frighten me, I have expected it & prayed about it so long. He says there is danger of it running into consumption.

Friday Nov 18th I still enjoy my company, Bro John Forbes came to see us, he brought official intelligence of the Commencement of hostile depravations that have been committed at Brownsville on the Rio Grande, that many Americans were slain. May it soon be stopped. O God preserve the ravages of war again.

[On September 28, 1859, Juan Cortina led about seventy-five men to Brownsville to punish the town marshal for past grievances. Cortina and his men killed between four and six people, released the prisoners from the town jail, took arms and ammunition, and fled.

On October 12, the sheriff of Cameron County, James Browne, led a posse and arrested sixty-year-old Tomas Cabrera, a close friend of Cortina's, who had participated in the earlier raid. When Cortina found out what had happened to his friend, he issued an ultimatum to the people of Brownsville, threatening that he would "lay the town in ashes" if Cabrera was not released.

Each side issued threats, armed themselves, and had outsiders join their forces. With Cortina's army growing stronger every day, the Americans sent for help and a force of Texas Rangers, under Captain William G. Tobin, was soon ordered to begin assembling in Brownsville.

On November 11, it looked as though the two sides were going to clash. People in Brownsville panicked, removed Cabrera from his cell, and lynched him in Market Square. In revenge, Cortina hanged three American prisoners and killed several rangers in an ambush. To get control of the situation, the US Army was sent to Brownsville on November 14. On December 13, the US Army, assisted by Texas Rangers, routed the Cortinistas. Both sides experienced small losses and the fighting came to a stop. This became known as the Battle of La Ebonal.]

Once in girlhood I passed thro' this fiery ordeal, we had to leave our peaceful homes. My father lost thousands of dollars in the loss of property. Now in my evening hours I feel ill prepared to go thro' such scenes again. O Lord advert the blow & give our lovely Texas land, peace (sweet has linger). But as yet mind is not excited on that subject at all. La Grange is fitting out squads to assist in protecting our western border.

Sat Nov 19th A lovely day. I dressed & returned to leave babe with Jeff, and Robert drove our carriage to church. I listen to a good sermon. I got in late, not like to have gotten a seat, turned to walk out & return home, but Dr McGown moved & his wife pressed in her "hoops" & gave me a seat for which I was very thankful.

But he has become estranged on account of a synodical church difficulty with his broth. Andrew J Mc Gown and I have recently been told that I offended his wife whilst I was sojourning with them, when our boys were sick.

If I could but talk with in regard to that matter, and he has not lost all confidence in my candor, I could I know remove those prejudices. But he has suffered his unreely disposition to run away with all his kind Christian feeling, and will not even speak to any of his old dear associates & Ministers. Today when I found myself seated so near one we had loved as an own brother, I prayed God to direct me.

I feared to offer him my hand, expecting he would treat me with indignity, it being the first time I had met him since his feeling became so turbulent & has refused to speak to my husband & hurt Bro Walker's feelings very much time of Synod. Who is one of our beloved ministers & a tried old loved friend of the Dr.

When the congregation arose to depart I spoke to his wife, she just observed, howdy you do Mrs Foster, it used to be (sis & sister Lou) with all love & kindness. Then I just took my station near carelessly watching the Dr who looked perfectly mad, although in the house of our God where we had gone purposely & professed to worship God.

When I got in my carriage to start home, I throwed up the curtain when I saw he was in his carriage right beside where we mostly drive. I determined that if I could catch his eye I would <u>make</u> him speak to me or back out. Our eyes met we both bowed spoken, but called no name.

O how sad, how hearts rendering that such a state of things should get up. Little did I dream that when we desired to live neighbors & have him as our family physician we would meet with so much brotherly & sisterly love, we would ever meet as we did today. Dr McGown would have to have injured me to some <u>awful</u> extend e'erever I could refuse to speak respectfully to him, it excited me very much. My health is so feeble I nearly gave out going to preaching after I was partly dressed. I returned home weak agitated & nervous, feeling worse than when I left home.

Times quite exciting in our town. The sound of the drum often salutes our ears beating up for volunteers to go and protect our frontier from the marauding Mexicans. I am told 50 men are ready for the campaign. [The events taking place in Brownsville had stirred memories of the fight against Mexico for Texas independence that took place twenty-three years earlier.]

Wednesday Nov 23rd I attended conference heard the Bishop read out the appointments. A large collection was made. I believe it was to pay their Christian advocate out of debt, several thousand dollars. But I perceive the Methodist ministers were the main subscribers how so many poor circuit riders could give $100 or $200 I could not tell. But they subscribed it and it all amounted to quite a sum.

Then they raised a subscription to publish a Sermon delivered by Bro John. They took up collection at last 5 or 6 times during conference. Well it is past by company is gone. I had a great deal, also 3 or 4 horses to feed. My friends left me with many kind words & smiles of affection & gratefulness.

Night had not closed in until here comes an acquaintance bringing with him a stranger and 4 horses for us to feed, for him to sell. Well it is hard for us to keep up at such a rate, but a minister must do all this & have no salary. Now this very trip Mr F has been preaching 3 weeks of his time & I presume he has not in lieu received $10, hardly $5. But in Eternity all will be right.

Friday Nov 25th I bought Jeff a coat at $2.75 to pay him for some molasses & potatoes I purchased from him. We looked at some nice furniture at Mr Rhode's & Mr Willcox's. Cousin walked on home & Finie with her. Tommie & I called on Mrs Powell, we found her a pleasant nice lady.

Monday Nov 28th Daughter is playing with Finie. I have Emma hired to wash. Jeff is making steps where the front gate was. My head aches, my cough is much improved & hoarseness most gone. 3rd of Nov last letter I have read from Mr F. I am surprised, uneasy & unhappy. If he is not sick or dead he certainly has written 2 or 3 since that date. O what shall I do unless I receive a letter soon.

If I only could get a letter and learn <u>all is well</u> I would be satisfied. Tommie & Robert are at school. Isham brought me some coffee this morning & loaned it to me. I told him I could do very well with tea. He said to me O no maam keep it, if any bad comes you would feel bad.

After all my anxiety I received a letter from Mr F but it was so short and was so indefinite that it was <u>little</u> or no comfort to me. I hope he has done <u>some</u> good. Up to the date of his last letter he had not attended to any business at all and he has been absent about 7 weeks in a few days. But it is all right if we can only get out of debt as such, and keep so. I am satisfied if I know my heart, I do not crave wealth. I want, <u>love peace</u>, happiness at home. A competent livelihood educate our children so they may do good in life and <u>all</u> our usefulness.

Wednesday Nov 30th A misty morning, but & went & spent the day, after Emma scoured my room, at Bro McFarland, found him sick for which I was sorry. On my return home Jeff had made $3.00 halling wood & had bought me one gallon molasses, best of all brought me a long letter from my absent husband, halled one load rails. He spoke tender of his children & said he was sorry to learn of my illness with cold, it was written last Friday 25th.

Sat Dec 3rd The ground is white, white, with snow, it looks beautiful to me from my window. We are all well and so thankful to God. Finie run in this morning all in glee, laughed and said, Mother, Cousin Robert was skating on the ice & fell sprangling on the ground, he was so tickled that it infused new life into me & I laughed heartily at his childish laugh. Isham had gone to kill hogs again. Jeff is going to hall one load of wood for us. Jeff came with the wood half after 10. Tommie made a nice trap, my old hoops knocked it over. The boys are having fun with their sweet sister Ibbie.

This is my 37th birthday. [She was born in 1821, so she is really 38 today.] I lament that I have lived to so little purpose in this life. O may I be more useful in the future.

Monday Dec 5th Weather is very much moderated, so warm that at bedtime we needed very little fire. Robert returned about 1 O clock and his brother with him. He had been absent in Germany 2 years, they seem affectionate & loving one to another.

Tuesday Dec 6th O such a cold snowy morning. So cold the boys will not go to school but I had to send Robert & Tommie up town to purchase for me some flannel & buckskin to make me some jackets. I ought to have made them & had them ready for this norther, but I was waiting for Mr F's return & for him to get them for me

I was so provoked this morning, when I had Tommie to get up and raise the window with, the bitter cold wind & snow pouring on his dear face & slender little chest to awake Jeff. And he could not raise the poor child had to wrap up and go out on an open porch to Robert's room, awoke him to get him to go to the kitchen, for Jeff was <u>absent</u>. He went up town and stayed all night, diametrically opposed to Mr F's orders.

I had Tommie to get up in half hour & call again. No answer. Then when breakfast ought to have been down, I had my poor child to call him again, he answered as usual. He told him to come make a fire, also asked him how long he had been up. He said only a little while, it then was about 2 ½ hours by the clock from the time I had him first called. Tommie went in the kitchen, Jeff said to him, you did not call me as early as usual, then he asked Tommie who had left his door open. He told him Robert. So the fellow saw he was trapped. He then said I just come home. Tommie said, Jeff why did you stay up town <u>all</u> night. Jeff replied with <u>great anger & indignation, just because I wanted to.</u>

I asked him where he stayed, he said Mr Tates. My next question is why did you not come home, when you know I am so feeble & Mr F gone. He said it began to snow. How delicate, fat as a bear cannot walk half or quarter of a mile in snow. I was so angry & hurt at him. I have prayed to be resigned to all such freaks, but O how hard after I have raised & instructed him all most like a child of my own, and his looks & manners speaks for this all around.

But he only laughed in my face & said he was doing no harm. I told him the bible taught servants obedience to their owners and he knew he was positively forbidden & always have been to stay away from home all night.

The next morning after Mr F left, the like occurrence took place I got up before day & went to the kitchen myself. Got Robert to go & look around the lots, after all our search he was seen coming from towards town. Said he had been after our cow, that always goes off the opposite direction. I suspected then this thing that happen last night. I fear notwithstanding <u>all</u> his <u>loud</u> profession of religion he will yet go to <u>ruin</u> in this world & the world to come.

I feel certain if Robert had closed his door, he would have stood it out to the last, that he ~~would~~ had come home at the proper time last night. But I presume it is best we have found out, another one of his tricks. O would that he be candid, and act from principle. It was so cold there was no school today.

Wednesday Dec 7th Dr Gregory called to see me he says he says he thinks I am doing pretty well when I get on my new flannel & buckskin and take my "Balsam & Tar." [The use of pine tar in medicine was first described by Hippocrates more than two thousand years earlier; it had been used to treat a range of skin conditions.] I will feel much better. I spit a pale yellow mucus. [This would be a sign that the body was fighting off an infection, possibly from pneumonia, bronchitis, or sinusitis.] I do not cough near so much.

We were compelled to eat in my room. Sun shone beautifully this afternoon. Today Finie left the window up after I distinctly have him shut it. I presume this bitter cold window blew on my shoulders an hour.

Thursday Dec 8th Emma is washing for me. Finie built me a nice fire I feel better, perhaps I let my room get to cold. I took a hearty sorrowful cry. O to be this left alone & sick, how doleful. I do believe if Mr F had been dead before me that I would have felt any worse than I did. If my husband was anything but a minister of the Gospel the world & church would cry out against him. But Ministers are expected to sacrifice home happiness & <u>even</u> the lives of their family, to go and preach. How many feeble delicate ministers wives have been brought to an untimely grave because the mind or body ere unable to stand up to the performance of both husbands & wives domestic duties.

Today I have read, better than I could have described, my symptoms in Dr O. Phillips Browms circular on first stage of consumption. I feel more certain than ever I have that disease, it caused me here <u>all alone</u> to weep bitter tears. [Tuberculosis has been variously known as consumption. It usually begins with flu-like symptoms that progress to a persistent cough, the spitting of blood, caused by lesions on the lung tissue, and consequent weight loss or general wasting of the muscles. It can be spread in families when aerosol droplets of infected sputum are ejected by coughing.]

To feel each foreboding of that fell destroyer, that seems to me is preying upon my very vitals & then my afflictions otherwise, my unhappy, lonely, sad, gloomy state of mind only makes it worse. O the thought of being taken from my wild, reckless boys and our sweet gentle, loving infant daughter it is all most more than a fond Mother's heart can bear. But my only hope is that it was years ago when I was similarly effected, only worse. I pray to my kind heavenly Father to spare me yet (years). Until my dear little ones are raised.

I was sitting at my work table sick, and gloomy, Mr F opened the door, stood there some time, then spoke to us. We all jumped & ran to the door, he pressed me in his arms and kissed me, the boys, daughter then awoke in a perfect good humor, I took her up, and her father took her & kissed, and she laughed and looked like she thought she knew her dear papa, who has been absent 8 weeks today, after we retired to rest she looked very uneasy & seem to think it not right to see papa in the bed and could not sleep until 9 or 10 O clock. She truly seemed excited.

As for Mr F & myself we did not sleep until after I O clock. Mr F bought a horse, he settled up all our debts up the county, brought Tommie a fine saddle price 12 dollars, he gave ten, it is a present for studying hard in his spelling class, at Belton school brought himself a pair of nicest Texas made jeans blue blk $1 per yard, 6 doz nice brown jeans for children. Tom Pats gave him a beautiful tortor [sic] shell handle knife. Bro Collier gave him a nice pr blk pants, $5.

The people gave him money enough for preaching to buy him a nice coat & hat save one dollar. Lord Sallers gave him a shaving brush, Benj. Dechard gave him a box of mixed buttons.

Friday Dec 9th I am so sick, I had to lay down a while. Mr F stayed with me all day long. I was so glad. O he has taken such a burden off my poor weak frame, nursing Sissie for me. I feel sure all most on my mind that I have consumption. I have cried most all day. I feel so bad, Mr F sent after supper for Dr, but he would not be found.

Sat Dec 10th It is half after 11 O clock, I have not been out of bed today. I felt so tired. I thought I would rest & see if it would help me. Mr F just went up town brought Dr Gregory, he examined my lungs & says there is no obstruction & not much effected. O may it prove so, he said he knew what would do me more good than any medicine, but he hated to prescribe it. It is the best brandy & loaf sugar 5 or 6 times a day. I do hate to have to keep in my house or take of, that fell destroyer. But when health wasted or waisting is to be restored, a body will take most anything. Jeff has halled one load got one dollar, collected one more, paid 75 cents on his wagon.

I kept my bed all day. Dr Gregory prescribed the best part brandy, said he hated to do so, but he knew nothing that would be so beneficial to my health.

Wednesday Dec 14th Finies birth. Today he is 7 years old. Bro Thomas came to day. We had Finie a cake at supper, it was nice.

Friday Dec 16th Sweet daughter is 9 months old to day. She is crying on the carpet, I must take the sweet thing for we are weaning her & I cannot hear her cry. I have attended to sweet little one, she is evidently talking, O she is all liveliness & goodness. I hope we will soon walk. She is a sweet light of joy & peace in our home this treasured babie.

Saturday Dec 17th Dr. Gregory called to see me a day or two since & then sent me some strange, meanest tasting power I ever saw or tasted. To combine with quinine to be taken 3 times per day, (O what a bitter pill) But they have removed those dumb miserable chilly feelings & my strength is so much greater. I am so thankful, my chest & cough is much improved. As I write Mr F is kindly nursing & singing sissy to sleep. O he has been so good nurse daughter since he returned home. But he has taken all most the entire care of her ever since. She is all most weaned and had been so little trouble. Mr F has been so kind I love him so.

Sunday Dec 18th Mr F has gone 14 miles over the river to fill an appointment, in Brother Jack Walker's neighborhood. Robert & boys as usual have gone to Sabbath School. I feel like if I could have gone to church today, it would have helped me very much. But poor me, it seems that I can never do that. But perhaps it will be better after a while, when sweet daughter gets old enough. But today I had no horses to work. Mr F & Bro T returned late this afternoon, with them a slightly norther. Bro & McFarland & Dechard attended with them upon the worship of God.

Tuesday Dec 20th My health is so much improved. I feel so grateful to the Great Giver of all good, also my good doctor. I cut out as much as 3 prs. of pants for my husband, and frock coat for Finie. Finished Tommies coat, it is a neat fit. He is very proud of it, and well he may be. I have been ashamed of his old ragged one, it was past patching and I had nothing to make the child a new one, until his Papa brought this jeans from Bell.

I feel happier than I have for a long time. <u>We all</u> do better, every thing seems smooth & lovely. Our sweet good baby girl, caps the climax of <u>all</u> our earthly happiness. She still prattles away, is all life & glee. Says, putty, putty, putty for pretty, we think. & she says it so sweetly & looks so cunning out of those sweet bright expressions, talking black eyes. O who would not love such a treasure. She has been so easy to wean, seems so contented without it. Drinks & eats anything that we <u>all</u> eat. I believe she loves sweet potatoes best. As I write she sleeps sweetly in the little cozy crib. Today Jeff halled Mr Dechard one load of wood.

Wednesday Dec 21st I failed to get a wash woman, so Jeff is fixing to wash. Daughter cried a good deal last night. But she is all life & play fullness this morning. As I write she is sitting on her rung, pratting so sweetly at her dear kind loved papa's feet, pating [*sic*] his legs. Robert & Tommie are now studying their lessons in the parlor, clothes washed & froze on the line this afternoon.

Thursday Dec 22nd A very cold day, so much so that Mr F & Bro T returned this afternoon late without looking at the country as contemplated on yesterday. School was dismissed this afternoon for the boys to enjoy the Christmas holidays. Tomorrow evening Mrs Dechard proposes having an exhibition. As it is the close of her term. I received a kind affectionate letter from my much loved La passes [Lampasas] spring friend & Sister M. J. Haynes which afforded me much pleasure. Daughter is so sweet, stood by a chair some time to day, she is so fond of Robert. Tom nice also & Finie, indeed she repays all our kindness with here precious love & sweet smiles.

Friday Dec 23rd Mrs Dechard's examination came off to day & to night I am told she had a very nice exhibition among her pupils. Mr F, Bro Tom, Robert & Finie all attended. I was very anxious to attend but the weather was so cold, I fear to go out as my health is not yet restored.

Sat Dec 24th A pleasant day. Mr & Mrs Dechard called to see us. Tommie has behaved so ugly to day, it has been with great reluctance he has obeyed the least of my commands, after I willingly & with a _pure_ pleasure, let him attend at every hour of Mrs Dechard's exhibition on yesterday & last evening, with the promise that he would cheerfully attend to his work to day, but every thing I have gotten him to do had been dragged out of him. O how sad it makes my poor heart to record it.

Sunday Dec 25th Christmas Day. The memorable anniversary of the Blessed advent of our Savior. But I am disappointed by ideas are gone, O what shall we do with Tommie. He will talk in despite of everything. When it is so improper & ill bred and impolite for children to speak, he regards neither Father nor Mothers counsels. O what shall I do. Will he break my poor heart, I fear his conduct will bring a black stain upon early piety. O my son, my son, would that I could induce you to act propily. [*sic*] O how it would swell my sum of happiness and doubtless lengthen out my days on earth. O you're wicked conduct at Sabbath, a few Sabbaths ago & then again to day on this doubly sacred Sabbath of the Lord, the precious glorious anniversary of your saviors birth.

Jan 7th 1860 I am sorry that I have neglected my journal so long. Since last I wrote in this sketch book, we have all been out to Bro Jacks in the country & spent near a week.

We found that while out there that little daughter had a rising in her head by its running out of her ear and we thought she had the thrush. [Most people have small amounts of the Candida fungus in their mouth, digestive system, and skin. When it grows out of control in the mouth it is called thrush.]

But Dr Gregory said it is sore mouth from a deranged state of the bowels. She has been very fretful, if it had not been for my husband's kindness in taking care of her at night, I expect I would have been sick.

But to day thank the good Lord she has been much better, and quite playful, and talking again. She can say Ball, tar, tea and day, also many other short words. Last night she slept from 2 or 5 O clock until day light without interruptions. Mr F got so sick he vomited in the night, and I the lay next to sweet daughter. He started this morning to fill his first appointment at Hamilton, a small village west of this some 30 miles. [Hamilton County was founded in 1856.] I have felt happy to day to think my husband has again started out to regular preaching.

Sunday Jan 8th Robert & children attended at the Union Church for Sunday school. But there was none, O such bad arrangements. Tommie has been kept one month at the same lesson, when he knows it well, just because his class mates don't know it. Then Bro Thomas, Robert & Tommie attended church, listen to a very good but a flowery one. At night Bro T & Robert heard him again, they said he preached pretty good again, but that he is not a "deep" man. This is what I have long since thought about him. I mean the Methodist pastor J. W. Phillips who has just arrived.

Tuesday Jan 10th Emma has commenced ironing & pouring water on my ash hopper to make soap. [The ash hopper was made out of wood because lye would have eaten nearly anything it was put in. In making soap, the first ingredient required was a liquid solution of potash commonly called lye. A ceramic or glass jug was needed to catch the lye drippings from the bottom of the hopper. One or two gallons of water were poured on the ash hopper until it just began to drip into the catch container. The lye, water, and grease were combined in a container over heat and boiled, stirring constantly. The soap had no unpleasant odor when it had completely cooled. Sometimes drops of peppermint were added to give it a nice smell.]

Monday Jan 16th Emma is washing & running down my ash hopper. Mr F has gone uptown to sell Isham to Mr Kavanough, at Ishams selection. To day our daughter is 10 months old. She is talking & walking by chairs. Take hold her sweet little hands & she will walk all over the house. O she is a treasure, she scolds & says ah daughter, it sounds so sweet, she is all loveliness, all sprightliness what could hearts desire more.

Well Isham is sold, $1400, we only lost $100 in the trade, and that is fine trading for us. We paid it all out for debt except 2 or 3 dollars. [Louisa did not mention Isham's wife. Both of them were bought to keep them together. I suspect she must have died.]

Tuesday Jan 17th Emma is finishing washing & ironing today. Aunt Phebe, Mr Carters black woman has made me $10 dollars worth of soap today I presume or more. It is half barrel at least, it is splendid soap. I think I will see to this, & see it is not wasted, as my last was, by careless hands. With those 2 or 3 dollars Mr F brought me, half dozen nicest plain white cups, & saucers, also plates I ever saw, price 50 cents each. Also a half dozen nice dinner knives, white handles price $1.50 I would have thought $3.00.

O I feel gratitude that so much so much of our indebtness is now liquidated. May we soon pay the last cent we owe, and go in debt no more for ever.

Wednesday Jan 18th/60 My soap maker arrived about 9 O clock, about ten at Finies earnest interest I smugly tucked little daughter in her little wagon, kissed her sweet ruby lips, whilst he pulled the little willow wagon with its rich invaluable treasure to the ditch where her dear Pa was fining the bridge. O what a messenger of love & peace she is in our "home."

Night has drawn her sable mantle around us. My grease is now all made into nice, choice soap. I have a large keg full, I presume nearly a flour barrel full. Must be 150 lbs. It looks like molasses candy, it is so thick & nice. I am to pay the woman one dollar for her work, the soap is worth bit a pound cash. [25 cents] I am so thankful about my soap. Mr Nichols gave Mr F the keg for to put soap in.

Thursday 19th Jan Mr F is cutting & I am cooking pumpkins. Jeff halled the tinnes [sic] one load of wood for which he was paid one dollar, and then, cooked us a nice dinner of chime & crackling head [probably specially prepared parts of a hog]. I enjoyed my dinner so much that I eat too much. My old symptoms from which I have suffered so much have returned.

LaGrange Courthouse built in 1856, as it looked when it was also used as Louisa's church. From Fayette County, by F. Lotto, published in 1902.

Sunday Jan 22nd A pretty day. Mr F preached at our place of worship here which is the court house.

Jan Tuesday 24th A lovely day. I set up with daughter until after 10 O clock last night. I have been troubled with headache all day. We set a hen to day on 17 eggs and sold 2 doz at 20 cents per doz, with the 40 cents Jeff bought me 2 yards crash for towels. [A crash towel was a blend of cotton and linen with a rugged, coarse weave.]

Mr Redding sold our Brooksville place, for which we gave $600 in trade, for $400, wagon $150, two horses one $100 the other $75 and 75 to be paid in money in six months. [Brooksville was settled in the early 1850s and became known as Florence by 1857. It was about thirty-five miles north of Austin.] A Mr Lumpkins just arrived with them. I am sorry Mr F is absent but I will send for him. I patched & darned Robert's coat.

Wednesday Jan 25th My symptoms all gone. I feel pretty well, except headache. I think that is caused by loss of sleep. I did not sleep a bit last night until after 11.

Thursday Jan 26th We closed the trade made and the man started home after dinner. I think it a bad trade for us. Paid expenses on horses 35$.

Sat Jan 28th We drove to Mr Wilcox's furniture shop & then to his furniture store. I wanted to purchase a China press, but he had none but what was sold. [These were two cabinets that are enclosed, one above and one below. The one below formed a tabletop.] We bought Sissie a pretty high cain bottom for her to sit up to the table and eat in price $3.

Tuesday Jan 31st Bro & Cousin Mc came up to meet in official capacity as a church session with Mr F (whom I believe they view as their pastor) to get a legally written document authorizing Mr James Haynie a member of this town. To solicit donations, during his business trip in New York & with those donations to purchase a Bell for our Church edifice that we are about building here. O may he succeed in so laudable an enterprise. Finies dressed clean & nice to go to school this morning. But in as much as his Papa could not go with him, he put it off until after dinner, as which time he is <u>very</u> desirous to enter Mr Dechards department as a regular scholar for the present session. Mr F was prevented attending with Finie on account of being present with Jeff at the commencement of our farming operations. Mr F gets the use of Grandmaw McAshans farm, 8 acres, 2 years for putting it under fence, which joins ours.

I am glad this session has opened with a full school, a good many new students. 6 O clock in the afternoon the norther is here, it is still dark & lowering in appearance. Mr F took our bright blue eyed Finie to school e'er they started. I retired with my precious boy alone to pray to go with my child, shield protect him from vice sin or folly in every form. To secure this endless pleasure you must be kind and loving to your playmates. Be affectionate dutiful & obedient to your teaching & parents, kind to your servants. Despise immoral & profane conduct. Act virtuously in <u>all your ways</u>.

Remembering your parents anxiety about you and especially your Mother's daily secret prayers, for & with her boy. O Finie how fondly this fond Mother's heart clings to you and prays & desires your usefulness & honor in this life & that life that is to come. Think of this my child, my child think of the responsibility that even now rests upon you & grows with your growth, the example you set before your little dear Sister, she watches all you do.

When you are at school you are tempted to act wrong, do not think that Mother cannot see me. But with reverence like a little Christian boy, remember that God is in the sky and watches & sees all that I do. Learn at once to act from principal, act like a man when you do a thing, do so because you know it is right. And ever have in view the great & coming day, when you have to stand before the Great I Am That I Am and give an accounting of all you do.

I stepped on the porch just ee'r the sable mantle of night was thrown oe'r natures works. And with inexpressible (Mother's delights) delights, I beheld our 2 boys for the first time in life returning side by side from school. Tommie walking next & manly, Finie skipping & playful as a lamb. O how pleased & happy I felt & thankful to the great donor for such a gift (of 2 boys) I stood in my door & watched them as they came in, they both ran into Mother's wide extended arms. I fondly pressed our boys to this fond throbbing heart & prayed & blessed them.

Wednesday Feb 1st Jeff is ploughing, our boys are at school, Emma is ironing for me to day. John is cleaning up the kitchen, daughter is standing by a chair near me saying <u>O don</u>, she means O John. She has one more tooth, she now has 5. Mr F set another hen for me on 15 eggs.

Thursday Feb 2nd We have had supper & family worship. Jeff & John washed dishes, & set the table, ready for breakfast, & neatly too. Jeff has gone to clean up in the kitchen & then to his book, he studies every night. I believe Robert & Tommie are at their studies in the parlor.

I dressed sweet lovely daughter for sleep. John walked & sung her to sleep. I laid her cozily in our bed, put sweet oil & wool in her dear little ear, then heard Finie's lesson, ready for him to recite to Mrs Dechard in the morning.

Mr F is sitting beside me at our fireside studying, preparatory to preaching an anniversary sermon next Sunday at our place of worship here, and trying to raise a missionary collection upon that day as it is our beloved churches <u>birthday</u>, fifty years since its organization as a church.

Sat Feb 4th We had such a shower this morning that half after nine Jeff had to quit plowing, then he put on the corn that Robert had shucked & nubed & Finie shelled, by so doing I had the rainy moments taken care of. I've had 2 hens setting and 30 eggs to set. I made 2 cup towels today, one for the lock room, one for the dining room. Finished Sissie's hickory eating apron that I made her of a scrap left of John's at his request. He said he wanted her to have one like his. So you see my children, Mamma by this has taken care of the scraps too. How important to take particular care of the <u>littles.</u>

Sunday Feb 5th Mr F preached the missionary sermon to a small audience, collected $10, I presume the inclemency of the weather perhaps prevented a large attendance. As a norther blew up last night I could not attend. I should have been glad to be there. But Mr F paid in my dollar, one for himself. Tommie & Finie handed in 50 cents each. Mr F paid 50 cents for one sweet precious Anna, thus attempting early in childhood to impress our dear children with a burning missionary spirit. Me thinks, I would gladly & proudly give both of my loved bright boys (which I fondly) think blessed with the brightest intellect to so good so holy a cause, if God should direct.

Monday Feb 6th Emma washed for me. Mr F after dinner walked up- town to hear the trial of Mr Burnes (a lawyer) that reside in 20 miles of La Grange, he is the murderer of Mr Bruen, his neighbor. [Cola Bruin was born ca. 1835 in Virginia and married Sarah Rebecca Rose. They had one son, Ryland, who was two when his father was murdered. Bruin's uncle, Joseph Bruin, ran a "slave jail" in Virginia. The jail was the basis for Harriet Beecher Stowe's *Uncle Tom's Cabin*.

Documents indicate that Cola Bruin was shot and stabbed by his neighbor, J. R. Burns. Family history cited the reason as Bruin having permitted a cow to wander into Burns's pasture. Burns was found guilty and was later issued a pardon by the Hon. R. T. Wheeler, chief justice, Texas Supreme Court.

The following was published in the *Alexandria Gazette* and *Virginia Advertiser*, November 24, 1860, page 3: "We learn from a gentleman who received a letter yesterday from Galveston, that Col. Burns, who was tried for the murder of Mr. Cola Bruin, formerly of this city, in Texas last spring has been convicted by the Court of Columbus in that State, but that he has applied for a new trial."[5]]

Mr Dechard & Drake dismissed their school and desired the boys to get leave of their parents and attend the trial. Tommie & Finie were so anxious to go. I had them to dress & go, as they said Mr Drake told them it might be a lesson to them thro life. O may it be a good one. I am told it is distress- ing to see Mrs Burnes there with her two little boys, one of them went to her father (who I am told wears a high head & iron face) and he kissed his little one & fondly patted his head. Had that been my condition before my child how awful I should have felt. But when mind dwells upon the picture drawn by my minds eye, of the poor bereft widow sitting there in her weeds of mourning. My heart sorrows indeed for her sad bereft heart & her little fatherless boy, that I suppose nestles upon her bosom for sustenance. O my soul is it not too bad. And Mrs Bruens brother in law gave evidence to

[5]Information on the Bruin family was found in Iris Rose Guertin, *Navidad Country* (Lulu.com, 2009), 1:98–102.

day, that he saw & heard the difficulty, that Mr Brunes was in sight of his own home and Mr Burnes shot at him, and Mr Bruen throwed up his hand and asked him if he was going to kill a man that had <u>no army</u> and he then stabbed him with his boweknife so deep until he put his foot upon him to haul it out, and when his brother in law came up to him, he found him weltering in his own heart's blood and Mr Bruen exclaimed "I am a dead man." O how horrid can such murders go unpunished? In our proud and happy state?

Our sweet baby stood alone to day, she laughed & seemed to know it was <u>very</u> smart. Her health seems better than ever in her dear life. Her papa purchased Sissie 50 cent worth of the very nicest sugar crackers I ever saw this afternoon, she is so fond of them.

Wednesday Feb 8th Mr F drove out to Bro Griff Killough's for a load of corn. Mr F returned late with 15 bushels. [This was probably Ira Griffin Killough, who was a farmer, stock raiser, businessman, and state representative. He was born in 1830 and served in the Civil War. When the war ended, he returned to his farm in Fayette County. In 1867 he moved to La Grange.]

Friday Feb 10th I feel badly had to lay down & rest. I am weak & nervous but it may be the influence of quinine that I have taken. But I decided to get supper so I rose and cooked biscuits and egg bread, had it most done when Jeff came from ploughing he milked the cow & made the tea & coffee.

I have commenced cooking supper for my health. I cannot find it in my heart to waste time every day to walk for sufficient exercise. I firmly believe that if I continue to sew as constantly as I have done <u>all</u> my life it will kill me. So to make my exercise profitable I have conducted to cook a while & see if it will be beneficial to my so <u>much desired</u> health, that I may live to assist in rearing my beloved olive plants [her children].

Sunday Feb 12th Robert Hodge, another preacher boy, one of Robert's classmates came home with him from Sabbath School, and also dined with us. He is a handsome nice <u>pious</u> young man.

O may the influence of the two young candidates for the ministry ever be for good. Tommie & Finie attended church, Jeff has gone to Darky meeting & is now absent. Our lovely Ibbie is all life, health & sweetness to day. She is daily, it seems, becoming fatter & firmer. O she is such a treasure.

Uncle Mahlon Renick came home with Robert to night. I was about retiring to my nights slumber, had my door locked, so I did not see him. I expect to see him & enjoy his pious conversation in the morning. When Jeff came from Darkey meeting. I had supper on the table ready to eat, he was surprised & pleased, so he milked & fed the good cow, Sissie's "friend indeed." Soon as we were done eating Robert & Tommie arose from our table, went & fed the horses. Jeff & John washed dishes & set table before candle lights. Robert attended church.

Wednesday Feb 15th A lovely spring. So much so it has invited us to begin gardening. Jeff is ploughing our garden. Mr F is cutting the last planting of potatoes to plants. I do hope we will succeed in raising irish potatoes. Most of our town folks have <u>many</u> vegetables up.

Thursday Feb 16th Tommie arose & washed off our porch floor before breakfast, had it nearly done when I got up. Now I think that's pretty smart for a 12 year old boy & it was his first effort & nicely done too. We are gardening, old symptoms returned.

Friday Feb 17th Finie made a speech at school & the boys applauded his so loudly as to interrupt Mr Dechard below, he had to come up to reprove them. Mr Drake said Finie did finely. Tommie perfect lesson all day.

Sat Feb 18th I could not with prudence arise & dress this morning until ten O clock. Our hired nurse tried to get Tommie to leave his work, preparing fuel for Sunday and go with him to see his (T's) dead cow. But he could not succeed then he tried Finie, he easily listened to his entreaties, so off they started, followed the trail where Jeff had dragged her near half mile. Finie in his candid manner came right & told me. Mr F whipped them both & then whipped Tommie for not informing on John for attempting to get him to disobey our fixed rules as a family.

I am so unhappy about Finis <u>disobedience</u>. O what shall I do it seems my heart will break. Mr F & Robert spent most all day gardening, planted May seeds, I presume my garden looks fine. O good Lord grow us a good crop, and we will try to praise thee. Jeff halled up one load wood Dr Gregory 2.00.

Sunday Feb 19th O how I wanted to go to church, but was not able to walk to day, or at last I feared the result. Tommie, Finie & Robert went. Jeff started to church after dinner, but only got to the door, then left & went a visiting, what he means I cannot tell. This his loving and promptness to attend church has ever been a redeeming quality to me. But perhaps he has often played truant as to day, for he pretended to me he had been to church. But as it happen Robert went to church & told me Jeff was not there. Jeff said he only went to the door & then went 2 or 3 places visiting.

O the strangeness or deception (as it seems) of the negro race, but I often hope in my kinder moments try to throw over their faults the mantel of charity, that it is their ignorance owing to the mannerisms in which they are raised. But this will not apply to Jeff. O no. Has had line upon line, precepts upon precepts here a little & there a little and I hope some good examples too, set before him. O with what anxious solicitation I have watched & prayed over him.

A child could not feel much nearer than he does to my heart, his fond religious mother died when he was little boy (she was sister to my own & my brothers nurse) she <u>loved</u> me fondly & truly, she proved this when she left her child (Henry) with my brother, of her free choice, preferring to have him & go with me than to stay with him & let me go hence with my minister, husband into they would up & leave her.

I have tried with Jeff to fill that mother's place. I <u>feel</u> I have done my duty. Surely this is enough to elicit faithfulness from a servant. A <u>Christian servant</u>, member of our own beloved Zion.

Tuesday Feb 21st Mr F corrected Jeff for some of his misdealings in the wood halling business. I am truly sorry Jeff acts as he does. I fear he is a ruined negro <u>& that</u> beyond remedy. Dr Gregory has returned, took tea with us this evening, he says daughter looks finely & greatly improved.

Wednesday Feb 22nd A lovely day again. Mr F has a sore leg, which cripples him considerably. He has a hope of selling a horse this afternoon. I was all absorbed in reading the "Banner," when I heard a noise, I was so frightening I knew daughter had fallen. I jumped & run, sure enough the little treasure had made her way to the edge of the porch & had fallen as Finie said "sprangling" on her face on the ground. I took her up she wept, then laughed so sweetly. I took in the house she cried to go out door again, she lives to be out, she crawls, she can walk any where by holding to something. She is the most cautious child I have ever seen I think. Not so forward as our first daughter, <u>Lou Clemmie</u>, she looked at 11 months old, but did not talk as Anna does at that age.

Friday Feb 24th Our children informed me that Mr & Mrs Dechard & Mr Drakes, departments all meet to declaim & read Compositions this afternoon. Although it is very cold through their urgent entreaties, I dressed took John & daughter over to Mrs McAshans who very cordially took care of her, thence I walked to the College. Heard Tommie & his class recite in Psyiology to Mrs Dechard, also a class in which 2 young ladies, Miss Julia Sinks & Miss Emma Gregory recite in a class of boys to Mr Drake in Algebra, all did pretty well. Then to class the climax Finie read & spelled a lesson to Mrs Dechard. He is only a beginner as will be seen in preceding parts of my journal.

Then we all repaired to Mr Dechard department and listen with interest to declamations & compositions. My biggest boy, as I term him (R. Willenburg) read a fine composition, subject, if I understood it, Teachers & Pupils Responsibilities & how important to recite good lessons & to dig it out ourselves & not obtain a superficial show. A number spoke well, some poorly.

Tommie spoke tolerable only. Finie althou he was so decided he would speak when he begged me to go to hear him when he was called he refused. It being the first time before the schollars [sic] twice. And knowing the full importance of a proper start for my orator boy, I felt all all a Mother's solicitude. I prepped him to me & whispered to him if he did not speak I would switch him. Tommie encouraged him like a little man. Finie then told Mrs Drake he would speak. Mr D told Mr Dechard he looked affectionately at Finie, said Finie will you speak now. O how this Mother's heart beat at this crisis. But my little man mastered his diffidence enough to arise, walk up on the rostrum, made his bow, and spoke,

"My head is bald, my face is small
Old woman is spinning
And thats the beginning
Kill the calf & that half
Knock him in the head with a mall
Throw him over the wall
And that's all."

But he was much frighten and excited and admit the loud cheers that rang thro' the College halls. To attempt to describe the excited & agitated state of my mind would be a vain one indeed. It was so great as to cause me to laugh & weep & the same movement, whilst my little boy was being so loudly applauded, & I presume every other face beaming with smiles & laughter.

Journal #8

February 29, 1860–April 30, 1862

Wednesday February 29th 1860 Jeff went out to the country to hall Bro McFarland a load of corn, price, I presume $2.50. It was near 5 when he returned but I thought I would fix supper & told him to hall Mr P Y McAshan a load of wood $1. This much by my industry.

And taking in sewing & sewing on until 11 & 12 O clock at night in our lonely dwelling, with my little beloved ones around me, in their little couches, soundly, sweetly sleeping. Your Papa off hundreds of miles preaching. Still I kept stitching, stitching until this late hour to get means to purchase for myself clothing, so my husbands <u>small</u> meager, pittance of a salary, which was often under $400 & often I presumed not exceeding $250 a year. [Here are some examples of average yearly salaries in 1860: laborers, $300 per year; privates in the army, $572; firemen, $468; and carpenters, $436.]

I said my children that perhaps I could have married a man that could have added more to my temporal comforts. But never could I have married a man that I loved so intensely, never, no never could I have married a man that could have done so much for my spiritual advancement as your beloved father has done. He has been my counselor, my guide, my companion, my friend all along lifes eventful journey, from the <u>earliest</u> part of my Christian race. I have never got into doubt, fears & conflicts I care not how dark the spots may have been. When I would listen to his counsel, but they have given way as the early dew & mist before the refulgent rays of the sun, that bright dispenser of natural lights to our often darken world.

I often think, Our Kind Heavenly Father brought about our "marriage" by a divine arrangement. This is your Poppa's own words & sentiment. My precious children, my loved manly boys always listen & take you dear fathers counsel. O I have tried it 17 years that is enough to know its value. O listen to your dear fathers warning voice go by its teaching, in will lead you in paths of rectitude, virtue & religion. The good fashion & experimental religion, "time & place religion."

My Anna you cannot love that Papa too dearly. Make O make his very wishes your delights and purest pleasure. I want my sweet little one to love my dear Mama, but you must love Papa best. Your little prattling tongue's accents sweet & mild. I have listen today with delight amid lives turmoil's, you seem little one an angel of mercy sent to us. Your dear Papa calls you our morning star. O May it ever be so, my child, my earth born treasure. Thou art our 7th babe and never did we enjoy before a babe so much, even before our cup seemed running over. Years my child will pass by ee'r you will know or imagine the length of our love to thee, thee our lovely budding rose. May your actions ever be fragrant with that mildness goodness & loveliness that characterizes thy daily young life. My baby girl.

Thursday March 1st This weather is fine for my vegitables [*sic*] that are up in my garden. Jeff has put on his clean white tidy lowels pants, which indeed look like spring. O I will be so glad when our lovely prairies become complete in <u>perfect</u> green. I want milk and butter. Mr F took wagon 10 bushels of corn started to Uncle Johnnie Rabb's mil.

Daughter has called her Papa often today. How fondly she loves this dear father of hers & how proud it makes him. Children have come from school. Tommie has made a fire ready to get supper, ovens lids, & water on ready to make bread, tea & coffee. Finie is attending to Sissie & swept the gallery. John took up ashes. Mr F has just returned, I quit, go & meet him, Sissie has already gone.

Friday March 2nd I felt a calm suborned this afternoon, that surpasses the power of my pen, but Jeff disobedience in not coming home as I bade him, disturbed & vexed me very much. And if this was the first act of disobedience of this kind (besides numberless others) I should not be offended. But it is almost daily occurrence, and to night our monthly concert night and wished early supper. And I have been enduring bodily suffering this afternoon that I feared to stand up long. So consequently I would not cook supper if I had felt disposed to do so. Yesterday he arrived here Quarter after 12 O clock to cook dinner, the evening most dark and so it is that our house is a perfect confusion and no system about it. Which causes me much dissatisfaction. If I had anything fixed with any <u>convenience</u> for cooking purposes,

I would be pleased to cook often to cook supper, but when I make biscuits or bread I have to get on my knees to work it. When I fry or bake anything it is the same, or sit flat on the floor on account of my lameness and then it is with constant suffering in my lame limb, that I perform the work. O the convenience and economy to have kitchen, meal soon, meat. House & dining room all close together.

But a man that has never had to do woman's work, <u>or attend to it</u> and that has had a wife & servant to run & attend to it, knows nothing about its realization.

Wednesday 27th Feb. My head aches, the turmoil within is I imagine the cause from which much of my sickness that has paled this once plump & rosy face & emaciated this form that was once so round and has descended the elasticity with which it used to gayly and pleasantly perform its domestic duties.

Bro Thomas Foster returned this afternoon, our boys ran clapping their hands & met him at the gate. I met him at the dining room door & gave his a welcome smile. Jeff & I were making a peach baked dumplings, peach pies & pumpkin custards for tomorrow, made 6 custards, one dumpling, 2 pies, had nicest luck. I gave Jeff a whole custard when we finished, which made him smile, and promised Tommie one.

Wednesday March 14th The sun has not shown out clearly yet although it is near 10 O clock. Emma has began ironing. I must close & begin my sewing. I have darned a little baby bonnet, daughter would hardly let me finish. She kept walking around my lap, which was side I would hold the bonnet. She would go say papa, papa, papa all the time at the same time trying to get hold of the little sweet white corded bonnet, that Emma had so neatly done up.

About half after 11 Mrs McAshan sent for Emma to come right home. I hated it & so did Emma, but away she run smiling & cheerful, did not return until late. So she did not get some ironing. We to day received 50 lbs lard. Jeff & I completed a 5 gallon jar of preserves into cans to get jars to put lard in. It was full & more than we put into another smaller jar. I cooked my preserves over and sealed them up air tight.

Just I was about finishing Bro & Sister Adkinson came in also with them Bro Paul Meashan, stayed a little while. I gave Sister Adkinson Julias copy book in which I had in compliance with their request written it full of copys. She seemed so pleased with it & praised and praised my writing until she plagued me. [A copy book was used in education and contained examples of handwriting and blank spaces for learners to imitate. Good penmanship at this time was considered an important business skill.]

Friday March 16th Dear old musty ledger, I again turn to your dear old treasured page and record with all a Mother's fondness the birth day of our own sweet Anna Isabella the sixth pledge of our conjugal affection. Today my daughter thou art one year old. Today my daughter your parents hearts are made happy when we gaze so fondly upon that rosy heartful cheek and sparkling black eyes, that expansive marble brow which surly indicates intellect dwelling within. Grand Ma McAshan & Mrs Drake dined with us. We had nice dinner. 3 kinds of cake, green peach dumpling, Pumpkin custards, short cake, Peach preserves, meat, egg bread, tea & coffee, all cooked well.

Emma helped us until dishes were washed. My precious little Anna, we look forward with intense interest to your next birth day. There we will feel the wait is over as we humbly trust & pray by that time those little dear eye teeth, the cutting of which we dread so much will be through.

Sat May 12th 1860 Death has again ravaged our home, and with his dark wreath bore from our midst, our home idol, our "household pet" the morning star of this home circle. The light of our home, Our angel babe, our sweet Anna Isabella is no more. No more will her sweet prattle greet us. No more will her sunny glance meet us. No more will her heavenly smile great us shewing to our enraptured vision her lovely snowy teeth. O no, she is gone, gone to eternity. She cannot return to us.

O my precious Annie Ibbie, would that we could have raised you, but a Mother's, father's & brothers fond intense love would not keep the young pure love wrapped spirit on these mundane shores. On April 30th it winged its way at early dawn, needless of a father's & brothers tears, or Mother wild "wail of woes." Deep do we feel our affliction, these former pages breath all the fondest purest love, that was lavished upon that pure fragile, angel one. It seemed she was the purest creature I ever looked upon. I have dreaded this task ever since her demise, which is nearly two weeks. To day is the first time I felt like that I could perform this painful duty. There is much I wish to write, my sad heart is full. I am all alone. Mr F gone to preach, Jeff to work, Robert gone, Tommie & Finie rode Ball to drive up Bill.

Mon Feb 25th 1861 [The Civil War will begin in less than two months.] The Sunday afternoon. Election held thro out the State for against secession. "Union or disunion of our grand "United States" came off her yesterday, on that account, my kind loving husband remained with us until this morning.

[The question of secession was voted on in Fayette County on February 23, 1861. The secession movement was defeated in Fayette County; 580 votes were cast for it and 626 votes were cast against it. Secession, however, carried in the state.]

O with what intense we await the election returns. O may "Union Forever" be the motto of our beloved state. If she secedes from our grand, once glorious proud and peaceful "Union." I shall feel for the first time in life like leaving her, and casting my lot elsewhere. Where the broad stars and stripes will wave and prove of olds, fanned by every passing breeze or evening Zephyr. But O will it be a mutilated flag, will O will it be shown of it brightest stars. Or will that "peace congress towards which every eye is now turned" with so much interest and intense anxiety. [The Peace Conference in February 1861 was a meeting of the leading politicians at the Willard's Hotel in Washington, DC. The politicians met in hopes of avoiding secession of eight slave states. The seven states that had already seceded did not attend.]

Finie has classed since I have attempted to write upon these dear old musty pages. After relentless death had torn from our fond embrace our idolized Anna, I could not summon courage to write only to mention her premature demise. Still fondly do I love her, deeply & indelibly are her sweet little serving ways engraved upon the tablets of our hearts. Truly yet do we mourn her loss in our little broken chain. But we say God has done it, "it is well."

God has given us another sweet infant daughter, she will be 4 months 15th of March. We call her Mary Nannce, [Mollie] sweet name endeavored to us by its bearer. She is lovely and promising, coos like a dove, talks & laughs, laughs a little aloud. We all love her she is our pet.

(Sabbath afternoon) March 31st 1861 To day Mr F's leg being very sore, and thus' being on the Sabbath, he kind remained at home to take care of Mollie, and as Tommie & I had cooked meat bread, custards and cakes plentiful yesterday, he had no cooking to do, I dressed, met the children half way home from Sabbath school. I sent Finie hastily to his Papa and Tommie returned with me to church. We got home at 12 O clock. Finie and Papa had warmed corn bread and made choice hot coffee. (already) Tommie set it on table with custard, cake and peach preserves, sweet & buttermilk, also butter. Whilst I pulled off my blk silk dress and put on my dotted calico skirt and brilliantine spencer and nursed sweet little daughter. Papa said she did not cry a bit whilst I was gone. (Sallie) the woman Bro Allen has hired came after greens for dinner, I had none. I gave a large pitcher of nice fresh buttermilk churned last evening. She kindly preferred of her own will, to keep Sissie every Sabbath, so I could attend church. Kindness I will thankfully if sister Allen does not object. And think it has certainly come from the Lord, as I have been wishing and <u>fervently</u> praying for some way to open up that my dear little treasure could be well taken care of, so that I could as I used to do worship my kind heavenly Father every Sabbath in "the great congregation." And feel sure that my little Mollie is well cared for by kind loving hands. O God grant that this may be the case now. O help me to trust my little angel "Mercy drop" out of my sight long enough to go up to the house of God and worship there and not deprive myself of such high & holy church privileges as I did whilst <u>our angel</u> Anna Ibbie tabernacle with us and blessed and made our household so happy. O may we not <u>idolize</u> this precious little treasure in the beautiful casket as we (<u>awfully fear</u>) we did. Our departed Anna, sleep sweet <u>sainted one</u> in that lovely village graveyard sweet consecrated spot. Go where we may on earth even that land of "gold and flowers" cannot, shall not, make us forget that dear little mound of earth that once contained one of earth's holiest little gems, & sweet thought we will all meet in heaven. The final happy resting place of the Lords redeemed host, there we will meet <u>our own</u> loved and lovely infant band, our five sweet little "white robed warblers" our two precious infant son; and three angel daughters (perhaps) and <u>doubt-less will</u> be the first to greet us on the heavens high coast, where no turbid, billowy tides will ee'r again disturb and almost founder our little tempest losses bark.

Monday 1st day of Apri We arose earlier than usual, <u>worshiped</u>, breakfast, all things cleaned up. Tommie gone to school, Mr F & Finie try to work a little. Our sweet babe is <u>crowing</u> so sweetly in her little chair in which she sits delightedly when tied in. O the merry laugh & winsome frolicsome glee of childhoods happy hour. Spring is here in all her loveliness, we are droping [*sic*] piece by piece our winter habiliments and putting on spring apparel. I could write more, but duty calls me to perform our dinner and to attend to the <u>pleasant</u> task of <u>pleasing</u> baby. Now an April sun shares light and splendor on all things. 12 O clock, dinner is near ready, Tommie has returned from school, he and Finie are out in the garden cutting down mustard & turnip greens for Papa to sow millets.

We received a letter from Belton containing a deed to a lot there of ours we have sold for $50, which to be paid over to our Agent Col Judge Walker who rents our house & farm there.

Tuesday April 2nd I arose as usual, children much earlier, now worshiped & praying over, <u>all</u> things cleaned up each to their vocation. Mr F cutting wood, Finie attending Mollie in her little willow wagon. Tommie ee'r he starts to school has stepped into the garden to plant a few melon seeds for "Mamma" dear. I must close, read my morning lesson in my commentary and go to my sewing. Tommie has returned from the garden and has started to school. Having no servants we <u>all</u> __?__ our time as much as possible. [Jeff has escaped from slavery.] Which I trust will prove I hope in after life of infinite value to our dear children.

Wednesday April 3rd A cloudy morning, fine for gardens, at family worship, breakfast, all things cleaned up. Tommie gone to school, Finie churning, Mr F attending his riding horse (Johns) lame shoulder, Mollie sweetly sleeping, I have been sewing. To day I commence Sissie the first dress. I am making it out of a beautiful French calico robe of mine which since I put on hoops, it is to short. I also cut out of it, Mollie, 2 morning gowns and strip them. I am robing her little dress, it looks pretty. I have made her a little white jackonet morning wrapper trimmed with pink stripes, a little yokee, [*sic*] the stripes extend into the yoke, it is a pretty thing.

Friday April 5th I have my paper ready to write to Mrs Pollie Quinan, a loved classmate of my youth in St Joseph Academy. [Pollie Quinan was born ca. 1823, and was first married in Matagorda County. Pollie and her first husband divorced, and she married George Quinan in 1850 in Wharton County. George was a lawyer, a judge, and a state senator in 1857 and in 1859. His portrait hangs in the capital at Austin.]

Mr F. & Tommie went fishing after Tommie returned from school, got home after sundown with 17 fish. I made Mollie a morning out of my French calico croppie, it looks pretty.

Sat April 6th 3 O clock, we arose, worshiped, breakfast as usual. Then Mr F cut Sunday wood, brush, took up butter after Finie churned, poured off the buttermilk into pictures, then washed horses shoulder and shaved. While Tommie & I prepared for Sunday, we cooked 5 custards, 3 cakes, stewed apples, boiled meat, fried meat, made coffee, biscuits and corn bread, Sat down to dinner ¼ after 12. Then Tommie cleaned up and now has just finished an answer to his Cousin Bella Leon's letter he received yesterday. Tommie swept the whole house, dusted furniture in parlor, had taken up ashes, wiped dishes and set the table.

Sunday April 7th As Mr F had no appointments he took care of Mollie. Finie stayed with him, Tommie and I attended church. Children & I cleaned up all the house and put all the dinner on the table, save the corn bread and coffee, and just as soon as we returned home, the warm corn bread and choice pot of coffee was set upon the table. After we and horses partook of dinner we harnessed up and drove to Bro Allen's, there we left Tommie & sweet little Mollie with Lauella Allen and Lucy Thames, took Bro and Sister Allen on board with Finie and we drove to Rutersville where Bro A preached to the students of that place, all seemed solemn & attentive. [This town was about five miles northeast of La Grange. In 1856 the college Texas Monumental and Military Institute was located there.]

Tuesday April 9th Tommie has just bid me good morning and left for College. Mollie is so bright & sweet this morning she slept fine last night. Tommie is learning fast says Mr Allen. Aunt Sallie has come and commenced preparations to iron. Sister Allen says I can have her for two days in each week, to wash & iron, every Monday & Tuesday unless company or sickness, then I can have her two other days in the week. I am pleased with this arrangement, she is so nice about her work and seems so kind, especially when she has offered so kindly to take care of Mollie <u>every Sabbath</u>.

Tommie and I after his return from school, dressed, went calling and shoping. We bought Mollie a neat marrow checked muslin dress 9 yrds clime domestic. Mr Shaw gave Finie a pocket handk, not 10 cts. I found each one of my boys a marseilles shirt bosom 25 cts cash, and myself 2 boxes, one neat work box $1 ½ and a portable writing desk price $3, a new journal .50 cents, half ream paper $1.25. When I returned and was told Mollie had cried so much during my absence <u>I could have wept</u> and <u>sincerely</u> wished I had not gone. O how sad I felt when the loved little form "nursed" and sobbed herself asleep upon my bosom. When I laid her down although so sweetly sleeping in the crib and came into the parlor I felt so much like I did when little Anna lay here a corpse. Aunt Sallie had got her ironing, baked me 3 nice love light bread and scoured the little bedroom & hall & gone home, and I presume had her supper done.

Thursday April 11th Mr F. proposed a visit across the Colorado river to Bro Ferrills whom we familiarly call Uncle "Hi". We sent for Sister Allen, she came early, we walked to the boat, crossed, I was tired by the time I got up that hill. We spent the day pleasantly, good dinner, Aunt "Hi" said she hardly ever wanted to see a baby so bad in her life. But her health was so poor she could not come. After dinner Sister Allen walk up to Bro Deharts and returned in time, and we all got home in time. I would not walk so far, so I <u>declined</u> and postponed my visit to Dr Dehart. [People in La Grange had to use the ferryboat to cross the Colorado River. In 1883 a bridge was completed across the river.]

Friday April 12th We are all well, Mollie seems improved, by her visit across the river. She gazed up the river with so much wonder and amazement in her little countenance. We spent this day pleasantly at Mr Sam Mc Clellans, Nephew to Cousin Mc.

After dinner Mr F and Tommie went and halled up a load of studding for our dining room. We on our returned visit for the first time the little dear ground where the infant loved from our Anna reposes. There we bowed with our Mollie around the concentrated spot and prayed for us all to meet with that dear angel one in heaven. There O there may we all meet an unbroken family.

[On this date, the Confederates attacked Fort Sumter in South Carolina and started the American Civil War.]

April Sunday 14th A cloudy morning. Tommie & Finie attended Sunday school and returned to Bro Deharts. We read talked about religion, afternoon we walked to monument hill, where 12 years ago (we sat in our boroush [carriage], on our way from Houston City to Presbtery to Austin City.) We listen to a funeral sermon delivered by Bro McKinney, M E Church south, at the burial of the bones of the chivalrous dead, Capt Dawson's company who fell in our struggle for liberty.

[In 1842 Mexican forces surrounded Bexar (later called San Antonio), and the local militia of La Grange, led by Nicholas Dawson, rode to the aid of the town. When they arrived at Salado Creek, just a few miles from the Alamo, they were surrounded by Mexican forces. After a short fight, the outnumbered Texans were left with the choice of death or surrender. Thirty-eight Texans were killed and the remaining fifteen were taken prisoner. In 1848 the remains of the thirty-eight Texans were returned to La Grange and buried at the top of the bluff, Monument Hill, overlooking the Colorado River.]

Now is a worse, Yes, a more dreadful war in progress has begun. At fort Sumpter and Pickens the contest has begun. O the sad consequences we can not tell. O Lord direct us in these perilous times what we ought to do. What we must do. Bro Dehart was full to overflowing at family worship, he scarce could close his pray for weeping. [As they say, "bad news travels fast." The news of Fort Sumter took only two days to reach Louisa in La Grange. Fort Pickens was located on Santa Rosa Island, in the Pensacola, Florida, area. An attack on the fort was planned before April 12 but not carried out because of bad weather. Fort Pickens was one of the few Union forts in the South to remain in Union hands throughout the war.]

Tuesday April 16th A cool day, pretty sunny day. Nearly flooded last night. Aunt Sallie is ironing for me to day, she scored the stove room & kitchen table. She is running down lye to make my soap. I am pleased with her so far. I hope she will continue to wash for me as long as La Grange is my home. Bro Adkisson dined with us to day. I showed him my "Escritor"—writing portable desk that cost me $3 ½, he says it is worth $5.

The typical writing desk had a tray you wrote on and under it you could keep extra paper. Ink and pens fit in the two trays in the front of the box. The desk would close up tight when you were traveling. Public domain.

I have taken cold & feel badly. Sissie seemed improved by her visit, she is all loveliness sweetness and beauty. Aunt Sallie is making me some light bread. My light bread is done it is very nice. My ironing done nice. Aunt Sallie milked our cows. From what Mr F learned of Mr Seymore, I presume Jeff was killed last of last June, the same month he ran away, if so he followed in the same precise footsteps of his father. He was shot down whilst runny away.

Wednesday April 17th 1861 I received an answer to Mrs Quinan my old <u>loved</u> schoolmate, she writes with such warmth and affection. She says she intends to send our little Mollie a dress before long. She spent last summer in New York on her return heard I had died during her absence and knew no better until she received my letter, which she wrote made her "heart beat with joy."

Friday April 19th Mollie is crying, I must stop. Mr F, Finie and I after breakfast and reading and cleaning up was over and Tommie gone to school, went into the garden with my nice little hoe and rake and worked about half an hour. I felt very tired.

Monday April 22nd A lovely day. We are cozily happily fixed in our "own sweet" home, after a most pleasant visit and I humbly trust not fruitless attendance at the house of God. We arrived at home a few minutes after 11, Soon after Bro McCallem and his dutch man, Mr Fink arrived. We dined a little after 12. All hands at work now making preparatory steps to build my wished for dining room. Which I presume is one thing that makes me feel so cheerful. Mollie is crying I must take her. Aunt Sallie finished washing a large one. A very warm day. Mollie is sorta spoiled. Sister Allen called.

Friday 23rd I feel all most sick. I think is sewing at night. I must quit it. I feel just like I am going to have one of my old nervous spells. Mr Redding is traveling thro' the country in the business of Rorabacks compound soap. Called to see us, he is an acquaintance of ours. He is very friendly & pleasant. I am sick today. [Isaac Roraback developed a new way of making soap and he used it to make two kinds of soap. One was called Roraback's Compound Chemical Toilet soap and the other was Roraback's Compound Chemical Washing Soap.]

Wednesday April 24th A rainy day, Mr Redding still with us. He has given Mr F all the recipes [for Roraback's soap] he can sell and appointed him agent and then Mr F appointed Bro McCallem subagent. I feel very weak and ill fit to sew but I must try. I made apple roll for dinner.

Sat April 27th The prospect fair for more April showers. Mr Redding is learning us to make Roraback Soap and also what he calls "Material" to make it out of.

Monday April 29th Cloudy morning. Since dinner the sun has shone out. Aunt Sallie is washing. I got dinner to day myself inasmuch Mr F told me Tommie might have half we could make by sowing our front pasture. So I made a present of my interest to Tommie and will help him all I can. Mr F is suffering with biles so he can hardly walk. We hate so much to take Tommie from school but he must learn to work too. [Biles was a type of skin eruption like boils. In the Bible it says that Job suffered from biles from the sole of his foot to his crown.]

Mr F and Mr Redding closed up their soap matters by Mr F swapping 1,200 acres of Prairie land east of San Bernard Wharton County for the rights to sell Roraback soap in this and Guadalupe Counties. Mr R bade us good morning and left for Bastrop.

[The average price of land in Texas in 1860 was around fifty cents per acre. This means that this soap deal might have cost the Fosters around $600. Since it was prairie land, it was probably worth quite a bit less. At twenty-five cents an acre it would have been $300. The Fosters would have to sell a large amount of soap to get their money back.

Selling the rights for making Roraback's Soap were being advertised all over the South. An ad appeared in the *Staunton Vindicatory* (Virginia, July 20, 1860, p. 4, www.loc.gov/item/sn84024653/1860-07-20/ed-1ol) selling the right to make the soap. It claimed you could clean muslins or lace with no rubbing. The soap was made with no grease or lye, and it could be made in ten minutes for less than a penny a pound.

In the *Yorkville Enquirer* (South Carolina, June 11, 1856), an article said the soap cleaned in both cold and warm water, and Mr. Westtonland would sell recipes to all who wished to make cheap soap and have clean faces. Other ads offered the rights to making the soap for the sum of fifteen dollars.

The recipe that was given to Mr. Foster for the soap was: six gallons water, three pounds opodeldoc soap of commerce, one pound of sal soda, four tablespoons full of spirits of turpentine, and four tablespoons full of spirits of hartshorn. This made fifty pounds of soap.

Since Finis traveled around so much, he could sell it went he when to preach. I can envision him riding into town telling people, "I can cleanse your souls with my preaching and your bodies with my soap."]

Wednesday May 1st A fairer prospect for fair weather, yet clouds & sunshine both prevail at times. William (colored) Anan is mowing our barley a poor stand indeed. Tommie ploughed all day again, he does finely for a little boy. He has made sign which makes this mother's heart proud. Finie and I took Mollie up to Bro Allen's and Sister Allen said she have her well taken care of. Until Finie and I would go uptown shopping & visiting sick and to see my lawyer Webb on business. I thank her very much indeed. We returned late with Mollie with a beautiful white silk and morino hat, trimmed <u>most</u> tastefully with white silk braid and white satin rosettes made of narrow white satin ribbon, cost $3, price was $4, Mollie 2 white needle worked lawn waists, price $1 and bit each. They are rich and handsome, very cheap, also 3 yrds beautiful pink calico, a dress for Mollie and one to send as a present to Cousin <u>Mandies babe</u>. Mollie a beautiful leather basket, it is made of black and red strips of leather, pleated nice handle and top with black buttons & india rubber loop. It is a pretty thing $1.50. One mosquito bar, to cut up for table covers to keep flies off, and cover for Mollies wagon. One dollar of opodeldoc soap of commerce, $1.00 of cochineal [Cochineal was used to dye textiles, drugs, and cosmetics.] $1.00 oil of sassafras. [This oil was used to treat skin problems, achy joints, swollen eyes, and insect bites or stings. Maybe Louisa got it to treat her husband's biles.]

Thursday May 2nd A rainy morning. Bro Mc & Mr Fink cannot work, so they are going fishing. Finie is churning, returned just before dinner worried a little and went home after want of plank to finish my room. He and Mr F had a settlement, I believe he still owes us $8½.

Sat May 4th A gloomy morn, especially so for a May morn. This green month of the year generally sets in with brightness & sunshine. War excitement high, for peace once more to swell in our land. How it disturbs the peace and quietude of the fireside to be thus harassed with the exciting war news of the day. O god bring order out of confusion, hear the <u>prayers</u> of <u>thy</u> faithful <u>few</u> and __?__ rule all things for thy <u>names</u> glory and let peace once more be ours as a grand peaceful and mighty nation. [On May 6 Jefferson Davis approved a bill from the Confederate Congress that confirmed that a state of war existed between the Confederacy and the Union.]

Monday May 5th An exceedingly warm day. Mr F was so cripples with his biles that he could not go out to Clear Creek to help Bro Jack, nor <u>even</u> attend church here.

Tuesday May 7th The sun shines brilliantly. After all got up this morning unsuccessfully for me. I a good nap I feel better. I need more sleep to make up my lost sleep which I have lost on account of the exciting times.

This morning is cool enough for fire. The clock has just struck six, breakfast is not quite ready. While it is cooking I thought I would take of the moments and write in my journal. Mr F is not done with milking our cows. Yes, he has come I must go and strain our milk. We had early dinner just as we got cleaned up Sisters Allen and Dehart came and spent the afternoon, to say I enjoyed myself I cannot. Sister Allen makes such uncalled for remarks that it makes me feel so unpleasant. Sister Dehart seem as usual very friendly and I could have enjoyed her company. She promised to come and dine with us tomorrow. [The discussion of the war may have come up, which Louisa would not want to talk about. The people in the county were split in their support of the war. Louisa was against it, and perhaps Sister Allen was voicing support for the Southern cause.]

Thursday May 9th A warm morning, breakfast about ready Mr F has just brought me the milk, I must go and strain it. Bro Hill came out spent the night with us, we sat up until midnight. Mr F sold him a soap recipe $10.

Friday May 10th We are all hurry to get ready to start to Mr F's appointments. O so hope the good Lord will bless us all abundantly [.] We drove 14 miles to Old Bro Green's. When we got here she had just got out of sight, going to sat up with a sick babe, old Bro G got back to late to go after her. He has two grown daughters here, we will do very well but regret that Mother Green is absent. He said and so did Martha that mother G "would be so sorry when she found out we were here and she were gone." Mr F sold a soap recipe to Bro G for a milk cow and a balance 5 for preaching.

Sunday May 12th Mr Wall came down and spent the afternoon and then had us all to go home with him and spend the night. Had nice supper near 12 at night, we were visited with a severe storm, hail, high wind, rain in abundance. We had to leave our little bedroom which seemed tottering to its very center and take refuge in Mrs Walls family room, the wind flashes of lighting and hail falling in our faces was quite a scene. Mr F told me to go to Mrs Walls room and he would bring Mollie. He said when the hail and rain fell in Mollies face she squalled, bless her dear little heart, she was so scared.

By this time Tommie & Finie awoke so frightened and hollering, their bed in so short of time was drenched in rain & hail. No one was hurt. We felt gratitude to God for protecting in such a storm and waring of elements.

Mrs Wall and I had many laughs over our first visit & first acquaintances, all mixed up in her room in our night clothes.

Thursday May 16th Dark and lowering as it looked to day we drove to Uncle Highs, the River was looming high. No crossing done at all. We were compelled to drive back to Uncle Highs and stay all night.

Friday May 17th A pretty Sunday morning. Mr F went over the river in a skiff but would not risk children and "Mamma" in it. Returned about 2 found all right at home to our pleasure we found our shacks had not been blown down. No hail her nor high wind, but heavy all most constant rain. Aunt Leigh had all my things done up just by the time we ready to start. Soon after we started we had quite a disaster with Bill [their horse] stalling, we all save Tommie the driver, we all had to walk up that that high rough rocky hill. Mr F packed Mollie, she looked so sweet & cozy in her papa's dear arms in the rain, and it rained on us all afternoon. When we came to the crossing of Williamson's creek it was impassable caused from the late rains. We drove back to Mr Cox's just in sight of the road, he told us Mr Alexander lived at another crossing, just before we got there Mr [F] told me Mr & Mrs Alexander were old acquaintances of ours. When we got there she met us with all the warmth of true <u>Southern friendship</u>. She knew us but could not call our names. I believe it had been ten years since we last met.

Wednesday 22nd Heard the river was impassible so we returned, Bro Mc's children helped Mr F & Tommie to set out our potato slips. We have a nice large patch between a quarter and half acre.

Thursday May 23rd Just as we were ready to go to Cousin Mac's, Cousin Amanda sent for us. She took the children in the carriage and away we went. Kind and pleasant visit. Made some nice Roarback soap, Made Cousin present of the recipe and gave <u>them all</u> a cake of the soap.

Friday My 31st Mr Dechard came over before breakfast and bought a soap recipe which paid Tommie's tuition. We drove to the store I purchased for Carrie one pr of shoes, cost $1.75 and 3 doz $2 calico and for Mollie embroiding for 2 dresses. & 2 shirts. Tommie got Finie a ten cent bugle, all at Ma Friedbergers.

Sunday June 2nd A pretty morning. Mr F still sick in bed and he is taking quinine, Mollie's cold is most well. Finie hoarseness has gone away. I was introduced to Mr Andrew Green this morning son of the old man. He has another fine cow for us. We had a more vegetable dinner.

Monday June 3rd A foggy morning, we have found this a very kind family. Mother Green is putting us up a nice bucket of butter, and she told Mr F last night if we remained in LaGrange next winter she would give us a nice fat hog and she gave Tommie a pr of guinea and Finie a guinea hen.

Aug 20th / 61 Mr F left us last Tuesday week at Jim Osburns, to go to Presbyterian 9 miles below Austin. I have not heard a word from him since he was to have returned to Mr Osburns last Wednesday. Well what must I do? I must start home and see if I cannot hear from my husband. I hope he will come this afternoon.

Monday Aug 21st I am so uneasy about my husband that I feel I can hardly sew at all. I do hope he will come to day, if he does not I must start somewhere and I don't know where. I had best go. I was so anxious to go to Columbus and see him and for Mr F, to see about our soap business there. Night has thrown her sable curtain around us. My husband has not yet returned. I have written a long pencil letter to Mr F tonight.

Thursday Aug 24th A very rainy morning, rain slowly all night. After 3 my dear dear husband came in love & smiles as I dreamed. I had just laid Mollie down to sleep. I took the <u>sweet thing</u> up and went to the fence to meet him, he affectionately impressed a lovingly kiss on each one of us. Bony came with him to take the horse back to Mr Taylor.

Sat Eve Aug 31st 1861 We are preparing to start in a few days for Bell County. I hope it will be a trip of profit, to soul and body. O may it be a benefit still to our now fat smiling pratting Mollie. We are planting a full garden.

April 1862 Wednesday Well here is my dear fathers old ledger again. I thought I would not neglect writing in my journal more. I am sorry I did not keep a sketch of our trip spoken of here on the foregoing pages. My fond hopes in regard to Mollie were realized, but during Gabriel camping she liked to have died. But Dr Owens happen to be there and cured my precious child. We went us as high as Bosqueville. Attended a pleasant Synod, precious revival there cheered many a weary soul, tempest looked upon the wary sea of life. [Bosqueville was a small town several miles north of Waco. Bosque Academy was about five miles north of Waco and was headed by John C. Collier, a Cumberland Presbyterian. In 1869 he was asked by leaders in Mansfield, Texas, to come and establish a school. Collier conducted the Mansfield Male and Female College from 1870 to 1887. He even dared to admit girls to his college.]

We returned to La Grange, found one of our little bedrooms broken open, a few bedclothes and a few buckets taken. We Sold out all our interest

Photo of John Collier ca. 1860s from the
Mansfield Historical Society

in Fayette, paid our debts, brought some articles that we needed and a little flock of sheep.

We moved to Bros Johnson's on Gabriel, stayed here one month, rented a 20 acre field and cabin one room 15 ½ feet square and a shed room about 8 feet wide., the shed __?__ like a riddle on one corner of the yard is a shanty we use as a lumber room. We halled up a small log cabin and fixed for a kitchen. We share planted corn, wheat, Barley. Oats, Sugar cane, Hungarian grass and a garden. Planted an irish potato patch, and a nice sweet potato bed, all things look well.

[Louisa did not share why they had left La Grange. The family appeared to be happy there, and Louisa was building the house she wanted. I suspect that the war may have had something to do with it. Currency began to dry up in La Grange as the war progressed, and money became tight. Cattle and other foods were needed for the war effort, so their stock and crops may have been taken. Since many of the men were away in the army, there was a fear that the large enslaved population might rise up and take revenge. These factors may have caused the Fosters to leave their home with very little.]

I am thankful that Mollie has got to be perfectly fat and rosy, she is running everywhere and is talking, begs so sweetly for tity, tity. Will kiss anyone to get tits, she eats hearty, likes fat meat bread and gravy better than anything else.

I am now convinced that I have been too tender with my previous babes and that perhaps caused their premature death. For after I came up here my friends and Dr Barton told me to let Mollie rough it. Dr B told me every pleasant day in the winter to let her play outdoors and one hour each day to let her stay out bareheaded in the sun. I did it fearing trembling. Thank kind heaven, happy indeed has been the result. I have given her only one-half tea spoon of Castor oil and little turpentine in it. And 2 or 3 doses of chalk mixture since I commenced pursuing this plan. She seems not as hard as a pine knot, she has a bad __?__ but it don't make her sick. Mr F and Tommie are ploughing the corn. I have kind neighbors. Monday a friend sent me a ball of nice butter. We had eaten most all up. I was feeling sorry it was so near gone and to day another friend sent a bottle of milk and a tin cup full of nice butter. My neighbors has often sent me honey combs, rib sauce, sausages and bones.

Sunday April Yesterday Mr F & Finie set out 280 sweet potato slips while Tommie and I made and cooked some Molasses cakes for Sabbath.

Monday April 21st A clear sun is shining but we really have a winters morning. Our corn looks like it is frost bitten. I fell dull and drowsy, it is not 8 O clock and Mollie has gone to sleep. Tommie complains of being sleepy.

I had 8 little chickens this cold spell has killed one. I have no coops as yet. Mollie has awoke after about 5 minutes nap, got out of the little trundle bed and came to me and asked for titty. O she begs so sweet for titty, some times says titty and will kiss anybody to get titty and cuts a heap of sweet shines over titty.

Sunday April 27th A bright sunny Sabbath has dawned on us again. Yesterday morning Mr F started to Round Rock to file Bro Flowers appointments there today, from there he expects to go to Belton on business if his rheumatism in his back gets better. And perhaps go on to Collins County Texas to see Bro Robert Foster's family, he has gone to the war. They recently fled to Texas as a place of refuge from the indian nation, admit the woeful commotions of this sad sorrowful war.

[Robert Foster lived in Collin County and joined the Confederate Army with his brother John on July 5, 1862. The brothers joined Company K of the Fifth Texas Partisan Cavalry Regiment, commanded by Col. Leonidas

Martin. Much of their time was spent in the Indian Territory in Oklahoma, until they were discharged after the surrender. Robert died in 1911 and is buried in Scott Cemetery in McKinney, Texas.]

Monday April 28th We are sad this morning, Mollie darling was sick all night vomited off and on all night, vomited twice this morning, the last time a great deal of bile. I sent Finie in a lope on Ball after Uncle Enoch. I had strong notions of sending for Mr F, but she took a nap, awoke better. I thought I had better not send for him as it was so important for him to take this trip.

Soon as Amelia heard Mollie was sick she told her pa she was coming up, so early after breakfast here come my <u>kind good</u> Amelia, about eleven Roena returned to stay all day and night with me. Bro Johnson sent Finie with a jug of milk to boil for Mollie. She could hardly wait until it was boiled. Amelia kindly fixed it with biscuits and a little black pepper in it. It now nearly 4 O clock. Mollie is playful and seems better, her bowels have moved twice to day. I was pretty sure this spell was caused by eating peas for dinner yesterday. Caroline is washing for me to day, her little boy <u>Gus</u> is now helping Finie cut stove wood. O I do pray the good Lord to spare our precious Mollie's life to us, she is so sweet, such light to our home she cheers every moment of our lives. Roena and Amelia are a going to stay all night with us.

Tuesday April 29th Sweet dear Mollie slept good all night, did not ask for tity all night, woke up and nothing would do but before I finished my toilet she had to have tity. She is quite playful. O I do think the good Lord that she has got well. It is 8 O clock at night Roena went home to fix her Pa off to hunt Indians. So she sent for Allie Price to come and stay with me. She is here now and will stay until tomorrow evening.

Wednesday April 30th Mollie was sick last night. Amelia rode Ball home before breakfast and sent her Pa up to see Mollie, he thinks she is not much sick. We gave her a teaspoon full of castor oil and 4 drops of turpentine. I feel so uneasy about her. I wish her poppa was at home.

Journal #9

May 1, 1862–April 8, 1866

———————

Thursday May 1st 1862 This morning is one of those bright anointing mornings that so often cheer our hearts in this lovely South-land of ours, that our kind heavenly father has lavished too much upon to beautify it and make it a comfort to us His people. If we would only in mass appreciate it and feel gratitude to the Great Donor of such benefits. But alas! Our national sins I believe has brought thus <u>dreadful war</u> up on us. O that this people would seek the Lord and learn righteousness and I firmly believe all would have peace and plenty. I am so thankful to say that Mollie is most well. She played last until ten O clock. She slept very well, but I had to let her suck in the night.

Sat May 3rd 1862 A beautiful morning, sunny and bright. Bro Johnson brought up his plough with 1 yoke oxen threw up 8 sweet potato ridges for Tommie & Finie to set out slips. I fear if we move from here we will never meet with such kind friends again.

Sunday May 4th Tommie had 3 boys to dine with him this evening. My feelings were indescribable O how I wished my husband was here. Mollie seems to be better. I had dinner ready when Tommie returned from Sunday school. I read several chapters in Parley's History. [Peter Parley had several history books out before 1862.]

Monday May 5th A bright & sunny morning but <u>all</u> is wet and muddy under foot and well it might be it rained nearly all night and we had 2 hail storms one just after nine, and one about 11 O clock. Finie has taken Roena home, and to get sweet potato slips. I received a letter from Mr Foster this morning dated Round Rock. His health is improved he thinks he will go on to Collin, I hope now he will, then that dreaded trip will be over. He hated to go on this trip so much but duty compelled him. [If this is Collin County, it is just north of Dallas and almost three hundred miles from Round Rock.]

I am so glad that I got a letter from my husband. He writes that he had bought me a flour barrel and a bottle of sarsaparilla at Mr Oat's. [Sarsaparilla in the United States was originally made from a blend of oil and sassafras, the dried root bark of the sassafras tree. It was widely used as a home remedy, and if enough taken, it induced sweating, which some thought had health benefits.]

1860s ad for Ayer's Sarsaparilla, from the Library of Congress

Tuesday May 6th 62 A coolish morning, all our company are gone home. Finie has gone and bought milk and now has gone after the wash board and some soap. Tommie is now washing, he and Finie are going to try their hand in washing up all the clothes.

Thursday May 8th I slept poorly last night, the cat got in the bed twice. I had to get up and walk about the room a thing I never had to do at home. When my husband is at home his kindness does that much for me. And when he is gone Tommie gets up, but here Tommie slept in an adjourning room. I had to go in there and awake him. I feel like this morning I had taken cold. I was afraid to take Mollie out this cold damp morning. I made and baked nice biscuits and fried meat. When Alex came his Ma sent me some nice butter but nearly sufficient last our little family one week. My neighbors are so kind to me.

The young folks say I must give them the History of the Mexican invasion of Texas at an early day and the Texians run a way scrape. [The Runaway Scrape took place in February 1836, when Antonio López de Santa Anna began his conquest of Texas. His army marched from the south-central portions of Texas toward the Houston area. Residents in this area fled, mainly toward the coast, from the Mexicans. Louisa was fourteen years old, and her family lived in the affected area.]

Friday morn May 9th/ 62 Tommie is hoeing out my garden. Bless his heart. Finie has gone after milk and acted badly to day. I had to whip him. My heart now aches about this way ward child of mine, that is so dear to me and for whom I feel so much deep solicitude. Will O will he ever do better. I fear every body will hate him.

Sat May 10th 62 Tommie is cutting wood cheerfully for Sabbath. I hope Finie will do better for me to write in my journal, than he did yesterday. I have cleaned up my room, bushed, put on clean all most snow white sheets and pillow slips, bolster do, Do, and toilette cover.

I have patched a pair of Tommie's & Finie's sheets also Tommie's hickory shirt to day, read my chapters. Tommie has worked well to day again. I read to Finie about what I wrote his misconduct, it cowed him, he looked serious a good while. To day in general only when I sent him to Bro Reed's for milk he has done pretty well, he said rejoicingly to me that now Mommie must write I have been a good boy, he said Mother why do you write that journal? I told him it was for My Dear children to read when Momma is dead, and then they could see how they acted when children. He looked serious a good while & then said I know you will be able tomorrow to write good about me.

Sunday May 11th Tommie stayed with me he has acted shabby to day. Finie went to Sunday school and brought Amelia home with him, she I believe visited me from pure love to her dear Aunt Lou. I hope I may do this kind Motherless young friend of mine good, and may she comfort me in my lonely hours. Finie has not acted as he promised. He has done badly and tolerable good at one time. I am much perplexed. I have the blues. I fear we will have no company especially girls to night. I sent Finie for Jane Hughe's her step mother told him she was not at home. Tommie said let him go for Myra Price. He did so but said she could not come.

Monday May 12th Finie acted ugly when he first got up this morning. Since that he has done pretty well. I hope he will be a good boy so I can write it in my journal. Tommie has been busy packing rocks out of the wheat all morning. He says he has killed one little rattlesnake, 2 centipedes, 2 scorpions, one lizard. I am so fearful my children will get bitten.

Mollie looks so hearty again she spends a great deal of her time in the yard. She can open the gate. She delights to get outside and pick up rocks she has just come in and said baby. She call her doll Amelia made her baby. Dinner is over, Tommie has returned to his arduous labor packing rocks. I feel for <u>my child</u>, but I trust he will get done this afternoon. Finie is doing pretty now. He is now a smart boy. I hope my dear little boy will continue to do good. Finie says that I must write that Mollie is sitting in the door calling papa and brother.

Wednesday May 14th Tommie, Finie and Mollie rode Ball, I rode behind Mr F home. I had not been on a horse for 5 or 6 years before I felt awkward, soon we got into the house. Mr F caught me fondly in his arms, embraced and kissed me with all the order of our faithful love. We talked until midnight. He had so much to tell about, Sister and the dear little ones of our loved relatives he says Bro Robert was sent to Corinth, and it is expected that he was in that last battle there. [The siege of Corinth, Mississippi, was an engagement lasting from April 29 to May 30, 1862. The siege resulted in the capture of the town by Union forces.]

Before Bro Robert left the nation the jayhawkers came in three days of lounging. Bro Robert, had it not been for the kindness of a friend that lived 40 miles off our dear bro' would have been no more. [Jayhawkers was a term that came to prominence in the Kansas Territory during the 1850s. The term became affiliated with gangs of guerrillas who clashed with proslavery groups from Missouri.] I fear O I fear we will never see him again on earth. But if not may be meet at the feet our blessed savior.

Tuesday May 20 /62 We dined early, had a nice biscuit butter and egg bread for dinner. Finie would make the egg bread and cooked it and the biscuit too after I rolled and cut them and all were very nice. About 3 O clock we had a terrible hail storm, stones as large and larger than a hen egg. We feared they would break in our capboard roof. [Clapboard was the word for long, thin boards that were used for walls and roofs. They were usually made of split oak, pine, or spruce.] Mr F put on his hat and took sweet little Mollie in his arms she was so frighten whenever papa put her down but seemed happy and felt safe in his arms. O the trusting confidence of a child in parental protection. Safe when in dear papa's or mama's arms.

I put my sore hand on my head. Thought that would not do to have it pelted with hail stones, for every moment we expected our old roof to give way. Then I put my hand on my head for a sorta shield but to our consolation the storm was of short duration and thank kind heaven no harm done our little family.

Thursday May 22nd Mr F read awhile and then slept a good while woke up in a great way about dinner. Tommie washed out 2 handkerchiefs and 4 aprons for Mollie. It is so wet and owing to my condition I feel that I cannot go into the kitchen without risking my health. So I will have to depend upon Tommie which makes me nervous. I find it best always to arise from our beds of repose by times, and then do some work at its proper time. This is like autumn, it is nearly 4, the rain has ceased. Mr F went to Bro Johnson's he informed him tomorrow was the last day to pay our tax at Georgetown.

In 1862 counties in Texas, in accordance with an act of the state legislature, placed a war tax on property above $2,000 in value. In Fayette County the tax was twenty cents on each $100 worth of property. The script raised money for destitute families of soldiers. The "War Tax Script" was issued in denominations of one, two, and three dollars. From the book, *Fayette County, Her History and Her People*, by F. Lotto, 1902, page 130.

Friday May 23rd A gloomy morning. My spirits partake of its dark clouds. Mr F has gone to Georgetown to pay his war tax.

I know he can find more things to take him from home and accomplish less by his absence than any person I ever have known. For we for the most part live from hand to mouth, but I suppose it makes no difference. A few more years at most and we will be done with the servitude of earth and if we gain heaven it will be enough, we will all be happy then.

Sat May 24th 62 Mollie has just taken a sweet nap and awoken laughing and got up herself, and is now playing with my journal. Mr F returned about 8 O clock last night from Georgetown, he was so tired he could not sleep until midnight.

Monday May 26th 62 Mr F & Tommie are hoeing. We sunned all our beds to day and anointed our bedsteads with corrosive sublimate to keep the bugs down. We are not troubled as yet. [For generations, people took their bedding outside to be cleaned and deodorized by the sun. Corrosive sublimate was a highly toxic chemical that was used as a wood preservative, rat poison, insecticide, and fungicide.]

Made Mollie a doll and dressed it. She cuts capers over it, calls it her baby, it has on a red skirt. I made the waist of my dress, after getting dinner washing some and nursing my sick little daughter. She was right sick this morning. I did not get to eat my breakfast until 8 O clock, but thank the Lord she seems as well as ever this afternoon.

Tuesday May 27th 62 I wish, I pray God to give us good leaders in political affairs. Me thinks if we as a Nation had been blessed with such leaders, never would the land be the scene of such carnage and bloodshed as has so recently drenched some parts of our south-land.

Finie and I cooked dinner, we boiled meat and greens and made and boiled gusse dumplings, made bread and one short cake. By the time I picked my greens, cooked read and wrote as usual. I sewed but little before dinner, I made my sleeves and sewed them in my waist. I hemed a little narrow ruffle for the pointed cuff at the hand, the sleeves are mutton legs.

Thursday May 29th I have washed my greens ready for dinner, and made up beds and cleaned up all. Finie fried meat & onions nice. We found a mouse nest she and her young in my cupboard. Tommie killed the little ones, put the cat in, she caught and eat the mama. I then got me a pan of hot suds, scoured the cupboard inside and out and washed everything that was in it and placed them back neatly. It looks clean and nice now, but I tell you I am so tired I feel that I can hardly live.

Friday May 30th Mr F and my precious Tommie finished hoeing the corn, came in and we had an early supper. Finie hunted the horses around could not find them, then he put a rope around the dog, Troops neck and so they merrily trotted off, after the fine sheep. When he got to Bro Johnsons he turned Troop loose. He arrived at home ¼ hour before Finie. I felt so uneasy about my boy, but ee'r dark closed in my precious Finie came with the sheep, his little shirt was right wet with sweat he ran so. I kissed and kissed my boy.

Sat May 31st Breakfast just over, Finie washing dishes, Mr F and Tommie gone to hoeing, before breakfast I made up the beds cleaned up and fixed my milk and greens all ready to cook for dinner.

I hope Finie will be a better boy to day so he can get to go a fishing after dinner. F or Tommie had worked so well this week he can get to go. Finie was so lazy I could not let him go fishing. Mr F and Tommie went and caught a nice mess of fish. Tommie caught some turtles, they had a nice quantity of eggs. I kept Finie stirring this afternoon with my sewing in hand I followed him round and round, but it was the only way I could get him to do his work, preparatory for the Sabbath. I nearly finished Mollies brilliant dress, I am robing it with some purple stripes I had.

Monday June 2nd 62 Mr F pulled at least 40 wild hairs out of my eyes and I feel drowsy and can not see clearly yet. I love dearly to write my dear children, fondly believing it will afford you pleasure to read it when you are men and Mollie a sweet little woman. But I must go to my sewing again. I love dearly to sew too for my sweet children and dear husband and make them look nice and comfortable.

Tuesday June 3rd 62 I am threatened with headache. Mr F and Tommie finished their sheep pen made of brush sufficiently to put the sheep in to night. And Mr F and Finie are now gone to Bro Johnson's to get 2 cow to milk. I washed the dishes and Tommie wiped them and set the table.

Sunday June 8th Rowena, Mary, Mattie, Amelia our two boys and myself. I got in the wagon with Ike and I am to wait upon us and drive and went to a Baptist foot washing. The old Bro said many good things which we might treasure up. I thought what a pity he had not been educated. But the other one that preached was grossly ignorant, they did not wash feet. We came home this evening.

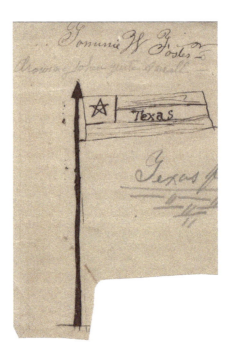

This drawing was found between this page and the next. Louisa wrote in pencil, "drawn when quite small." This was drawn by Tommie, but the signature I believe was written by Louisa. On the back was the same signature and Louisa wrote, "Best flag in the world." The only Texas flag with the single star in that position was between 1836–1839. It was also prominently featured on the $10 and $50 notes of the Texas dollar.

[Baptist foot washing in some groups meant the practice of bathing the feet of a fellow church member. It was usually followed by words of support and fellowship between the people involved in the ceremony. The custom of foot washing was based on the Gospel of John 13:4–15.

A "foot washing Baptist" could also have another meaning. Miss Maudie, in the book *To Kill a Mockingbird*, said that it was a person who followed the "laws" of the Bible while missing the overall mission that Jesus taught his followers, to love one another greatly.]

Sat June 14th Mollie is sorta ill to day, I expect she is cutting another sweet little tooth. I have not sewed any yet I have been busy straightening things up.

Sunday June 15th Mr F and Tommie went to Sunday school, it is too far for me to walk there and back and then cook dinner and perhaps for a crowd.

So Finie and I stayed at home had dinner ready when they came home. Tommie had company, Mr Williams son little Frank.

Tuesday June 17th Work as usual, all very well. I have baked a cake all afternoon, I am tired. Late this afternoon Sister Gardner came and kindly offered to assist me cooking tomorrow.

Thursday June 19th This bright sunny morning 10 hands mostly white men, our neighbors & members came of their own accord to help Mr F to cut his grain, they cut until dinner. Finished all but the wheat the rust had ruined it so it was not worth cutting.

I had the best dinner I could scarcely set down the whole morning. I am tired indeed. I had no help but Tommie and sister Gardner. After dinner the gentlemen went on a deer hunt, children and I went to Bro Gardners and stayed all night.

Friday June 20 The hunters did not return until late in the afternoon. They killed two deer and divided them equally. Myra spent this night with us, we had such nice stash for supper. Mr F has rented the Pastors house & farm and got the refusal to buy it.

Sunday June 22nd A beautiful day, but I am sad & gloomy. Mr F & Tommie gone to Sunday school. I wanted to go but I could not walk there and back in the heat of the day and do justice to myself. Finie Mollie and I are at home.

I am so perplexed in my mind. Mr F wants to stay here at least another year or until the war is over, or all ways. I see no hope of a school here and being so near the frontier and the whole country abound in Terantulas, centipedes, various kinds of snakes, copper head, cotton mouth water Mocherson, rattlesnake, and many kinds of destructive animals on stock. O I don't know what to do. Lord direct in Thine unerring wisdom.

We had early supper then milked, then we took a long walk around the farm over to the Procter house and then back home. Mr F killed a big diamond rattlesnake.

Monday June 23rd A pleasant morning. Milking, churning, prayers, breakfast cleaning up as usual. We have a new young lamb this morning its form is good, wool fine. As the wheat has ripened Mr F & Tommie have gone to cutting & shocking. [Shocking was an arrangement of sheaves of cut grain stalks placed so as to keep the grain heads off the ground while in the field before collecting for threshing.] I must start to pick my wool today.

Tuesday June 24th Jim & Ike are helping Mr. F cut the little wheat that came to perfection, got done long before night. Tommie & Finie then helped me pick wool. I have had the headache most of the day.

Thursday June 26th Sent Mrs Westfall & Mrs Reed a nice mess of irish potatoes. My neighbors are so kind to me. I am glad I have got something to send them in return for their kindness to me.

Mr F rode over to Dr Westfall's to see if he could go hunting with him. He took dinner there, I took Mrs W a mess of irish potatoes, in return she sent me a gallon bucket nearly full of very nice honey comb about 4 O clock. Mr F started in all the life, glee & excitement of boyhood to try to kill a deer. I do hope he will succeed. The children and I went to Mr Gardner and stayed the night. I rode part of the way behind Tommie.

Friday June 27th A pleasant morning, we returned home early. Ball had jumped out of the lot and on our return we found him in our field. Tommie says he had eaten nearly 2 shocks of oats. Caroline is here washing for me. I feel dull and tired my walk was too much for me.

Sat June 28th Mr F returned, he killed a fawn. Dr Westfall killed 4 large deer. I have suffered with my eyes so much, this morning Mr F pulled out 50 wild hairs which I believe has somewhat relieved them. Tommie, Finie and I besides doing many other things, and my taking two naps, which is very unusual for me, but I was obliged to do on account of my eyes. We picked a whole long fleece of wool. Mr F has been out all day hunting some missing sheep, but is now returning without them. It is after 6 in the afternoon, Bro Johnson sent Jim and Ike up to hall our wheat to his thrasher, he is indeed is kind friend to us.

Tuesday June 30th Mr F went to Bros Enochs after our wagon we had loaned him to go to muster last week. Amelia and Mag came up and helped me pick wool a little while. We then all rode over to the Proctor house in the wagon. O they got the wagon bed so greasy when they went to muster. Mr F and Tommie halled rails with Jim and Ike's aid and built a pen to stack our grass in. Jim and Ike halled all our wheat to day to the thrash yard.

Friday July 3rd. I feel headachish. I have read as usual and rounded up domestic affairs, now to my dreaded wool picking. I did think I could get some of the young folks to help me out thereby lighten the burden on my all ready bowed down shoulders. But I presume I shall have to go it alone what catched up moments Tommie and Finie can help me.

Sat July 4th I am so sick I did not get up at all today. Mr F was gone all day only eat dinner, until night finishing thrashing our wheat also bro Johnsons and brought our grain home. We raised 30 bushels of oats, 36 bushels barley, 17 bushels wheat. We think we will raise corn enough for bread.

Monday July 6th I am a little better. Another sad day to me, roll from one side to another. Mr F after trying all our won skill and remedies went after Dr Westfall. He was not at home but he left word for him to come see me on his return after dinner early he came. He is a pleasant gentleman. He gave me some morphine and some other powder combined which relieved my back in less than 2 hours. So much for knowing just what to give.

Wednesday July 8th I am still very weak.

Thursday July 9th I am still poorly.

Friday July 10th Poorly

Sunday July 11th I feel so weak and infirm but I went to Sunday school.

Monday July 12th I don't seem to improve hardly at all.

Tuesday July 13th I did to day what I never did before in my life, leave Mr F at home at work and go visiting, but he wanted me to do it. Finie drove me to Bro Williamsons about 2 miles, that was something new to him and made him very proud. I borrowed and brought home 50 lbs flour and brought home one of our lambs that had strayed off there.

Thursday July 15th I slept better last night since I have before I got sick. I feel some better. Mr F and children came at dinner time. John Owens killed a fawn and Mr F brought a quarter home.

Friday July 16th I feel a little better but I have no appetite but I must try to iron today. Amelia came and helped me, by 10 we ironed all the things and then she partly put the blocks of a quilt together, she did about half days work during the day.

Sat July 17th A pretty day, we all went over to the Proctor house, spent the day scouring and cleaning up. Which was a heavy days work. Mr F, Tommie and Finie complained of being so tired. O I feel so sorry that they have to work <u>so hard</u>. I feel tired and I feel less than any of them.

Sunday July 18th A pretty clear sunny day, warm, all seems well but myself. My work yesterday has lain me up. My old dreaded symptoms have returned again, only 2 weeks since I had an attack. I fear my health is now gone forever. Surely there is something very wrong about my system.

Children attended Sunday school, then at its close Mr F went to preach to fill one of Bro Flowers appointments, as he has not yet returned. And we heard that he engaged to preach one of his old places of preaching at a salary of $500 per year. $400 of which Bro Colliers brothers have bonded to pay him.

Monday Sept 1st 1862 To day Mr F and I have been married 20 years. Many changes have occurred since that happy evening. Today we are at Bosqueville, [located a few miles north of Waco] have moved here after 5 or 6 year trial, have started our boys to school to Bro Collier. O May they improve this start.

And continue to improve until they are properly to act their part in a useful peaceful, and happy life. A life the results of which may make them happier in heaven. Then my fond aim will have been accomplished, and I will die happy and fondly and expect to meet all my loved ones in that pure world on high.

Mr F drove to Waco bought me out a fine walnut bedstead as an anniversary present. Cost $20 it is beautiful, engaged the man to make me a fine walnut sofe [sofa] price 35$ and if he can get means he will get man to make me a $35 dollar wardrobe, then I will be so glad as I need them so much. He also purchased a molasses barrel containing 21 gallons molasses with a gate all ready to draw molasses he paid 1 ½ $ per gallon, the molasses are very nice. Also he bought me a nice folding leaf walnut breakfast table $10.

We drove 12 miles bought 150 weight of nice brown sugar 25 cents per pound, bought it home. We have market twice a week, get nice fat beef, we get meal at the mill 80 cents per bushel, 1 ½ miles off, flour there also 20$ per barrel.

Sunday Sept 21st 1862 We had 5 boarders to begin to board with us the last day of August. Their names, Mary Sadler. Mary Jones, Billie, John and Dack Sadler. They all went with Tommie and Finie to the college to go into the organization of a sabbath school except Billie he was going but took a spell of Phthisic, to which he is subject. [Phthisic is a wasting illness of the lungs, such as asthma or tuberculosis.] All my boarders are irreligious, I hope I pray, Yes I believe they will every one embrace religion before the ten months session is out. Mr F has been gone since Wednesday to attend a camp meeting on Gabriel and bring our sheep up.

With deep heart rendering regret I must write Tommie is not learning as I fondly wished and sanguinely expected. But to my surprise Finie is learning fast. The children formed themselves in a line last night and asked me to give out their dictionary lesson. Finie would spell with them for the first time and when he began he was fast and he left nearly head. I'm prouder of my boy tonight than ever. O my Dear loved boys. O do study hard, and improve each golden moment as it swiftly passes by.

The school was organized, Bro Collier was elected Superintendent, Assistant Sup., Bro McSpadden, Miss McMulling Librarian. Bro Collins wife called to see us this afternoon. [John Collier married Mary Ellen (Mollie) on August 26, 1858. In 1863 Collier resigned his position at the school to become a scout in Ross's Brigade, one of the most famous and active Texas military units of the Civil War.] Bro Jimmie Sadly [Sadler] came to see his children, it made my heart glad to witness his children's joy.

Tuesday 23 My health so feeble that we were compelled to hire. I hated it but could not help it. Bro Wil's son Harvey came and stayed all night. They have moved to the place Mr F rented for them 5 miles from Waco, 9 miles from here.

Friday Sept 26th Mollie has hurt herself, I can't write much it is near dinner. I have spent this morning reading, looking over old papers, which job I completed, and patching. Sarah is spinning but slowly indeed. I feel discouraged about her, I feel she is a real eye servant from what I am told. [An eye servant was one who worked only when being watched.]

My paper job was so great, that I did not finish Tommie's drawers until late this afternoon. Had early supper just as we were done joy to tell, Bro Robert his dear wife and his 2 sweet little girls came also Sister Jinnie's Mother a good kind old lady.

Sunday Sept 28th Bro and family returned home after breakfast. Bro Wils and Roberts are speaking of purchasing homes in Texas. I hope they will be satisfied if not I would rather that they not be here.

Sat Nov 15th My beloved little daughters 2nd birthday. to day our sweet Mary Nancy is two years old. We have never been permitted to look upon a little infant daughters face, at that age, <u>death</u> (cruel monster) before two years of the little dear had expired, snatched those other three lovely buds of ours from comfort & embrace. O I cannot express by deep sense of gratitude to God for blessing us so long with this dear little inestimable treasure of a baby girl.

Today we baked Mollie 3 nice cakes, ate them for dinner, drove home after supper. Sarah, Johnnie Sadler and I made Mollie three more cakes and baked a little one for Johnnie. Tommie learned to reel for me to night, he reeled about 4 hanks of wool filling for jeans for me.

Sunday Dec 14th 62 Today is a day of thrilling interest to me, as it is the tenth birthday of my precious boy Finie. Bright child of promise. May you in after life read these lines penned by a loved Mother's hand. When you arrived at manhood and mix and mingle in society. Always seek the best and purest men and women for your associates. Never become too intimate with any person, particular a woman, yes a lovely fascinating woman <u>until</u> you find out their character and that it is <u>good</u>. My child you must be good and meet dear Mamma in heaven, that land of repose the abode of the blest, the rest of the family faithful.

Mr F started early to preach, at Bro Jones to day. Tomorrow he leaves there on his way to Brownsville on the Rio Grande and Matamoras in Mexico, in company with Bro I. W. Smith, Bob Smith, and Col Singleton for the purpose of buying supplies for family use and to sell to the neighbors. Mr F borrowed a little over a thousand dollars, they are sanguine of success. I fear the trip will prove a failure, but trust not as our comfort and that of our neighbors are involved to a great extent, as this blockade has deprived us of nearly all the comforts of life. [The Union's plan was to blockade all Southern ports during the war. The principal seaport—Galveston—and the entire Gulf was blockaded for four years, and the county was occupied for three months in 1862.]

May heaven's smile attend them. May they all return in health. And O may in their return greet every loved in each family circle. May death not enter our dwellings and desolate our homes whilst they are absent.

When my husband drove off this morning at an early start, My heart, O such a sad gloom oe'r spread my heart I felt like <u>nearly</u> one of my family was being borne to that long as lasting place, I feel this is a presentiment of evil. O My kind Heavenly Father prevent it, prevent. My fervent pray is in peace health and purity, may we all meet on earth.

Mamma has made her little boy some nice cakes, as a fresh ernest of her undying love to him. So if these should be my last words to you is, I <u>dearly</u> love my noble boy. O be a good boy, and at last become a good <u>useful</u> man, and Mother will be glad.

Sat Dec 20 Tommie has been very disobedient since his father left. I cannot get him to cut wood or make fires or take any interest to attending to anything. O how it makes my heart ache to write to sad stubborn fact, but it is true. Children and I are alone with Minerva the woman Mr F hired before he left. She had 2 little children. I like her very well.

Dec 25th Thursday We have baked a fine lot of fine cakes, family pound cake, and soft ginger bread. Baked 3 nice loves of wheat light bread, one large corn loaf, baked and dressed a hen, baked pork and pickled beef & apple custards. Finie hung up his and Tommie's socks last night. This morn they were found with a large cup cake in each one and some brown & white sugar. And I should have enjoyed their bright eyes very much, but when Finie awoke first and caught Tommie's Christmas gift, Tommie got <u>mad</u> and cut up so it killed my joy, more my peace all day. O my children when will you do right and respect your Mother's feelings that are so tender toward the children of her love. My feelings are so hurt that I cannot command them to write as I desired to on this <u>blessed day ever memorable</u> day.

Dec 30 As I was sitting to day sewing, Mollie was at my feet sitting on the carpet with the slate in her little sweet lap, she looked up to me and said I want to write a letter. I asked her what she said, she remarked plainly "I want to write to <u>my father</u>." I was so struck and surprised I would have given $100 to have her papa to hear her just as she spoke, so sweet, childlike earnest & plain. We never hear her say My father before. Yesterday Tommie wrote to his father. I reckon she heard us talking about it.

Jan 10th Last night after sewing so constantly, I felt so much oppression in my <u>whole</u> chest that I feared that I was going to be sick, about 8 at night I layed by my sewing, had prayers, and retired to rest my feebly body. Finie was asleep, Tommie was reading, Mollie pratting, to our joy and great surprise Bro Smith and my husband rapped at my room door. I could not tell what it was but great was our excitement and gratification when we heard those well known voices. O Mollie was the gladdest little thing she knew him, said papa papa, they brought some things.

Jan 11 Mr F thinks this trip will enable him to save for ourselves what we need, and pay all our little debts here. Mr F and Tommie have gone to church. I desired much to go but the carriage is broken and I had such a headache I feared to walk.

March 1863 Tuesday I have been sick ever since, have not been out of bed a whole day since, I suffered great deal with by chest and stomach, have no help but the children. Mr F has a negro man hired by the year $300 and now he has a white boy hired 75 cents per day and another negro man hired for which I expect he will have to pay $2 per day, which makes the cooking heavy on my children, but still they are compelled to do it. If I was well and able to cook I would rather do it, than to see these boys cook for these negroes.

April 1st 1863 For a few days I have had a young ignorant girl to do my work. Yesterday I hired her out and hired Mortee from Mrs Susan T.

Woodword, a lady who with part of her negroes fled from Louisiana to this neighborhood as a tempory place of safety during our <u>devastating</u> war. She is said to be a good cook, ironer, washer, soap maker, milker and seamstress, raised in the house and fond of house work. Spins but little, but says she will and can learn. Loves me very much, and desires to live with me. She made the first effort towards being hired here, her mistress said I was the only person Mortee was willing to live with she has seen in Texas. Mrs Woodword says Mortee fell in love with me first sight. She has two children a little boy Nep big enough to nurse Mollie, feed horses and hogs, make fires, pack chips and a little girl named Loulov just the age of Mollie. I give $10 per month, gave Mortee 2 suits and clothe Nep and Loulov with our children's old clothes. I am happy in the prospect in having a good trusty servant during my feeble health to attend to my house business. O may I not be disappointed but may we live happy together. She is so kind to Mollie and Mollie loves her so much. I feel so relieved that my health seems much improved. I am fixing Mr F to start to Brownsville on a halling trip. My dear kind old friend Aunt Mc is to day coloring Mr F a pr of jeans pants that I purchased at $15 a pattern from Mrs Woodward yesterday, expressly for the trip as I could not get my jeans ready. Sister Mitchell has promised to put 25 yrds in the loom to weave for me this week at $1 per yrd. This was a sad disappointment the negro was anything but what I desired. I kept her only one month.

Jan 24th 1865 [Twenty-one months have passed since the last entry.] To-day my heart and home is sad and dreary. Altho' the sun is shining in brightness and beauty. This morning my husband in compliance with an order of Synod started with the army on the Rio Grande River and coast country in West Texas as army missionary to preach to the soldiers.

[There was no major fighting in Texas during the Civil War. In West Texas in 1865, where Louisa's husband was going, there was little danger. The closest fight occured in January near San Angelo between Confederate forces and the Kickapoo. In April General Lee surrendered his army at Appomattox. Small skirmishes continued in Texas for several more months.]

I felt he was wrong to leave me in my feeble health, to go so far and stay so long (three long weary months is the time set by Synod for him to labor among the soldiers.) But if I am wrong and selfish O Lord forgive me. Never shall I forget how long he embraced his little Mollie Nannie and said to her to be good to <u>Mamma</u> and then how he bent over the little willow basket that held our last little one, our sweet John Collier [born October 12, 1863].

He was sweetly sleeping unconscious that, that dear father he loved so fondly, was biding him a long farewell to go so far away upon our extreme western border, there to traverse those western wilds and preach to a needy few.

Mollie of her own accord said now father you must preach good to the poor soldiers. He replied, "I will my daughter the best I can." Finie wept bitterly and said, I don't believe Brother (that is Tommie) is sorry that father is going away at all, for he don't cry a bit. I did not catch the parting of Mr F and Tommie. I presume it took place as Mollie and I knelt so long after Mr F left his position near the little willow basket.

Feb 7th 1865 After a siege of cold rain, sleet and snow, about 1 O clock my son, my dear Tommie bade us all adieu with many a parting kiss and fond embrace to go where he is ordered as a member of the reserve corps under Capt. Berry & Lieut. E. S. Johnson. Yesterday he went to Austin and had his likeness taken for his dear Mamma. Paid $3 for it. O I am so proud of it, it is very striking, it looks so sweet, mild and gentle to this fond Mother he surely is a nobly looking boy. O what word is sweeter than My boy. [Tommie was seventeen at this time.]

I have just arisen from sitting about an hour gazing with all a fond mother's love upon this dear image. We don't know where the authorities intend to send these precious blessed youths. The fond mother's love cannot stay them at home. O if this could have been done, my poor inexperienced boy would not have been forced from his parental roof thus, his foot is so sore he could scarce or ride. He suffers intensely but still the cruel tocsin of war had sounded and he was compelled to obey its summons. A week ago to day he received his orders to meet his Capt & Lieut at Camp Eayly 15 miles distance from here, Round Rock Texas to night and from there to march to Houston. Since that I have learned that they are ordered only to port Sullivan, there they are supposed to remain several months to drill, but the Lord only knows what will be the issue. When first heard that my child was ordered out to buffes with all of the trials, hardships, and temptations of camp life in this most horrid of wars, it seemed that I could not stand it. I have wept and prayed day and night ever since. I have prayed with all my heart for resignation to this as I may safely say saddest trail of my eventful life, a life that has been fraught with so much gloom and despondency. Sad indeed and broken hearted have I been all week. I dreaded to see this morning down I feared it would kill me.

I wrote to Capt. Berry and Lieut. Johnson with a full heart, my feebleness and with all a mother's fondness I begged for my cripple boy a furlough, and then with a mother's pathos with all a mother's undying love. [This was the first time she ever wrote that Tommie is crippled.] I wrote a long letter to Genl Walker of Houston beging, pleading for a detail for as many months as he would grant for my dear boy to stay at home, take care of me, my little ones in my feeble health, and go to school. I feel that I have left no key untouched, that I could think of to get my child to stay at home, until his soft growing bones become stronger. O never have I prayed harder, even for religion, I don't believe. This day I dreaded so much I am surprised at my feelings. They are so calm, so clear, so peaceful.

O God put into the Capt's heart to let him stay at least one more month with his poor mother. And grant that he may be permitted to go to school at least one more session. I am more anxious for that from the fact that his teacher said he stood such a good examination a few days ago and I am sure Tommie would apply himself and would study harder and would learn more than he has in his life before.

O what an interest I feel for my boys education. Lord bring it about. Thou cans't do it, and of thou dost's it it will be right that my child that thou gavest me, may be permitted to go to school at least one more session and that his father and mother may witness with heartfelt pleasure his last examination. O God close this horrid war in thine own appointed way. Grant my kind heavenly Father that all this fondness mother's hopes in regard to her childrens education and usefulness may not be lost, especially this dear boy my eldest living son, my Tommie.

[Early in 1865, President Jefferson Davis knew that the cause was lost. Many of the Confederate forces left in Texas and Louisiana were ordered to Hempstead, Texas, in March. There, they awaited Davis's arrival to make the last stand of the Confederacy. A "fighting commander" was needed to command the men in Texas, and General John Walker was sent. He was given command of the district of Texas, New Mexico, and Arizona.

Local militias had been formed in February and sent off to train for the final event. Tommie Foster was one of hundreds of young boys drafted into the local militias. Few records remain of these units since they were not members of the regular army. There may have been many mothers like Louisa who had their young sons taken from their homes. They probably knew that the cause was lost and that their sons might be needlessly killed in the final days of the conflict.]

Wednesday Feb 8th O I miss my dear child so much. I needed him so badly. I have been sick all day, so I could scarce walk across the house. O this has been a day of deep anxiety to me and almost one ceaseless prayer has gone up to God for my child to day. It would beggar human language to try to express the complicated agitations of this fond mother's heart to day. Surly it has been the saddest sorrowfulest day of my poor life. O God may my faithful prayers be answered. My Dear boy returns to take care of his old feeble mother and her dear little ones. The sun has set behind the western horizon. My home is sad and lonely. My boy has not yet returned. Finie has gone to see if he could meet him. Finie returned in sadness & said he could not find him.

Friday Feb 10, 1865 About 1 O clock to our great joy unspeakable joy my Dear Son returned on detail under Leiut Stewart with 15 others to buy up cavalry horses, perhaps he will stay at home 2 or 3 months. I am sick in bed to day. This detail was obtained by my kind friends with the express understanding that he is to stay at home with me all the time. Thank God.

March 4th 65 Sab. To day Tommie received orders to meet his Capt at camp or near Capt Mankins, close to Georgetown. Ready for marching orders with gun if possible. Tommie started about 4 O clock to see Capt Berry so as to find out the cause of this order on him as the carrier said the balance of the detailed horse buyers were not ordered in.

Capt Berry received and treated Tommie very kindly, insisted on his remaining all night with him at his residence, but Tommie declined, telling him that he did not want to stay away from home, only when compelled owing to my poor health. Capt explained to him that Genl Robertson would grant no more details only by individual application. So Tommie is ordered to go up and in person apply for his detail, all my friends seem so anxious for Tommie to remain with me in my feebleness. O I hope he will. [General Jerome B. Robertson was transferred back to Texas in 1863 to command the state reserve forces.]

My feeling were not like they were before, they are calm, peaceful, and trusting. I believe he will get a detail. I have such confidence in our good kind friends, the officers of our acquaintance that I believe the good Lord will grant my earnest prayer and my dear boy will be permitted to stay and take care of mamma and go to school at least one more session. O God grant these fond hopes that I our son are right may not be disappointed.

If I should be disappointed in this, it will come down crushingly upon me in my feeble state. But I hope and pray that my dear child will be permitted in the benevolence and wisdom of an <u>all wise</u> God to remain at home and go to school at least until 18.

Sat 11th 65 The day has arrived. My child was notified to be in company, Makings springs five miles from Georgetown. Soon after breakfast I told Finie to go and bring out his brothers horse, and saddle him. Tommie said it is not time yet. But I had it done, for I wanted by child to go by and see Bro Cadwell about our oxen, and go by Georgetown, and try and borrow a few dollars from Bro Mc Reynolds as I had only 5 dollars to give to my poor dear boy to start on, this made me so sorry but I don't know what we will do for we have no hope of getting money. And then Tommie lingered along, within his home, around his poor old Mother, would look around the room, and would kiss and hug again his poor old mother and his little brothers & sister. He would say O I hate to go so bad, I don't feel well, I feel bad. Sister he would say. But Tommie would not go and leave his little sister if he could help it. Took his slate sit down in our plain neat little parlor and said I will write all our names. He did so and then drew Mollie with his pencil wrote under her picture, Mollie, my sister. He started two or three times then would come back and hug and kiss us. Last he said I must go. We knelt kissed and embraced each other, prayed to meet soon. (O god grant to hear our prayer) Finie held his brothers horse, his brother pressed to him to his bosom said brother, be good and take care of mother. O how strong and tender that tie binds our little broken family circle together. Cruel war that takes from me my last hope and protection. O God rule and over rule all things and bring about a speedy peace, in Thine own appointed way. Then we know it will be right. Please in thy wisdom give us a peace or make it so my child can stay at home take care of me in his fathers absence. And in my feeble breath and go to school. O God if consistently with thy will put it into the hearts of his officers to give him a detail until he is 18 years of age.

I do hope he may be permitted to return. I felt calm and prayed for resignation, but when this sad morning dawned all resolution was gone. I wept, prayed and talked to my loved boy until he was gone. We stood and watched until that loved form was out of sight. O how sad I felt when this thought was revolved in my mind perhaps I'll never see that loved form again. But directly Finie said yonders brother, he dropped something and had come back in sight to get it. He was down fixing something. We watched him with gloomy feelings but this circumstance trivial as it was, gave me hope that I would again meet my child within the hallowed precincts of his own loved home, and again enjoy his dear society, that is so soothing and see him look loving upon his dear old mother when'er she speaks approvingly of what he does well or chides when he does wrong. O I believe he is the best boy in the world. I thank God for such a child, I thank God that he has given me knowledge, firmness and grace to be strict with my child and raise him so circumspectfully. I feel that I am being repaid for all my trouble. My children are my souls delight. I love them as dear as life itself. "I spare not the rod." I have ever corrected and that severely when I felt to be my imperitive duty. My life ever since I became a mother and been one of never ending anxiety, scarce a moment has passed in my long eventful life without a prayer being offered for my children. If Tommie continues as he is, and improves as time adds steadiness to his course, and my precious Finie, sweet Mollie my only daughter and then my last little boy my John Collier, that papa and mamma loves so will be good quiet and religious children, the first and dearest aim of my life, that has been so full of trouble will be obtained and my happiness will be indisciribable, my own, my loved children. My four treasures.

As I read this to Finie when I came to his dear brothers last words to him he hid his face in my lap and wept bitterly. More of the mournful effects of war, but after all at dinner my dear Finie behaved very ugly, which caused my saddened heart to ache afresh. My little boy when will you learn to be good to mother as Tommie requested and thereby soften the many sorrows that is hastening her death. O my dear children be good to mamma, so her days may be lengthened out. So she can be permitted with her own kind hand to rear the tender olive plants that God has given her to daily surround her table.

Sunday 19th 65 I feel so sad and lonely, how I miss my Tommie this morning when the sabbath bell called the children to his loved sabbath school. But he was not here to answer the call.

The war has taken him from all his dearest most loved ones. Times still becoming darker and darker. Houses have been entered, money demanded, Mr Ruble taken from the midst of his family, between midnight and day a few nights after his return from a long absence, and shot with 3 bullets thro' his head. The cause no one seems to know. [Near the end of the war, some soldiers knew that the cause was lost and began to live by the rule of every man for himself. These groups of men began to commit acts of crime and violence throughout the state.]

Finie is sick with a dreadful rising on his lip which has swollen his face until he can scarce open one eye. Mollie and Collie are so well and playing so sweetly. O I know Tommie would be so glad to see them this morning.

Sunday night 11 O clock Our dear Tommie returned. He started Sunday morning last by order traveled to Mosbys Ferry on Brazos. Got there Tuesday night, stayed a day to let his pony rest, then came the first of his traveling on sabbath, so more of the sad effects of this cruel war we have brought upon ourselves by an injudicious, impolite step. [Moseley's Ferry operated on the Brazos River between Burleson and Brazos Counties at the crossing of the Old San Antonio Road. It was called Boren's Ferry until 1849, when Daniel Moseley, a plantation owner on both sides of the Brazos, began to operate it. Toll fees were set by the Burleson County Commissioners Court.]

March 27th 1865 Monday—alternate clouds and sunshine, last Wednesday Mr F returned. He said when he received one letter from which told of my ill health and our deranged business matters, he could not stay away. Tommie's detail arrived by Yesterdays mail. It permits him to remain at school until he attains the age of 18, unless the Reserve Corps of Texas are ordered out in a body in that case he is to return to duty with his command. By order of Brig Genl Robertson.

In a short time Mr F will return to the army, he says the soldiers hated for him to leave and come home. He feels that he can do good among them.

April 5th 1865 My eldest boy Tommie and Finie are in our little parlor studying Finie his speech, Tommie his Latin and Philosophy. My littlest ones Mollie and Collie are sweetly sleeping, feeling perfect security as Mother is near. My husband as usual is absent. He is gone across Colorado, beyond Austin to Bro Youngs on business.

My dearest sons, have closed their studies for this night and come into my room and washed all over to bed. Tommie beside Collier on the trundle bed, Finie on the lounge in the corner by the fire. [The Civil War effectively ended on April 9, 1865, when Confederate general Robert E. Lee surrendered his troops to Union general Ulysses S. Grant at Appomattox Court House in Virginia.]

March 2nd 1866 Twelve months ago O how different my feelings. Altho I am in nearly as feeble health as I was then. Then we were in the midst of blood and carnage expecting daily our state to be fully invaded, and our whole land to be deluged in human gore. But thank God it was not so. The rebellion was conquered by the Northern army. Peace has returned and the old U.S. flag floats again from Maine to the Rio Grande.

And I hope we will never again hear of a conscript law that will force from lived homes the beardless guileless unsuspecting youth to sicken and die, or return a wreck in body and morals. Also the aged and infirm. O such a devastating war, sad and gloomy are its effects. Still we are under military rule, cannot express perfect peace and quietude until we return hearts and hand to our old tried and true paternal Mansion. And be willing to pleasantly acquiesce in the order of government this war has inaugurated. Altho Southern born and southern raised and educated, with all my prodivities at the beginning of this war truly southern to the letter, I feel that I can see the hand of the Almighty in it. And I bow submissively and most cheerfully to it, without a murmur of sigh for the return of the darling institution of the south. The South had surely made it their God.

Startling murders, Burglaries, robberies are rife all oe'r the land. [Texas did not suffer as much from the war as other Confederate states. Still, the blockade resulted in many shortages during the war, and these continued after the war. In addition, an extended drought from 1857 to 1864 devastated the wheat crop and wiped out many cattle raisers. These shortages, combined with scarce jobs, created a climate of lawlessness and violence that affected much of the state.]

Our convention is in session here to remodel the constitution. O may an all wise spirit preside o'er that body. May they fully realize the sacredness of the trust committed to their hands, their peoples lives homes and interest. Their countries good. O that all may work together for good. That perfect peace quiet and security may be ours as a people, as a great national government. May we soon again become the admiration of the whole world. May these scisms be done away with. May peace love and harmony triumphant.

[The Texas Constitution of 1869 was quite different from the past Texas government. It centralized and expanded governmental power. New social welfare programs were brought in. For example, it created the first statewide public school system financed by public lands and taxes. It abolished slavery, allowed Black people to be citizens, gave them the vote, and allowed them to hold office. The majority of Texans grudgingly accepted these changes in order to get rid of the hated army of occupation.]

We had no house servants for two months until yesterday. Ann Johnson colored came to live with us $10 per month. [Despite the formal end of slavery in Texas, laws and restrictions were enacted for African Americans that severely limited their rights. Most had few resources with which to start a new life. Many, like Louisa's servant Ann Johnson, found that little had changed, except now she received limited pay for the same work she did when enslaved.]

Mr F is writing in Comptrollers Office at $75 per month currency. Bro Latimer one of our Elders is Comptroller. Tommie and Uncle Joe, colored, are cultivating 40 acres land we pay 3rd rent and pay Uncle Joe $10 per month. Finie is droping corn they have sowed 10 acres in wheat, have about 8 acres corn planted. We need rain.

Monday 5th I have just slapped Collie for tearing my papers, Mollie is peting him so sweetly. Finie is fixing my box. Tommie and Uncle Joe building a cow lot, as it is too wet to plough. Mr F in the office. I feel much improved. Finie is winding me a bale of knitting cotton. Mollie & Collie are sweetly sleeping in the trundle bed beside mine upon which I have slept over 20 years. I have knit Mollie's stockings to day, crimson clouded fine morino, homespun wool, vert pretty. I am still feeble must retire to bed as we have had prayers some time ago.

Tuesday 6th 1866 At our Austin rented home, o that it were mine, a dark cloudy morn. We must try to wash. I can not go to the breakfast table. I am waiting for my butter cakes. I knit Mollie's stocking to toe, could have finished but felt tired & weary and feared it would make me worse again as I did myself once by sewing this spell.

Wednesday 7th Prayers, breakfast over, rainy morn. Ann is ironing, Tommie & Uncle finishing lot and gate for horses, they started to the farm but it commenced raining. Finie is jobing around as usual can't get much out of him.

He went to the blacksmith shop and sold 1 pr of socks for 50 cents that I knit, got my chest lock fixed at 15 cents and the balance to be paid in black-smithing. I am to knit him 1 pr socks for his grandson at 40 cents. I have then just commenced. I am glad every cent I save, feel I an thou' so feeble helping that much.

I don't think I feel quite so well as I did yesterday. I reckon on account of knitting too steady and the damp weather.

Thursday March 8th 1866 Our farmers Tommie, Finie & Uncle Joe went to the field planted one row of corn and watermelon seed, found the ground so wet, they returned they have employed themselves very profitable cleaning up the yard. The aspect of our front yard this evening is very different, clean as a pin. Ann commenced spinning carpet filling to make me a homemade carpet. Last Sat evening we put down our parlor carpet. Ann cleaned up all my tubs and set up on a place prepared for them beside the kitchen. They look so nice. I finished my sock to day for the dutch boy and knit the rib of the other, bound a ball & patched Tommie's old pants. They are putting up a long nice horse trough in the new lot. My dear Finie has gone to drive up the horses. Lord please take care and guard our little boy from evil.

Friday March 9th Finie is sawing a plank for me, made me a nice pretty pan cover and is now making me a plank to fix my mustard plaster on as I have to have one on my chest or spine every night. [The usual recipe for making a mustard plaster was to use ground mustard seed, with flour mixed with water. The paste was then wrapped in a piece of flannel or other cloth and then placed on the affected area. Some people claimed it could cure all varieties of diseases. It was, however, mainly used for colds and congestion or temporary relief of pain.]

Ann is washing, Mollie has just brought me in a basket of chips, but sad, I had to whip her to obey me, 3 times to day. Collie is ploughing, Mr F at office, look for him in 25 minutes.

Sat March 10th All well as usual. Tommie, Finie and Uncle Joe gone to the field. Ann going to scour clean up & cook for Sabbath. Capt Anderson and Bro Richardson sent me word they would be around to tea. I must try and have something nice. Mollie and Collie out at play. Mollie brought me in two eggs. I am knitting on Mollies last crimson clouded stocking. We are looking for Bro Roach here to day as he wrote to that effect. I had as nice a supper as I could yet. My cook did her best. I had cold boil meats, Peach pie and custard, biscuit custard tea cakes, corn hoe cakes tea & coffee.

Sunday March 11th 66 My chest and eyes ache. Mr F's appointments for the day is 9 miles off, Hornsby's school house. Bro roach accompanied him and will preach for him.

The delightful sounds of the church bells are ringing as I write. My trio, my eldest three have gone to church at the Presbyterian church as we have no preaching at our church to day. O god bless my dears. I went to the door of my bed chamber and with all a mother's pride and gazed upon those three not mature loved forms, as they loving and pleasantly, neatly attired walked hand in hand. Mollie between her two brothers church ward. May God bless my children to day and <u>all</u> along besides life's pathways.

O I am so sorry to record here that my dear little daughter <u>that</u> looked so sweet walking between Tommie & Finie, you have spoiled all your pretty dressings. I am so ashamed and <u>so</u> sorry. What shall I do. As you my dear walked onward to church Mamma, dear old Mamma that was too feeble to walk there to day prayed for you. O what shall Mamma do with little ugly Mollie. I'm so afraid every body noticed you and the dear good preacher too, and if he knew you were a preachers child how sorry he was, for all good preachers love <u>good</u> preachers children.

And O Mollie God saw you my little love. And then I am so fraid the great good God that made you to be good is angry with <u>my daughter</u>. You told me when you started to church that you would be good. So you see my child, the great dilemma into which you have fallen. You promised me to be good and failed.

O my child remember that the other day you told your sweet little bro' that the "bad man" tried to make you be bad so he could get you to burn you. Now my little girl that is a good way to go to the bad world and be burned <u>forever</u>, to misbehave at church.

As I was reading this to Mollie she says O mamma I saw a lady have on a dress just like yours, it was just like molasses. I asked Mollie if she was sorry for her ugly behavior at church. She looked sad, said I don't want to talk about that, company might be in. Ann dressed walked down towards Aunt Lile's, Uncle Joe is in the kitchen. Very pretty afternoon. Our session met. To Mr F's great pleasure he saw a bell already hung at our church which our members had purchased and hung since our last appointment. Which encouraged him truly.

We walked near the Capital then Finie Mollie & Collie went into the Capital grounds to the atesian well where they saw Bro & sister Jimmie Smith our nearest neighbors.

Tommie and I walked around out north edge of town and back home. O I was so tired I had to lay down. Mr F returned, very hoarse, he preached at 3 to the negroes after visiting by request a sick and dying friend and the wife of an old eastern Texas friend and son of one of our preachers, Mrs Dr J J

The limestone capitol was built in 1853. One publication called it an "architectural monstrosity" because of its dull design. It burned down in 1881 and the plans for the new capitol were rescued from the fire. Photo from the *The Illustrated American*, January 16, 1897, "The Evolution of a Great State's Capitol," page 109.

Moore. She is the last daughter of old Mr Hornsby and she was formally the wife Jessie Burdily. She is dying with consumption.

Monday morning 12th March Cloudy, damp. I mended my gown, have knit some on Mollie's hose, Ann washing. T, F & Joe gone to the field as usual. Mr F fixing to go to the office, dear sweet Mollie and Collie playing.

I have just finished a letter to Sister Mollie Collier desiring they come and visit our city with the view of moving here to build a high Cumberland school. [Mary Ellen (Mollie) Fowler married John C. Collier on August 26, 1858. At that time they were living in Oakland, Texas, about three miles from the present town of Grandview. John opened Oakland College there, and several years later it was moved to Alvarado, Texas. In 1869 Collier moved the college to Mansfield, Texas.]

Tuesday 13th 66 A gander got in our yard a while ago. Collie said I'll take my sword and shoot him. He frighten Mollie so she ran up on the pavement. Mr F as usual at the office. Finie had a lump of sugar, he didn't divide it with his little sister and bro Collie cried for more. Mollie said don't cry son, too much sugar will make you sick, come here and I'll give you this, it was a needle that I had given her. She sooth as she often does his little child troubles.

Tommie put a lock on the east seller door also on my flour chest. Finie rode out to Mr Herst's to tell him that Cousin Farmer wrote that he would here to day or tomorrow with 75 or 80 head of mutton for him, he is an old butcher here, and told Finie he was much obliged to papa for sending him and was glad they were coming and then Finie looked at and priced some furniture Rev Charles Gillette has for sale as he is going to move to Stubensville, Ohio. [Rev. Gillette (1813–69) founded Wharton College in Austin in 1858. Named for his wife, Mary Ann Wharton, the school closed in 1865. Gillette, an Episcopal minister, moved to Steubenville and became rector of St. Paul's Church.]

He has a small mahogany secretary, he sent Mr F word he could have it for $15.00, Mr F had wanted to buy a very fine one uptown at $55, but I told him I thought these time and our circumstances demand we buy plainer furniture, and so we get neat, good furniture, we ought to get the most we could for our money, he said yes it looks so. And then said for the $55 we could get that little secretary, a cottage bedstead & sets of cane seat chairs. Or the little secretary, a neat bureau and glass and bedstead. Certainly this is the best or taste would say purchase fine furniture matters not how costly but my better judgement says furnish as plainly, neatly and cheaply as possible until we purchase us a home, have an annual income, sufficient for our sustenance and an overplus. Then take our plain pieces of furniture for bed rooms and for our childrens use, and furnish my parlor and my family room with splendid furniture, prices according to our ability to pay for it.

Wednesday March 14th 66 When I wake Collie this morning and dressed him, it made him mad. I said I see that bright eye, he said you shan't talk to my eyes, hid his face but he soon got in a good humor and laughed and played with his usual sweetness,

Tommie wrote to his Uncle Andy he described Finie as thirteen, a real Foster feature, has ways like his father, Mollie description he gives this, "My little sister is getting to be very much like a little lady, about 3 feet 8 inches in structure black piercing eyes, a brunette, mind keen as a brier, she has a warm affectionate heart, with a great desire to be loved."

This is a good description of my little angel daughter, I had no idea Tommies descriptive powers were so good. He then adds "I have a little brother 2 years old, he is a blonde fat as a pig named John Collier, the John is for Uncle John, the Collier for one of our preachers." Mollie and Collie are now in the yard playing so sweetly. I dressed and visitied Sister Smith.

Finie like a little man went up to Rev Mr Gillettes and examined and priced their furniture they wish to dispose of before they move to Ohio.

Then in the afternoon he, Mollie and his papa went up, Mr F found Finie's description true. We have engaged of him a neat small monogamy secretary $15, nice walnut bureau $30, 6 nice cane seat parlor chairs $8, 2 large gentleman's arm chairs $2. And a very neat little bible stand with drawer $5. This little stand I purchased with money than was given to my children. The above prices with the proceeds of things I have sold out of my house and by sewing such as a matrass, blanket, coats, pants, vest socks & c. My safe and little plain pine varnish book case I bought the same way. Also my cow and one horse feed for the whole winter.

Friday March 16th 66 I am reading the correspondence of Bishop Gregg of the Protestant Episcal church and Rev M Chas Gillette Rector of St. David's church Austin Texas. [In 1859 Alexander Gregg became the first elected bishop of Texas. His diocese covered the entire state of Texas. St David's Church was formed in 1853 from the merger of two other churches.]

Photo is of Bishop Gregg, taken from
The Bishops of the American Church
by William S. Perry, 1897.

During the rebellion Bishop Gregg being a hot secessionist, Mr Gillette a stanch Union man of the conservative cast, a perfect gentleman, and a Christian. I met him first, 20 years ago, he and his wife at their marriage, lived in Houston and the same time Houston was our home, which was 18 years ago. We have ever heard Mr Gillette spoken of a Christian minister of high standing. I remember in Houston they had ministers prayer meeting, all denominations met there. Well do I to have heard Mr F speak of the perfect fraternal union spirit manifested by Mr Gillette on that occasion.

Sat March 17th One of Ann's old fellow servants came to see her. I was glad, treated him kindly and made him to feel (I think) that he was welcome to visit Ann. I think servants ought to be permitted to enjoy their social relations and friendships. I believe in conforming to this new order of things (that has by the late war been inaugurated) as far as rights, Rectitude and deep piety favors and the common weal and perpetuation of a <u>pure white race.</u> The negroes are free it is true but I cannot but conceive that they are an inferior race and that most of them ought to be servants, it seems to my mind that it is very obvious that nature designed to fill that position.

I do not say as slaves, O no I would not, I dare not say so, when God so lately shown us the time has come their bondage to end. We ought as a Christian people to bow submissively to the will of the Great I am that I am. Let it, or education, or former habits of early life that makes such lasting impressions on the human mind. O Lord rule and over rule <u>all</u> our scisms that jar our land and that so much <u>mars</u> our peace, and bring order out of confusion, light out of darkness, may every troubled wave cease to roll its turbid waters across life's great arena.

Late this afternoon I finished reading Bishop Greggs an Episcop protestant Clergyman strictures on Rev Chas Gillette Rector of St. David's church in this place. The Bishop was a confederate in the full import of that term. I conclude from his correspondence with Rev Gillette. The latter a good pure union man, one as there was thousands such in the south, that would rather give up our loved institutions, tho it was dear as a right eye than to see our once proud and happy Union severed. Further remarks I forbear at least for the present. My children love the Union.

March 24th Sat 1866 Sickness, sickness, Measles, dying, many deaths young and old, never such mortality has been in Austin before. [During this period, Texans experienced numerous epidemics. Outbreaks of cholera, yellow fever, dengue fever, measles, influenza, diphtheria, and whooping cough occurred in the various communities. Some of the diseases were brought in by soldiers sent to Texas during Reconstruction.]

Some think it was caused by soldiers being camped so near, so many dead horses, some say it is abating. The hearse has just passed us, I was writing returning from that lonely but loved place because some loved form reposing there, underneath a little sacred mound of earth and beneath a spreading tree.

I finished another sock for sale. Mr F purchased me a nice walnut bureau with beautiful glass, set cane seat chairs, 2 large office chairs, mahogany secretary bible stand for $60. I sold things out of my house to pay for most of them. Mr F started yesterday to Presbytery in Round Rock. Got leave of absence from comptroller until Monday.

Sunday morning 25th 66 Tommie Finie and sweet daughter Mollie Nannie have gone to church. I felt if my servant was not willing to wash a few more dishes if company should come (I expect none but I always wish to be prepared) that of course she would be unwilling to be troubled with the watch care of my babe. So with great pain and disappointment indeed I had to give up my fond desire to hear Rev Mr Gillette preach and stay at home and take care of my dear little boy myself. My John Collier is so noble, so bright, so promising that he is worth taking care of.

What will we do. I am too feeble to do my work. My little daughter is too little, I hate to have my boys to do so much house work. They hate to do it. When they have it to do they disturb my mind so it makes my health more feeble. All physicians say the most that can do me good is rest and quietude.

But how can I have that without a good trusty, willing, kind sympathetic hearted servant. I have prayed hard for such a servant. When Ann came here I hoped I had found that very one. I told her at the beginning that if I gave her $10 that exorbitaut [sic] price, she must hard all the week, and do what was obliged to be done on Sunday. She said she was willing and would do it. But right away she complained and I never had given her a task, but a few times only have hurried her. She is very slow, but does her work well and goes out attending to her daily __?__ time of daily duties, incumbent upon family affairs without being told every day. Which delighted me and I would not care for anything if she would not grumble and only seemed to appreciate my lenient manner and kind treatment. It is a pleasure to my heart to be kind to a servant and have them express appreciation like good old Anthony used and that kind old servant aunt Betsy. I know I try and want to do for the best. I altho' truly Southern, taught to believe in the divine approbation of the former almost idolized institution of slavery, from my earliest most infantile days, have been convinced let it have been ever so divinely approved in the past as many suppose. The time has come and God has permitted the freedom of this degenerate race, they are among us. They must live, they are immortals, they have souls, feelings and sensibilities. O God forbid that we should injure the _feelings_, the prospect or the interest of one of these immortal beings as regards time or eternity. O no, let us whose minds are enlightened bear with the infirmities of the ignorance of these poor creatures, whom we as a Southern people with a misguided view have helped to keepin ignorance.

O God give us wisdom from on high to enable us a act with propriety toward this inferior race now in the beginnings of this new order of things that has been inaugurated amongst us, we are the last people that ought to complain. The south struck the first fatal blow. Yes, they sounded the death knell to slavery, their idolized institution. The _Great_ I am has said "there is no God beside me." Need we be surprised that slavery has passed away with us, ought we kick against God. O no let us arise in mass as a mighty nation, and say by our public acts, our legislation, our converse, _our lives_, that the Great I am that I am is "God and there is none else." And if we would do this how great would be our glory as the mightiest, most peaceful and happiest nation upon this broad green earth.

To do this let us bow submissively to God, let our fondest and most favorite wishes that has all along life's pathways clung and clustered around our hearts and seemed interwoven with our very being itself be swalled up in the will of God.

The African race is freed among us, they are here, let us do all we can to elevate in morals and in piety thus assist them in this new era to become good useful citizens.

How can we do this? We cannot whip them as when they were slaves. O no I do not wish to do this. This has as in Rev Mr Johnsons speech in our convention said for years giving way to milder and more elevating incentives to labor. And I feel that if the whole nation in pureness of hearts would join Judge Paschal in this prayer written in a letter to a friend here, for divine aid at this sad juncture, he would bring order out of confusion, light out of darkness, _peace_ out of discord, and this sad chaos that surrounds us, and threatens a portentous storm would be hushed. And we could all enjoy peace in the full import of that word, and I feel that would be enough for earth.

Tommie and Finie put up the horses, waited for Uncle Joe to come home and feed, they did not mind feeding them, but we don't like to hire a servant pay them before hand and then have their work to do. Ann begged my pardon, said she had not to have talked that way. I freely forgive.

Tuesday 27th 66 We have but little flour, and I had been thinking we were out of debt. But Mr F had neglected to pay a small debt for 5 or 6 years now it has run up to $300 and he owes his relations some $100. I feel atho' he is getting good wages that we must save every dime and deny every indulgence wish until the last cent is paid. I wish I could get him never to go into debt again. I have tried so often and he has resolved & reresolved, but always breaks over, but if he don't quit it we will be untimately ruined. We are nearly that now, because he is no financier and scarce ever can make ends meet. From almost a little fortune left me by my dear papa, but a small fragment remains.

Sat 31st March I walked to Aunt Leila's an old col [colored] friend, also Finie, Mollie and Collie accompanied me as they were so anxious to see Aunt Leila. We spent the morning there pleasantly. I have known her 18 years and over, she has long proved herself to be a woman of principles and good Christian character. She is one of our members, and one of Mr F's useful members when we lived in Austin before.

Before we left she brought me in some nice light bread and preserves and gave the children honey and light bread. Told me she was much obliged to me and the children for coming to see her. She has been sick, quite feeble. Like myself her healthiest days are past I presume.

Altho' she has always been so faithful, true and honest, had dressed at the 1st dressing of 380 some odd babies, nursed their mothers, and when slavery was in vogue, I never heard of her doing ought but what would impress upon them the duty they owed their masters. I had often heard her say that she was happier when she belonged to Dr Mayberry, than she has ever been since. During the rebellion the Confederacy took $50 in specie from her, took her to the county house, tried to sell her and all her property she had worked so hard to obtain.

They kept her $50 but she saved her home just because the title happen to be in the name of a white friend. How she saved her person from being sold I don't know, but I believe it was by showing her fidelity to the cause of humanity and nursing the sick, by the interposition of white friends I presume. What an outrage upon law & justice to have poor offensive but useful members of society abused thus.

We had a fine churning to day, got a nice saucer of golden butter. I sent Sister Smith a picture of butter milk. Also some to Aunt Leila. She told Ann she was much obliged to me. Such a thing is a treat in town. I paid Ann her months hire $10 in specie she looked so proud. I felt so much better to pay her for her faithful work than to hire as formerly from some aristocrat the negro work, faithfully, and then I be compelled to pay the hire over to the hands of the owner, that had thousands without. I felt really happy when I looked at Ann's gratified countenance, and I felt more & more confirmed in my former convictions that the Lord had freed the slaves and that we would yet see better times than we have done in this sweet sunny southland of ours.

Many of course will have to labor more but for the youth of our country this will prove a benefit as it will give strength to limb and muscle. We old folks may perhaps suffer by it. But I firmly believe that eventually it will work out for the good of our race.

I hope the colored members for whom Mr F labored for, for years will not desert him now. For they <u>say no</u> other minister during their years of bondage labored for their souls eternal interest as my Dear husband did. Surely they ought to rally to him help, amid the crash & crush of things to bear up and rebuild again. I called and pleasantly spent an hour with sister T Smith. Finie went uptown and bought 1 box blacking. Mr F at 12 heard Gov. Hamilton speak, at 3, Ann heard him speak to the darkies, two freemen spoke too, how changed the scene.

Tuesday April 3rd 66 Ann received a letter from Peter, her husband, who is in Arkansas. Ann was completely overjoyed and said Mrs Foster I can't iron today, I can't see, but before night notwithstanding rain and she had 7 or 8 dresses to iron for me and one for herself and 2 window curtains, nice pillow slips besides the regular washing, she finished before night. Such a servant is truly a comfort. And I feel such an one is from the Lord. I observed to Mr F that Ann is not like a negro but has principle like a white woman. I have no trouble housekeeping now Ann is so forth and true. I fear I shall never get such another. But maybe I will, for I thought this when Aunt Betsie left me. But now in Ann I find her equal, I never expected to see a superior to either.

Thursday April 5th Well I am a little tired tonight. Finie & Mamma have been on their feet nearly all day, unpacking and repacking trunk boxes, wardrobe, bureau secretary & c, lots things done up pretty nicely about 5 in the evening. Mr F returned horse fell with him hurt him badly, had a nice wedding supper. The groom gave him $5 in specie, for which we feel grateful.

Mr F read to me in our city paper that Rev Mr William Baker, former resident of this city, who I am told had to support his self whilst preached people, has since his late removal to Zaynesville, Ohio received 15.00-$500 in specie, $100 in goods. O how encouraging it did my poor saddened heart good would this could be our happy lot ee'r we die. That my dear husband could be untrammeled and devote himself to his holy calling that is so dear to his heart.

[William Baker became the pastor of the Presbyterian church in Austin in 1850. A Unionist, he moved his family to Zanesville, Ohio, and remained there until 1872. When he died in 1883, his body was returned to Austin to be buried next to his father.]

Ann told me last that she loved, did not believe any other lady would have done by her as I have done, that I comforted her in her distress and that she would never forget me in this world. And that she could not help loving me that I have been so good to her. I told her that she had really comforted me in my feeble health, and I did not think I would have been as well as I am if she had not come to live with me. Because her course has been such, that my mind and body has been relieved and quietude and a partial restoration of health has been the happy results. O it does my heart food to feel toward a servant as I do toward Ann and especially as she constantly proves to me that she loves me and mine.

To day I commenced giving her writing lessons for 50 cents a month. And hearing her in reading and spelling for 25 cts per month. I made her and sold her a copy book for 25 cents. Finie hears her lessons every night for 25 cents per month.

I felt it a pleasure to teach Ann. She is a woman of a strong good mind. Capable of receiving instruction and I intend to do all I can to aid her. I always believed that the negroes ought to have been taught to read their bibles at least. I never raised but one, a boy that was given me, soon as he was born, by my parents. I taught him around my knees to read, gave him a handsome testament and hymn book. He could read them both. Ann still spinning.

Journal #10

January 24, 1867–June 5, 1867

———

In January of 1867 the ages of the Foster family are as follows: Louisa will
be forty-six in December, Finis will be fifty-one in February, Tommie will be
twenty in November, Finie will be fifteen in December, Mollie will be seven in
November, and John Collier will be four in October.

* * * * *

Thursday, Jan 24th 1867 Austin Travis County After this afternoon
we commenced a female prayer meeting in <u>our</u> parlor. Sisters Cummings,
Dignon, & Harrington were the only ladies that came to the meeting. My
sister across the street did not attend. I thought surely she believed in females
thus retiring to pray for their loved ones and especially the dear children of
our love. Of course we would have been much happier and more encouraged
if we had have more in attendance. But still <u>our</u> hearts are fixed and as ever
we feel that as for <u>me</u> and <u>mine house we will serve the Lord</u>.

I hope, <u>I believe</u>, I humbly trust this book will prove a sweet remembrance
of our little female prayer meeting, that we had such an humble beginning in
the poor, way ward anxious hearted ministers home. I don't feel discouraged.
I <u>know</u> in whom I have believed. I know his promises are <u>Yea</u> & <u>amen</u>. I have
tried Him so long, and ever found him true to His <u>promises</u>. So my poor
soul is buoyed up with the humble trust and hope that He has in reservation
for us a great blessing.

Tommie is studying his lessons for school tomorrow. Finie also, they are
going to professor Baker, an Episcopalian, they like him very much. Sweet
Mollie and Collie after a fine healthy romp, have gone to sleep. Collie says he

is my bird hunter and he will climb up in trees and catch <u>lots</u> of them and bite them and kill them.

Sweet lively child how comforting to me is his dear little prattle. Collie says when he kills the birds they will be for me to eat, especially the feet. Mollie churned her butter today and took it up herself. I salted it and put in the little yellow jar. Finie sold $1.35 cents worth of beef, milk and eggs to day for himself after school hours.

Friday Jan 25th 1867 We had prayers, breakfast before 7. Children gone to school, I washed the dishes. Mollie wiped all the dishes, swept the floor, has washed her face, is combing her hair, will then dust & tidy up my room & parlor.

Sat 26th /67 Finie and Colie Lackett had a fine play until Mr F returned. Mr F preformed the marriage ceremony between a federal officer and Miss Fomie Peck, a Frenchman and german lady, this eve at 7 O clock, he gave Mr F $5 in gold, Mr F gave me $2.50. I handed round coffee and cake. The groom and bride promised to attend our church and weekly prayer meeting. O that good may result from this event. The groom Mr M. Charles LaMore of his own accord promised to call round with his bride some evening next week, bring his guitar and play for us, he is a teacher of music.

Tuesday 29th We had about 25 persons at our prayer meeting, a sweet calm refreshing time, three young men prayed, Bro Dick Castleman, Ceph Cummings, My Son Tommie. O how sweet the hours passed with me.

Sat 1867 All well, we look forward to tomorrow with deep interest as it is the anniversary of our beloved Zion and Mr F will preach (no preventing Providence) a set discourse upon the Distinctive Doctrines Rise & Progress of the Cumberland Presbyterian Church.

Feb Wed 13th We have had several dark days, altho' last night was so dark and <u>dismal</u> we had 14 at our weekly pray over meeting.

Feb 14th Thursday Mr F mailed my letter I wrote yesterday, one to sister Ginnie, one to Rev J M Halsell, Editor of Pearl, one of inquiry to Wheeler & Wilson, one to Sidney E Morse Jr & Co. The last one contains a draft of $42 and his receipt of $21, in all $63 for which he has promised me a $55 sewing machine, but I don't like the bronze one. I want to make another club and get a higher priced, silver plated one, because they are preferable.

[Louisa wrote to the Sidney J. Morse Company (brother of Samuel F. B. Morse, who developed the electric telegraph) and Wheeler & Wilson. Both companies made sewing machines. Louisa paid $63 for a new machine, which in today's dollars would be over $2,000. This was a large amount for this poor family.]

Sabbath morn May 4th 1867 I am so fearful Mollie will not behave at church to day. Lord, do grant to let the good angel take the seat on her little sights, shoulder, descend thy spirit into her little heart and while mama is at home, feeble and praying for her little daughter, may she be by so many kindly influences, be induced to behave like a little lady then I will be so happy. O do kind Father take possession of Finie's heart, keep him awake, may he exercise a proper brother's Watch care over his dear little sister. Help papa to preach good, help us all to pray right, up into heaven, and bring the blessing from above.

Tuesday May 7 1867 Last evening, although there were fewer present than ever before, yet we had a soul cheering meeting. Three ladies prayed, two spoke a little.

I ask Mollie to bring some fuel to my fire, before she left me to go only out into the yard to get it. I talked to her about doing right, and if she met anyone in the yard to be good. She then looked sweetly at me and remarked, she would to be good so she could meet her sweet little sisters in heaven. She went off and soon returned with the pare of cobs to burn to make coals, to make my coffee boil for my dinner. She said to Collie I prayed at the hog pin when I was out, Oh! I was so touched, I took the sweet little girl in my arms, embraced, kissed and blessed her. O God grant that my daily teachings may be as a "nail driver in a sore place" as I begin to feel under Gods spirits may influence my constant anxious watching over my boys have been. Bless the Lord. He is a covenant keeping God. Last night Collie was sitting on my lap, all was silent. I looked in his sweet baby face, he looked so serious and thoughtful, so much like a sage as Tommie wrote about him. I ask the sweet little one what he was thinking about. He said I'm thinking about God. I inquired of him what he was thinking about God. He said I was thinking God loves me.

Wednesday morn May 8th /67 Our old, dear kind friend Bro & Sister Gray came from Lampassas springs [about fifty miles north of Austin]. Stayed all night with us, they are always so kind to us, she brought me 4 or 5 lbs of nice butter, steak enough for breakfast. She told Bro G he must get us some flour to day. They have gone to the stores to purchase their supplies. Our little parlor was nearly filled, and we had a blessed good meeting. Bro Steele the dear old baptist minister led for us, he told us that we were commanded to worship God with our <u>bodies</u> and <u>souls</u> and said the churches in Austin were so lazy in their worship, that they could not stand up and sing, nor even open their mouths wide enough to sing. And he supposed that they would soon have their feather beds and couches in church so they could worship God at their ease.

Sat May 11th 1867 I am much better except a hacking cough which annoys me very much. We have just read a letter from Bro T C Anderson, Lebanon, Tenn. containing a $100 check, for Mr F he writes the missionary board sends it to help the church session here, pay for Mr F for ministerial services rendered.

We do feel so grateful, it is much needed <u>right now</u>. The board has not appointed a missionary for Austin, but will wait until after the Genl Assembly. He writes he thinks Mr F will be appointed. In this regard we feel greatly interested.

I made Mollie a pink, striped calico jacket to day, commenced about 12 O clock, trimmed it all around with black worsted braid, in a chain. It looks very sweet. Patched Mr F's linin drawers, read as usual, and attended as is my custom to my domestic concerns. Mr F accompanied Finie, Mollie and Collie to see a man walk a rope on the avenue. I doubt the propriety of children going to such places, but they were so anxious that I reluctantly gave my consent, perhaps I may be too strenuous, but when I think of my youth, my misspent time that I whiled away on sin and folly, I desire to press upon my precious children's minds the importance of improving every golden moment.

My heart has been pained since the children came home. They talk more about the feat they witnessed than any thing else. Tommie hoed out the irish potatoes, he was so tired he did not wish to go. He looks feeble. I am more feeble myself. I ironed 4 garments felt like I could not stand up to iron any more. Uncle John came and told me his wife would iron for me for some cotton I have in an old matress [*sic*]. So I fortunately got all the articles ironed that I needed to day. I do feel we have great reason to thank God.

Sunday 12th of May 1867 Tommie and I are too feeble to go to Sabbath school or church. Mr F, Finnie, Mollie and Collie attended early. Finie nodded at church. Mollie behaved ugly. O it makes my heart ache, when will my children <u>"learn to do well"</u>. I will be compelled some way to break up such misbehavior in the house of God.

Collie behaved so sweet at church which made my heart so happy. O he is such a treasure, God has blessed him with such a sweet disposition, which

This photo was taken of John Devier walking a tight rope across Congress Avenue in Austin Texas, 1867. Somewhere in the audience were Mr. Foster, Finie, Mollie, and Collie. Photo from the Austin History Center, Austin Public Library, public domain.

is such a comfort to my <u>very</u> soul. How a sinful mortal can be so lovely and passes such an angel spirit, I can not tell. I daily feel the influence of this child's, calm, placid disposition on my own heart and <u>every</u> day life. What gift could have been so opportunely bestowed upon me as this dear child of <u>mine.</u>

Mollie is bright and lovely girl when she tries to do right, which she neglects to do often enough. O blessed holy Father I beg, I implore thee to help my little girl to learn to govern her disposition and become more lovely in spirit and behavior like her sweet little blue eyed brother she loves so dearly, so that she may be enabled to shine in "the home circle," as lovely, lovely woman is designed to do. Then Mama will be so happy. Won't you try my dear daughter? Go alone every day and pray to God to help you to be a comfort to dear old gray headed mama, that loves sweet Mollie so tenderly.

I wrote this to benefit you my loved little daughter, called her and read it to her. She got so mad, stuck out her mouth and pained my poor fond heart afresh. O what shall I do? Mollie won't you curb that high hateful temper of yours? That throws so many hot fire bonds into our home circle where naught but <u>love</u> should reign, love to each other, love to our fellow man. If you won't listen to me, now perhaps when I am gone, forever gone, you may read this and be profited. If so Mama's dearest wish will be obtained.

Tuesday morn 14th May 1867 O I am so pressed, I have some sewing I <u>must</u> do for my children, and I want to read, and there are several letters ought to be written, one to order my sewing machine that I need so much to help me make up my sons shirts and many other things for our little girl and boy. O I wish I had nothing to do the balance of my life, but to read and write and improve my mind so as to be useful.

But I dearly love to sew and make up nice clothing for my dears. I feel that I have lost much of my precious time, embroidering, braiding, ruffling and trimming my children's clothes and beds. Still I have to see trimming and all things neat, but we should be very careful how we spend our time.

Mollie has just come in and asked me to write that she is good "<u>some times</u>" and brings Mama flowers. I asked Collie, my sweet little baby boy, what made me love him so, he paused a moment then he reply, I <u>reckon</u> it is God that makes you love me so.

Thursday 16th May/67 Mollie hurt me so much this morning she was so mean about saying her lesson. I had to slap and scold her. Collie said his little lesson sweetly as he always does. I must retire now alone to pray. O for heavenly guidance to be the better enabled to train me.

Mollie has been so <u>naughty</u> and tedious about her day and Sabbath school lessons, that I will be able to perform but little this forenoon. Which I hate as time is so precious with me, as I <u>feel</u> I <u>must</u> devote more time to reading and writing than I have <u>ever</u> in the past. And my sewing must be done for six persons, whose taste seem to require neatness in the workmanship. I feel that I can do it up all nicely, and with the help of my children do all the house and kitchen work to, as the old woman has gone. We have no servant. A kind, black Christian woman does our washing for 50 cents a week. And takes pay in corn, meat, or our partly worn clothes. Sometimes Mollie, Finie and I do the ironing. Sometimes we hire it for dry roasting corn, or fish or something we have in the house.

I hope soon to receive my sewing machine, that I am entitled to for sending on a club of 16 names for that most excellent paper. The New York Observer. [The *New-York Observer* was a weekly religious paper founded by Sidney E. Morse in 1823. It ceased publication in 1912.]

Finie, my noble, my darling Finie has been so naughty to night, I have just finished hearing his lesson in geography, when he ought to have it perfect an hour since. I always when able to sit up to hear his spelling in the fourth reader and Webster's spelling book and Geography before I permit him to retire. I know just how he is progressing.

Friday May 17th 67/ Finie arose early, went to market to purchase some very nice steak, 15 cents worth which makes us three meals. Tommie spoke so roughly and unkindly to his sister that I was duty bound to seat him before me, as is my custom as to lecture him. O he has such a hateful disposition with his morale conduct, he embitters every day of my life.

The outside world knows nothing of the deep heart trouble this child's unkindness causes me. By my friends he is held up as a pattern of sweet disposition behavior and kindness to me. But O could they lift the veil and view his lowering, angry looks at me and his harsh words he speaks to the mother that has arisen at the midnight hour to administer to his wants when he was helpless, how different the aspect. I feel that I have done my duty by him. I hope he will. I cannot say I hope. I would be glad if he would return kindness and shows that he appreciates all my deep untold solicitude for him. But alas!

Mollie lost her first reader, she said if I go to God and pray I think I will find it. I said my daughter go. She went came in smiling look thoughtful a minute or two, then said I know where it is, she ran off into the parlor and then brought it into our room. Mollie and Collie have said their Sabbath school lesson.

Collie looked at me so sweet, got out of my chair in which he had sat all the time, met me at my west door. I took him in my arms, we kneeled in a secluded part of own apartment, there he offered up his original prayer, prayed for the whole family, naming each one out, the whole world, he concluded by saying bless budda Finie make him say his lessons good and not go out of the school house 'till school is out. O my heart was devout raised to God in silent prayer for this dear little last boy of mine, and mine house hold again. I feel to adore the good Lord for His amazing goodness in winning my thoughts of late, more from earth than ever before.

Mollie had a chill has a hot fever. Lord please bless and sanctify my child's affliction to her good. O how unhappy, deep and pungent are the feelings of my sadden heart to night. Tommie, O Tommie when will you do right and act from principle in religion and all the minor obligations of life. You made me heart sick this morning and the last thing to night is to add almost poisoned daggers to my already stabbed and bleeding heart.

Sat May 18th 1867 First Finnie arose without being called, awoke his brother Tommie, Finie then went to market, purchased some tolerable nice steak and soup bone for which he gave 20 cents.

Then went to professor Clingers by 6, a German teacher in day school, whose little sweet bright blue eyed daughter is my little Sabbath school scholar, a class mate of my only little daughter Mollie, he, professor Clinger sent me two most beautiful bouquets out of his flower garden.

Mr F, Tommie and Finie cleared off the yard nice. I gave Finie money, he went to purchase for himself a pattern of neat brown linin pants and a pencil one half red and one half blue. I must do Tommie the same way. This morning Finie bought himself two pencils with his own money and one nice one he gave me with idea rubber on it, which I am writing with. [On March 30, 1858, Hymen Lipman received the first patent for attaching an eraser to the end of a pencil.]

Monday morn May 20th 1867 I write in this diary with dear Finie's colored pencils, thinking it will please him. They're at school. Mr F is gone in to the city. [The population of Austin at this time was nearly four thousand people.] Mollie is learning her Sabbath school ticket when she gets a certain number of red tickets then so among blue ones, she will receive a present from the school of a pretty book. The number of tickets not decided on yet.

Mr F gave children & me a parting kiss and started for the neighborhood where he preaches every 3rd Sab, there he proposes spending the entire week visiting his members and endeavoring to prepare their hearts for the approaching communion season. As usual almost his last words were, to me to pray for him.

May Tuesday 21st 67 O I wish I had any machine home to help me out of this press of sewing. Lord help me to do good today. Mollie has read and spelled her Sabbath school lesson so well. When thro' she said I may quit, for you said I might if I said my lesson well, and you tell the truth, then she looked so sweet and remarked the good Angel is on both my shoulders now. She has also almost learned her pretty red ticket she drew Sabbath. Lord do bless our only little girl, that God has permitted in His wisdom to dwell with us. Had about 30 persons at our meeting.

Wednesday May 22nd 1867 My washer woman came and took my washing off. I hope it will be neatly done up. I made some nice soup for the children's dinner from the bone Finie purchased at market this morning, and now we have the meat off the bone to make hash for breakfast. 20 cents worth of meat has served us all day and will do for breakfast. I am determined to be just as economical as I can.

Thursday May 23rd 67 A pretty day, but rather cold. Sarah a col [colored] girl ironed, washed up my lock room, scoured my kitchen, ironing & kitchen table nicely. I am to pay her in corn.

Mrs Southerland said she had some work for me to do, and that she had confidence that I could do it. That was to talk to Miss Dinah, her only child, on the subject of religion. O I feel so grateful for this sweet indication of the widening influences of our little sweet, social prayer meeting, as Mrs S has only been present once last Tuesday evening. It seems she has already gotten her pious heart, carefully aroused to the <u>interest</u> of her uncovered daughter's <u>precious Soul</u>. Lord bless and help me talk just right Sat eve as Mrs S told me on this afternoon she intended to bring her daughter around so I could talk to her. And try to get her to attend our female prayer meetings.

Friday 24th of May 1867 A friend and brother brought me a cow and calf this morning for which he had received the pay a month or two since, when he sold me the cow, he said he intended to give Mr F a beef. But this morning he remarked kindly he had given Uncle <u>Fine</u> enough, let the members here support him.

Now again I feel the buddings of that same pride, from which I have suffered so much or natural feelings or whatever you may call it, that has so often cause me to feel and say, before I would live <u>poor</u> and <u>nearly starve myself</u> and family, I would go to work and make a good living. We do have to <u>live</u> so hard it has been two months or more since we have had, except for part of a dollars worth, of flour in our house it was given us by a Sister Gray that came and stayed nearly two days and nights and eat with us most of the time.

Finie has returned and says he has spoke his speech and that Professor B very well only he did not place stress enough at some places. He is foot [bottom] in grammar he has been head in most of his classes. I feel so bad to think Finie is foot. I shall see hereafter in regard to his grammar, as I have been doing in his other studies. I have neglected his grammar but I shall awake. O my boy, my noble boy, the pride and joy of my heart must learn all his lessons.

Sab, May 26th/67 Such an ugly morn, looked like rain, but I felt I must risk it. I could not bear the idea of not meeting with my sweet little class. Mollie and Gussie had perfect lessons. Mattie pretty good. Sarah Shepherd was not that far advanced. I had to put her in Tommie Cummings & Collie's class.

Tuesday 28th 1867 Strange weather for Texas. All the family I believe feel improved in health. We are now seated around our family alter ready for prayers, this is ever a sweet spectacle. This has been another sweet day to me, one replete with interest. After I got all cleaned up, and came in my room, Mr F told me two gentlemen and just driven up to the gate and told him they had the deed from Mr and Mrs Miller for the two lots adjourning the two we had perched he went down to Bro Smiths office and had the paper legally arranged, paid every __?__, which we had been nearly __?__ to save for this purpose, we now own a half block, bless the Lord.

Wednesday 29th 1867 Mr F. Finie, Mollie and Collie are practicing singing. "I want to be an Angel," to sing at Bro Lacketts lecture in Sabbath school next sabbath' ["I Want to Be an Angel," was written in 1845 by Sidney P. Gill.]

Thursday 30th /67 I have cleaned up breakfast things, milk things, peeled irish potatoes, enough for a nice mess for dinner. Have them now washed ready for dinner. Children at school. It has rained ever since breakfast. Four of my little dears came to see me to day.

Frank and Jessie Pitman the last mentioned, brought me some beautiful vines to set out around my west gallery. Judge Miner sent me several madeira vines, sister Smith gave Mr F four.

Finie sold his buttermilk for 25 cts. And with it he purchased Mollie a buff jacket. I have cut it out since dark. I intend braiding in a rich pattern with the braid Sister Collier gave M when she was my babie. Finie did up his little jobs, played painting with Frank, and has just recited his third perfect lesson to me. I think God for such a boy. Mr F trained the little ones singing again.

Sunday June 2nd 1867 Mr F, preached a good sermon, on "We shall grow up as calves of the state & c." Mallichi last chapter. At three we attended preaching at the blind Asylum of this city by Rev. Lackett. [In 1856 the Texas legislature built the Texas Blind Asylum at a price of $12,390. At the end of the Civil War, the campus was commandeered by General George Armstrong Custer as his family's residence during the occupation and reconstruction of Texas. In 1866 the asylum was restored, and in 1915 it became the Texas School for the Blind.]

Monday 3rd 67 Fine weather, nothing could have cheered us more than our good female prayer meeting. We had about 15 anxious <u>weeping</u> mourners. In our meeting for requests, Sister Smith, Southerland Finie and myself spoke.

Wednesday June 5th 1867 I have written three letters, one to the Howe Machine Co., one to the Empire S M. Co. [This was probably the Empire Sewing Machine Company in New York.] One of request for prayers again for God to bless more abundantly here in converting power. And to order my Wheelers & Wilson sewing machine. O my heart was sadden this afternoon when Sister Smith came over for me to assist her to finish Nannie's white dotted swiss for her to wear to a dancing party. Her argument in favor of Nannie's going, was that nice little girls her associates had begged and begged again and again for her to go, and she had refused and she thought it was wrong not to let her go, and that Mr Johns at whose house the party was to be held his family was considered very pious. I could not refrain from telling her that I felt it would be a blight upon the church for an elder to go, take or permit his daughter to attend a dancing party. She laughed and said Parson Philips, a methodist south, was going to let his daughter go. I remarked that no minister or no ministers in the world permitting their children to go would affect me, that we ought to take the bible as our guide and it taught us to shun the very appearance of evil.

Journal #11

June 10, 1867–March 3, 1870

———

Monday June 10th 1867 I have been <u>very</u> feeble, was <u>compelled</u> soon as I washed my dishes, to lie down. I rested 'till dinner, fearing if I did not I would not be able to attend the religious duties of the day, as it was my time in course to lead our dear little ladies prayer meeting. O how blank I felt at dinner. I felt I could not hold it profitably. I begged my husband to lead it for me, he said he could not, he must go down into the city. I retired alone and asked for guidance. O I begged God to teach me to be plain and just what to do.

Thursday 13th 67 I have not been up to day. Mr F would not consent for me to go, as he said Sister C was washing and I needed to rest. So I did not go altho' I wanted to go and felt I could hardly stay away. All right I presume. Old col [colored] Aunt Lila is worse, Mr F called and talked a long time with her and her son Jerry.

Wednesday July 17th I am so sorry dear children, that the press of religious and domestic duties, with feeble health, has prevented the continuation of my journal.

Friday July 19th Our home devotions as usual, secret prayers yesterday, and this morning at 9 as Bro Lackett requested, he told us last night that he felt the efficacy of prayer, and realized we had all obeyed his request, I have offered up a constant prayer for that young Mr Moore. I hope, I almost <u>believe</u> that he will find consolation in Christ in this nights services close. I feel almost sure of it.

I am so tired I have just finished a letter to Mr W W Williams, a photographist of our city, who had to close his gallery on account of ill health, and repair to the Lampasas Springs to recruit. [W. Wirt Williams was a photographer in Texas for approximately forty years.] My theme was his return to God whom he once professed to have found in believing.

Sat 20th 1867 I fried the steak out and attended to the egg bread, children are now taking up breakfast. I made the pot of coffee. I hope it will be nice. We expect all to attend the meeting at 10 at Father Hall's. All the family attended the above mentioned meeting.

Sat Jan 4th 1868 We have not so much as a light kindled on the hearth this evening. The moon is shining brightly. Harrie, Finie, and little Alfred Smith are having a nice time at play. Mr F is done studying and he and Mollie & Collie are playing Santa Klause. O they are so happy. Tommie is still reading and I am at my loved, and pleasing tasks, writing.

Sabbath June 19th 1868 I was too feeble to attend church, which made me very sad, the more especially on account of being absent from my sweet little Sabbath school class. All our dear family attended the precious dear Sabbath school and the blest sanctuary of save Collie and myself. Collie behaved very sweet and amused our servant woman very much, so much that she came several times to tell me of his sweet childish, funny sayings. One time she came laughingly and said Collie sat down on the oven and said if I had some fire I could fry myself.

Jan 27th 1868 Prayers & meals as usual, excepting Mollie made up the batter, and put it into the little oven, put fire under the oven, and on the lid, attended to it, and baked nice egg bread for dinner, had it ready on a nice clean plate, when her papa came home to dine, from the court room, where dire <u>necessity</u>, compels him to serve on the jury so as to add a little pittance to his meager salary.

O it made me so happy to see Mollie's dear papa so proud of his little daughter's cooking. I think it was enough to make any parent proud, a little girl 7 years and old to cook as nice bread as my precious little Mollie did to day.

It gladdened our little sweet girl's heart to hear her precious papa, she loves <u>so dearly</u>, speak in commendation of what she cooked expressly to please his fond heart, and O it was a pure pleasure to me <u>too</u>, to see him eat it so eagerly, and smile so lovingly on our only sweet little living daughter, that we so much desire to raise for <u>usefulness</u> in life, and we have thus begun to prepare her for its realities. She also washed the sweet potatoes, I cut them up, and put them on she attended mostly to them.

Sat 28th 68 Tuesday As usual our family devotions, meals & Mollie made up and baked bread again. I am so delighted that our loved little girlie, loves to do such work. She washed her papas woolen socks out as nice as any body could do. Very, very cold, notwithstanding, we had a doz persons at our precious weekly prayer meeting, several spoke & prayed.

March 22nd 68 As I have of late been more fully permitted to feel that all my afflictions in feeble health, loss of children and the little estate my own dear sleeping papa left me at his demise has all been necessary to humble this poor proud heart of mine, and to draw my soul (that is priceless on its value) still nearer to God who created it for some purpose.

March Friday My sad fate, I have been sick all week, lost so much time from my pressing sewing and house work, tho' dear children attend to the house work very well. Mr F bakes me nice batter cakes, but I have poor appetite. Collie made a chime, papa said I must write it down. It is "Now old big head, go to bed." O may my son become a great religious Poet. We had a sweet ladies prayer meeting Monday. I was scarce able to sit up.

May 5th 1868 Home, City of Austin Tex. The day is here, the solemn hour to our "home circle" has passed. The fond husband, the affectionate father is gone. But sweet thought! He has gone to obey the mandates of the beloved church of his choice.

I had felt that I was very firm, and really wished and believed that I would not shed a tear, feeling so willing for him to go, Yes! I was anxious for him to go, for I felt it was his duty to bow to the obligations laid upon him at the last presbytery, by his dear brethren, when they voted that he should be our delegate to the Genl. Assembly at Lincoln Ill.

When he got to the door he turned fondly embraced & kissed me again, that last fond pressure will never be erased from memorys leaflet, but will stand as a green spot in this wilderness of gloom as well, spring of untold pleasure, both to his heart and mine. Finie bore for him his neat valise, that he purchased with money that dear precious Sister Cope raised expressly to fit him for this trip, to the stage office, from there Finie went to school and has not yet returned. Mollie & Collie would run after dear papa about 100 yrds, he stopped kissed & talked to them with all the fathers love, that characterizes his noble soul. Tommie went to the east gallery whither I followed him. I found him weeping, so full he could scarce speak, there Mother and son engaged on that lovely manly form.

My old cough has returned I am very feeble this wild agony was more than I could bear, after all my resolves to be composed, which I thought I could be without an effort, I was overcome by the children's wild excitement that I wept for about one hour. I was compelled to go to bed.

Tommie went to work, I was so overcome that I fell asleep. When I awoke, the plaintive grief of my little sad prattles that was borne to my ear, and their child expressions, rather amused my sorrowful heart. Collie would say two months an't anything, then he would say I wish he'd staid here one month longer, 4 big fat horses will take papa away, they can kill every thing.

Then Mollie says I'm glad he's gone, I wish he would stay away. Collie says I'm glad he's gone, because he's gone to preach and I know he'll come back.

Well Mollie says I don't care if he is gone if the boat is nice, and big like a house. Mollie says but I think he ought to have staid at home. I am not glad he's gone. Collie says he's sorry because papa's gone, he wants to see him. Collie would look so sad and say, I can see papa now preaching.

Finie has returned from school he says he wept on parting with his dear father at the stage office, then went to the school room, it was play time, he then returned, and stayed with his father and saw him step in the stage and it depart.

Monday July 20th /68 We all attended Sab. School & church, once more, Collie having gotten well of whooping cough. O! how I did thank the good Lord. About six weeks since the sweet little blue-eyed one has been to Sab. School or church. Uncle Henry preached a good sermon at 11. Mr F in the evening. In the mist of Mr F's sermon I was so sick. I was compelled to get Tommie to come home with me. I hated it so bad. I suffered intensely could scarcely walk home. At to sit down and rest on a rock on the way.

O how I hated to walk out of that crowded church. I feared some would say I was not interested in my dear husband's discourse but it was not so. My suffering was so great I was compelled to do what I never did before in life, leave the house of God during preaching. It almost killed me.

July 23th 68 I am more feeble than usual, at this season of the year, but much better than I was a month ago. Mr F is quite feeble, not recovered yet from his attack, brought on by fatigue, traveling home from the Genl. Assembly which met at Lincoln, Ill. O what a happy morn was, the day down of the 1st July 1868 to our little family for at that hour the <u>loved</u> husband and dear father returned from the holy mission to bless his precious house hold.

Tuesday July 28th 68 Your father, dear children remarked to me before our marriage. He had thought if he ever loved "it would burn him up." Notwithstanding all this there was a strange confidence in our secret prayers, which neither knew about till after we were united in this <u>dearest</u> of all bonds. Each fervently prayed, with all the soul for God's will to be done, and if God saw any cause why we should not be united in marriage, if it was not best for our souls interest, that God would prevent it, if no other way, by death.

The appointed day came, we were alive, spared. We married almost with this prayer on our youthful lips, I was about 20, my companion 26. <u>I know</u> two fonder more warm, impetuous, congenial hearts, ever loved, & come together in this dearest <u>sweetest</u> strongest union on earth.

Sunday Aug 30th Mr F started to a camp meeting yesterday eve, altho' he was suffering badly from a fall from our upper room, to the basement floor. He looks pale like he had had a severe spell of sickness. Every one of our children went to Sab. School. I staid all alone, save our faithful dog Lion.

We haven't a dime buying meat and a few vegetables on a credit, right against our rule. But we had to do, or eat dry corn bread. I had to sell my eggs and chicken to buy sugar & coffee or do without, hence not an egg. We have not had a sack of flour since Christmas, Mr F made the money independent of his salary to get that. Since he came from the Genl Assembly, we bought $2 worth nice flour with money the church gave Mr F, whilst on his late visit to his dear kindred. We not perhaps have meal enough to last a few days. Sugar to do 4 days, may be coffee to last a few days. Holes in both my shoes so if I step out my feet get wet. Finie has no decent shoes, neither has Mollie.

What will we do without relief, in a few days we will have nothing to eat. O how it hurts us, to have our poor little Mollie & Collie beg for biscuit and non to give. Isn't it hard? But perhaps it's for the best. Would God permit it were it not for our good?.

But I married a minister, my private feelings are nothing. I shall lay them aside and drop, and go with him where ever he says go, altho' it may be far from my hearts desire. Eternity will reveal my sacrifices, my heart troubles, my lonely sad hours, my hopes, and my fears. But all this is nothing compared to the sufferings of my Savior & his apostilles. Then hush my heart be still, look up trust in God, step out, do your duty.

Tuesday Sept 1st 1868 City of Austin Texas Another anniversary has come, 26 years since I became the wife of a minister of the cross of Christ. Little did my youthful heart dream of the trials that were all o'er life's great arena. I don't see how I could have lived 20 years and been so trusting, so unsuspecting,

Altho' I had been a child of sorrow, and had with bursting heart, just about 2 1/2 years earlier buried my first kind, dear husband. Soon after my mother, father, my first born child, my treasured little Isham Benjamin Clopton, then the dear kind old man that father left in care of his homestead, & servants. Where his only two orphan children dwelt in sadness and gloom, though surrounded with kind relatives and dear friends..

My children, it is for you that mother is writing this. With a view to benefit you & nerve you on to duty, and enable to bear with Christian fortitude, life's bitterest trials. I shall attempt to enter into details, more than usual with me in my diary. For you alone it is written. I had in past life a few dear friends, that begged so hard that I permitted them to read my journal, but very few. I feel a great diffidence in letting anyone read my writing, they seem so imperfect to me.

Little did I dream, 26 years ago when I was a youthful bride, that on the 26th anniversary of our marriage, that my fond heart thought would bring to my life, perfect peace, and complete happiness, that in a land of plenty, I would be in the midst of my children, My husband gone to Camp meeting, we too poor to own a conveyance or to hire one. No shoes without holes to wear, not a dime, in debt for beef market bill & vegetables, no nice meal, not flour sufficient for one meal, and we dine on a few potatoes, not enough to satisfy hunger, and one or two table spoons full of milk filled the glass with water. And my soul wept when sweet little Collie said I love the milk so I wish I could have another sup. The milk was left from breakfast coffee, it was given me by a German Lady, a Roman Catholic, the potatoes by my ever dear friend Sister Cummings. O I sadly ate my bare dinner. I enjoyed it, with a mournful pleasure. I was glad my precious husband was not here, he can't bear such, as well as I have learned to do.

Our kind and esteemed friend Bro Cummings, voluntarily sent me $3 in currency this afternoon. and my old valued friend his dear wife without solicitation sent me word she could loan me a bucket full of flour. Bless God, for our friends in the hour of need. I fell upon my knees and thanked god for this little valued, needed gift, that would keep me and my darlings from want.

Sept Sat 5th /68 We too poor, to own a conveyance, or to hire one, no shoes without holes in them to keep Finies, Mollie's, Collie's feet dry. Not a dime to purchase any thing with. Against our long established rule, we were compelled to go in debt for beef & vegetables, or eat dry corn bread, made up with water.

No meal but, a little musty meal, eating the musty bread made Mollie quite sick. Not flour enough for a meal. We dined on a few potatoes that Sister Cummings my old tried friend sent me. But it was not enough to satisfy hunger & one or two table spoonsful of milk filled the goblet with water, which served Mollie, Collie & myself. My soul wept when sweet Collie said I love the milk & water so, after it was all gone I wish I could have another sup.

The milk was left from breakfast coffee, if was given me by a kind German Lady, Mrs Wiser from the cow, by our breakfast time the cream rises, and by it I can prepare me a nice cup of coffee. I cannot relish coffee at all without cream in it. In my feeble health my cup with a spoonful of nice cream seems to strengthen, and help me so much.

Sunday Sept 13th 68 Mr F is absent attending presbytery in Washington, [between Austin and Houston] he will meet my dear cousins there, for some have resided there many years. I was not able to walk to church. All went to S. School but Collie and me. My head aches so I can hardly sit up, I am feeling very badly. Last Friday Sister Smith sent me a nice fresh saucer of butter it was a nice treat, as we cannot often when we have money get new butter.

3 Octob. PM.

Mollie was quite sick all night, she says she ask for her papa to nurse here, he took in his arms, sat on the bed side and nursed her. She was so feeble she could not walk so duty compelled me to stay with my only living daughter, for I feel my first duty is to my children then others next.

Friday 18th 68 I was to have spent the day at Bro Cummings, but I was scarce to walk, having a return of my disease that enfeebles me so much. I fear I shall not be able to get to church. Mr F has not returned yet. He is very precious to me. I hope God will spare us to live long & useful lives together, and after our last little one is grown & settled in a religious life if it is the Lord's will die near or at the same time in the full triumphs of the Christian faith and go to glory to dwell together there forever, amen & amen.

Sunday 12 O clock Feb 7th 1869 See how time has flown apace, how I have filled my resolves. When last I wrote in my journal I thought I would keep it up. But to think of all my joy and happiness on my moving into my new home, after being a houseless wanderer for years, and to think we commenced to moved home last Oct 12th.

O how grateful I was for my home once more. But dire necessity compelled to go to my needle, to make money to buy, Mollie and self dresses

& amid the press of home duties, Finie at school, Tommie off at work, my sewing. I have neglected every kind of writing and from my views of my incompetency I have smothered almost every desire to try to write.

All alone with beloved Finie in his sick bed, all the rest at church. My mind has been busy with my past impressions to write. I fear I have sinned. I am sick & feeble, been for a week I can scarcely sew at all. My mind is so troubled about my dear Finie. O if he were to die what would I do, he is such a treasure, help and prop to dear old mama, in my house of feebleness he is the dear one I go to for everything. Mollie is great help to me, but no one can I think can fill his place in waiting on Mama & cast light & joyousness over our home circle and it don't stop here all seem to love my darling Finie.

Wednesday 10th Feb 69 Finie has been <u>so sick</u> & I had so much anxiety of mind beside watching & nursing him & sewing day & night to finish Mrs Corleton's work 'eer I got down sick as usual in the spring, so I would not owe her anything. The effect of which you see dear children is I have neglected my journal. I have finished making & braiding Lena's skirt sent it home 75 cts. So I am relieved I am not in debt to Mrs C, but she I reckon owes me a little.

March 5th 69 O how grateful this sunny March afternoon to be able to arise from sick bed & write dear children for you in my journal. I have been quite sick about 2 weeks.

Wednesday March 17th /69 How sad! How sad & here I am sick & we so poor, not money to buy even some little nice something to brace my frail decaying body. Kind sister Dr Horne sent me some fresh butter made so nicely with her own dear hands and they <u>too</u> are poor like us but kind & loving. God bless them.

Thursday March 18th 69 Mr F got up before breakfast and went to Bro Golden's, one of our dear ministers, who has recently move here to send his loved children to school to Rev. F. J. Smith, Finies kind teacher. Bro Golden loaned him a horse cordially, kind Mr Harrington loaned him $15 in currency & Mr F bought 2 bottles, 1 of wine, 1 of brandy, cost $2.25, he told us keep half & send half, so I did. I sent Sister, for Aunt Betsie some tea, loaf sugar, blk pepper, spice, nutmeg & morsden expectorant, & a little rice all I had. Finie, Mollie and Collie went to Mr Harrington's & brought the 6 hens & Sister H sent me half doz eggs, but declined sending the rooster.

Tuesday 23rd March /69 I feel badly. My shoulders ache so bad I went to the door several times to talk to Finie about business & the north wind has effected me thus. O how bad to be such a frail reed so little account. I was so glad the ladies meeting was here on the very day I heard of dear sisters sorrow, for I felt I needed prayer for me to become resigned and I asked the dear sisters to pray for my loved bereaved ones & they did it.

April 7th 1869 As usual I have neglected to write in my journal. Mr F's visit was soothing to poor dear afflicted sister, when he started home he left her & children weeping.

I have just received such a sweet letter from dear Bro Blake. In that letter he writes, "I have heard much of you as one of the best specimens of female devotion to our church in the country. Heaven bless you. Ever your bro." O what sweet words, how precious were the words, "Heaven bless you." But O, how humble and thankful I felt that such a good, great man esteemed me a devoted daughter of the Church I <u>love so intensely</u>. And I thought if he could see me, and see how little, frail, ugly & ignorant I am he would change his opinion.

April Sab morn 11th /69 About sun set Robert came, O I had no idea he would be so proud to see us. He caught Finie in his arms, hugged & kissed him. I met him at the front parlor door. His face was full of the pure love & affection of a child for his mother. I had no idea that my heart would be so glad. He grasp my hand with all the fond manifestations of purest Christian affection & said kiss me. I from the excitement of the moment kissed him. It was the fond kiss of a mother for her long absent son. It was the only kiss that I have ever imprinted on any gentleman's lips except my devoted husband & dear & men kindred. Bro McGown always kissed me when we met or parted. When I look upon Robert's manly form & view his bright intellect mellowed by his devotion & remember in the past the little orphan german boy, I can but wonder & adore.

Monday April 12th /69 Last night after Robert preached in my ever beloved husband's pulpit, he returned home with Mr F & Tommie. Feeble as I was I sat up & talked a long time before we retired to rest.

This morning as Dear Robert read at prayers, my mind was busy with the past, present and future. I ran back to the poor little orphan german boy going around hunting work to make money to satisfy natural wants. Then how God impressed strangers to act the part of loving friends & educate the poor orphan boy. And as I sat with my eyes riveted on the tall manly form seated at our desk reading in clear, beautiful, distinct tones (beautiful thought) clothed in humility the precious words of God, my old eyes were suffused with tears, tears of joy, tears of love to that God.

Then another sweet thought occurred to me & made my happy tears fall on apace. It was brought plain to my mind, if God could call this poor orphan boy, that by some means had been cast upon our shore, from his native Germany, raise him up true and loving friends of American birth and bring about his preparation for the holy ministry, clothe him in such humility, fill his heart with such love for his adopted country and its countrymen and such devotion to our own beloved Zion & her interest certainly the same God, can & will hear this people when they unto him & ask him call qualify & send forth many more faithful labors into his vineyard, that is so white unto the harvest & the labors so few. All these thought pass in review before my mind during the short space of time of morning family prayer.

Tuesday April 13th I am very feeble, old bronchitis bad, so hoarse I can hardly talk. Mr F, Robert & Tommie have gone to dine with Mr & Mrs Castlema. Robert wound himself around our old hearts, so that we hate to see him leave us. It does me good to look at my husband's face, since dear Robert came and told us of our influence exerted over him in establishing him in his pious course. Such encouragement is worth more than gold and precious diamonds, to my weary soul, whose constant wish & <u>dearest</u> aim in life is to live a devotedly pious life and to win souls to Christ.

Wednesday 14th 69 Precious Finie is smilingly baking poor sick mama nice batter cakes. Mollie mad & pouting is bringing of my things for me to eat out of. I have no appetite. I feel so bad this morning. Dear little Collie is sick a little. He rose up in the bed & says Mama write about me. Write about my being sick. This evening Collie, said to me, mama I know why God gave me to you. I asked why my darling? To comfort <u>you</u> was his sweet baby reply. Then I said dear darling where do you think you would go if you were to die. He sweetly, smilingly remarked to heaven. I said why my Dear do you think so, He replied because you say I am so good. Then he said Mama I know why God made me so good. I asked him why he replied to comfort you.

Sat April 17th 69 Sister Herrington sent me about half gall. Of lamp oil, & a nice glass jar & gave Finie a hen on yesterday. When I was sick she brought me a jar of preserves. Mrs Wynne yesterday, gave Finie a setting of eggs, 1 egg a piece for Mollie & Collie to eat. I roasted them & the dear ones had a feast. Finie sold the setting & bought a hen for Collie. With money I saved for he bought Mollie a hen.

Children & I have 14 hens & 2 roosters. Bro Gracy gave us a nice bacon ham enough for breakfast & dinner. I sold him my bedstead, that I gave $17, for $10 in gold. But however it is a $12, bedstead.

May 9th 1869 Sabbath Day I feel I had to have dinner cooked on Sunday. But we are too poor to hire our work, little daught is <u>too</u> little to cook much yet. I am <u>too</u> feeble to prepare dinner on Sat for Sunday as I used to do.

But I am determined as soon as we get the little house built to rent, that this shall be in the bargain the colored woman that rents from us shall work for us every Sat, so as to have none if any cooking to do on Sab. Lord prosper us & hasten the time for this to be accomplished, if thou seest it is best for us. For my constitution is so frail I never expect to be stout & able to do much.

May 13th 69 Thurs morn Mr F prevailed on me to let Mollie go with him & spend the night at Bro Steel's Mothers. But to do justice to history, I must say my home is <u>much</u> more quiet since Mollie left, for she gets so mad when I tell her to do any thing & quarrels & dear Finie & sweet Collie so much. I write this to see if it will help dear daughter to do better.

June 10th 1869 Mr F came home this morning just after 8. When I told him our little daughter Mollie got up & cooked the entire breakfast for the family, he looked so proud of his little 8 year old girl, & said Mama you must be sure to write it down. Mr F took his seat in Court yesterday as Juror, he hated to do it and would not do it but dire necessity compels to do something to make a little money, & this interferes less than any other business as he has nothing to do but sit in Court from 9 a.m. to about 11. Some days only 1 hour. Sometimes the judge merely calls Court & adjourns, & each day he gets $2.00 in currency.

June 20th 1869 Our Church blinds & pews have been very neatly painted, the blinds a beautiful deep green, & the inside of top molding of pews cherry, the backs & ends oak, finish. Tommie helped to paint it. He is an apprentice, under Mr Orr, the fine Painter that bossed the job, he gives him $1.00 per day, while he is in his first six months apprenticeship.

July 12th 1869 After our dreadful overflow, & distress caused from loss of property, and a few deaths of persons. We are this morning blessed with bright sun shine in all its loveliness and <u>cheering influences</u> the dreadful rain prevented. [During the flood of July 1869, water levels reached fifty-one feet above sea level. The water from the Colorado River spread across Austin and into Bastrop and La Grange.] Since I began to sew after I got well I have made $6 or $8. O it does my heart good to bring into the family for its comfort fruits of my own labor.

Dec 31st 1869 After 10 at night. Mr F has gone to Washington County Texas in a missionary tour. Will be gone about 1 month. May God bless him & make him useful.

January Friday 28th 1870 I am very feeble with my lungs & throat this morning. So much so that I must keep close in my room. Home is a little heaven to me this morn.

Sweet baby Collie just now came with smiling face all beaming with love & embraced me again & again. Then lay on my fond bosom locked in embrace & would look up in my face and say over & over to me this is a heaven to us & I love God for giving us such a dear good mama. O how these baby remarks thrilled this loving heart! This Mother's heart!!! Then he said "if they all loved you as I do it would be heaven." We can't bear to think of anyone loving mother more than he does or that I love him better than he does me. Such a dear child. I do believe God is training my dear last boy for this precious work. God grant it. Amen & amen.

Finie is at school. Mollie is acting the lady, she has cleaned up kitchen & dining room & with a happy smiling face is preparing thickening for mama's turnip soup which I hope will make me feel better. My precious & dear husband has not returned from his last missionary tour.

Feb 6th 1870 Sab. Morn. Again I am sick, too sick to write. But I must say something about my new affliction. I am surprised at my calmness when I reflect upon my impetuous nature.

I received two kind letters one from Cousin Mc in La Grange, the other from Miss Amanda Athinson, mailed Rutersville [about six miles northeast of La Grange]. Both telling me of my dear husband's illness which has been severe but that he is better. I hope from these epistles my dear one altho' very weak out of danger. [Finis had been gone from home on a missionary tour.] I feel sad our congregation are getting to be so small, not more than ¼ as was last year. I felt Mr F was too old & feeble for so arduous a work as he has chosen.

Collie thicken the soup had a great time loving me & calling me pretty. I do not believe the little thing really thinks I am pretty with all, my sallowness, furrows, no teeth, & harsh cough. God help my last boy. He says if I live long enough I'll hear him preach. I observed that you must not preach unless God tells you to preach. The dear little angel boy voluntarily remarked God has told me. I remarked how has he told you. I felt an anxious curiosity to hear his infant reply. He remarked he told me in my heart.

March 1st 1870 Bro Robert is very kind & good to us he is going all around getting subscribers for an Organ for the Church at 3. He had $55.00 subscribed. He has just returned a half after 4, has subscribed $85.00. With a fervent prayer I handed him $10.00 in gold.

I received a letter yesterday from Tommie telling me father was sitting by the fire looking more like himself than he had for some time. Bless God. O Lord help Tommie to be <u>ever</u> watchful and kind of that dear precious one. O that we may meet again on earth!.

Finie has had measles and is well. Mollie & Collie are to have them. Finie & Collie visited Jess & Tommie Cummings this afternoon. Collie said a little boy that was there cursed so bad. Sweet Collie remarked to me I could not stand it, and I left him and went up to the house where Aunt Cummings was.

March 3rd 1870 A lovely morn, yesterday was interspersed with clouds & sunshine. Dear Aunt Sallie Bates & her amiable daughter Dr Mrs Westfall called on me, they seemed so glad to see me & expressed so much sympathy for us & so much love for Mr F that their visit was like a cool refreshing shower in a hot summer day.

O what a rich <u>mine</u> of untold heavenly joy is there to be found & enjoyed in our holy religion! O how wise & good is our Holy God been to us, in its adaptation to the wants happiness & interest of the immortal soul! In time & thro' the ceaseless roll of eternal years. God help the dear precious sinner to lay hold of the immortal hope set before them & look & live e'er it is <u>too late!</u>

[This is the final entry of Louisa's journals.
She will pass away in October 1871]

John Collier Foster Journal #1

March 2, 1882–July 31, 1882

The next three journals were written by Louisa Foster's youngest son, John Collier Foster. When he began this journal, he had just turned eighteen years old on October 12, 1881. Both his parents had been dead for some time, and he lived in Marshall, Texas, with his brother Finis, who was twenty-nine. Both boys worked at a drug store during this time period.

John Collier Foster's journals are transcribed as he had written them, with no changes to content or spelling. I have also underlined words that he chose to underline, and if I could not determine a word, I indicated it by "___?__." Any comments inside square brackets are made by me to explain what was written or to make a historical observation.

* * * * *

Marshall, Texas March 2, 1882 I have been reading some in the Journals written by my <u>dear</u> departed <u>father</u> and <u>mother</u>, also some in one written by brother Tommie, and have concluded to write one myself hoping that it may help me to live a <u>better</u> and <u>more</u> Christian life, and to come nearer living up to the fond <u>wishes hopes</u> and <u>prayers of my dear sainted mother</u> who has long since left this world of sin and sorrow and gone home to be with Jesus forever and ever.

Thursday March 2 1882 We should take a lesson from them and thank God for sparing us to see the breaking forth of another Spring. Marshall is all excitement on the subject of Prohibition. [Marshall, Texas, was first settled in 1839. By 1860 it was the fifth-largest city in Texas, with around fourteen thousand people. By 1880, when John Collier lived there, the population had shrunk to a little over 5,600 people because of the effects of the Civil War. But by this time, the town had started to expand and again prosper.]

The Probations are working hard to carry Local Options in our county, while the whiskey men are working hard to defeat it. [Local options meant allowing decisions on some controversial issues within their borders, decided by a popular vote.] It is going to be a hard fight, but I trust we will gain the day. I attended a meeting on the subject last night or rather the night before at which I heard several good speeches on the subject, among them & the main speaker of the occasion was a gentleman from Paris, Texas [about 114 miles northwest of Marshall] by the name of Mr H. H. Latimer. He spoke about an hour and a quarter, and it was the best thing I ever heard on the subject.

Friday March 3 1882 I am now serving an apprenticeship under Dr. Sears a druggist in this place and while I am writing this I am keeping store while brother Finis is gone to breakfast.

4th This morning isn't as pleasant as the previous ones as it is cloudy and looks very much like rain. I went to a sociable given by the "Little Helper" a little Missionary society last evening. [There was a Baptist missionary group by this name during this period.] I went with Ida and of course had a good time. Made the acquaintance of several young ladies.

March 5 1882 Sunday Evening I have just returned from a temperance mass meeting held by the "Womens Temperance Union" of Marshall. Before which I went to our Boys Missionary Society which I enjoy very much. In it was sing read scriptures and have prayers and reading of Missionary Selections that is pieces on Missionary work in different parts of the world.

6th Tomorrow the election comes off which says whether or not we are to have Saloons and Gambling Halls in Marshall. I walked home with Ida which I enjoyed very much. I also wrote to Miss Maggie tonight.

March 7th 1882 Tuesday I have been reading a great deal today in one of Mamas journals written in 1856. In it she speaks of the birth and death of little Katie and Lou Clemie, it seemed so hard for her to become resigned after their deaths. [Louisa spoke of this in her second journal.]

March 8th 1882 I have been reading more in one my own dear mothers Journals. It seemed to be her chief aim to raise her children so as to prepare them to meet her in that "land of pure delight where saints immortal reign."] Oh! How sweet it will be for us, an unbroken family, where we shall have all been gathered home at last, for my dear mother desires and prayers have been answered in that all of her children who are living are Christians, and our <u>dear sister</u> Mollie who left this world for a better one on high, last August 15th after a long protracted illness, was a most earnest Christian. She used to write me such <u>dear good Christian</u> letters in which she showed such a <u>meek submissive</u> spirit to God's divine will. She used to say if it was God's will for me to live on and suffer, for she had become almost an invalid, she was willing to do it.

Her death was one of the hardest blows I ever received, for I had not seen her, only while very sick, a few months previous to her death, when she was not expected to live and Finis and I were telegraphed to come at once, for nearly two years, and it was about the first time we had ever been separated any length of time. But I became resigned for I knew her death was only a happy change for her, and that though she could not come back to us, we could go to her. Just two years and one day before her death on the 14th of August 1879 my <u>dear dear</u> father took his departure from this sin cursed earth, and went <u>Home to Heaven</u>, to receive his reward for a life's labor for the master, his to was but a happy change, for he had suffered long from heart disease and other troubles. I think God that I had such <u>dear good</u> parents to teach me in the way I should go.

March 9, 1882 Thursday morning We have not heard from all the voting places yet but the expectation is that the Local Option is lost this time, but we can try it again in 12 months.

March 10 1882 Friday morning I wrote a good long letter to mother (my step-mother) last evening also sent her some pictures for a scrap picture Book [The Rev. Foster had remarried the year after Louisa's death.].

13 Monday morning Before the church commence Ida gave me my album. She had written a very nice piece in it. After church I walked home with Charlin Talley and had a time. Left my album for she and her sister to write in for me.

March 14/ 82 Tuesday morning I saw Ida this morning as we came from breakfast, but didn't get to speak to her as I was to far off and across the street. I wrote a long letter to Alfred Dechend last evening, hope he will answer soon as I like his letters.

Well I must stop as Finis wants me to do a little errand for him, and then we want to make "syrups" today in the store. I have returned from prayer meeting had a very good meeting. I went over after Miss Hattie Roberts to take her to prayer meeting.

March 16/ 82 Thursday Well we got our Syrup made did not rain any yesterday. There was a temperance Lecture at the C. P. Church [Cumberland Presbyterian Church] last evening. Finis went so I had to stay at the store, but about 9 oclock I closed up and went down thinking that it last 'til about half past 9 or 10, but I just got there in time to see them blow the lights out.

March 17/ 82 Friday morning I made up 324 pills yesterday wearing and raised a blister on my finger during it.

18 Saturday morning We had our party and had a splendid time. Adury Allen says for me to write down that I had a nice game of Dominoes with Ida, she and I were partners and A. J. & Miss Gruevier was, we beat them. . . . Had a very nice time with Chorlina also had several little chats with Ida.

Sunday morning March 19/ 82 This evening our Boys Missionary Society meets, and I have to read a piece. I am the Secretary of the society and have to keep minutes of every meeting. Well I went to church this morning. After church I had the pleasure of seeing Ida home. I went in and sat a while and had a very pleasant time.

Monday morning March 20, 1882. We are having the room upstairs over the store that Finis and I occupy, Calsomined and the doors and windows to be painted. I think it will be quite pleasant when it is finished.

11:40 a.m. I have just returned from a fire. I was called to front of store by the ringing of the Fire Bell, it was said to be the residence of one of the proprietors of a firm just across the street from us by the name of VanHooks. I saw him running for his delivery which was standing in front of his store, so I made for it also to save having to walk down and just as I got there it started of in a run, but I got in, but just then another man wanted to get in and caught hold of me and pulled himself in and pulled me out but I got in again although she was going very fast, we got there in a few minutes found the fire up between the ceiling and the roof, but it soon began to blaze through the roof. We all began carrying up water in everything we could find that would hold water, through the ceiling up into the loft by a narrow passage, they then cut a hole in the roof and then went out with water as the fire was at a different part of the house from where the stairs led up in the loft it was soon all put out.

March 22/ 82 Wednesday morning After services I walked home with Miss Hattie Roberts and had a very nice time with her, and had just returned to the store and it was now bedtime, so goodnight.

March 23/ 82 Thursday I attended the convention this morning and was well pleased with the exercises. Miss Charlin, Miss Della, and I constituted the choir again, we got along very well and made very good music. Finis went this afternoon and I kept the store, he has gone again tonight and I will close up and go down about 8:30 p.m. as there isn't much business after that time.

March 24/ 82 Friday Evening I went to church this evening, had Ida for my company. After service we over and Ida Belle and I played consequences and talked until about 10 when I came home and Finis and I retired. [Consequences was a parlor game played with pencil and paper. Each player was given a paper and wrote down a word or phrase that contributed to a story. Once written down the player folded the paper to hide what was written and handed it to the next player to do the same. At the end of the game, the final story was read out loud and usually with funny results.]

Monday morning March 27/ 82 Evening We moved up to our room today it begins to look right snug although we haven't arranged things yet. I think it will be quite comfortable when we get through. A norther blew up late this afternoon late, and it is quite cool tonight. I have just put on a pair of then light pants but guess I will take them off again tonight as it is almost to cool for summer clothing yet for a while.

March 31/ 82 This has been a bright sunny day. A.J. and I walked to Ida & Belle take them to the sociable at his house tonight.

April 1 Saturday We had our Sociable and I took Ida and as usual while with her I enjoyed myself very much. The moon was shining brightly so we took quite a promenade up and down the sidewalk in front of the house. I read her some in a letter I had just read from Miss Maggie in regard to her it tickled her muchly. With all it was a very pleasant evening.

April 4/ 82 I met Ida this morning at the Post Office and walked a part of the way to school with her and she gave me a lovely little bouquet, and as I write I have it sitting in front of me and it perfumes the whole air around me, it is awful sweet.

April 5/ 82 I have been making pills most all day, have made 648 today. The weather pretty warm has been pretty cloudy all day looked something like rain.

April 6/ 82 morning I went to see Blind Tom the great musician by ear, he is surely a wonder.

I didn't think I could go and Finis wanted to go and I would have to stay at the store, but at the supper table last night Dr asked me if I would like

Thomas "Blind Tom" Wiggins, May 1849–June 1908, was an American pianist and composer. He was born a slave, and because he was blind he could not preform the usual work of a slave. At the age of four he began to play the piano by ear and by five had composed his first tune. In 1875 he went on an eight-year tour around the United States. Photo public domain.

to go saying he had 2 tickets for himself and a young lady, a niece of his and if I wanted to I could take them and go as he didn't care particularly about going, and he would stay at the store. I thanked him and told him I would do so with pleasure, if it suited the young lady as well and she said it did, so we went and enjoyed it splendidly.

April 7/ 82 We are going to have another sociable tonight at Mrs Van-Hooks. I have engaged Miss Genuiun Richardson company for it. I recd. a long letter from mother today. She was not in very good health, said if she did not improve soon she would have to quite teaching.

April 8/ 82 We had our sociable. I took Miss Genuiun and had a very nice time, Had several nice little chats with Ida, we went out on the porch to promenade and when we got tired of walking we took seats in some chairs out there and had a long talk by ourselves.

April 13/ 82 It cleared off today so they had the supper tonight, but as I was suffering from a severe headache I did not go up. I was very sorry for I wanted to go very much, and I didn't feel like eating anything and I didn't want to go up unless I could eat something. They haven't broke up and Finis has not come back yet so I guess I will read a little.

April 17/ 82 Today has been a very pleasant day. The doctor and I went over to the hotel, with a drummer [salesman] to look at his samples and buy some goods this afternoon. Finis has gone to call on a young lady so I am alone at the store. Our new Mayor was sworn into his office today and the first thing he did was to fine a negro $50.00 who has been in the habit of riding and breaking wild horses on the square. It was a good step for him to make, as it had been quite an annoyance to ladies, as well as gentlemen walking around the square, as well as a very dangerous on account of children be liable of being run over.

April 20/ 82 I went to Miss Sue Rains today, engaging her company for the sociable tomorrow evening. Got a good letter from Alfred Dechand today, I like his letters very much. I have had lots of fun today with one of the electric batteries that we have in the store. It had run once or twice so that I couldn't turn it a loose at all. Finis has gone down to the church to practice for a Temperance meeting tomorrow evening, has not returned yet. It is getting late, almost 10. We purpose making Syrup again tomorrow, which is a pretty warm job.

April 22/ 82 The wind blew most terribly blowing down a large tree near the store. I heard this morning that it took the roofs off of several houses in town. It has cleared off and the sun is shining brightly now, it was a good season for the crops. We made syrup yesterday morning, in the afternoon I went and had my hair cut for the social.

At the sociable we had a very large crowd and had a splendid time. Ida gave me the cutest little pin cushion, made to represent a little fan, that she had made for me. I appreciate it very highly indeed, because she made it for me and because it is so nice.

Tuesday April 25/ 82 It is just 6 a.m. I arose very early for me this morning have just opened up the store. Finis has not arisen yet from his bed of slumber. He starts today for Dallas [about 150 miles west of Marshall] to attend a S.S. convention, after it is over he will run down to Tehuacana [where he went to college and where the family lived after the death of Louisa] for a few days to visit home.

Oswald Hargrove has just come in and handed me his sisters Autograph Album to write in, she ask me to sometime since and is just getting her album back from some of the girls. I must try to get up something for it.

April 27/ 82 There was a good deal of burglaring going on in town last night. Several houses were invaded and went through, they got $100.00 in one house, haven't heard what they got from the rest only some clothes. One of them was caught this morning with some of the things he had stolen, on his person. I am a little afraid they will try me some night, as I sleep in the store by myself. I would not be afraid if I wasn't so very hard to awake, they might take all I have got and got out before I would wake up. I have one consolation though, they wouldn't get much if they were to get all I had.

April 28/ 82 A very lovely morning though pretty warm. It is going to be a very warm day indeed. There was a supper given by the Baptist church in the court house on last evening, but I didn't go. Haven't heard how much they made. I wrote a long letter to Alfred Dechand last night and received one from Craig Johnson this morning.

Evening Finis returned this evening. Mr J. L. Thompson a New York drummer from whom we buy goods and who we all like very much for he is a splendid gentleman is here on his way to N.Y. We bought a small bell from him. He is going now to get out his samples for next fall and the holidays. He spent quite a while with us this afternoon in pleasant conversation. Ida was at the store this evening.

Sat. April 29/ 82 Today has been a very pretty day, have been tolerable busy. I wrote a long letter to bro Tommie he is teaching school at Liberty Hill down near Austin is getting along finely with his school. [Liberty Hill was about thirty-three miles northwest of Austin.]

Sunday April 30/ 82 I got a letter from Harris my step bro, yesterday, all was well at home.

Monday May 1st 1882 The Church or rather the "Ladies Aid Society" of our church are going to give a Moonlight Festival of Ice Cream Dew Berries on next Wednesday night in Mrs Sanders yard. All anticipate a good time. I expect to go and spend a few dollars in the good cause. Finis has been posting the books as this is the first of the month. He will draw off accounts this evening and collect tomorrow. So I will have to run the store, which is a very easy job however.

Thursday May 2/ 82 I went up to see them skate some last evening on the Rink, some of them look very gracefully, while some fall all around. It is lots of fun to see them fall. This morning Harry Allen was around at the store with a pair. I tries them on, and at first I couldn't do a thing, but I soon got so I could get around pretty well without falling. I only fell once, I believe I could learn in a little while.

Roller skating first boomed all over the world from 1880 to 1910. This photo of skater ca. 1905, from the Library of Congress.

Thursday May 4/ 82 The supper came off last night. I had a splendid time. I took supper with Ida. The young folks got off in one corner of the yard and played games. I went down in the evening to help fix-up for it and worked liked a good fellow all evening and will go down pretty soon to help return everything. I only ate one saucer of ice cream and it made me sick at the stomach so I didn't eat anymore, I was sorry for I wanted to take cream with several of the girls. [Before milk was pasteurized in the late 1880s, sickness from ice cream was a common occurrence. There were accounts in newspapers of outbreaks of illness at picnics, county fairs, and parties. Also, sickness resulted from the reuse of glassware at these events. Disease was spread by washing glassware in dirty water and drying it with a dirty cloth.]

Sat. May 6/ 82 Well I didn't wrote in my journal at all yesterday. I was pretty busy in the morning making up preparatiores in the store and in the afternoon I had a bill of good to help mark and put away and at night went to a party, so I didn't write at all. I went with Ida to the party and had a very nice time with her, as well as some of the other girls. There seemed to be a rain storm coming up so we broke up pretty early and I came by the skating Rink on my way home and tried a pair for a little while. I only got 2 falls, got along very well, think I could learn in a few nights. It did not rain to do any good after all.

I got a letter from cousin Eva Ratcliff yesterday she said she was going to the Indian Nation this summer to visit friends and to see to her and Bobbins property there. [This probably was in Oklahoma.]

Sunday May 7/ 82 A very dark gloomy morning and pouring down rain, last night we had a most terrible rain and wind storm almost a cyclone it blew down a great many trees in town and a house or two I overheard. A gentleman came in from the country this morning to get hands to help him put up his fence which was all down and the stock in his crop. It came right through a window near our bed so that I had to get up and put a blanket over it.

Monday May 8/ 82 After church I went home with Miss Ellen Tally. Had a very nice time. Last evening Ida sent me 2 cape jasmine. I have them in water on my desk and they perfume the whole room, they are just lovely.

Tuesday May 9/ 82 I walked up to the Rink and skated an hour last night. I got some pretty good falls, but I can skate pretty good, until I try to go to fast, and then I fall down. It is lots of fun after any one learns to skate good. I enjoyed my skate very much only I got very hot.

May 10/ 82 I went around to Bro Allens and had him fix my shoes, had then sewed up when they were riped and a button sewed on. I got a letter from Alfred Dechand again today.

May 11/ 82 I went up to the skating Rink last night and skated about an hour and a quarter. I am becoming very fast, I only got a few falls. Well I must stop and clean up the store first thing I do.

May 12/ 82 Last evening I had a long walk with Ida, as I went down to supper saw it was not supper time and she and Miss Chamberland were just starting for a walk, so I ask them if I might go with them and they said I might so we walked about a quarter of a mile and back, and Miss C went in at home with Ida. I enjoyed the walk very much indeed, so did Miss Minnie for it was her first walk about for she has only been here for a short time.

May 13/ 82 A very pretty morn though pretty cool yet. Last evening was public skating for both ladies and gentlemen. I went up and got a pair of skates and at first I fell a good deal, but after a little, I got started all right and got along finely.

Finis got a letter from Miss Emma McDaniel yesterday, stating that she was to be married soon. She is stepping off pretty soon, as she isn't 18 years of age yet. I got a letter from Tommie this morning he was well, he complemented me on my improvement in writing, my writing doesn't look much like it, but this isn't very good paper, and it pretty hard to write on as it has no glaze, business very dull for Saturday.

Monday May 15/ 82 We had our boys prayer meeting last afternoon and there was a Mr. Haynes present, a young man I used to go to school with about 7 or 8 years ago at Tehuacana, but he moved away and yesterday was the first time I have seen him since.

After our meeting I came back to the store and stayed until after the girls meeting, when Miss Minnie and I went down after Ida and we took our walk. We went first out to the Bishop Baptist College, a college for educating the Negroes, there I saw the president and asked him if we might get in and he went around a got a key, and showed us all through the building. It was a beautiful building made of brick and splendidly furnished on inside. It is either 3 or 4 stories high with basement, I forgot which after having gone all through we departed after thanking Dr. Culeen for his kindness in showing us around. [Bishop College was founded by the Baptist Home Mission Society in 1881 with the intent to build a college for African American Baptists. The college remained in operation until 1988, when it closed and its buildings were purchased. It later opened as Paul Quinn College.]

Wednesday 17/ 82 Mr Webster brought around a proof sheet of my Photos today, they are very good. Finis has gone up to the skating rink as this is ladies and gentleman night. I have written a long letter to Alfred thanking him for sending me 50 cents to become an honorary member of our Missionary society, in response to a circular that I sent him, I being on the committee on membership.

Thursday May 18/ 82 After writing the above in my diary, about half past nine I went up to the Rink and skated ¾ of an hour without falling at all, only I was knocked down by a boy running against me twice, am learning pretty fast, it is splendid exercise and pleasant amusement.

Friday May 19/ 82 We were to have a sociable tonight but a young man, a son of the gentleman whose house it was to be, got hurt on the railroad, so of course it was postponed, haven't heard how badly he is hurt, as he hadn't gotten in at last accounts. I think he was brought in last night. I had an engagement with Ida to go so we will go up to the skating rink instead.

Sat. May 20/ 82 We went to the Rink last evening, and had a very pleasant time. There were some very pretty skaters on the floor. I took Ida home about 10 oclock or a little after and then I went back and took a half an hour skate, only fell once I believe.

Sunday May 21/ 82 I got my Photos yesterday, every one says they are splendid, they were taken with my first moustache, I have cut it off since.

Tues. May 23/ 82 A lovely May day I wrote to bro Tommie last night and sent him one of my photos. I also wrote to Eva this morning and sent her and mother each a Cabinet Photo. [A cabinet card was a style of photograph that was popular after 1870. It consisted of a thin photograph that was mounted on card stock about 4 x 6 inches. Many times the reverse side had information about the services of the photographer.] A boy came along today and had some very nice Plumbs and I bought some of them, they was very good.

Wednesday May 24/ 82 I had just a splendid time last evening. I had an engagement with Ida to take her to prayer meeting so I took her down one of my Photo's in a handsome Plush Olive colored Frame, she had asked for one of my Photo's and I thought I would like to give it to her in a nice Frame, she thought it was a splendid gift and thought the frame was elegant and thanked me <u>over</u> & <u>over</u> again for it. She told me she had given up her trip to Virginia and was going to Millsap Springs in western Texas, for her health. [Millsap was about 230 miles west of Marshall.] I hope it will fatten her up, as she looks very poor, has fallen off in the last few months.

Thursday May 25/ 82 Well I have got a good deal of work to do now, soon I must clean down and rework the store and wash a lot of bottles and put up some Castor Oil, so will be pretty busy for some little time. I put up and labeled 4 doz. Castor Oils this morning and washing a lot of bottles insides. A. J. was down tonight telling me about a fine bottle of cologne having been voted off to Ida last evening at the fair, as the most popular young lady in the house. I was glad for her to get it and I don't object to voting but I do seriously to raffling.

Monday May 29/ 82 I had the pleasure of seeing Miss Hattie Roberts to church she was a member of the M.E. Church choir so we went there to service. Heard Mr. Wagas their minister preach a good sermon, she gave me a Cape Jasmine which I have in water on my desk now.

May 31/ 82 I asked Dr this morning if he would let me off to go up to Mr Awalts and take a fish this summer, he said he would so. A. J. Allen and I wrote to Mr Awalt this morning that we could come any time between the 15 & 25 of June just as it suited him.

Evening I sent mother one of my Photos, she said it was very good, said the moustache became me, only it didn't look like Collier.

June 1/ 82 A note from Ida this morning stating that there would be A sociable on her home at tomorrow eve, and asking me to tell all the boys I saw, and to be sure and favor them with my presence, "for with out you", she said, "it would not be a success."

I wrote her an answer telling her I was glad she thought my presence would add to the enjoyment of the occasion, but was sorry to say, that on account of Finis having an engagement for that evening, I would have to stay at the store, though I may go down about a half past 9 or 10 after closing.

Sat June 3/ 82 Well I did go down to the sociable last night, after cleaning up, and had a splendid time, I had some nice talks and promenades with Ida, this is her last sociable until she returns which will be 4 to 6 weeks. So I was with her a good deal. I walked to Mr Dechand last night and sent him one of my Photos.

Tuesday June 6/ 82 I wrote to cousin Nannie McCollene yesterday morning and sent her one of my Photos. Finis sent her one of his. She lives down near LaGrange on a farm. She is 14 years old and writes a good letter. I have never seen her in my life, I wish I could.

June 7/ 82 I took Ida home from prayer meeting last evening. I also took her cup to the ice cream parlor and got her cream it was very good, but it was her company that I enjoyed more than the cream. After we went home we had a long chat on the sofa, she told me she had asked her mother nice if she could correspond with me and she seem perfectly willing, she had already told me she would correspond with me when she went off and she said she was afraid to ask her mother for fear she might object, for she would hate to do it against her mothers will, but said she was going to tell her ma if she wouldn't let her write to me, she couldn't write to her.

This was probably the photo Finis sent to Nannie. It was taken January 3, 1881, soon after he moved to Marshall, Texas. The tie pin looks similar to an Alpha Omicron fraternity pin. Finis belonged to that fraternity while at Trinity University in the late 1870s. Photo from Mansfield Historical Society.

Thursday June 8/ 82 Ida gave me this rose on the 25 day of last May and I brought it home and put it in press to keep it and this morn. I took it out and thought I would pin it here in my Journal and keep it as a reminder of the pleasant evening I spent with the one that gave it to me. I have borrowed a pair of skates and this morning I took quite a skate after I opened the store before business opened up.

Friday June 9/ 82 We received word that Mr Awalt wanted us to come up a week from today, on our fishing excursion, but as we can't leave our stores on Saturday, we wrote him if it suited him we would go up the Monday following. We anticipate a good time. I have been reading some in the Dispensatory this morning. [This book contained the description of drugs and of preparations made from them.] I am going to read more and inform

John's journal with a pinned rose

myself more than I have for some time, this summer so if I have an offer any where else when my time is out here I will be better qualified to take it. I have been very negligent in my reading, haven't read ½ as much as I have ought to have done, though I am somewhat excusable on account of my eyes, as they do bother me a good deal if I read very much.

Sunday June 11/ 82 I read some in Mamma's Journal this morning before breakfast, which I enjoyed very much.

Monday 12/ 82 We got a card from Mr. Awalt saying it suited him as well for us to come today week the 19th, so we will go on next Monday.

Wednesday June 14/ 82 We had 3 of the hottest days I most ever felt it seems to me, but I guess it is felt so much on account of the sudden change rather than the extreme heat as the Thermometer had only reached about 90°. I must get to work and do some more cleaning up, I am mostly through, hope to get through today. [The highest average temperature in Marshall in June was about 89°. So the weather John had experienced was typical.]

Friday June 16/ 82 I walked to Jennie Stokes night before last and sent her one of my Photos. I guess I will have to wash a few bottles today so they will not get out while I am gone. I washed 6 doz. Bottles so haven't anything more to do now in particular, but to attend to the wants of customers, between now and 11:35 a.m. next Monday when we will leave on our grand fish, I have got my tackle ready, we thought we would take guns at first, as Mr Awalt wrote for us to, but we have come to the conclusion that they will be more bother than they are worth to us, as we don't expect to hunt much. Ida told me she thought she might go Monday on same train we do, hope she will, for it would make the journey that far more pleasant to both of us.

I recd. a Postal from Alfred this morning, he said he had read my letter with Photo, would have written a letter, but for want of time, said my Photo didn't look much like I did when he saw me last, about 5 or 6 years ago, I guess not.

Saturday June 17/ 82 I had the pleasure of taking Ida up to the speaking of the boys of Marshall University, at Opera House last night. Some of them that I had heard speak last year showed quite a decided improvement.

Monday June 19/ 82 I had Ida for my company after church I staid a little later than usual, as it was the last time I would get to see her for 5 or 6 weeks. As I learned today and she will leave for Millsap Springs before I return, we had a very pleasant time. A. J. Allen was with her sister Belle, after our fish he expects to go on out west on a trip for a month or so.

Later We left Marshall at 11:55 A.M. for Willow Spring, where we are to get off and got from there to the River. As I went down to the train I passed Ida's house, she was sitting in the window, I called her out as I wanted to tell her good by, as I was leaving she told me she wouldn't go until Saturday, so I will get back before she goes.

We boys all went out on the platform of the car to wave our handkerchiefs to the girls on the "Hill." We reached Alney's Station 5 miles from Marshall at 12:07 didn't stop there, nearly stacked up so any one could get off if they wanted to.

Longville Junction 1 p.m. Trains stops here 20 mins for dinner, we ate dinner before leaving M so will not take any now. A. J. has steped to see some parties he knows here. I will go out and walk around some and see if I can get some Lemonade Soda Water or something as I am very thirsty. I could find none without going in a Saloon and I wouldn't do that, but I found some ice cream, which though it was not very good, helped to allay my thirst, left the Junction at 1:24 p.m.

At Mr. Awalts 3 p.m. when we steped off the train at the station, one of the boys was waiting for us, so we walked up to the house about ¼ mile from the station Bro Quait was there seemed glad to see us all. After having been introduced to the boys and a few preliminary remarks, we began putting the hooks and leads on our lines getting ready for action.

Sabine River June 20/ 82 We got us this morning at 4 oclock and moved down and fished until it was light enough to go to our hooks that were set out but found nothing on any of them. Our lines had caught something which had broken the pole into and the line also, but he was gone. As soon as it was light enough for us to walk along without falling in the water, A.J. and I started up the river to see if we could but catch enough fish for breakfast. We fished and walked until we were out of bait and only caught a few little pearch.

At Mr Awalt's June 21/ 82 We arose this morning about 5 oclock feeling much refreshed by our good nights rest. We will start pretty soon for Longview where we will wait for #4 this afternoon, which is due at 1:20, on which we will sail for old Marshall.

Longview Tex 1 p.m. at depot Train reported 35 or 40 minutes late. About 2 p.m. the train rolled in and we rolled out.

Marshall We reached here all O.K. soon after leaving Hallville. We boys went out on the platform & rode and sang "Golden Slippers" the brakeman was standing out with us and he seemed to enjoy our song. When we passed the Hill we all got out to walk but could see no one, so we didn't. But Miss Ellen told us since that she was at a window waiting for us. Just before we got to the depot, we met Jim Dopplemayer and gave him a wave the train was going so fast that he didn't know us, but waved to us all the same. He thought we was the Barry boys of Dallas. Everyone was surprised to see us back so soon.

June 22/ 82 This has been one awful hot day. I went down to the festival last evening and had a splendid time. Had several nice talks and promenades with Miss Ida and Miss Hattie Ford, of Shreveport La. She is awful nice, I had the pleasure of seeing her home. The only trouble was that it was not far enough, only across the street. After seeing her home I went back and seeing Ida standing out in the yard by herself. I went up and took her to a seat and we sat and talked until nearly every one was gone when I took my leave.

Sat June 24/ 82 Ida did not get off this week as was expected, but expects to go next Monday. I shall be very sorry to see her leave, for I have some splendid times with her, but she will not be gone but about a month.

10:30 p.m. I had the pleasure of seeing Miss Hattie Ford, a mighty sweet little girl from Shreveport, out to church tonight and had a nice time. As Ida did not get off Saturday as was expected, and is going tomorrow. I went down to see her and tell her good bye, we sat in the parlor and talked a while and then took a stroll down in the grave yard and then back for the house when I sat a few minutes and then bid her good bye as it was getting late. I had a real nice time with her which will be nice and I think improving to both of us.

June 28 At prayer meeting last evening Hattie Ford returned my album having written in it. I went home with her to bid her goodbye as it was the last time I would see her as she goes home tomorrow, but expects to come back soon and maybe spend the summer up here. I guess Ida is in Ednaville. Wish I could hear from her & know how she is & how she likes the place. I missed her last evening as she is a pretty regular attendant at prayer meeting. I will write to her tonight as she made me promise to write in a few days, for she said she would be lonesome and a letter from me would be pleasant to receive.

June 29/ 82 Still hot & dry, that is about all I can write nowadays it looks like. I wrote a long letter to Ida last night. I didn't think I would write more than a short one so, but I kept writing, and first thing I knew I had finished my 4th sheet and could have written more, but thought I had better stop.

June 30/ 82 It is quite windy this morning making it very unpleasant as it is so dusty. Today Geutlo hangs, for the killing of President Garfield. I think it is nothing but right that he should. [On July 2, 1881, Charles J. Guiteau shot President James Garfield twice at a train station. The president died on September 19, 1881, following complications. Guiteau went on trial for murder in November, and was found guilty on January 25, 1882. He was executed on June 30, 1882.]

Monday July 3/ 82 I met Miss Belle Sanders thru Ida's sister. She and Miss Hattie Roberts ran in the house when they saw me coming for they were not dressed up. I took Miss Belle to church last night. Had a very nice time, they had recd. a letter from Ida. She said she was not very pleasantly situated out there being in a room 6ft. square and with only one small window, she said if she didn't have a better room, we might look for her home any day this week.

7:11 p.m. The rain is about over, though we have had a good one, one of those severe sparks of lightning struck the rod on the Court House, several persons saw it. I didn't see it but could tell from the peculiar sound that it had struck some rod and thought likely it was the Court House.

July 5/ 82 I recd. just a splendid long letter from Ida yesterday afternoon. She is not very much pleased with the place, the accommodations are not very good out there. And the wells not having the desired effect, so they said she will start home today or tomorrow.

July 7/ 82 A cloudy morning, looks like rain, I hope it will. Well Ida did not come, we had the sociable and I had a very nice time. I had the pleasure of walking home with Miss Matti Twyman. Last night was the second time I had ever met her. I enjoyed the walk very much. I made 324 pills yesterday afternoon for amusement, guess I will make some more today.

1:35 p.m. I went down to church and before church I saw Ida, and told her howdy. She looked as sweet as ever. She seemed somewhat glad to see me, and I am sure I was <u>very glad</u> to see her. I think she has improved some during the absence, at least she looked better to me.

July 14/ 82 We had just a splendid night for the sociable. There was not a very large crowd there, but just enough to make it pleasant. About 10 oclock we were invited to the dining room to partake of refreshments consisting of Ice Cream and cake, both of which were splendid.

On last Wednesday evening one of the most terrible things occurred at TexArkana Ark. that I ever heard of. There was a 4 story brick building in course of construction. 2 stories being finished and not being wall built when the wind struck it, which was blown over right on stop of a 1 story building, a Saloon and Gambling Hall, killing about 50 men. As soon as the walls fell the lamps all exploded and set every thing on fire, some parties who were there and witnessed it said they never heard such pitiful groans and cries for help in all their life. But nothing could be done as it was all in flames and 6 or 8 ft. deep in brick. Some were begging to be killed if they couldn't be gotten out. They have been at work yesterday and today digging them out, and have gotten about 25 out so far, and are not near through yet. The most of them are burnt beyond recognition. One gentleman from this place was in it and could be recognized only by the specks (eyeglasses) found sticking to his burnt and charred skull.

O! How terrible to think of 40 or 50 men going from such a place into eternity, and what a warning it should be to those who are pursuing such a course, people who saw it, said they never witnessed any thing to compare with it.

[The Paragon Saloon was located on Broad Street in Texarkana. It was a wooden structure, and on its flank was a three-story brick building. A storm blew in on the evening of July 12, 1882, about 6:30 and began to intensify. The wind picked up, and the wall on the new brick building came crashing down on the saloon roof and the people inside.

Kerosene lamps used to light the saloon were overturned and set the wreckage and the trapped people on fire. In the end, twenty-nine people were identified and verified dead, but the count may have been over fifty. Many were never identified and were buried in a mass grave at Rose Hill Cemetery. Two other buildings were also destroyed in the fire.]

Saturday morning July 15/ 82 I have finished my work. Finis has gone to breakfast. Marshall is on somewhat of a <u>boom</u> in the way of improvement just now. The streets are being put in better condition than I have ever seen them since I have been here. Culverts being built where necessary to carry off the water when it rained and thus prevent so much mud. And a nice substantial brick is going up just across the street from our store it will be quite an addition to our side of town. There is also a company organized and have filed their charter to build a street car line through some of our streets. It makes us feel a good deal better these dull times to see so much improvement going on. [When the railroad came to Marshall in the 1870s, the town began to grow. By the 1880s, it was one of the South's largest cotton markets. With this growth came improvements in the city services and newly built structures.]

10 p.m. It is almost time to retire so I will close up. There was a sociable near here tonight and several of the boys came by after me to go down with them. But I didn't care about going and besides I heard they were going to turn it into a dance.

Tuesday July 18/ 82 11:20 a.m. I have just finished labeling 6 doz. Bottles of Castor Oil and Turpentine, that Finis filled up yesterday afternoon. [Turpentine oil was used topically to treat rheumatoid disorders, muscle pain, and toothaches. People would inhale the vapors to reduce thick secretions caused by bronchial diseases.] The masons are at work again this morning just across the way and I can every now and then hear them call out, "More Mortar." The building is going up very fast.

2:45 p.m. We made out the orders for Dahals Pill & Powder Boxes, and Finis had gone to mail it. During the rain the lightning struck the Catholic Church and tore it up considerably. It also struck a horse belonging to Mr James F. Taylor, a gentleman living a few miles out in the country killing it instantly. The horse was tied out in Dr Taylors yard of their place at the time. [James Franklin Taylor (1812–89) was a planter, state representative, and state senator. He had a plantation about six miles outside of town.]

The saying is "an ill wind brings good to some one," so it was with us and the storm yesterday. It caused parties to want lightning rods so we made a sale of all the Balls we had on hand. [Lightning rods had glass balls on top. This was done to provide evidence of a lightning strike by the ball breaking or falling off.] They say the Church is damaged about $500 worth, where it caught fire, but was soon put out by the Priest.

Thursday July 20/ 82 I tell you I worked like a good fellow pretty well all day. Only I had to stop a time or to help to put up some Prescriptions and I had cleaned down all one side of the store, taken down all the bottles dusted off the shelves, whipped every bottle and put them back, so I am pretty tired.

This afternoon late I went down to the Ice Factory to get some Ice and when I came back I found Miss Ida Sanders & Hattie Roberts in the store so I put the ice in the basket and came back and had a little chat with Ida. [During the winter, ice was cut from lakes or rivers and then taken into the ice house and packed with insulation such as straw or sawdust. This kept it frozen for use during the warmer months.]

She told me she might go to Virginia and that she would start next Sunday. I want her to go for I know it would benefit her health, but I will miss her mightily.

Friday July 21/ 82 It is terrible hot, looks a little like rain, hope it won't for we are going to have a Sociable this evening. I have Miss Charlin Talley's company engaged for it. I finished cleaning up the store and went up and dressed for the party.

Saturday 22/ 82 A very pleasant day so far only misty. Well we had the Sociable, there was a very large crowd there and all seemed to have a good time. I had a long talk with Ida, which I enjoyed very much indeed. Guess it will be the last time I see her for about a year.

Monday July 24/ 82 I am partly early had the store open before 6 oclock. We are going to have a Sociable at our house tonight. Complimentary to Ida and I am to have the pleasure of her company, we want to make it as pleasant for her as we can. As it will be the last time we will have the pleasure of seeing her for a long time.

July 28/ 82 Awful hot this morning. There was a big festival out in the

College yard last night. The proceeds to improve the College's building, but as there was a ball upstairs in the building I did not go. I don't propose to go when there is dancing is carried on. [John's mother, Louisa, was very much against parties that had dancing.]

Monday July 31/ 82 I have been reading some in Mamma's Diary this morning. I enjoy it so much. What a dear good mother I had. I read just a splendid letter from Ida today, she reached Va. all right, though worn out by the long journey. I have written a long letter to her, which I will mail tonight after I write a little more in it.

John Collier Foster Journal #2

August 1, 1882–February 1, 1883

————————

Marshall, Texas, August 1, 1882 Bro Finis has gone to breakfast and I have finished cleaning up the store and am now ready to go to mine, when he returns. Business has been better for the last few days than for sometime past.

Wednesday Aug. 2/ 82 After prayer meeting I walked home with Miss Belle Sanders and had a very pleasant time with her and she gave me her Autograph [book] to write in. [As] I came back by the Opera House they was having a rehearsal for a play to be given for the benefit of the "Womens Christian Temperance Union" and just as I got there Eugen Browlitte told me Miss Ethel Turner wanted to see me so I went over and she told me she wanted me to take the part of Jumpman in the play and I told her I would see if the Dr would let me off and if he would, I guess I would take it, and let her know this morning whether or not I could take it. I guess the Dr. will be willing and as I think it is a worthy cause, I will lend my assistance.

Later The Dr. said it was alright so I went down and told Miss Ethel I would take the part and try and have it ready by this afternoon when there will be a rehearsal. My part is not very long and I have about learnt it.

Friday August 4/ 82 We had a Social down at Dr Sears house last evening, for the benefit of the Little Helpers, they raised $4.05 it was a very pleasant affair. I had the pleasure of Miss Belle Sanders company. Miss Turner sent me over word about dark that there would be a rehearsal of the Dickens Play at her house and for me to be sure and come down. So I took my girl to the Sociable excused myself and went down for the rehearsal, but a good many didn't come, so we had none. So I went back to the social. I had the pleasure of meeting for the first time Miss Pula Hog. I like her very much, she is very pleasant and entertaining.

Photo of Cousin Eva, early 1880s, who John wrote to several times. The back of the photo said, "To Collie from Eva." Photo from Mansfield Historical Society.

Saturday Aug. 5/ 82 Well this town is crowded with negroes, "come to see de sho!" the procession has just passed through it was not very good, for such a large Circus as this proposes be. [Steven & Begun's Circus toured through Texas, Arkansas, Missouri, and Iowa during this time.]

Miss Maggie Whaley was in the store this morning with a cousin of hers from Longview, and introduced her to me, and invited me to call on her while she was here. She seems to be a very nice young lady, and I think I will try to call and see her before she goes back. I read the sad intelligence yesterday of the death of cousin Eva's little baby Lula Kathrina, but I try to feel that "God does all things well."

Sunday Aug. 6/ 82 This morning I have been reading some of the letters I recd. from my <u>dear sister</u> before she died. I also read the manuscript of a Piece on "The dangers of Card Playing," showing the history of a young man who, began card playing as an amusement only, but who ended a regular Gambler and a drunkard. But when was finally reclaimed by the prayers of pious parents.

Tuesday Aug. 8/ 82 A nice cool morning as it is somewhat cloudy. Looks somewhat like it will rain, hope it won't for it might interfere with our play this evening. We had a good rehearsal last evening. It was the first time I had rehearsed with them. I got along very well.

I have been reading letters from my dear sister before she died. I enjoy them so much. O! how I wish I could have gone to see her before she was so sick. The dear girl seemed to have loved me so much. In every one of her letters she said she didn't how she could stand not to see me, much longer. But she is now in a Better and Brighter World, where loneliness is no more, but where all is joy and happiness.

I recd. a postal from Bro Tommie this morning his school class closes on the 18. He didn't say what he was going to do next. I wish he would come over and see us, as I haven't seen him in nearly a year.

Monday Aug 9/ 82 A cool cloudy morning. The Dickens Entertainment came off and was a success, had a good crowd. I don't know exactly how much was made yet.

Monday Aug. 14/ 82 This has been a tolerably cool day though pretty warm at times. I took Miss Lula Whaley to church last night, heard a good sermon and had a very pleasant time after church. I wrote to Ida this morning. I recd. in a letter from her or rather just a note accompanying there an of her Photo and a lovely Hat mark that she embroider with her own hands for me. The Photo is a splendid one of her, and I tell you I appreciate it. I also wrote to Miss Sallie Young of Tehuacana my old teacher when I used to live there and go to school.

Tuesday Aug 15/ 82 A cloudy morning, it is cool & pleasant. Bro Finis has just gone to breakfast. Sad is the event recalled by this the 15th of Aug for one year ago today we laid our <u>dear sister Mary</u> away in the tomb.

18th We had a sociable at Mr Allens last night. I had the pleasure of taking Miss Ganniura Richardson, and had a very pleasant time. I recd. a splendid long letter from Ida which I enjoyed ever so much.

August 19/ 82 There came near being a serious difficulty in town this evening between two political leaders on different sides. Mr Pope and Mr. Singleton, they got to quarreling over a congressional convention which had just been held, and Mr Pope drew his pistol and had it right in Mr Singletons face when Mr Fry, a banker here who was standing by, knocked it up and then took it away from him. I haven't heard all the particulars so don't know which one was to blame. It is a pity that men will quarrel over such things and get so angry as to take the life of a fellow man.

Aug. 21/ 82 This has been a very pleasant day, though I have not been well at all, have the headache now. I read the news this morning of the death of Will Pool and Conrad Ferrill, two boys I knew well at home. Conrad was riding by our house on his horse and was struck by lightning and killed, he and his horse. I wrote to Ida this evening. It is bedtime and I am sleepy, so goodnight.

Aug. 26 /82 This morning a nice little job of putting up, or rather labeling 137 bottles of Castor Oil. Business moderately good so for today and the afternoon is always the last part of the day the negroes all stand around and talk to one another until 4 or 5 oclock in the afternoon and then buy what they want and start for home.

Reports from every part of the state are that crops are very fine though the cotton worm is appearing in some sections. Though it is said that if the worm do come still there will be more cotton made that can be gathered and we are all looking for a boom in trade this fall. We bought the other night some of the finest goods for our Xmas trade that I ever saw such as Plush and Rusbice Leather Dressing [a crème for leather goods] and Perfumery Cases. The retail price range from $5.00 to $15.00 a piece. [During this time perfumes were rarely applied to the skin. Instead, they were used to scent handkerchiefs, gloves, and other articles of clothing. Most of the scents used were florals, such as rose, violet, or lavender.]

Wednesday Aug 30/ 82 We recd. a letter from brother Tommie this morning. He has engaged to teach a ten months term near Georgetown, beginning Nov. 1/82. So he will have 2 months vacation yet. He says he can't come over and see us though. I wish he could.

Thursday Aug. 31/ 82 I had quite a job this afternoon of sorting a big sack of different size corks, they were all mixed up together and I sorted them out. Not much business today. If it keeps dry and a good cotton crop is made, business will begin to boom pretty soon.

My year will be out on the 24th of this month, and I expect a raise on my salary which is at present only $35.00 per month. I am going to strike for $50.00 and I think I will get it for Dr don't want me to leave him. And I would rather not if I can do as well with him, for I have become attached to the place and people and the Dr is a very pleasant man to get along with. [The following were monthly salaries in Texas in 1882: the average teacher, $24.00; average worker, about $35.00. John was making a decent salary, and his working conditions were probably better than most places.] Well I have been going out to a most too many parties and entertainments this summer. But I am going to hold up now and knuckle more closely to my business. Of course I may go to occasionally to the Sociable for the Little Helpers. Well the water is pretty icey yet so I believe I will take some Citric Acid and make me some Lemonade.

Friday September 1st-82 I went out collecting this morning and had a very good success. Collect most all the bills I had. I got a letter from Ida today it was written on the day she left Va. For Nashville. She said she had improved wonderfully having gained 10 pounds in a month.

Sept 2/ 82 We read the sad news the other day that Doctor Beeson the President of Trinity University was very sick and not expected to live. His whole body being paralyzed except his right hand. [Rev. W. E. Beeson was president of Trinity University, except during 1877–78, from 1869 until his death on September 5, 1882. He was stricken with paralysis while at the dinner table.]

Monday Sept 4/ 82 I went down to the church to help Mrs. Maulding organize a Band of Hope, acting as secretary and for organization for her. [The Band of Hope was a temperance organization for working-class children. The members enrolled from the age of six and were taught about the "evils of drink." They met once a week to listen to talks and take part in activities.]

It kept me pretty busy for about an hour & a quarter, writing out or rather filling out the Pledges for the 35 who joined. Oswald Hargrove helped me filling out the stubs.

Sept 6/ 82 About 12 oclock I was taken with a swelling of my right foot right at the joint only in front, so I went ahead went to prayer meeting and when I returned my foot was paining me so that I soon went to bed.

This morning the Doctor pronounced it Erysipelas, [an infection of the skin near the surface] so it has kept me in bed almost all day. I am keeping it painted with Iodine. And this evening the swelling seems to have gone down

Band of Hope membership card, public domain

some. It not only pains me to walk, but irritates it and makes it worse being as it is right on the joint. I also continue to have the headache so I am going to take some pills tonight and try and stop this headache.

Marshall. Texas September 13/ 82 This is the first time I have returned to sit up long enough to write in my diary. Since last Wednesday I was not able to leave my room and walk enough to get my meals until Sunday at noon, when with the aid of a walking cane I got down to the house for my dinner it being only 2 blocks distant. But I still have to lay in bed all the time as it injuries my foot to sit up, for it has to be up even with my body. It has been a pretty bad case my foot and nearly half way up to my knee, being swollen up. I kept it painted with Iodine until it stopped spreading, painting the part just above my ankle to guard against spreading up any higher, so that part was severely blistered and that is the really the only sore part now. The swelling having about all gone down out of the lower part of my foot. I think and so does the doctor that I will be alright in a few days.

While I was sick nearly a week ago the sad news came to us that our beloved Dr. Beeson was no more. There was a memorial service at our church in memorial of him which was a most interesting and impressive one. had been under his care for the past 3 years preparing himself for the ministry. Having thus being associated with Dr Beeson whom to know was to love.

Sept. 15/ 82 I am going to take a dose of Pills again tonight and then I think I will be all right. As my foot is about entirely well.

Geo. Leachman was in town today and came around to see me this morning. He is now Secretary of the Longview Marriage Association and is located at Longview. And I saw and had quite a long talk with Miss Maggie W. When I started to leave she pinned a nice little boquet on my coat for me. She likes Mr Leachman very much, he likes her very much, in fact I think they are engaged. But the "old man" doesn't like Geo. at all, and would not let him come near the house. I am a kind of a confidant of both parties, carrying messages from one to the other for them. I carried one for George this evening.

It is against the rules for the girls to write to the boys, at Ward University so I haven't heard from Ida since the 29 of Aug, the day she left for Va. I would like to hear from the "old Girl" mighty well. She said she would write me a long letter during Christmas Holidays, but that is a long way off yet.

Saturday Sept. 16/ 82 We have been pretty busy today. Good deal of cotton in town selling at from 11 to 11 ½ cents per lb.

Sunday Sept. 17/ 82 I attended the Episcopal Church this morning and the Baptist this evening. And had the pleasure of Miss Hattie Ford's company, a young lady from Shreveport.

Monday Sept. 18/ 82 It has been pretty warm today and we been quite busy marking and putting in order in the shelves a bill or two of school books, business quite brisk. Bro Finis has gone to supper, I have just finished arranging some things in the store. I have got lots of work such as putting up different kinds of medicines that we keep put up, things of that kind get behind while I was sick. So I will have to work fast to get even again.

Sept. 19/ 82 We had a large fire in our town last night. A whole block of frame buildings (the only block in town) was burned down. They were so far gone before any one got there. And the engine was out of order and took some time to get it to work. So they could do nothing with it, only get all the things out and let it burn. It was mostly occupied by negroes, one of the houses a Saloon and gambling place. It was an eyesore to everyone, so all are glad to see it out of the way. Now if someone will build it up with good bricks, it will add greatly to our town. Our store and an old livery stable are now the only Frame Stores on the square. It is wonderful how houses have burned all around and still it is here, one of the oldest houses in town being about 35 years of age.

Another circus was in town today so all the negroes was out of course as usual. As a great many white folks. Several young ladies came to our store, situated as it is on the west side of the square, to see the procession. The procession was very good and there was one curiosity that I would have liked to seen. There was the two headed woman in fact she had two whole bodies joined together about the small of the back. She can talk with one head on one subject and on another with the other. Can sing alto with one mouth and soprano with the other and so on.

[Millie and Christine McKoy were African American twins conjoined at the lower spine. Various people enslaved them and exhibited them at numerous freak shows and fairs. A wealthy merchant, Joseph Pearson Smith, who had earlier held the girls in slavery, found them and united them with their mother. They were freed by the Emancipation Proclamation in 1863. The girls were educated and taught to speak five languages, dance, sing, and play music and enjoyed a successful career.

Advertisement for "the Two Headed Lady" ca. 1880. Photo in public domain.

In the 1880s, they moved back to the farm where they were born, which their father had purchased and left to them. They later founded a school for black children and supported, anonymously, a number of colleges. They died of tuberculosis at the age of sixty-one on October 6, 1912. Christine died twelve hours after Millie.]

But I didn't go and thought I could put my money to a better advantage, besides I didn't care much about seeing any more of it. I had the pleasure of seeing Miss Hattie Ford to prayer meeting.

Sept. 20/ 82 A. J. came in and he and I took a few games of checkers and he beat me 3 to one. Then Eddie Buck and I tried it and I beat him 6 to 1.

Sept. 22/ 82 It is quite cool this morning so much so that it is quite pleasant with a winter suit on. Geo. Leachman was in town again yesterday. I went down to a sociable at Mr. Evers last evening. Met several young ladies and had just a real nice time.

I heard from Ida the other night through Miss Fannie Richardson, her aunt. She was quite well and pleased with everything. I also was introduced to a Miss Sexton, a cousin of Ida's from Va. where Ida was staying. Of whom Ida frequently spoke in her letters to me. She is quite pretty and apparently very pleasant though I didn't get to talk to her any as I was introduced just as I was leaving church. I would like to call and see her if she was only a little younger. But she is a little too old for me.

Saturday Sept 23/ 82 Still cool. Bro Finis has gone to his breakfast. I have just finished cleaning up. I went down to the sociable last night and got acquainted with several young ladies. But they began to dance in one of the rooms, so I came home. I didn't know there was to be any dancing, or I wouldn't have went down at all.

Today is one of the Jew's holiday, so they are all closed up. They closed at 6 oclock last evening and will open at 6 this evening. [The holiday was Yom Kippur, the Hebrew year was 5643. Many Jews moved to Marshall after the arrival of the railroad in the 1870s, and the first temple was erected in 1900. Meyer Dopplymayer and his brother, Daniel, came to Marshall in the 1850s and started the first Jewish business in town. Meyer's son, Jim, was a good friend of John Collier, and he is mentioned several times in his journals.]

Monday Sept 25/ 82 Yesterday was the last day with Dr. according to the contract. So Saturday afternoon we talked about business a little but didn't agree much. He wants me to engage by the year and I don't but I don't want to tie myself down for so long of a time. For I might have a better offer for what he is giving. So I would like to have it so that I could give him 30 days notice in which time he could get someone to take my place. And I give him the same privilege if he can get someone to fill my place for less money give me 30 days and do so. He told me to give him until today to decide what he could give me and if he could take me by the months. So today will decide whether I stay in Marshall any longer or not. I have another place in view if we don't make a trade. Though don't know for certain whether I can get it or not.

Later Dr and I had our talk. He made me the offer of $40 pr. month if I would stay with him for another year. But I told him I would not engage for a year, but that I would stay with him at that rate on the condition of giving him 30 days notice and quitting and I gave him the privilege of doing the same if he thought he could get someone to fill my place for less. So when he saw that I would not engage for a year (for I would have quit first) he came to my terms and we agreed on $40 per month. It is not as much as I think I could be worth to a man with a good live trade, but with his trade, it is as much as Dr. is able to pay me. Well I am very well satisfied, for I expect to do better before a great while.

Tuesday Sept 26/ 82 After prayer meeting I went up to Weismans to look for some clothing. Found a suit from $15.00 that I liked very much, a business suit so I think I will get it tomorrow. [In 1878 Joe Weisman and three of his brothers came to Marshall and opened the first department store in the state.]

Sept 27/ 82 Business has been very good today. I went up this morning and bought the suit for $15.00 also a pair of Shoes spending 20.00 with A. J. & Weismans.

Sept 29/ 82 Well I was pretty busy putting up Castor Oil, Turpentine and in the evening I attended a Sociable at Dr. Johnsons and, by the way, I had the pleasure of having Miss Lula Evers for my company. It is real queer about she and I, we were never introduced. The way it was is, that I have known who she was and she has known who I was for 2 years or more. For she attended our church but we were never introduced. So of course never spoke, but last week there was a sociable at her home and I was asked, by others who were getting it up to be sure and come. So I went down expecting to have someone to introduce me to Miss Lula, but she met me at the door, spoke very cordially to me invited me in and introduced me around to all that I had never met. And she and I were together a good deal through the evening, and she made it so pleasant for me, that I felt like I had known her a good long time. And when I went to leave she invited me very cordially to call some time so I wrote to her to go with me last evening and she went and she said she liked the way we came to know each other. It seems so odd and I told her I did too.

We had two drummers in this afternoon, we bought a bill of glass ware and Druggist Sundries from Whithall Tatum & Co's man. But didn't buy anything from Mr Practon, Mayer Bros and Cb's man, as we were not needing enough in his line to make an order. [Whitall Tatum and Company mass produced prescription bottles for drugstores around the country. The company's plant was in operation from 1806 through 1938.]

Geo. Leachman was in town this afternoon and there was a Sociable at Mr. Pierces residence and he went to see Miss Maggie and as the old Man don't allowed him on the place, I went down and got her and he met us on the way and took her on, and I returned as I didn't intend on going, but did it just to help Geo. I guess he and she are having a nice time by this time, somewhat in the corner by themselves. I heard from Ida again the other day through her mother. She was quite well pleased, with the school and every-thing and enjoyed good health.

Business just ordinary today. Well it is ten oclock, time all honest people are in bed, so goes the saying.

Saturday Sept 30/ 82 Bro Finis leaves Monday morning for a visit to Tehuacana and Austin and several other towns making quite a trip. Will be gone about two weeks on such a matter. So I will be alone for a while. Will have to run the store by myself for most of the time as doctor will be attend-ing the fair which commences next Tuesday lasting 4 days.

The other night when I was promenading with Miss Lula Evers when she said "just let me compliment you on your splendid voice, I just think it is splendid." It kind a got away with me. I knew I have an ordinary voice, but I don't think it is any thing extra ordinary. The trouble is, though, that my throat bothers me so much that I can't sing much at one time. It just stops up and won't go on all handily.

Bro Tommie wrote us the other day that he had an offer for some land we three boys own out in Burnett Co. to sell it. I will have to be made of age by a process of court, which I guess will be done at the next term of the district court, which meets here next month. For if we don't conclude to sell it now, we might have a good offer for it sometime again before I am 21. So if we do, then I will be of age and we can sell it. Bro Finis will see Bro Tom at Austin and they will talk the matter over and see if it is best to sell now or wait. I told Finis I would leave it to their judgement to do what they both thought best.

Monday Oct 2/ 82 This has been a very busy day with me. Bro Finis got off this morning and I have been collecting pretty well all day. Have collected about $70.00 pretty good for the amount I had to collect for I got nearly every one I asked. And what time I was at the store I was kept pretty busy putting Prescriptions and waiting on customers. I guess business will lull a little tomorrow, and the fair commences and nearly everyone will be attending.

Oct 3/ 82 There has been a very large plain comet seen for some time now, and I have been up to see it for several times before but failed to see it on account of its being cloudy until this morning when I woke up and thinking it was about time to see the comet. I got up and went to my window and there it was over in the east near the horizon in full blast. It is an immense one the tail being very big and very plain.

I was filled with wonder and admiration as I sat and looked at that great body suspended in the air, apparently so near the earth, and yet so <u>very far</u> away.

[The Great Comet of 1882 was perhaps the brightest comet that had ever been seen. It was first spotted in the Southern Hemisphere on September 1, 1882. By the end of September, it was noticed that the comet's nucleus had enlarged and had split into two shiny balls. By October 17, the comet had broken into at least five fragments.]

This is a photo of the comet of 1882 that had the interest of John Collier. Photo in public domain.

I was a little late at prayer meeting tonight and I walked home with Miss Vera Johnson and we had a nice little talk.

Oct 5/ 82 There is a traveling Theatrical Troup in town and their Band makes just elegant music. Tonight as I came up from supper as I was waiting for the mail I heard them play a piece. They have been in tour 2 days now and have given us music through the streets both days. The fair have the colored band from Shreveport playing for them but this band beats them so bad I have to hear them.

Oct. 6/ 82 This morning Dr told me that if I wanted to go to the fair today that he would stay at the store and let me go. So I went over this afternoon and seen some very fine stock, mostly horses, this being the day for stock. There was one or two very good races, but the part I enjoyed most was a chat with Miss Mattie Twyman for about an hour. I also walked home with her. I saw Miss Lula Evers, but didn't get to talk to her any as there were two gentlemen with her most of the evening. I wanted to get a talk with her too, but couldn't.

Oct 7/ 82 Tonight I ordered some catechins from A. L. Paxon St. Louis and some stationary and books from Shorb & Boland of same city. [Catechins was found in some fruits and types of tea. It was taken to improve overall health. A. L. Paxon was a pharmacist who had moved to St. Louis from Indian Territory in Oklahoma. James Shorb and John Boland ran a book and stationary company in St. Louis.]

We have had a good rain this afternoon about 5 oclock, it began and it quit about half past nine. I lost the store key tonight, as I went to supper, but found it. I just slipped on my coat and put the key in my pocket and there being a big hole in the pocket it just went on through, so that I didn't miss it until I got to the store after my supper and ran my hand in my pocket after the key and found none. So I got a lantern and found it, as I suspected only a few steps from the store.

Oct. 10/ 82 Business moderately good today. I washed about 200 bottles this afternoon. Joe Hendrick kept store for me. I will fill some of them with Turpentine tomorrow if I have time. I read a card from Bro Finis yesterday. He is in Austin where he will see Bro Tommie.

Oct 11/ 82 I have closed up and gone to my room to retire. Eddie Buck is going to stay all night with me. We are going to get up and see the Comet in the morning. I was up to see it this morning in all its splendor.

Oct 12/82 This is my birthday, I am 19 years of age and I recd. a lovely present from one of my lady friends. I had been off from the store and on my return I found one of the prettiest boquets you ever saw with a note containing the following. "With complements & best wishes of a friend." But I recognized the writing at once, so sat down and wrote her a nice little letter of thanks in reply to which I read a <u>real nice</u> little note from her stating that she sent these as a token of her respect and esteem for me, and was glad to know that I appreciated them so much.

[During this time, the type of flower conveyed a special meaning. For example, Aster was a symbol of love, and a pink Camellia was longing for you. If a ribbon on them was tied to the left, it meant the flower's symbolism applied to the giver; when tied to the right, the symbol was referenced to the recipient. If the flowers were wilted and dead, there was no need to send back a kind note. Many homes at this time had guidebooks explaining the "flower language." The message depended on what book was used. It's a shame that John did not mention the type of flowers he received.]

It is a lovely boquet and very fragrant, it perfumes the whole store nearly. The young lady was Miss Lula Evers. I have found her to be much pleasant company indeed.

Oct 13/82 Eddie is staying with me again tonight and we will try to see the comet again in the morning. I was up to see it again this morning.

Oct 14/82 I got a letter from Finis today written from Austin on the 12th. He met bro Tommie there on business matters. He said bro Tommie was looking well, said no one knew him hardly.

Oct. 17/82 I have been very busy this afternoon in putting up prescriptions. And tonight I wrote a letter to Jim Dopplemayer and helped Dr. buy a bill of drugs. Finis got in about 9 oclock.

Oct. 19/82 I bought me a nice Hat this morning and had Miss Della to put the Hat Mark Ida gave me in for me and it looks just as pretty as it can. Bro Finis struck a splendid thing while he was gone in the town of Cleburne, two doctors have a drug store and they are going to give him one third interest in it to manage the business. It will be under the name F.A. Foster & Co. He will take charge the 1st of December I suppose. If bro can get off from his school he is going to go and learn the business under Finis. And I guess I will stay with Dr. for another year. But if bro can't go I will go out in a month or so and see be with him. I hate for us both to leave the Dr. at once. [Cleburne was about 195 miles west of Marshall. In the early 1880s, the population was around five thousand. It began to grow in 1881 when the Santa Fe railroad line from Galveston to Fort Worth passed through the town.]

Bro Finis went down to Dr Johnsons tonight and hasn't returned yet. I wrote an order to Shorb & Boland of St. Louis for a book for one of the boys tonight and went and mailed it. I returned the suit I bought for $15.00 as it didn't fit me and got a better one for $20.00 [.]

Oct. 20/ 82 I have been reading some in the Dispensatory tonight. I am going to try and read some in it every night. now that Finis is going off. If I stay the responsibility of filling prescriptions will fall upon me. So I must study up more, it will be all the better for me. For I can see that having to do all that work while he was gone two weeks did me good.

Sunday Oct. 22/ 82 I have been reading in Mamma's journal of the fall of 1859 & spring of 1860. It almost brought tears to my eyes when I read where she thought she was going into consumption and papa was away from home on business, and how she would feel so lonely and sad at times when she would allow herself to think of being taken from her children.

Oct 24/ 82 A very pretty day, business not very good. I cleaned our largest showcase this afternoon quite a little job after I had cleaned the glass I took some oil and rubbed up the walnut frame nicely.

Later We had a very good prayer meeting. Miss Lula Evers was there without an escort. So I walked home with her and engaged her company for the sociable at Mr. Rains house. After I came back some boys came in so we played a few games of checkers.

Oct 25/ 82 This morning I washed a lot of bottles and then opened up and helped mark up a bill of Autograph & Photograph albums and other goods for Christmas such as Fancy Ink Stands, Perfuming Cases, Picture frames and so on. I tell you we have some elegant goods. This afternoon I took everything out of our nicest case and cleaned it inside & in the morning I am going to arrange the goods in it.

Oct. 27/ 82 Am going to a sociable, have Miss Lula Evers for my company and I expect to have a good time generally. Finis got a letter from Bro Tommie this morning stating that he could get off from his school and go with him to learn the business, so I guess I will stay here another year.

Nov 5/ 82 It seems as if I had about forgotten about my diary, well I haven't. Only it seems that if I don't get time to write in it. This evening we had a "Song Service" besides the organ we had a Cornet and the choir which added greatly to the music. There was a very crowded house and all seemed to enjoy it so much. I went with Miss Lula Evers and took my "Auto" for her to write in, she also gave me hers to write in.

Nov. 10/ 82 I went to a little party at Mr. Rains house last night and had a very nice time. I took Miss Lula Evers, she gave me my album having written a nice piece in it. I wrote in hers today, she passed the store 2 or 3 times in a buggy this afternoon. I got a letter from Harris Taylor [his stepbrother] tonight. He had just gotten back from his trip to Mountain City with Miss Nellie Roach who was called home on account of the sickness of her mother.

Sunday Nov 12/ 82 I finished reading of Mamma's Journals today in it she speaks of bro Finis first speech in public. It was when he was 7 years old and he was going to school to Mr & Mrs Dechand at LaGrange. Mr Dechand now has a good school at a town by the name of Weimar near LaGrange [about fifteen miles southeast of La Grange].

Thursday Nov 16/ 82 I applied yesterday for a Certificate of Membership in the Youth and Aged Mutual Endowment and Benefit Association of America. I take a Five thousand policy and the plan is this—I am assessed $1.50 at every death or often enough to pay off the benefits. If I live nine years I draw out Thousand Dollars ($1,000) and so on every nine years until I draw $5,000. If I die, at my death, whoever I name in my certificate as my beneficiary receives $1,000. In the event of my decease I think it is a good thing. As according to the death rate. It cannot cost me more than 25 or 30 dollars a year. Which in nine years will only be between 200 & 300 dollars, at which time I will draw $1,000. It will be no trouble for me to pay 25 or 20 dollars a year and it will be pretty good interest on the money.

And should I die before I draw all it will be $1,000 to Trinity University which will do some good. Dr. Sears examined me & I wanted to pay him but he would not let me. So that makes it a dollar less that it would have been, had Dr. Taylor their regular Examiner me which would have made it cost me $7.00.

Tuesday Nov 21/ 82 There was to be a Pink T. Party at the residence of Mrs Gregg tomorrow evening at which there will be music recitation & so on and a nice supper. The admittance being 25 cents each, a general nice time is anticipated by all. It is gotten up by the Ladies Aid Society of our church and the proceeds are to go towards fixing up the church. So I hope it won't rain so all can attend who want to. Thursday evening Miss Evers is going to give a Sociable at her home.

Wednesday Nov 22/ 82 We will have a nice evening for our T. Party. I helped Miss Della make the Pink T's out of Pink card board this afternoon.

Thursday Nov 23/ 82 The Pink T. Party last evening was quite successful & there was I guess at least 50 or 60 people there & all seemed to enjoy themselves. The supper was very nice indeed. I anticipate a nice time this eve. Miss Lula said she wanted me to assist her in serving that everyone has as nice a time as possible. Miss Vera & Hattie Johnson were in just now looking at some Photos albums. Miss Vere said I <u>must</u> give her one of my Photos. So I guess I will when I have some taken.

Friday Nov 24/ 82 There was very nice crowd out last evening at the sociable & we had a splendid time. Once in the evening we were all out in the hall paying when the door opened and in came a crazy man I suppose. Dolph Evers was at or near the door & ask him what he wanted but he didn't seem to notice him but started to come on in when he took hold of him & put him out. He was muttering something all the time we couldn't understand what he was trying to say. When Dolph put him out & told him to go he went on off. He was either crazy or Drunk & I don't think he was drunk, because I couldn't smell whiskey on his breath at all. Miss Lula was kept pretty busy acting as Hostess so I didn't get to talk with her a great deal.

Tuesday Nov. 28/ 82 But just as the service began the fire bell began to ring so Dr Ward dismissed the meeting and we came up to the square to see where the fire was and found it. Over south of town out in the suburbs a negroe house.

Wednesday 11/29/82 Well the electric light has been running all this week, it makes a most brilliant light. But I think it would ruin my eyes to work where it is on account of the glare. [One light bulb was installed in the Texas and Pacific Railroad depot. This made Marshall the first city in Texas to have electricity.]

We had quite a little scare down at Drs. House this afternoon about 5 oclock. A gentleman came into the store & told us that one of the chimney's at the house was burning and though he didn't think there was any danger, that some of us had better go down as Mrs. Sears would likely be frighten. So I ran down and up stairs when I got there, there was two gentlemen on the roof. So I took off my shoes and went up also taking up water and salt for them to extinguish the flames. We wet the roof all around as the sparks were falling thick all around. All was out in a few minutes and I returned and dried my feet.

Tomorrow is the day set apart by the President for the thanksgiving to God for his many blessings towards us during the past year. How thoughtful we should be indeed for every good thing that we possess for it all comes from the Great Giver of All Good. Goodnight.

[Thanksgiving had been celebrated nationally off and on since 1789. The dates for celebrating Thanksgiving ranged from as early as September 9 to as late as March 16. President Chester A. Arthur set the date for Thanksgiving in 1882 as November 30. In 1941 President Franklin Roosevelt signed into law a bill from Congress making the fourth Thursday in November the legal holiday for Thanksgiving.]

Sat Dec. 2/ 82 The alarm of fire was sounded this evening just after dark. And in running to the fire I struck a stump with my foot, fell and almost tore my thumb nail loose. It was very painful and I can hardly work with it. And after running myself nearly to death I found it was only a brush fire out in the suburbs of town.

Wednesday Dec. 6/ 82 My dear old diary does seem that I neglect you. Today was the day for the transit of Venus across the suns disk and it will not occur again for 120 years. It has been cloudy nearly all day but this morning I smoked me a piece of glass and when the sun would come out from under the clouds I would look and there I saw it a time or two, the star looking like a nice speck on the sun's face. A wonderful world in this that such a thing occurs and yet none of these great bodies of which the universe are so full, ever get off their track but all move at their enormous speed as if working by clock work. And man, frail feeble man, is made to exclaim how wonderful are the works of God.

Sunday Dec. 10/ 82 After church I went down to the house with bro Finis where we sat a little while before telling them all goodby as he leaves tomorrow morning before day. He goes up to Emit Ark [about 120 miles northeast of Marshall]. To see a particular lady of his, Miss Hattie Brown before going to C. Every one seems very sorry to see him go. I tell you I do for it will be awful lonesome for me. And then I always go to him for advice in everything. So I will miss him more than anyone else. I guess it is for the best to both of us that he should go. So I bid him God Speed in his new enterprise and where he goes my prayers go with him.

Tuesday Dec. 12/ 82 I have been pretty busy today. I filled a prescription this morning containing some "Camphor Water" which was about out so I

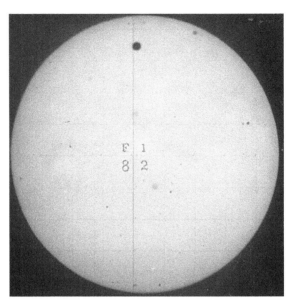

The 1882 transit of Venus on December 6, 1882, would be the last until 2003. This event only occurs as one of the interior planets, Venus, or Mercury, passes across the face of the sun. This photo was taken of the 1882 transit of Venus which showed up as a black dot near the top of the sun. Photo in public domain.

had to make some before I could put up the prescription. [Camphor water was usually used to alleviate coughs.]

I made up quite a number of prescriptions yesterday morning among them was Spts. [spirits] Camphor, Tr. Gingen, Tincture Culabus and so on. Mr. J L Lovejoy was here today and Dr. bought a little bill of drugs from him. [Mr. Lovejoy represented the Richardson Drug Company, which was headquartered in McKinney, Texas.]

Tonight is our regular prayer meeting evening. I went up and got Miss Charlie Talley and she played the organ and led the singers & Miss Hattie Roberts sang Alto and I sang the Bass so we had pretty good music. After she and I had returned to the Capitol Hotel, her home, for some time Eugen Brouielittle came in and I sat longer than I otherwise would have down, had quite a nice time.

Wednesday Dec. 13/ 82 I put one or two Tinctures to filter this morning. Put up some Laudanumin 25 cents bots. [This was a medicine that contained opium and was used as a painkiller.] Put up several prescriptions & so on and at 12:40 I went down and Miss Della & Hattie went down with me to see bro Finis as he passed through. [Finis was returning from Arkansas.] He said he had quite a pleasant visit. Joe is coming to help us until after Xmas I think. I guess he will be here tomorrow before he will for it keeps me a going. Some Xmas goods going.

Wednesday Dec. 20/ 82 Last night was a night long to be remembered for me as I acted for the first time in life as a waiter or groomsman at the marriage of Miss Clara Foster, though not any relation is a real good friend of mine. It was right funny the way I came to be one of the waiters. It was this way—Miss Clara came to me and told me that she had invited a certain young lady and wanted me to bring her for if I didn't she would not get to come for there was no other gentleman invited to bring her. And though I was slightly acquainted with her I never having called on her I told Miss Clara that I would bring her. So I did, well we were all out there in the parlor when Mr. Brown who was first waiter called me out and told me that one of the waiters had failed to get here and I had been chosen to fill the vacancy and stand with Miss Lulie Hog. So I told him I didn't see how I could under the circumstances, having on a sack suit instead of a regular dress suit and that I had no gloves. [A sack suit was a leisure or business suit for men. It was not considered very formal.]

But they all said that made no difference. So I agreed to act, but it happen that there was another young gentleman there just about my very size who had on a dress coat black so he said he would let me wear it. So I was all right and as one of the other groomsman had no gloves we all went without. So every thing went off nicely. Mrs. Rainny at whose house it came off gave a nice supper. I called to see the bride this evening and had the pleasure of walk home with Miss Lulie Hog who was there also after the call. Miss Lula Evers was in today and when she started I took my hat and went by the post office and walked home with her which I enjoyed so much.

Miss Humphries was in the store when I returned tonight and I walked home with her. I had just bought a couple of apples as I came down the street and was eating one and had one in my pocket and I told her and Miss Jessie Marton that the one that got it out of my pocket first might have it. So Miss H got it but Miss Jessie took it away from her. So I bought her another one as we walked on down home.

Thursday 21, / 82 I had a letter from Finis last evening he said he had been recd. very cordially by every one. We got our Garden Seed in this afternoon and tonight Joe & I opened and marked them up and got them all about put away.

Friday Dec. 22/ 82   I packed a box of presents for Bro Finis tonight, to ship tomorrow, consisting of night scenes in the Bible by Mrs Sears bound in Morocco a very handsome present. The Jones Family by J.G. Holland, a nice embroidered neck tie by Miss Dellie, a Napkin ring with the name Fissis on it, the name little Hattie always called him by Hattie and Bay Path by Holland by me. [Each family member usually had their own napkin ring. It not only showed that it belonged to you but was also important for sanitation. Most homes did not wash their cloth napkins after each meal and might not for several meals. The napkin ring, with your name on it, ensured that you would get the same napkin you had used at the last meal.]

Saturday Dec. 23/ 82   We have been in a rush all day today and have sold lots of Xmas goods, the boys are popping fire crackers and shooting rockets making it sound very much like Xmas.

Dec. 25, 1882   This is Christmas day, anniversary of our Lord and Savior Jesus Christ and how thankful we should be to our loving Heavenly Father that our lives have been spared to see another return of this day.

I had quite a little bit of experience in which I prevented the burning of a residence and perhaps the life of a young lady friend of mine. It was this way, I took Miss Lula Evers to the song service and I having a curiosity to attend the Catholic service, she and I were going to sit up and go to midnight mass. About half pass ten we were in the parlor talking when Mrs Evers who had retired seeing a light in the kitchen through a window near her bed called Miss Lula and told her to go to the kitchen and see what it was. So Miss Lula went and when she got nearly there she saw that the house was afire. The wood box full of wood being all ablaze also the mantelpiece, the plaza porch nearly to the celling so she hollowed to her ma that is was fire, as soon as I heard these words I jumped and ran and got to the kitchen door just as Miss Lula opened it, and run in, the air was almost suffocating the room being all closed up, so that Miss Lula ran across to another door to get out and to the well which was on the galley just outside the door. She got to the door and unlatched it but was so near suffocating that she didn't have power to open it. And she says she believes she would have fainted had I not come to the rescue. I was right after her seeing that she didn't or couldn't open the door. I threw my left arm around her waist which supported her almost fainting form while with the other I yanked open the door and as soon as she got a breath of fresh air she was alright and we lost no time in getting water out of the well and on the fire. And soon in a few minutes had it all out. I tell you Miss Lula didn't staid around and hollowed like most girls would have done but went bravely to work assisting me to extinguish the flames by drawing of water from the well while I took it up and dashed it on the flames.

In the meantime Mrs Evers ran down to Mr Brautleys her son in laws and brought Mr Brautley and his son Dolf Evers and 2 ladies up. But they got there after we got the fire was all out. It seemed providential that I was there for if Miss Lula had run in the way she did alone, she would undouble have fainted before she could have gotten out. And might have died before any one could have gotten to her.

Mrs Evers thank me over and over again for my kindness and promptness in putting out the fire. I told her I was very glad I was there and had been able to render the assistance I had. We went back to the parlor after all was right and had a nice time until about 15 minutes of 12 and when we went down to the Catholic service and I would have enjoyed it very much if it hadn't been so long but an hour and half was pretty long to sit and listen to a service that I couldn't understand. While I don't believe in so much outward ceremony it made one feel solemn to sit and listen to it.

I made Miss Lula a present of an elegant Old gold colored Plush Ador case which she said was the prettiest thing she ever saw of this kind. And she gave me one of the loveliest Silk Handkerchiefs I ever saw. I tell you I appreciate it very much coming from the source it has. This morning at breakfast table there was quite number of presents exchanged. I recd. 3 elegant books from Mrs Sears Dr & Miss Della. The one from Mrs Sears entitled "Our Fathers House" [written by Daniel March, 1869] is elegantly bound in Moroccan also a Silver Napkin ring from Little Hattie with my name engraved in it. All of which I appreciated very much.

Dec 26/ 82 I recd. letter from both bro's Finis & Tommie. Bro Finis said he was spending a very pleasant Xmas in his new home, said he had recd. before breakfast the Pkg. we sent him. Had responded to an invitation from a Rev. Mr. Gilliam to take Xmas dinner with him and had enjoyed the dinner much indeed. Said he had received most of the goods for his new store. Bro Finis said he didn't think he like city life as much as country life having lived in the country so long. [In 1880 Cleburne had a population of 17,911 and Marshall had 5,624.]

Said he couldn't tell how he liked the business yet. I hope he will be pleased with both. Oswald said he had rather a dull Xmas not being much acquainted with Fort Worth [6,623 population].

Saturday Dec 30/ 82 I have neglected to write in my diary again for several days. It just seems like I don't have time I wrote a long letter to Finis tonight and a short one to bro Tom, Miss Lula was in the store last evening just before dark and I had the pleasure of waiting on her and walking her home afterwards, which of course I enjoyed very much. She said she spent the day very pleasantly at Texarkana. Said she had brought something from Texark. for me but didn't tell me what it was.

Monday Jan. 1st 1883 I have been drawing off accounts preparing to collect up to the first as near as possible from all our customers. A pretty cold job for today but it has to be done.

I had an engagement with Miss Lula for Church, but as it rained so we couldn't go. We staid at home and spent the evening very pleasantly reading and in pleasant conversation. I took down my "Beautiful Snow" to let her keep it and read it and she made me read some in it for her. [This may have been *Beautiful Snow and Other Poems* by J. W. Watson, published in 1869. I read the poem and thought it was very nice.]

She gave me that "something" she had brought from Texarkana with her for me and it was one of her Photo's. And I tell you I appreciate it most highly as I was anxious for one. I had to stop just now and put up a Prescription and I tell you it is pretty cold handling graduates & bottles & so on today. But that is my business.

Jan 4/ 82 [3] I have missed another day somehow, well I have been pretty busy getting my accounts ready and trying to collect up the first of the new year. I have had very good success so far have collected nearly all I had out. Today while collecting I came up with Miss Lula who was out shopping and so I had the pleasure of walking home with her as I was going down her way anyhow.

Jan. 5/ 83 Dick Guorrett, the young man that used to be the clerk at the Capitol Hotel here, and who is now in a large wholesale Groceries store in Houston now, was in to see me a few minutes today. He used to be one of my best friends when he was here. He goes from here to Cleburne before returning to Houston and said he was going to see bro. Finis.

Mr Bowman who is engaged in the T. & P. Shop here was in tonight and is just from Cleburne where he saw bro. Finis and also met bro Tommie he said Finis had a very nice large store room and had every thing fixed up nicely and expected to get opened up by Jan. 1st or 2nd so I guess he is getting things in working order by this time.

Sunday Jan. 7/ 83 5 p.m. Another Sabbath day has come and almost gone and I have enjoyed it very much. This morning just after breakfast according to a request of Mrs Sears I went down to the church to have placed in order 3 elegant pulpit chairs which was presented to the church by the ladies of the church.

At the Band of Hope we had no lesson the books not yet having arrived so Will was asked to give us a talk, I mean by Will, Rev. Mr Preston. I have known him so long and so well that I call him that all the time. We all enjoyed his talk very much indeed. After the Band of Hope Dr. Ward Mr. Preston and quite a number of others including myself went down to the Jail by request and sang a song or two and Dr. Ward read a chapter and gave them a short talk and prayed for them. All of which they all seemed to appreciate.

Jan 10/ 83 I called on Miss Humphreys as it would be my last opportunity, as she left for her future home, Mississippi City, today. I spent a very pleasant evening with her. Last evening was our regular prayer meeting & will Preston had the meeting. I had the pleasure of seeing Miss Lula to prayer meeting. We had a splendid meeting and afterwards Miss Lula and I had a very pleasant time. A short time ago I was there and saw some copys of the "New York Weekly" on the table and she said she subscribed for it and read it. I told her I was sorry to know that she read such papers, for I told her that she knew they were not improving by any means. I told her that I liked to read them as far as my inclinations were concerned but would not permit myself to do so. [John may have considered this Northern "big city" newspaper too liberal to be read by a small town young woman.]

So last night she told me she had stopped taking it and had not read the ones she had. So I told her that I was <u>truly glad</u>, if it was in accordance with my wishes that she had quit and she said it was. I am glad to have influenced her in this way. I sometimes tell her how much I would like to see her become a Christian and she says she wishes she was. May God help her to be is my prayer. I took her down a Hat Mark I had embroidered for her (just for fun) and she thought it was awful nicely done for a boy to do and would handily believe I had made it. She passed the store this afternoon and I had the pleasure of seeing her.

Geo Leachman and Miss Maggie Whaley were married this morning and left immediately for Fort Worth their future home. Geo. is in the P.O. there now. I was invited by both to be present. About the time for me to go down I had 3 prescriptions to put up so didn't get to go. I wrote to bro Finis again today. Haven't heard from him for over two weeks.

Jan. 17/ 83 Will Preston came over again Saturday to begin a service of meetings here. Sunday evening he preached both morning and evening 2 of his impressive sermons. At the conclusion of his sermon in the evening, he then asked all those who wanted to be Christians and wanted the prayers of Gods people to get in theirs and quite a number did. The meeting was dismissed and on the way home I asked Miss Lula why it was that she had openly denied wanting to be a Christian, by not kneeling, when she had previously told me that she had wanted to be a Christian. And she said she didn't know why she didn't kneel hardly. Well I talked a good deal with her on the subject telling her that I had been and would continue to make her a special object of prayer that she might be converted for which she thanked me.

Well yesterday I recd. a little note from her saying that my words were still ringing in her ears and she could not get away from them if she would and saying she had resolved to try and live a better life. I hope and trust that she be truly converted. Oh! How happy I could feel if I could know that I had been the instrument in Gods hands of bringing about her conversion.

I would feel that my life had not been in vain. As now as I was there Sunday night, Dolph her bro, came in the parlor and he and I had quite a little talk on Hell. He advancing the idea that there was no such place, I of course taking the opposite side. I of course as most any one on that subject would, got the best of the argument. But was afraid that my talk would not have much affect on him. But in her notes Miss Lula said that, although he had not said so, she thought my words had more affect on his mind and belief than any sermon that he had ever heard. I humbly trust that they may do him good.

I got a letter from bro. Finis yesterday he said he was selling more goods that he had expected to begin with had filled 6 inscriptions, he sent me one of his cards. It was very pretty the style of the firm being "Foster & Logan."

Later 15 minutes of six I feel I have reason to thank God for having answered my prayers in the conversion of my friend Miss Lula at the regular hour this afternoon. She was at our prayer meeting and Will asked any who desired the prayer of Gods people to please kneel and she knelt and after a prayer while we were singing, Will went over to her and ask her if she felt that she was a Christian, and she said she was, and then he proposed that we all extend to her the right hand of fellowship. It was indeed a happy moment to me, as I had for sometime been making her an object of prayer and I feel that God has heard my prayers. Oh! May this be but the beginning of a glorious revival in Marshall is my earnest prayer.

Marshall, Texas Jan. 26/ 83 I recd. the sad intelligence Wednesday morning that Jimmie Doppelmayer was dead, it is indeed a sad occurrence. He wrote his parents that he was suffering from a sour throat and they wrote him to come home and they expected him Wednesday and instead recd. a telegram saying that he was dead. Joe Weisman went up after his remains and will get here tonight with them. And the funeral will take place tomorrow on Sunday owing to the state of the body. I am going to act as one of the pallbearers. It looks strange all the pall bearers except one are American boys and he a jew. And Dr. Ward is to conduct the funeral services. His father is not much of a Jew and Dr. W was a favorite of Jim's and so that is the reason for that.

[Jimmie Doppelmayer was one of the earliest documented burials in the Marshall Hebrew Cemetery. His name was mentioned on a historical marker at the cemetery. Many Jews were living in Marshall, and they made an effort to integrate into the community. At times, however, they did resist, as demonstrated by the following story told in the Texas section of the *Encyclopedia of Southern Jewish Communities*: Rabbi Saft's daughter, Hattie, attended a Catholic school in Marshall. One day she brought home an award to show her father. It was a small cross on a chain that she won for being the best student of the week. Rabbi Saft politely returned the award saying that Jews do not wear such things.]

Sunday Jan 28/ 83 It has been somewhat cloudy all morning and pretty cool. I have just returned from paying the last tribute of respect and esteem to the lifeless body of Jimmie Doppelmayer and it was a very imposing scene a great many were there both Americans & Jews. Dr, Wards remarks on his life and character were very nice and appropriate. His father after Dr. Ward had finished read in hebrew some kind of a service at the end of which all the jews came forward and threw in 2 or 3 spades of dirt then the Pall Bearers threw in 2 or 3 each and then the grave was filled.

I was very much disappointed in not getting to see him, but when I reached the house this morning the coffin had been closed and was opened no more, so that I didn't get to see him at all. This should be a warning to all to be prepared for the monster death come when we least expect, thus its important to be prepared. This is only the second time that I have been called upon to act in this capacity. Tis surely a solemn duty to perform.

Monday Jan. 29/ 83 We sold a big bill of paints today and didn't have enough oil to fill it so had to get it out in town. I got a letter from bro Finis yesterday, he and bro Tommie were both well and everything moving on nicely so far.

February 1st. 1883 Well I got off last night at about half past 8 oclock and though pretty late, I thought better later than never. I went down to see Miss Lula and low and behold when I got there found two other young ladies and two other gentlemen there. Which was quite a surprise to me as I expected to see Miss Lula alone, but it was not her fault that it was so, for it was this way. After I seen her in the morning and made an engagement to call, the two young ladies came from Texarkana to see her before she left and they being there she of course must entertain them and knowing that it would be better to have two other gentlemen there, she had asked Tom Clemmons to come and bring another friend of his. Which he did. Although it might have been more pleasant for Miss Lula and myself alone, still I enjoyed the evening.

John Collier Foster Journal #3

February 3, 1883–November 11, 1883

———

Marshall, Texas, February 3/83 Last night was very warm and today up to about 10 or 11 oclock when a norther came in and now it is sleeting some at intervals. I don't think I ever saw as sudden a change in the weather in my life before. I started to write to bro Finis tonight but had to order some Reward Cards from a Drummer and by that time it was so late and I was not in a humor to write so I thought I would put it off until Monday night. [During the Victorian period, schoolchildren (both public and Sunday school) were given cards for good behavior. At the top of the card, it might say "Reward for Merit," and below was a place where the name of the student could be written. Usually there was another space for the teacher to sign. Sometimes parents would save these cards in a family album.]

Sunday Feby 4/ 83 A customer just came in and wanted some whiskey and I could not supply his wants and I am glad we don't keep it, for although he said he wanted it for medical purposes, I don't want to have any thing what ever to do with the <u>vile stuff</u>. For I think that whiskey is the greatest curse that the world has ever known. I have just carried the Show Bottles which are filled with colored water, all those preservatives which consist mostly of water, and all the inks and so on. Goods that are liable to freeze tonight I have carried them to the rear room of the store where I have a good fire and thus avoid the danger of having them freeze and burst. But our old store is so cold it must be done.

Monday morning 2/5/83 It sleeted a while this morning and then sleeted and snowed both together for a while and then got to snowing in real earnest and snowed for an hour or two, but is snowing but little now. Seeing the snow fall reminds me of years past when I used to sit by the hour out in the snow watching a trap to catch snow birds and still did not feel the snow, so much I was enthused with the sport. It makes me want to get out and play in the snow. Drummers have been quite numerous today. But all have failed to get an order from the Doctor, as we are all well supplied with the goods which they represented.

Thursday 2/8/83 Mr. Jno. Stuart a young man who used to be cashier in the bank of E. J. Fry of this place was buried here yesterday or rather Tuesday. Another case of the effects of whiskey. He was almost always under the influence of Liquor to some extent. A short time since he went to Hot Springs, Ark for rheumatism and while there recd. something of a paralytic stroke and also became deranged and was brought home in an insane condition, in which state he remained until his death took him hence. It is sad to see one in the prime of life who is so well qualified to be useful, thrown themselves away this way and worst of all lose their immortal soul.

Saturday 2/10/83 It turned quite warm this afternoon and is pretty warm yet. It was telegraphed by the Signal Service that a norther was coming this way and was expected to have reached here today. But as yet it has not come and I am in hopes it will not, for it looks as if we have had enough bad rainy weather for a while. [The Signal Service's years were around 1870 to 1891. One of its responsibilities was weather observation and prediction. The Pikes Peak region in the Rocky Mountains was used to observe the weather patterns. The weathermen thought they could observe weather patterns there and predict the weather as the systems moved toward the east. Like today, their predictions were not always accurate, which led to much public criticism.]

Notwithstanding the inclemency of the weather there has been quite a number of the "Darks" [African Americans] in town today and business has been pretty brisk. I am going to trim out my beard on my chin, for the first time in the morning, just for the fun of it to see how they will look. They are very thick, much thicker than my moustache. Tom Clemmons was in tonight and he and I talked quite a good deal on different subjects. The Girls being (of course) one of them.

Today I filled a prescription containing Salicylak of soda after the party had gone I took the Dispensatory and "read it up" and found that the reports of different physicians as to its efficacy as a medicine were very conflicting. [Sodium salicylate acts as a nonsteroidal anti-inflammatory drug.] Some having used it with utmost success in inflammatory Rheumatism, gout and so on while others used it with no success whatever. Its principle effect being that of diminishing the beats of the pulse and lowering the temperature. I think this a good plan of every time I fill a prescription which contains some ingredient whose medical properties I am not acquainted with, getting the Dispensatory and reading up the medicine.

Sunday morning 2/11/83 I have just finished filling a somewhat difficult prescription, it contained both Strychnine and Arsenic and so I had to be very careful it was to be made into 40 pills and consisting mostly of Quinine it was somewhat hard to make into a good firm pill mass, which however, I accomplished by using Confection of Rose. [According to the *Dispensatory of the United States of America*, the book John uses, this confection provided adhesiveness for the formation of pills.]

Monday 2/12/83 I recd. a letter from Miss Lula, she had just reached Miss. City she had written it last Friday and has been all this time getting here she said, if she might start next Saturday I mailed her a lovely Valentine today.

2/15/83 Business has been very good indeed today. Valentines still selling. I recd. a letter from Finis today and in it some of his labels showing his style. I went down to call on Miss Lula last evening and had a very pleasant time, though for some reason she seemed rather cool toward me.

Saturday 2/17/83 About 4 p.m. a big bill of Stationary was brought up from the depot and I have just finished opening and marking it and it is now 10 oclock. It was an awful cold job but it had to be done. We have in some lovely box papers and envelopes. The latest style is very dark papers.

Monday 2/19/83 I was with Miss Lula at church last night and Mr Hawley the Bass in the choir failed to put in his appearance so I had to seat her in the audience and go up and sing bass for them in the choir. After church I was made the recipient of an elegant present. It was a gold pen and pencil combined presented to me by Miss Lula and I appreciate it most highly indeed. First because she gave it to me, and second of its beauty and excellence, it is just lovely.

Tomorrow is Miss Vera Johnsons birthday and they is going to give her Sunday School class a Sociable at her home and has told each one of them to invite someone of the boys to come. Miss Mary Brownrigg invited me to come and I accepted the invitation and returned the compliment by asking her the pleasure of escorting her down tomorrow eve. To which she asserted and so I will see her down. It is my first time with her as my company as I have only known her for a short time, but she seems very pleasant.

Tuesday 2/20/83 11: oclock P.M. I have just returned from Miss Vera's birthday party. The evening was passed most pleasantly indeed, tho' I was disappointed in not seeing Miss Lula there. She was in the store this fore-noon and bought a real nice present for Miss Vera which I saw tonight and I ask her if she intended on going and she said she didn't know whether she would or not. We had quite a deal of pulling candy. Miss Mary Brownrigg and I pulled together. I recd. a letter from cousin Bob Foster today contain-ing one of his Photo's. He has grown so I hardly knew him, he has gotten to be quite a young man.

This is the photo that John received from Bob. On the back of the photo it said, "R. W. Foster Tehuacana." The photo was dated 1883, which would have made Bob eighteen years old. Mansfield Historical Society.

Wednesday 2/21/83 This morning early broke forth like a spring morning but it soon clouded up and has been more or less cloudy all day. Tonight other boys and myself met here at the store at 9 oclock to organize ourselves into a kind of literary society for our good as well as our amusement. We adopted as our name "Phive Phunny Phellows or account of there being 5 of us present and because we had quite a good deal of fun with the organization. Eddie, Buck, Neal Granberry and myself even appointed a com. to draw up a constitution and bylaws.

Sunday 2/25/83 It is about breakfast time so I will read a chapter in my Bible (one that my <u>dear father</u> used many years in the sacred desk) and go to breakfast.

Thursday March 1st 83 I met Miss Lula on the street and walked her as I was going that way to see a party. I tell you I feel pretty well played out tonight. I recd. a paper sent by Ida from Nashville containing a piece about the school she is attending. I wrote to cousin Eva and Bob tonight.

Sunday 3/4/83 Had a good sermon, Dr. Ward spoke feelingly about the life and death of William E. Dodge the great Christian philanthropist of New York drawing a comparison between his life and the good he had done and the life and character of a great theatrical actor who had also lately died without hope for a better world. [William Earl Dodge (1805–83) was a politician, businessman, and activist. He supported Native American rights and was the the president of the National Temperance Society for eighteen years, a congressman, and founding member of the YMCA.]

In connection with this great man, he chastised parents against saying that their children were too young to be Christians, saying that this great man was a Christian at the age of <u>twelve.</u>

Saturday 3/10/83 Vegetation under the effect of these nice warm days is putting forth very fast. Peach trees and so on are in bloom. We had a tea party at Drs. house the night before last given by the ladies aid society of our church. The proceeds being for the benefit of our church. I couldn't get off until after I closed up which was 9 oclock, but I had made an engagement for that hour with Miss Lula she knowing that I couldn't get off any sooner. So we went and had quite a pleasant time, had a very nice supper. We recd. a nice line of Birthday & Easter cards a few days since and are selling a good many. Business has been tolerably good today.

Marshall, Tex 3/16/83 This has been a lovely day bright and sun shining though cold. I had a letter from bro Finis yesterday. He was well and

William Dodge, public domain

everything going on nicely. There is to be a sociable at Mrs. Brownriggs about closing up time so I believe I will go down.

Monday 3/19/83 I went to church with Miss Mary Brownrigg last night after hearing one of Dr. Wards practical sermons we had a very pleasant talk. We had a little discussion on dancing as she dances and seems to think it strange that I don't dance. She said that was all the objection she could find with me. I thanked her for her high opinion of my character and told her that I thought that a good objection.

I recd. a beautiful note of thanks today from Miss Lula for a copy of "Lucile" by Owen Meredith which I gave her as a birthday gift. Her birthday was the 15th but she wouldn't tell me until yesterday when it was. So yesterday I sent it down. [*Lucile* was a narrative poem published in 1860. The heroine, Lucile, was beloved by two bitter rivals.]

A young gentleman from Longview had made an engagement with her for church last night but failed to get her and I am going to tease her good about it. Have been marking up a bill on two of goods today.

Marshall, Tex 3/24/83 I had a letter from bro Tommie a day or two since. He seems to like the drug business very much, so far and is keeping well. I received today through the mail a lovely decorated Easter Egg and I think, yes I am satisfied Miss Lula sent it. I attended a concert last night by the students of the Negro college here and was very highly entertained for they made some splendid music.

Sunday Mch. 25/83 Mr Stricbanger who is traveling and organizing "Young Mens Christians Associations" [YMCA] through the country is in our town and is to lecture or rather speak on this subject this afternoon at the M.E. Church and I was in hope he would have a good attendance. I hope he will succeed in organizing one in this place for I think it would prove beneficial to the boys and young men and they do need it so much. [The YMCA arrived in North America by 1851 and was staffed mainly by volunteers. In the 1880s it began putting up buildings in large numbers across the nation staffed by paid workers.]

Tuesday 3/27/83 I made an engagement with Miss Mary for the Little Helpers sociable Friday night to be at the residence of Mr. Elgin. Have been at work pretty hard today putting up and Labeling Oil & turpentine so I am somewhat tired tonight. Wrote to Finis last night.

Thursday 3/29/83 I have been making Syrups today hand made Simple Syrup, Syrup Squill [used mainly for coughs] & there is a good deal of work making them so I am pretty tired tonight.

Sunday April 8/ 83 It has been over a week since I have written in my diary. It is not because I had forgotten it, for I have not. But it just seems like I don't take the time. A good deal has transpired during this time which it will be impossibly for me to recall at this late date.

A night or two since I had an unknown visitor at the store, it was a burglar. He made his entrance by cutting one of the glass out of one of the front show window and went through the store as I saw next morning from the fact that he blew out the lamp I always leave burning in the store. And also left quite a number of drawers open not taking time to close them in his haste to make the rounds. I sleep in a room upstairs at the rear of the store but heard nothing of it as I sleep very soundly. But he didn't get anything but a large family Bible which was missed from the store the next day.

I heard from both bro's Finis & Tommie last week. Both of them are well. Also a letter from cousin Eva. Just after dinner I took Miss Witherspoon a young lady who has been visiting Mrs. Sears down and saw her off on the train for her home. Then I attended an open meeting at our church and assisted them with the singing. Having an engagement with Miss Lula to see her to a Temperance lecture at the Baptist Church.

Monday Apl. 9/83 I recd. a letter from cousin Nannie McCollum today containing a Photo of herself and sister Ida together, it is very nice. I had never seen them and of course didn't know how they would look. I intended to write to Purci Paul tonight but have just finished a job of making up 324 pills and I am a little tired.

Apl. 27th 83 I recd. a letter from bro Finis a few days since stating that bro Tom had found that he could not stand the confinement necessary to being a druggist. So he has quit and will seek some more active employment and bro Finis wants me to come out as soon as possible which I expect to do. But will wait until Dr. to get someone to fill my place for I would hate to leave him alone. If possible I want to get off by May 15.

Such a time as I have had this rain began, this old store sprung about a dozen leaks and I was trying to catch the water and save the stock. We now have the "Telephone Exchange" in our town and we have one in the store. It is very convenient indeed as well as lots of fun to talk with your friends & so on after business hours. Though the electric light hung in several places where Telephones are, its buzzing sound can be heard at night all over the wires thus making it very hard to hear on the telephone. Finis writes me they all have to have an Exchange there and he is to have one. [The first Texas telephone exchange was opened in Galveston on August 21, 1879.]

There are reports of a great many tornadoes all over the country during this month. The likes were never know before, in fact we are having a very strange spring, very backward which is injuring crops very much it stays so cool. [There was a large outbreak of tornadoes in the southeastern United States on April 22 to 23, 1883. Over one hundred people were killed and nearly eight hundred injured.]

Miss Lula made me just a lovely hat mark and put it in my new straw hat for me. She seems to be sorry I am going to leave. My friends generally seem to hate to see me leave.

Cleburne, Texas Oct. of 83 Dear old Journal again after a silence of nearly 6 months I take my pen in hand to communicate to you a brief sketch of what I have been doing since my last writing on the 27 day of last May.

I left dear old Marshall with all its pleasant associations and many friends there for Cleburne to make it at least for a time my dwelling place. I went by way of Ft. Worth at the urgent request of Mrs. Geo. Leachman, (Miss Maggie Whaley) who now resides in Ft. W. Arrived at the city of Ft. Worth at 4:25 p.m. was met at the depot by my friend Geo. Leachman and who took me at once to his house. But on the way down we met Miss Lula Hogg with whom I was well acquainted and who was very much surprised to see me in Ft. Worth.

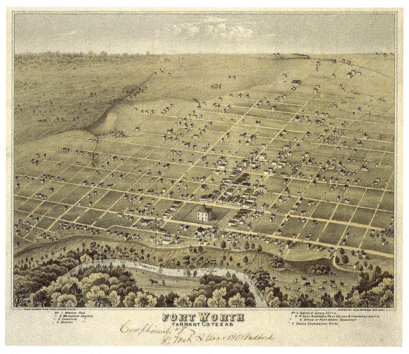

This was Fort Worth in 1876, looking south from the courthouse. It was so sparse it would have been easy to meet friends on the street. Map in public domain.

I spent the night very pleasantly with Geo. and his lady. Next morning I met Oswald Hargrove also formerly of M, on the street and he and I "took in the town" visiting the "water works" and other places of interest until 10 a.m. at which time I took the train for Cleburne at 11:22 a.m.

Being met by bro Finis at the depot who was expecting me. We came up and I was at once initiated into the position I now hold, as Head Clerk in the city Drug Store of Foster and Logan. From that time to this I have served them to the best of my ability in that capacity, having had charge of the business one week during the absence of bro Finis on business. And at this writing I am managing the business while bro Finis is on a trip to La to bring with him on his return Miss Hattie Brown, his wife. If nothing occurred to prevent, he was married this morning at 9 oclock. He will take a short trip up to Ark. for his wife to see her parents and a sister living there, whose health would not admit of their being at the scene of their marriage which occurred in La. at the home of another sister with whom Miss Brown has lived with for years. They will also stop a short time in M the scene of their happy courtship days and see their friends. Then and from thence to Cleburne. So it will be some time before their arrival here.

I am very well satisfied with C. Think I will like it more once better acquainted ho. I am getting pretty well acquainted, know quite a number of the young ladies and find them very pleasant. Our business prospects are splendid. We of course are not doing any large business at present, for we are strangers in these parts and of course will have to get acquainted before we can do a larger business. But our business is on the increase all the time. In fact we have far exceeded our expectations for the first year.

I am not at present a member of the firm and only clerking for them, but I have about $1,000 in the business on interest, money realized from the sale of our Austin property, they are also owing me some, I expect next fall to enter the firm at which time I become of age.

I took a trip down to Tehuacana last June during the Examination exercises of the school and had a splendid time, meeting a good many old friends that I hadn't seen for years. Those meetings are so pleasant. Every now and then I strike some one over in this part of the country I once knew before.

Had a letter from Lula this morning. She is now visiting friends and relatives in Texarkana Ark., and having a nice time. The young gents there are many, it most pleasant for her. It is very natural that they should, she is such pleasant company.

I had some Photos taken last week with my mustache Side Burns and Goatee on my chin. Will send her one as she has never seen me with my beard that way. The photos are very good. Mr Logan who is out helping me in the store during Finis' absence, though he is not much help for he knows nothing of the business. Had some new Photos taken at the same time and he and I had 2 taken together. There is quite a difference in our size. He being 6 inches taller than I.

I had a letter from Bro Tom this morning wishing to know the exact dates of Mothers and Fathers death dates as recorded in our dear old family Bible. I don't know his object unless he is writing a sketch of their lives or something of the kind. He is getting so peculiar and distant that I don't know what to think of him. He never writes to Finis nor I. Only letters of business like anyone else would. I am sorry he is so. Well I must now write him the desired information as regards the dates.

Oct 12 1883 Today is the 20th anniversary of my birthday. Still I can hardly realize that I am that old. At the same time I am as mature in looks as most men are at 22 or 23 years of age. As everyone guessing at my age takes me to be. The older we grow the faster time seems to fly round. It only seems like a short time since I left home over four years ago. Then a mere boy to begin the battle of life in earnest. Having thrown on my own resources but being blest with a kind older brother to whom I could go for advice any time and still we are together and if nothing happens I expect we will remain in business too then until one or the other is called from time to eternity.

Had a card from bro Finis this morning he said every thing passed off pleasantly and as merry as a "marriage bell." He was married as expected at 9:30 a.m. Wednesday morning Oct 10/83. And by this time up in Ark. His card of the 10th was written from Shreveport La. The "Cleburne Chronical" of this morning stated that bro Finis had gone to Louisville (Ky. I suppose) and on his return would introduce to his friends Mrs. Foster. How these newspapers get things mixed up. It is much cooler this morning, is pleasant with winter suit on.

Had a letter from Mother yesterday. She said her health was not very good, though she is still in school. School prospects very good. She has quit keeping house rented her place and is boarding at Mrs. Ratcliffs which is much more convenient to the college that at home. Mr Logan and I took advantage of the week spell and cleaned down all one side of our store. A pretty good job too for we have a quite a large store room.

Oct. 14/ 83 Had another card from Finis this morning written from Emmet, Ark. [southwest Arkansas] stating that he would be back with his bride next Wednesday evening. I will be glad to see them, more especially the "Better Half."

Cleburne, Texas October 21/ 83 Bro Finis got in with his wife Wednesday eve as was expected. Mr Logan and I met them at the depot and saw them to bro Gillians their temporary home.

Thursday evening A reception was given them by bro. Gillian at which we all had a splendid time. Mr Logan and I being the only unmarried gentlemen present having for our company Miss Minnie Jackson and Addie

Goodwine. My new sister is much pleased with her new home. Their house will be ready for their reception tomorrow one week.

Oct. 28th 1883 I received a letter from mother, Miss Nellie Roach an old time friend of mine of 10 or 12 years ago, and from Lula all were interesting. I had sent Misses Lula and Nellie a Photo. Both thought them excellent and seemed to appreciate them most highly. Nellie promised me one of hers in return as soon as she could go down to Austin and have some good ones taken. She is teaching school in Hays Co. below Austin.

Also had a letter from bro Tommie he is teaching at a new school again, don't suppose he will ever do anything but teach. Mr. Logan left us for M last Thursday after having been with us 1 month, he hated to go, had begun to feel at home here.

November 11th 1883 Sunday evening Bro Finis has just gotten moved into their new home and he has had to be away from the store a great deal of the time and consequently I am kept pretty busy during the day and up to 10 oclock at night.

Bro Finis has at last gotten home, has been there one week tomorrow and are getting very nicely fixed up now. I am boarding with them and we have lots of nice times. It is more like home to me than anything has been in sometime. Sister Hattie is so sweet and nice to me all the time. I enjoy it ever so much.

It is true Finis and I are never there both at the same time only on Sunday as we both can't leave the store at once. But Sister Hattie is with both of us at our meals. Haven't got to read much today, read my Bible some and some in the Observer and Cumberland Presbyterian. I think I shall read some "Stepping Heavenward" and retire pretty early as I must be up early tomorrow, as have a lot of goods to mark. [*Stepping Heavenward* was written by Elizabeth Prentiss and published in 1860. It was a story, told in journal form, of a woman who learned that true happiness was found in giving oneself to others.]

[This is the end of John Collier Foster's journals.]

Epilogue

Now that the journals have been completed, it becomes necessary to uncover what later happened to the main characters.

* * * * *

Malvinia Louisa Foster

There are probably no adult photos of Louisa hidden away in a trunk, desk, or antique shop. She never mentioned having one made, or even a desire to do so. Louisa was tight with money, and for her the thought of paying for photos would have been an unnecessary luxury. Unfortunately, one can only speculate on what she looked like. Louisa wrote of an early life of gaiety, so it might be safe to assume that she could have been an attractive young girl. Since poor Louisa had health problems for much of her adult life, her appearance would have suffered.

She preferred to be involved with indoor activities such as writing, reading, and sewing. This could have resulted in a woman who was pale and did not have the dry, weather-beaten skin of the typical frontier women of the period. Louisa was probably a short woman, perhaps underweight because of her illnesses and, at times, harsh diet. Based on the appearances she described of her children, she probably had dark hair and blue eyes.

In the last years of her life, her late forties, she admitted losing most of her teeth and she likely became very thin and frail. During the last year of her life, she described herself: "Collie thicken the soup had a great time loving me & calling me pretty. I do not believe the little thing really thinks I am pretty with all, my sallowness, furrows, no teeth, & harsh cough."

Her last journal entry was dated May 3, 1870, and with her health declining, she may not have had the desire to continue writing. Domestic duties

Louisa's tombstone is supposed to sit in the top groove on the base. The tombstone is a few feet away from the grave. Photo by Jack Crowder.

were probably completely given over to her children, who were ages seven to twenty-three.

According to cemetery records, Louisa died of consumption. In most cases this referred to what we today call tuberculosis. In the 1870s consumption was a common catch-all term for any disease that caused the body to waste away. Louisa was buried in Oakwood Cemetery in Austin, Texas, on October 23, 1871. This would indicate that her actual death date was probably October 21 or 22.

It is perhaps fortunate that Louisa died before she had to experience the death of another child. Her daughter Mollie died August 15, 1881, at the age of twenty after a long illness. John wrote of her illness in his journal, "She used to say if it was God's will for me to live on and suffer, for she had become almost an invalid." It is unfortunate that Louisa did not live to see her three sons become productive and good men in their communities.

Louisa's grave can be found in the southwest section of the cemetery, about twenty yards north of the Jewish section. There is a small gravel road that leads to this section, and her grave is about ten yards east of the road. Looking west from her grave, you can see the Texas capitol building. Her tombstone has been separated from its base by roots from a large tree pushing up on it.

Louisa wanted to be an accepted writer. She wrote in July of 1868, "The greatest is my <u>entire</u> want of confidence in my ability to become an acceptable writer. I don't mean a fancy, showy writer, but a useful writer, one that would stir & move the hearts of men & women, one that would reflect credit upon the blessed cause & not disgrace."

Near the end of Louisa's last journal entry she was in poor health and probably felt depressed when she wrote, "And what I have written, I have written. I don't expect it to mitigate my sad fate. I expect to die unknown."

Rev. Finis Ewing Foster

Finis was the mystery person of the family. Little was known of his life before he met Louisa, and there was no written description of his appearance. It is known that Finis was born on February 26, 1816, in Wilson County, Tennessee. His parents, Robert Foster and Virginia Elizabeth Johnson, were both from Virginia.

Like many men during this time, Finis probably came to Texas seeking adventure and opportunity. Since the Cumberland Presbyterian Church was one of the principal religious denominations in Wilson County, it would explain why Finis became a preacher. Finis and Louisa fell in love shortly after they met, produced nine children in fifteen years, and remained a devoted couple until death separated them.

In 1872 Finis, now fifty-six, married a twenty-five-year old widow, Mary Fannie Taylor, who had at least one child, Harris, around seven years old. The couple married in Hayes County, which is several miles southwest of Austin. It's possible Finis met the young woman while preaching in the area. Sometime after the marriage, the family moved to Techuacana, Texas, which gave the children an opportunity to go to a Cumberland Presbyterian College. The school taught children from grammar school age all the way to college. Many times the older students were engaged to teach the younger ones, and since Mary was a teacher, she may have taught there.

During this time Finis's health began to suffer, and he died on August 14, 1879. John wrote in his journal, "On the 14th of August 1879 my <u>dear dear</u> father took his departure from this sin cursed earth, and went <u>Home to Heaven</u>, to receive his reward for a life's labor for the master, his to was but a happy change, for he had suffered long from heart disease and other troubles." Mollie, his daughter, was probably buried at the same cemetary. However, I found no record of her grave.

According to the 1880 census, Mary remained in Techuacana teaching and raising her son, Harris, and stepdaughter, Mollie. John Collier Foster remained in contact with his stepmother after the death of his father. He last mentioned Mary on October 12, 1883, "Had a letter from Mother yesterday. She said her health was not very good, though she is still in school. School prospects very good. She has quit keeping house rented her place and is boarding at Mrs. Ratcliffs which is much more convenient to the college that at home." Mollie had died by now, and Harris, who was now eighteen, may have left home.

The grave of Finis is located on the west side of the cemetery in Techuacana, near the fence line. It stands off by itself. The inscription is on the bottom left side of the marker. Photo by Jack Crowder.

Thomas Wilson Foster

Of the three boys, Tommie was the most mysterious. His brother John summed it up when he wrote about Tommie in his journal, "He is getting so peculiar and distant that I don't know what to think of him. He never writes to Finis nor I."

Only a small amount of information was learned about him in the census reports from 1870, 1900, and 1910. The last time Louisa mentioned Tommie in her journal was on February 6, 1870. "Tommie is off on business tho' legal & right makes his life in danger. I shouldn't be surprised if I never see his again." She does not mention in what business he was engaged. According to the 1870 census, there was a twenty-two-year-old Thomas Foster working on a farm on a property owned by Mr. White in Fannin, Texas, about 130 miles south of Austin.

Louisa recorded in her journal that on December 31, 1869, her husband had gone on a missionary tour to Washington County, which was about fifty miles east of Austin. Then, on March 1, 1870, Louisa wrote, "I received a letter yesterday from Tommie telling me father was sitting by the fire looking more like himself than he had for some time. Bless God. O Lord help Tommie to be <u>ever</u> watchful and kind of that dear precious one."

It was not clear where Tommie was in 1870 or what he was doing. He was never mentioned again in Louisa's journal. The next reference to Tommie was made in John's journal on April 29, 1882, "I wrote a long letter to bro. Tommie he is teaching school at Liberty Hill down near Austin."

In January of 1883, Tommie had left teaching and joined with his brother Finis in Cleburne to work with him at his drugstore. I suspect the reason Finis asked Tommie to join him, rather than John, was maybe to reconnect with his older brother. Regardless, Tommie became restless with the drugstore business and soon left to go back to teaching. John wrote, "I don't suppose he will ever do anything but teach."

Nothing was found of Tommie until the 1900 census reported that he was a farmer in Burnet, which was about sixty miles northwest of Austin. He had married Lela Pauline Dennis on October 4, 1894, in Burnet. When they married, Lela was seventeen and Tommie was forty-six. Could this have been a former student of Tommie's? Lela outlived Tommie by thirty-six years.

The 1910 census indicated that Tommie was still a framer but that the couple had moved to Iredell in Bosque County. This was about forty-five miles southwest of Cleburne, where Finis was currently living. The census mentioned no children.

According to the death certificate for Thomas W. Foster, he died at five in the morning on November 11, 1919, on his eighty-second birthday. His cause of death was an abscess on the jaw that he had suffered from for four months. In the final month he was treated by a doctor, but it was too late and apparently it developed into sepsis, which caused his death. He was buried in Irdell, Texas, but I found no record of his grave.

Finis Andrew Foster

Finis was living with the family in Tehuacana, Texas, in the late 1870s. The small town had a population of nearly five hundred people. In an 1850 election, it had been the second choice for the new Texas state capitol. While living there, Finis attended Trinity University in Techuacana for three years and was a member of Alpha Omicron fraternity.

Trinity was founded by Cumberland Presbyterians in 1869, and for the first few years the elementary, grammar, high school, and college students from the area went to Trinity. There were over one hundred college students when Finis attended. Women could take a less rigorous curriculum, for example no Latin and Greek, and graduate with a diploma. A few women accepted the challenge of the harder courses of study and graduated. In 1902 the university moved to Waxahachie, Texas.

Trinity University in Tehuacana today. The building is vacant and parts of the roof have caved in. Photo by Jack Crowder.

In 1880, twenty-seven-year-old Finis was living in Marshall, Texas, and was working at a drugstore. He lived upstairs in the store and shared a room with his younger brother, John. His job was to run the store and fill prescriptions for the owner, Doctor Sears. Finis was dating his future wife, a young music teacher named Harriet (Hattie) Brown, who was rooming at Mrs. Maulding's house. Eighteen-year-old Hattie had been living in Arkansas and going to school. She later returned to Arkansas to live, and Finis continued to date her long distance.

In 1882 Finis received an offer to become the druggist and part owner of a drugstore in Cleburne, Texas, which he accepted and moved there in December. The name of the store became Foster and Logan. The store was a large one, so he asked his older brother Tommie to come work with him. By early spring of 1883, Tommie discovered that the druggist's life was not for him, so he left. Finis wrote to his younger brother, John, and had him join him in Cleburne in the summer of 1883.

Finis married Harriet Brown at nine in the morning on October 10, 1883, in Caddo, Louisiana. The marriage took place at the Sheborn home of Hattie's sister, whom she had lived with for several years. Due to poor health, her parents were unable to make the trip from Arkansas. The happy couple went to Arkansas to visit Hattie's parents and from there traveled to Marshall, Texas, to visit friends. The couple arrived back in Cleburne on October 17, and a few days later moved into their new home at 503 South Anglin Street. John Collier moved in with the couple.

In 1895 Finis and Hattie moved to Nashville, Tennessee, and Finis took a job in the Book and Bible Department of the Cumberland Presbyterian Publishing Company as an advertising manager. The couple rented a house at 27 Maple Street until 1904, when they moved back to Cleburne, Texas. Both moves were probably prompted by the desire to improve their financial conditions.

Finis took a job at the Foster-Fain Drug Company on East Henderson Street. The store was owned by Otto Foster (no relation to Finis) and Blair Fain. Finis was hired as a bookkeeper. The Fosters first lived at 313 Caddo Street and later moved back to 503 South Anglin Street. Both homes were just a few blocks from the drug company.

Finis and Hattie were the proud parents of four sons and one daughter. Unfortunately, Hattie died from paralysis (according to her death certificate) on July 6, 1914. Finis remained in Cleburne until he retired in 1924, around

A photo of Finis and his grandson taken ca. 1924, when he retired
and moved to Forest Hills, Texas. Photo courtesy Harriet Caroline Pepa,
the great granddaughter of Finis A. Foster.

the age of seventy-two. He moved to Forest Hills and lived with his daughter,
Ruth, and her family at 506 Forest Hill Drive. Ruth's husband, Sam Collier,
was a bank teller.

In May of 1940, around suppertime, Finis suffered a fall from a chair and
fractured the top of his right femur. He never recovered and died in the hospital eight months later on May 29, 1941. He was buried in Cleburne next to
his beloved wife, Hattie.

Based on photos of Finis, and John's and Louisa's description of him in
their journals, he appears to have had dark hair and blue eyes, was lean, and
around six feet tall. Louisa would have been happy to know that he was a
hard and useful worker who remained a religious man all his life.

Tombstone of Finis Foster. Photo by Jack Crowder.

Finis Foster's Illness Fatal

Pioneer Texan, Resident of Forest Hill 17 Years, Was Former Cleburne Druggist.

Finis A. Foster, 88, pioneer Texan and resident of Forest Hill for 17 years, died in a hospital Thursday at 6 p. m. after an illness of eight months.

Mr. Foster, a druggist in Cleburne for many years, moved to Fort Worth 17 years ago when he retired from business to make his home with his daughter, Mrs. Sam Collier of Forest Hill. He suffered a hip injury eight months ago and had been confined to the hospital since.

Born in Austin, Mr. Foster received his education at Trinity University. He moved to Cleburne in 1882 and the same year was married to Miss Harriett Brown. In 1895 the couple moved to Nashville where Mr. Foster served as manager of the book and Bible department of the Cumberland Presbyterian Publishing Company. They moved back to Cleburne in 1904.

Other survivors are three sons, Frank and J. Ward Foster of California, and Paul Foster of Washing-

Obituary of Finis Foster

John Collier Foster

John was educated at Trinity College in Techuacana, and quit school after the eighth grade. At the age of sixteen, and after the death of his father, he left Techuacana and moved to Marshall, Texas. There he lived and worked with his brother Finis as an apprentice druggist at a drugstore. John became very active in the church and particularly in the temperance movement. While there he remained in contact with his stepmother, Mary, and his stepbrother, Harris, who was around fourteen when John left home. In Marshall, John became quite the ladies' man and went out several times a week to socials.

I can only speculate about John's physical appearance based on descriptions in the journals and one photograph. He was probably around 5 foot 6 inches tall, since he wrote that brother Finis was six inches taller. In his photograph with Mary Etta next to him, he looks to be just a couple of inches taller than her. Etta appears to have been a small woman, probably around five feet three inches tall. I suspect that John had blue eyes, most likely maintained a trim body, and kept his beloved facial hair.

In the summer of 1883, John left Marshall for Cleburne and once again joined with Finis at a drugstore. When Finis got married in the fall of 1883, John was invited to board with the couple in their home.

According to John's obituary in 1951, he moved to Fort Worth in 1890. I could not learn the reason for the move, although he did have several friends there. A fire destroyed many of the US census records for 1890, and unfortunately, John's were among them.

While in Fort Worth, he met Mary Etta Feild, whose father was Captain Julian Feild, a wealthy and important man in Fort Worth. Julian served as the first postmaster of Fort Worth, set up the first general store there, and cofounded Mansfield, Texas. The Feild family lived near the courthouse at 5 Taylor Street. Mary was born on May 16, 1866, in a log cabin near Mansfield, Texas. She studied music at the Mary Nash School in Sherman and at the New England Conservatory of Music in Boston.

I believe it is safe to say that John and Mary, both being Cumberland Presbyterians, met at the First Presbyterian Church in Fort Worth. Both came from a strong religious background, and this probably helped draw them to each other. On September 29, 1892, the couple were married. Over the course of their marriage they had four children: Julian (1893–1981),

"The Captain" Julian Feild. Mansfield Historical Society.

Mary Louise (1895–1980), John Jr. (1897–1978), and Robert Feild (1899–1980).

Sometime before 1900, Mary Etta, John, and Julian moved to Nashville, Tennessee, and lived at 65 Carroll Street. Also living in Nashville, having moved there in 1895, was John's brother Finis. Perhaps the two families moved at the same time. According to the 1900 US census, both men worked in advertising. The census reported that John worked as a manager for an agency, and Finis's obituary said that he was advertising manager for the Cumberland Presbyterian Publishing Company. I suspect both men worked at the same company, perhaps as equals or one over the other. Remarkably, both families returned to Texas in 1904. John's family had an addition of three children born in Tennessee. Finis and Hattie had three boys and one girl, all born in Texas. This, however, would be the first time in many years that the brothers would not be working together. John's family moved back to Fort Worth, and Finis took his family and returned to Cleburne.

Finis returned to the drugstore business, while John embarked on an entirely new career. According to the 1910 US census, John was working as

This is a photo of Mary Etta and John, probably shortly after their marriage. It was taken at a studio in downtown Fort Worth owned by Charles Swartz. Around this time his brother, John Swartz, who also owned a studio in Fort Worth, took the famous and only known portrait of Butch Cassidy's Wild Bunch. Photo courtesy Harriet Caroline Pepa, the great granddaughter of Finis Andrew Foster.

This is probably the Christening photo of their son Julian in 1893. Photo courtesy Harriet Caroline Pepa.

a cotton seed product's broker for a cotton seed producer. Mary Etta's father, Julian Feild, had died in 1897, but his name probably still carried some weight in Fort Worth. It was possible that this would have helped John land a good job as a cotton seed broker.

In 1910, and for the remainder of his life, John and his family lived at 1114 West Cannon Street, across from what is now Harris Hospital. It had to be a large house, since it had to accommodate John, Mary, four children, now 10 to 16 years of age, and their cook, Bessie Ferrel.

By 1920, living in the Foster home on West Cannon Street were John, Mary, and John Jr.; two servants, William and Ada Harris; and two boarders, Mary Lou Curtin, twenty-six years old, and Hennie Boothe, an eighteen year old steno writer for the railroad. John was still prospering in the cotton seed industry.

In the 1930 census, the Foster home was valued at $6,000, which was a pretty good price since the country was in the grip of a depression. John had retired from the cotton seed business and was busy selling real estate. Living at home with John and Mary was their unmarried daughter, Mary, who was thirty-six years old. They had one boarder, Annie E. House, who was a forty-nine-year-old widow and a life insurance salesperson.

Mary Etta, now sixty-seven, passed away at 1:10 in the morning on February 6, 1934. She suffered an illness for several months caused by heart and kidney problems. According to the 1940 census, their daughter had remained living at the house helping to take care of her seventy-six-year-old father. She was also teaching, which paid her $1,624.00 a year.

At 1:30 a.m. on August 20, 1951, John, the ladies' man from Marshall, passed away at the age of eighty-seven. He died in a convalescent home after a three-week illness from heart and kidney failure. He was the oldest elder in the First Presbyterian Church at the time. Like his brother Finis, his mother Louisa would have been proud of John, for he was a good, useful man and remained very active in his religion. John and Mary were buried next to each other under a large oak tree at Greenwood Cemetery in Fort Worth.

Mrs. Mary Foster, Ill 2 Months, Dies

Mrs. Mary Etta Foster, 67, born in a log cabin near Mansfield and the daughter of the late Capt. Julian C. Feild, died at 1:10 a. m. Tuesday at her residence, 1114 West Cannon Street. She had been ill of a heart ailment for two months.

Mrs. Foster was the daughter of the Tarrant County pioneer who was the first postmaster of Fort Worth and for whom Julian Feild Masonic Lodge is named. She was born May 16, 1866, and came to Fort Worth in the early seventies. She studied music at the New England Conservatory of Music at Boston, Mass., and was graduated there in 1855. Before her marriage in 1892 she taught music in the Mary Nash School at Sherman, which later became Kidd-Key College.

In 1895 Mrs. Foster moved to Nashville, Tenn., returning to Fort Worth in 1904. A member of the Presbyterian Church, Mrs. Foster was active in church work until the time of her illness. She also was active in musical circles of the city, having been among the first members of the Harmony Club.

Survivors are her husband, J. C. Foster Sr.; a daughter, Miss Mary Louise Foster of Fort Worth; three sons, Julian Foster and John C. Foster Jr., both of Dallas, and R. Feild Foster of San Saba; a brother, Dr. Bingham Feild of Enid, Okla.; a half-brother, George M. Feild of Dallas; a half-sister, Mrs. John Walraven of Dallas; five nieces, Mrs. W. R. Edington, Mrs. G. V. Morton and Mrs. J. M. Collins, all of Fort Worth; Mrs. John W. Sandidge of Aledo, and Mrs. C. C. Abbey of Hemet, Cal., and three grandchildren, Julian Feild Foster and Mary Ann Foster, both of San Saba, and Jean Marie Foster of Dallas.

Funeral services will be held at 10:30 a. m. Wednesday at Gause-Ware Funeral Home, Rev. James K. Thompson officiating. Burial will be in Greenwood Cemetery.

Obituary of Mary Etta in
Fort Worth Star-Telegram

John Collier Foster's grave. Photo by Jack Crowder.

ABOUT THE AUTHOR

Jack Crowder is a retired teacher and administrator with forty-plus years in the classroom. He received a B.A. and Masters from Texas Christian University. He has written numerous books on the American Revolution and given presentations on the Revolutionary War to many organizations in the area.

www.ingramcontent.com/pod-product-compliance
Lightning Source LLC
Chambersburg PA
CBHW051813110425
24985CB00018BA/1182